T0291312

Emerging Patterns and Behaviors in a Green Resilient Economy

LAB FOR ENTREPRENEURSHIP AND DEVELOPMENT

Series Editors: Bruno S. Sergi and Cole C. Scanlon

Lab for Entrepreneurship and Development is Emerald's innovative book series on the study of entrepreneurship and development, striving to set the agenda for advancing research on entrepreneurship in the context of finance, economic development, innovation, and the society at large.

The Lab for Entrepreneurship and Development (LEAD), a now-independent research lab that first started at the Institute of Quantitative Social Sciences (IQSS) at Harvard University, with the overarching and ambitious aim of using the book series as to synthesize interdisciplinary research by academics and students to advance our understanding of modern entrepreneurship and development across cultural and disciplinary boundaries.

Previous volume:

Entrepreneurship and Development in the 21st Century – Edited by Bruno S. Sergi and Cole C. Scalon

Entrepreneurship for Social Change – Edited by Bruno S. Sergi, Cole C. Scalon and Luke R. I. Heine

Entrepreneurship Development in the Balkans: Perspective from Diverse Contexts – Edited by Veland Ramadani, Sasho Kjosev and Bruno S. Sergi

Entrepreneurship and Development for a Green Resilient Economy – Edited by Adriana Grigorescu and Jean Vasile Andrei

Emerging Patterns and Behaviors in a Green Resilient Economy

EDITED BY

JEAN VASILE ANDREI
National Institute for Economic Research "Costin C. Kirițescu," Romanian Academy, Romania

and

ADRIANA GRIGORESCU
National University of Political Studies and Public Administration, Romania

United Kingdom – North America – Japan – India – Malaysia – China

Emerald Publishing Limited
Emerald Publishing, Floor 5, Northspring, 21-23 Wellington Street, Leeds LS1 4DL.

First edition 2024

Reprints and permissions service
Contact: www.copyright.com

British Library Cataloguing in Publication Data
A catalogue record for this book is available from the British Library

ISBN: 978-1-83549-781-4 (Print)
ISBN: 978-1-83549-780-7 (Online)
ISBN: 978-1-83549-782-1 (Epub)

Printed and bound by CPI Group (UK) Ltd, Croydon, CR0 4YY

Contents

About the Editors

Jean Vasile Andrei is Full Professor at Petroleum-Gas University of Ploiesti, Department of Business Administration, Managing Director of Center for Renewable Energies and Energy Efficiency within National Institute for Economic Research "Costin C. Kirițescu," Romanian Academy, and PhD mentor in Economics at Bucharest University of Economic Studies, Romania. He is Co-founder and Scientific Coordinator of the Research Network on Resources Economics and Bioeconomy. He holds a PhD in Economics from the National Institute of Economics Research – Romanian Academy of Sciences. He has earned a BA degree in Administrative Sciences (2005) and in Banks and Finances (2007) from the Petroleum-Gas University of Ploiesti. He has an MA degree in Economics, Administrative, and Business Management (2007) earned at the same university. He is also Associate Editor of Economics of Agriculture (Serbia), Scientific Reviewer, and Committee Member for numerous international conferences. He is a member of scientific organizations: The Balkan Scientific Association of Agrarian Economists, Serbia (2008), DAAAM Vienna, and Information Resources Management Association (2011). Issues like agricultural economics and rural development, energy and resource economics, and business economics are among his research and scientific interests.

Adriana Grigorescu is a Full Professor and PhD Supervisor in Management at the National University of Political Studies and Public Administration, a Senior Researcher at the National Institute of Economic Research Costin C. Kiritescu – Romanian Academy, and a Full Member of the Academy of Romanian Scientists. The research area is management and marketing in business and public administration, innovation and knowledge transfer, circular economy, labor economics, education management, and especially integrated, interdisciplinary studies of global economy and governance. The last published studies explored the digital transformation side effects of various aspects of business models, education, and the world of work. Sustainable development and environmental protection also represent a significant part of her work from the perspective of their impact on education and skills or business models. Moreover, she is preoccupied with finding models to measure people's readiness for the nowadays challenges and spatial analysis.

About the Contributors

Prof Roshan Ajward, a Distinguished Academic with over 15 years of experience, currently serves as a Professor in Accounting at the Faculty of Management Studies and Commerce, University of Sri Jayewardenepura in Sri Lanka. Holding a PhD from Waseda University, Japan, he is a Fellow Member of the Institute of Chartered Accountants of Sri Lanka and the Institute of Certified Management Accountants. As the Co-chair of the Research Council and Coordinator of the Master of Professional Accounting Degree Program at USJP, he demonstrates strong leadership. He, a Mon-buka-gaku-shu scholar of Japan and a Monash Fellow of Monash University, Australia, has numerous international research publications in esteemed journals, focusing on corporate governance, auditing, ethics, and financial reporting. His contributions extend to serving as the chief editor for several journals.

Mohammad Javad Amiri is PhD and an Assistant Professor at the University of Tehran, Department of Environment. He is also the Executive Vice President of Aras International Campus of University of Tehran. He obtained his PhD in Forestry and Land Preparation. He holds a Master's degree in Forestry and a Bachelor's degree in Environmental Engineering. He has done research on social studies and tourism as well as research with statistical data analysis and remote sensing. He has also participated in several national and international conferences.

Hareendra Dissabandara, a Distinguished Finance Expert, currently serves as Finance Professor at the Faculty of Management Studies and Commerce, University of Sri Jayewardenepura in Sri Lanka. With a PhD from Nagoya University and Chukyo University, Japan, he has achieved a high level of academic excellence. He has played key leadership roles within academia, serving as the head of the Department of Finance and as a council member at the University of Sri Jayewardenepura. His membership in the Chartered Institute for Securities and Investments (MCSI, UK) reflects his commitment to advancing the fields of finance and corporate governance. His research portfolio encompasses significant contributions to areas such as corporate governance, financial literacy, and dividend policy. He has further demonstrated his leadership and expertise in finance through roles such as vice-chancellor and CEO of Saegis Campus and deputy secretary-general of the National Economic Council of Sri Lanka.

Homa Irani Behbahani is PhD and a Retired Full Professor at the University of Tehran, Department of Environmental Design. She has also been a Professor at L'ecole polytechnique d'architecture et d'urbanism d'Alger in Algeria. She obtained her PhD in Architecture from the University of Florence in Italy. She has done research in landscape architecture, heritage sites, and most specifically on the subject of Persian gardens. She has authored two books and several papers in national and international journals and conferences.

Isidora Beraha, PhD, Institute of Economic Sciences, Serbia. A Senior Research Associate in the Innovation Economics Department at the Institute of Economic Sciences. Her expertise encompasses business economics, small- and medium-sized enterprises' operations, industry clusters, value chain analysis, and innovation policy. She held the position of president of the Scientific Board from 2019 to 2023 and currently leads the Sector for Fundamental Research at the Institute. She has authored 2 scientific monographs and over 60 papers in various publications. Engaged in numerous national and international projects, she actively participates in conferences, workshops, and professional events globally. Additionally, she contributes as a reviewer for several domestic scientific journals and is affiliated with the Serbian Scientific Society of Economists, Society of Economists of Belgrade, and Entrepreneurship Research and Education Network of Central European Universities (ERENET).

Gholamreza Nabi Bidhendi is PhD and a Full Professor at the University of Tehran, Department of Environment. He has focused on the subject of environmental research and impact assessment. He has obtained his PhD in Chemistry from Delhi University in India. He has been active in the academic sector as well as the executive departments in Iran. He has 3,426 citations in Scopus as well and 6,965 citations in Google Scholar. He has been in the editorial board of several journals, authored papers in scientific journals, and participated in numerous national and international conferences.

Snežana Cico, PhD, JKP Prostor Sombor, Trg Cara Lazara 1, Sombor. Title: Doctor of Social Sciences (PhD); scientific title: Research Associate; education: University in Belgrade: doctoral dissertation completed in the field of economics. University of Novi Sad: Faculty of Economics, postgraduate studies. Work experience: Starting from September 2021, she has been employed as a director of a state-owned company JKP Prostor Sombor. Before that, she was the Director of state-owned company Severtrans for eight years. She has been engaged in several projects of the Ministry of Science and Technological Development, numerous public policy projects, and domestic and foreign private companies. Scientific and professional activity: her research is primarily focused on the topics that deal with the study of the world economy, marketing, investment management in order to achieve competitive advantages, finance, with special emphasis on studies in the field of matters related to corporate governance, corporate restructuring and restructuring, acquisitions, privatization, international agreements, etc.

As an author, she has published over 70 bibliographic units. She was involved in the development of numerous projects, which were put into practice. She speaks English. She collaborates with numerous research and educational institutions in the country and abroad. She is the president of the board of directors of the Association of Auditors of Serbia.

Nikola Ćurčić, PhD, works as a Senior Research Associate in the field of Economic Sciences at the "Tamiš" Research and Development Institute in Pančevo, Serbia. He is the author of over 70 scientific papers that contribute to the domestic and international literature in the field of business economics and marketing. He is the Executive Editor of the *Ekonomika* journal; a member of the Editorial Board of the *Agricultural Economics, Economy – Theory and Practice* and *The Annals of the Faculty of Economics in Subotica*. He is also a member of the "Ekonomika" Scientific Society of Economists Niš and the Serbian Marketing Society "SEMA" Belgrade. He has also actively participated in the organization of numerous scientific meetings as a member of the scientific and organizational committees.

Drago Cvijanović, PhD, is a Full Professor and a Dean at the University of Kragujevac, Faculty of Hotel Management and Tourism in Vrnjačka Banja, working within the Department of Management and Business. He has many awards such as FIRST ANNUAL AWARD FOR 2008 – on the occasion of the day of the Belgrade Chamber of Commerce – for successful scientific research work in the field of agriculture and food industry; ACKNOWLEDGMENT 2019 – on the occasion of marking the 70th anniversary of the Institute for Agricultural Economics – Belgrade, for many years of successful management and contribution to the work and development of the institute; CHARTER 2022 – Ministry of Agriculture, Forestry and Water Management of the Republic of Serbia, in recognition of their exceptional contribution to the development of consultancy and agriculture in the Republic of Serbia. He was employed at faculties, institutes, factories, agricultural cooperatives, agricultural combines, and the Ministry of Agriculture. He was engaged in scientific and research work on a large number of projects (44), in the capacity of project manager, research team leader, expert coordinator, and member of research teams in the country and abroad. He has written over 50 monographs, books, and textbooks. He published over 500 papers in domestic and foreign journals, proceedings at domestic and international conferences. He was a member or president of the selection committee for scientific and research positions more than 50 times. He is editor in chief of two journals (international and national) and participates in the editorial boards of 15 domestic international journals.

Hassan Darabi PhD, currently holds the position of Assistant Professor of Environmental Design at the University of Tehran, where his area of expertise lies in the research of regional landscape. He obtained his PhD in geography and rural planning from the University of Tarbiat Modras in the Islamic Republic of Iran.

At present, his research primarily focuses on regional landscape changes, planning, and tourism.

Hiranya Dissanayake, a Senior Lecturer at the Department of Accountancy, Wayamba University of Sri Lanka, is a PhD candidate in Management (finance) at the University of Sri Jayewardenepura. Holding an MSc in Applied Finance and a BCom (special) second-class honors degree from the University of Colombo, Hiranya is a passed finalist of CIMA and a notable recipient of the CIMA Research Excellence Award in 2022 and Second Runner Up and People's Choice Award at the National Pitching Research Competition in 2021. Having served as the head of the Department of Accountancy (2018–2019), Hiranya's teaching interests encompass corporate governance, strategic management accounting, sustainability reporting, financial statement analysis, and research methodology. With a research focus on corporate governance and sustainability, Hiranya has made substantial contributions to both international and local journals, addressing critical topics in finance and management.

Sonja Đuričin, PhD, Institute of Economic Sciences (IES), Serbia. A Senior Research Associate in the Innovation Economics Department at the Institute of Economic Sciences. She has authored/co-authored more than 100 research papers, multiple books in business economics, financial management, and competitiveness. Engaged in various national and international projects, her expertise spans financial management, market research, restructuring, value assessment, business development, local economic development, innovation, agroeconomics, and value chain analysis. She is IES' transformation team leader in the World Bank's SAIGE project – Serbia Accelerating Innovation and Growth Entrepreneurship. She is also the editor in chief of the IES' publication on medium enterprises in Serbia and serves as the deputy president of the IES' Governing Board. She is a member of the Scientific Society of Economists of Serbia and the Entrepreneurship Research and Education Network of Central European Universities (ERENET).

Vasilii Erokhin is an Associate Professor, School of Economics and Management, Harbin Engineering University, China. Since 2017, Dr Erokhin is a Researcher at the Center for Russian and Ukrainian Studies (CRUS) and Arctic Blue Economy Research Center (ABERC), Harbin Engineering University, China. He is an author of over 200 publications in the areas of macroeconomics, sustainable development, green development, and food security. His major book titles include *Contemporary Macroeconomics: New Global Disorder* (2023), *Shifting Patterns of Agricultural Trade: The Protectionism Outbreak and Food Security* (2021), and *Handbook of Research on International Collaboration, Economic Development, and Sustainability in the Arctic* (2019).

Tibor Fazekaš, PhD, is an Assistant Professor at the University of Novi Sad, Faculty of Economics Subotica. He is working within the department of trade, marketing, and logistics. He has worked as general manager of Subotica–Trans, a public transportation enterprise. He is an expert witness, expert forensic evaluation of traffic accidents. He is involved in the realization of the teaching process for basic and master studies. He is an author and co-author of several textbooks, scripts, notes, and compendiums. He has published or co-published many scientific and professional papers in both national and international journals in the field of traffic and economic science. He has participated in the work and has presented his scientific works at more than 30 scientific meetings. He coordinated the IPA "DitranS 2011" project and many local projects about sustainable development in transport.

Cristina Gafu holds the position of Associate Professor in the Department of Philology, Faculty of Letters and Sciences, Petroleum-Gas University of Ploiesti Romania. She has published more than 30 international papers in outstanding journals (h-index 4), and 4 authored books, being interested in ethnology, Romanian culture and civilization, and folklore. She also participated in research projects in the field of entrepreneurship.

Tianming Gao is a Professor, School of Economics and Management, Harbin Engineering University, China. He is a Director and Chief Expert of the Center for Russian and Ukrainian Studies (CRUS) and Arctic Blue Economy Research Center (ABERC) at Harbin Engineering University, deputy head of the Heilongjiang International Economic and Trade Association, and leading consultant of governmental bodies and commercial organizations in the sphere of economic collaboration between China, Russia, and South Korea. He is the author of many publications in the areas of economic development, industrial policy, and investment. He is a member of the Scientific Board of the Research Network on Resources Economics and Bioeconomy (RebResNet).

Ileana Georgiana Gheorghe holds the position of Associate Professor in the Department of Business Administration, Faculty of Economics, and Petroleum-Gas University of Ploiesti Romania. She has published about 60 international papers in outstanding journals (h-index 8), 6 book chapters in edited books, and 2 authored books, being interested in human resources management, green economics, social responsibility, and organizational culture. She also participated in research projects in the field of human resources development.

Aleksandar Grubor, PhD, is a Full Professor at the Faculty of Economics in Subotica, the University of Novi Sad. His field of interest is marketing. He has authored 3 textbooks, 18 scientific papers published in the *Prominent International Journals* ranked in the Thomson Reuters JCR, and more than 80 scientific papers published in the *Journals of National Importance*. Besides, he has participated in more than 40 international scientific conferences. He teaches global marketing, services marketing, and the principles of marketing. He is the project leader of the University of Novi Sad team in ERASMUS+ projects: the Implementation of Dual Education in the Higher Education of Serbia – DUALEDU, and the Professional Development of Vocational Education Teachers with European Practices (PRO-VET). Also, he is a project member in the Advanced Data Analytics in Business (ADA) ERASMUS+ project. In the period from January to March 2004, he successfully completed the International Faculty Development Program at the Free Market Business Development Institute, School of Business Administration, Portland State University, Portland, Oregon, USA. Currently, he is a member of the Serbian Marketing Association (SEMA). From 2010 to 2016, he was the editor in chief of *The Annals of the Faculty of Economics in Subotica* journal. From 2016 to 2022, he was the editor in chief of the *Strategic Management* journal.

Gheorghe Dan Isbăşoiu is Lecturer at Faculty of Economic Sciences within the Petroleum-Gas University of Ploiesti and holds PhD in Industrial Engineering. His research is focused on social and economic statistics as well as on entrepreneurship.

Nataša Kljajić is a Doctor of Economic Sciences. She has been engaged in scientific work for a long time and has so far published many articles and books in the field of rural economy, organizations of agricultural production, and agricultural development. Also, she has participated in numerous domestic and international agriculture and rural development projects.

Vuk Miletić, PhD, an Associate Professor and Research Associate, is employed at the "Dositej" College of Academic Studies in Belgrade, Serbia. He is the author of more than 60 papers published in journals of various categories, including papers in relevant international journals in the management and business economics fields. He has authored the monograph titled *Leadership in a Contemporary Organization*. He is a reviewer of the *Ekonomika* international journal for economic theory and practice and social issues and a member of the "Ekonomika" Scientific Society of Economists in Niš. He has actively participated in the organization of numerous scientific meetings as a member of the review teams and the editorial boards of national and international scientific conferences.

Vesna Paraušić is a Doctor of Economic Sciences. She has published many scientific and research articles and participated in numerous rural development projects. The focus of interest and scientific work is directed predominantly on the following areas: sustainable rural and local development, strategic planning, networking and associations in agriculture, and local development initiatives.

Prof Wasantha Perera, a Distinguished Academic, currently serves as a Finance Professor at the University of Sri Jayewardenepura in Sri Lanka. With a PhD in Finance from Victoria University, Australia, he received the "Best Research Student Award" in 2015. He holds a first-class Bachelor of Commerce from the University of Sri Jayewardenepura and an MBA in Finance from the Asian Institute of Technology, Thailand. His accomplishments span publishing in esteemed international journals, supervising students, and serving as a peer reviewer for numerous journals. He also authored widely used finance textbooks and assumed various academic administrative roles, including postgraduate program coordinator, department head, international conference chair, and chairperson of the Board of Study in Management Studies and Commerce in Sri Lanka.

Prof Dr Catalin Popescu is Professor of Management at Petroleum-Gas University of Ploiesti, Romania. His research and consulting interest includes project management, quantitative methods for business and management, operations management, statistical analysis, energy management, and sustainable development. He has 32 years of experience in higher education. Starting with 2016, he is PhD Advisor in the Engineering and Management domain. He has published over 230 articles, 9 books, and 12 book chapters, he participated in 45 international conferences (in more than 27 different countries), and he was involved in more than 30 scientific research grants and international projects. He was also a member of scientific committees within more than 50 international conferences, and he was six times plenary speaker. He is editor in chief of two scientific journals: *Journal of Innovation and Business Best Practices* (JIBBP), Stamford Publishing, USA, and *Economic Insights Trends and Challenges Journal*, Romania.

Irina Gabriela Radulescu is Professor at Petroleum-Gas University of Ploieşti, Dean of Faculty of Economic Sciences, Vice President of Export Business Center Association from Bucharest, Member of the coordinating team of European Digital Innovation Hub – Wallachia eHub for South-Muntenia region, and manager of Danube Engineering Hub Cluster. She is author and co-author of 80 scientific papers presented at national/international conferences and/or published in recognized journals, indexed ISI Web of Science, Scopus, EBSCO, Ulrich, or other international databases and 10 specialized books published at recognized national publishing houses. She is involved as member or coordinator in national and international projects related to international trade, entrepreneurship, or digital transformation processes.

Ljiljana Rajnović, Institute of Agricultural Economics, Volgina 15, Belgrade, Serbia. Title: Doctor of Social Sciences (PhD); scientific title: Senior Research Associate; education: *University Union – Nikola Tesla Beograd:* doctoral dissertation completed. University of Belgrade: Faculty of Law, postgraduate studies. Work experience: Starting from April 2003, she has been employed at the Institute for Agricultural Economics, Belgrade (Institute), as a Research Associate. Before that, she worked in state bodies and the Government of Serbia on jobs related to economic subjects. She has been engaged in several projects of the Ministry of Science and Technological Development, numerous public policy projects, and domestic and foreign private companies. Scientific and professional activity: her research is primarily focused on the topics of legal and economic science and profession, with special emphasis on studies in the field of matters related to business law, corporate governance, corporate restructuring and restructuring, acquisitions, securities market, privatization, international agreements, etc. As an author, she has published over 80 bibliographic units. She was involved in the development of numerous projects, which were put into practice. She participated in expert groups on drafting several laws. She speaks English and Russian. She collaborates with numerous research and educational institutions in the country and abroad. As a lecturer, she participates in seminars and other professional forums and promotions.

Mahta Saremi, PhD is an Adjunct Professor in the Alborz Campus of the University of Tehran. She has done research in the fields of tourism planning, management, design, and modeling tourist behavior and has presented several national and international papers. She has also done research on World Heritage Sites (WHS) for their development with limiting the negative impacts of unmanaged visitations as well as the intangible aspect of WHS. She has her PhD in Environmental Planning and has two Master's degrees in Environmental Management and Environmental Design and Engineering. She has work experience with the United Nations Development Program (UNDP) and Department of Environment on the subject of Environmental Impact Assessment in Iran. She has been one of the main members of the Sport and Environment Commission of the National Olympic Committee in Iran. She has also worked with different nongovernmental organizations (NGOs) as well as organizers for various conferences and forums. Her recent research works are on new technologies for tourism development.

Otilija Sedlak, PhD, is a Full Professor at the University of Novi Sad, Faculty of Economics Subotica, working within the Department of Quantitative Methods. She has worked as the Vice Dean of studies as well as ECTS Coordinator. She is a Member of the following scientific and professional associations: AEORS (Association of European Operational Research Society) and EuROMA (European Operations and Management Association). She is involved in the realization of the teaching process on basic studies, master studies, as well as on PhD studies: operational research, financial and actuary mathematics, business mathematics, quantitative methods in economy and management, and risk management. She is an author and co-author of several textbooks, scripts, notes, and compendiums. She has published or co-published over 35 scientific and professional papers in both national and international journals. She has participated in the work and has presented her scientific works at more than 80 scientific meetings.

Violeta Sima holds the position of Associate Professor in the Department of Business Administration, Faculty of Economics, Petroleum-Gas University of Ploiesti, Romania. She has published about 70 international papers in outstanding journals (h-index 9), 6 book chapters in edited books, and 4 authored books, being interested in marketing research, consumer behavior, green economics, and social responsibility. She also participated in research projects in the field of entrepreneurship.

Ilyas Sozen is a Professor at Dokuz Eylul University. He received his MSc in 2006 and received his PhD in 2010 from the Department of Middle East Economics at the Marmara University. He focuses on the regional studies and energy and environment in the context of international economic issues.

Dragan Stojić, PhD, is an Associate Professor at the University of Novi Sad, Faculty of Economics Subotica. He is working within the Department of Quantitative Methods as a Head of the department. He is a member of the following scientific and professional associations: AEORS (Association of European Operational Research Society) and EuROMA (European Operations and Management Association). She is involved in the realization of the teaching process on basic studies, master studies, as well as on PhD studies: operational research, financial and actuary mathematics, business mathematics, quantitative methods in economy and management, risk management, and financial and actuarial mathematics. He is an author and co-author of several textbooks, scripts, notes, and compendiums. He has published or co-published over 35 scientific and professional papers in both national and international journals. He has participated in the work and has presented his scientific works at more than 40 scientific meetings.

Mustafa Batuhan Tufaner is an Associate Professor at Beykent University. He completed his MSc in 2015 and received his PhD in 2019 from the Department of Economics at the Marmara University. His research focuses on the economic development and renewable energy in developing and developed countries. He is the author of various international articles.

Răzvan Vasile is a Researcher at the National Institute of Economic Research "Costin C. Kiritescu" – Romanian Academy. The main research topics are the digital transition, labor market disequilibria, skills mismatch, financial inclusion, energy transition, sustainable development, cultural heritage interpretation, digitalization, and socio-economic evaluation. He has good international cooperation as a team member in interdisciplinary research projects. As a member of the Center for Renewable Energies and Energy Efficiency, he is involved in interdisciplinary studies and publications related to today's challenging topics.

Nikola Vasilić, MSc, Institute of Economic Sciences, Serbia, is a Research Assistant in the Innovation Economics Department at the Institute of Economic Sciences. He is a PhD candidate at the Faculty of Economics, University of Kragujevac, Department of Macroeconomics. Currently, he is in the process of writing a doctoral dissertation titled "National innovation system efficiency and economic growth in developed and developing countries." His primary areas of scientific research interest encompass science, technology, innovation development, entrepreneurship, and applied econometrics. He has published over 20 papers in prestigious domestic journals, as well as in international and domestic monographs and conference proceedings.

Dana Volosevici is Lecturer at Faculty of Letter and Sciences within the Petroleum-Gas University of Ploiesti and is specialized in Labor Law, researching mainly the impact of labor legislation in industrial processes and transformations.

Foreword

In a context of environmental challenges and the urgent need for sustainable development, *Emerging Patterns and Behaviors in a Green Resilient Economy* may represent a reference contribution to understanding this new economic and societal landscape, bringing together a series of in-depth analyses and discussions that together point the way to a future where economic growth is seamlessly aligned with environmental responsibility.

This edited volume explores the strategies and innovations that are shaping the global economy, focusing on the intersection of environmental sustainability and economic resilience. It comprehensively explores new business models, policy shifts, and technological advancements. The volume explores and presents a range of perspectives from different fields to illustrate the path to a more sustainable and resilient economic future. Policymakers, academics, and industry leaders who want to understand and contribute to developing a resilient green economy will find this text a vital resource.

With contributions from diverse experts, this book maps out a path toward a sustainable and robust economic future, making it an indispensable resource for policymakers, academics, and industry leaders. It begins with analyzing China's journey toward carbon neutrality, exploring the hurdles and successes that offer lessons for other economies. Further chapters delve into sustainable marketing strategies in tourism, the gender gap in entrepreneurship, and the nexus of CO_2 emissions with manufacturing growth, among other critical topics.

This book delves into the role of rural entrepreneurship, as discussed by Vesna Paraušić and Nataša Kljajić, and the intricate dynamics of scientific output in environmental science, as analyzed by Nikola Vasilić and the team. "China's Pursuit of Carbon Neutrality: Roadblocks and Greenlights" by Vasilii Erokhin and Tianming Gao sets the tone with an in-depth analysis of the world's largest emitter's journey toward carbon neutrality. It is a story of challenges and triumphs that offers valuable lessons for other economies. From China's journey toward carbon neutrality to the insightful examination of marketing strategies in historical tourism by Mahta Saremi and colleagues, this book traverses a broad spectrum of topics.

In "Marketing Strategies in Historical Tourism," authors like Mahta Saremi and Hassan Darabi explore the intersection of tourism, a significant economic driver, with sustainability principles. This chapter is particularly relevant in preserving cultural heritage while fostering economic growth.

Addressing crucial aspects like gender gaps in entrepreneurship, corporate sustainability, and the intersection of CO_2 emissions with manufacturing growth, each chapter contributes unique perspectives and findings. This book also ventures into the critical discourse of gender and entrepreneurship. Gheorghe Dan Isbăşoiu, Dana Volosevici, and Jean Vasile Andrei examine the gender gap in entrepreneurship, offering insights into developing competitive economies that are inclusive and diverse.

In addition to these, this book covers a broad spectrum of topics ranging from the LEADER approach in rural entrepreneurship, the relationship between CO_2 emissions and economic growth, to the development of smart cities, and the dynamics of scientific output in environmental science.

This book also includes in-depth discussions on corporate sustainability, offering operational frameworks for sustainable corporate practices, indicative of the evolving role of businesses in a greener economy. Covering a wide range of topics, including rural entrepreneurship, the relationship between CO_2 emissions and economic growth, and the development of smart cities, this book is a forward-looking collection that reflects and anticipates the future dynamics of green economies.

Cristina Gafu and her co-authors discuss women entrepreneurs' challenges, while Nikola Ćurčić and colleagues analyze personnel policies in Serbian organizations. Ljiljana Rajnović and Snežana Cico explore the possibilities for sustainable business operations in extraordinary external conditions.

Hiranya Dissanayake and colleagues present "Salience of Corporate Sustainability," a chapter that proposes operational frameworks for sustainable corporate practices. This chapter is a testament to the evolving role of businesses in leading the charge toward a greener economy.

Furthermore, chapters like the one on green energy paradigms by Răzvan Vasile and Adriana Grigorescu indicate the breadth and depth of this book's coverage. This forward-looking collection reflects the current state of green economies and anticipates future developments and challenges.

Each chapter presents unique perspectives and insights, contributing to a rich narrative that underscores the importance of inclusive, diverse, and competitive economies. Discussions range from rural entrepreneurship and scientific output in environmental science to the challenges women entrepreneurs and sustainable business operations face under extraordinary external conditions.

Emerging Patterns and Behaviors in a Green Resilient Economy serves as a call to action, inviting readers to engage with pioneering ideas and practices that are pivotal in steering societies toward a more sustainable and equitable future. It is a valuable resource for those in entrepreneurship, economics, environmental science, and sustainability studies, providing in-depth insights into the emerging trends shaping contemporary economies. This book weaves together a narrative more significant than the sum of its parts, representing a mosaic of strategies, challenges, and innovations crucial for shaping the future of resilient green economies.

The editors
Jean Vasile Andrei,
National Institute for Economic Research "Costin C. Kiriţescu,"
Romanian Academy, Romania
Faculty of Economic Sciences, Petroleum-Gas
University of Ploiesti, Romania

Adriana Grigorescu,
National Institute for Economic Research "Costin C. Kiriţescu,"
Romanian Academy, Romania
Faculty of Public Administration, National University of Political
Studies and Public Administration, Bucharest, Romania
Academy of Romanian Scientists, Romania

Acknowledgments

The editors wish to express their deepest and most heartfelt acknowledgments to everyone involved in making this book project possible. Our sincere appreciation also goes to all the contributors to this book project and the Emerald Editorial team, whose support was invaluable in publishing this edited book. Your invaluable contributions, each idea shared, every piece of constructive criticism, the invaluable insights, and the support have brought this edited book to printing.

We extend our profound gratitude to the National Institute for Economic Research "Costin C. Kiritescu" of the Romanian Academy, Petroleum-Gas University of Ploiesti, and the Research Network on Resources Economics and Bioeconomy Association. The development of this book would hardly have been possible without their support.

We are also immensely grateful to Professor Bruno S. Sergi, the Lab for Entrepreneurship and Development coordinator, for providing the opportunity to expand our research. A special acknowledgment is reserved for Ms Sashikala Balasubramanian and Ms Lydia Cutmore whose direct involvement was crucial in bringing this book to fruition.

Chapter 1

The Dynamic Interaction Between Scientific Output in Environmental Science and Energy and Carbon Dioxide Emissions in G7 Countries

Nikola Vasilić, Sonja Đuričin and Isidora Beraha

Institute of Economic Sciences, Serbia

Abstract

Due to excessive carbon dioxide emissions, the world is facing environmental devastation. Energy and environmental innovations are considered to be critical tools in combating the growing CO_2 emissions. Developing these innovations requires extremely high investments in research and development processes, where knowledge is generated as one of the important outputs. This knowledge serves as a basis for innovation development and raising awareness among all relevant stakeholders about excessive environmental degradation. One of the significant sources of knowledge is scientific publications. Therefore, the aim of this research is to examine whether increased CO_2 emissions stimulate the scientific community to publish a greater number of papers, as well as whether the knowledge contained in these publications is utilized in reducing CO_2 emissions. The sample consists of G7 member countries. The time frame of the research is 1996–2019. The dynamic properties of the vector autoregression (VAR) models were summarized using impulse response function and variance decomposition forecast error. In most G7 countries, it has been determined that an increase in scientific production in environmental science and energy leads to a reduction in CO_2 emissions. On the other hand, increased CO_2 emissions affect higher scientific productivity in environmental science and energy only in Canada.

Emerging Patterns and Behaviors in a Green Resilient Economy, 1–30

doi:10.1108/978-1-83549-780-720241001

Keywords: Scientific output; environmental science and energy; carbon dioxide emission; impulse response function; variance decomposition forecast error; G7 countries

1. Introduction

Climate changes caused by irresponsible and environmentally unsustainable human behavior have devastating impacts on public welfare and population health (WHO, 2018). Starting from the 1880s, global average surface temperatures have increased by 1 °C because of the increase in greenhouse gas emissions (NASA, 2019). The consequence of this increase is significantly altered weather conditions (Difenbaugh, 2020; Đuričin et al., 2016). Droughts, heavy rainfall, and even in areas where such events were rare until recently are becoming more frequent. Further temperature rise and ocean acidification, as well as an increase in the average sea level globally, are almost inevitable (Petrović & Lobanov, 2020). Such forms of climate change lead to the spread of infectious diseases, reduction in available reserves of clean drinking water, and deterioration of air quality (Montgomery, 2017). Under such circumstances, the sustainability of the ecosystem is being questioned. Experts from relevant organizations estimate that 75% of all greenhouse gases are carbon dioxide (CO_2) emissions, which significantly contribute to the increase in global surface temperature (NASA, 2019). If prompt measures are not taken, it is predicted that with this pace, the global average surface temperature will reach a level of about 1.5 °C between 2030 and 2050 (Petrović & Lobanov, 2020). Therefore, to slow down the process of global warming, it is necessary to reduce CO_2 emissions. Various initiatives have been launched globally to find effective mechanisms for addressing the issue of excessive CO_2 emissions. Two of the most notable agreements are the Kyoto Protocol, established in 1997, and the Paris Agreement on climate change, adopted in 2015. The primary goal is to successfully mitigate global warming by ensuring that the temperature increase remains well below 2 °C (UNFCCC, 2015), through the promotion of energy efficiency principles worldwide. Also, in 2015, the United Nations General Assembly formulated the Sustainable Development Goals, which are projected to be achieved by 2030. Two out of the total 17 goals are clean energy and a less-polluted environment. The implemented measures have not yet yielded the desired results. CO_2 emissions have continued to rise, and in the meantime, a record increase rate of 2.7% was reached in 2018.

The main challenge for environmentalists, the scientific community, policymakers, and other stakeholders is to uncover the main drivers of CO_2 emissions and develop innovative solutions to mitigate them.

Many studies have been conducted to determine the causes of CO_2 emissions. Economic growth, energy consumption, international trade, population, and urbanization have been recognized as the primary factors contributing to the increase in CO_2 emissions (Acheampong, 2018; Apergis & Ozturk, 2015;

Cai et al., 2018; Dong et al., 2018; Mahmood et al., 2019; Sadorsky, 2014; Zhang et al., 2018). The desire of both advanced and developing economies is to achieve increased economic growth and long-term development to improve national well-being. However, this cannot be achieved without serious consequences for environmental quality, as economic growth is likely to be the leading driver of CO_2 emissions. Given that economic growth encompasses a wide range of structural changes and effects (Többelmann & Wendler, 2020), the question is which is the dominant channel through which economic growth affects CO_2 emissions? With increased economic growth, there is a higher demand for output and a greater need to fulfill various human desires through energy-consuming activities. As economic activities expand, there is a corresponding need for a larger energy supply (Raghutla & Chittedi, 2021). The more energy is consumed, the more fossil fuels are needed to generate that amount of energy (Többelmann & Wendler, 2020). It is estimated that fossil fuels accounted for 60% of worldwide CO_2 emissions, with coal accounting for 46%, oil for 33%, and natural gas for 20% (Alam et al., 2020). These data undoubtedly highlight fossil energy as the forefront contributor to environmental degradation.

After identifying the primary source of CO_2 emissions, it is now necessary to develop an appropriate mechanism for mitigating the negative effects of energy on the environment without compromising future economic progress.

The continuous growth of CO_2 emissions globally and the necessity to achieve the goals set in the 2030 Agenda for Sustainable Development place a demand on countries to make a change in the current trajectory of economic growth and development, which has predominantly been based on the use of fossil fuels. Analyzing the findings of the report "Mission Innovation Beyond 2020: Challenges and Opportunities," the International Institute for Sustainable Development emphasized the need for a greater focus on innovation, particularly in the field of energy, in order to fully achieve the goals of the 2030 Agenda (Beraha & Đuričin, 2022; Cheng et al., 2021). Energy innovations support the transformation of countries whose economies heavily rely on fossil fuel use into sustainable economies where priority is given to renewable energy sources. Renewable energy sources, such as biomass, sunlight, wind power, waves, hydro, and geothermal, result in lower CO_2 emissions (Chiu & Chang, 2009) compared to fossil fuels, which are widely recognized as the primary source of CO_2 emissions and global warming (Stern, 2007). Renewable energy production innovations, such as solar and wind energy, reduce energy consumption-related emissions. New types of biofuels or more efficient vehicles may reduce mobility-related emissions (Többelmann & Wendler, 2020). The consumption of renewable energies is a real sustainable economic alternative that could limit the depletion of natural resources, reduce air pollution, ensure energy security, and finally create jobs (Mongo et al., 2021). Hence, the use of renewable sources of energy is considered one of the most important strategies to reduce CO_2 emissions (Gessinger, 1997). Successful implementation of such a strategy requires substantial investments in energy-related research and development activities (Alam et al., 2020) to create conditions for the development of new or the improvement of existing clean energy technologies. Even though increased research and development activities are likely to result in new and improved clean energy technologies, experience has shown that governments have not been willing to increase funding for these purposes in the past few decades. Furthermore, the amount of funding for energy-related R&D has been declining since the 1980s in both developed and developing economies. In 2014, public energy-related R&D investment in the world was approximately 17 billion US dollars, which is even 3 billion dollars less than 40 years ago (Alam et al., 2020). A possible explanation for the negative trend in energy-related R&D investments is the insufficient awareness among policymakers about the benefits, as well as the consequences of limited investments in this field. Given the devastation that further uncontrolled increases in CO_2 emissions can have on people's livelihoods and the rate of global economic growth, it is imperative that all those responsible for developing and implementing environmental policies aimed at reducing and preventing environmental degradation collect and thoroughly analyze existing theoretical and empirical findings in the field of energy. Scientific publications on relevant topics in this field can be the most reliable source of knowledge for developing effective evidence-based policies (Đuričin et al., 2022). Furthermore, the theory of endogenous growth highlights that R&D sectors create technological innovation through the utilization of human capital and the stock of existing knowledge (Romer, 1986). Basically, scientific publications provide and disseminate knowledge that can inspire new innovative ideas or technological breakthroughs, which researchers and firms can utilize to develop new energy-friendly products, services, or processes that simultaneously stimulate economic growth.

In addition to energy innovation, it is important to highlight the significant role of environmental innovation in abating environmental degradation. Environmental innovations include novel or substantially enhanced products, manufacturing techniques, organizational strategies, or marketing approaches that foster environmental protection, enhance sustainability, and prevent or minimize adverse impacts on the environment (Aldieri et al., 2021). Environmental innovation encompasses a broader range of solutions beyond energy. The following six types of environmental innovations can be distinguished: reducing material costs per unit of output; reducing energy use per unit of output; reducing total production of CO_2; replacing materials with less hazardous or non-hazardous substitutes; reducing soil, water, noise, or air pollution; and recycling waste, water, or materials (Aldieri et al., 2021). These innovations synergistically collaborate with energy innovation to foster a more sustainable and environmentally friendly future.

Taking into consideration the importance of the topic, many studies have analyzed the impacts of energy and environmental innovations on CO_2 emissions. However, research is still limited and far from reaching a consensus (Mongo et al., 2021). Based on their findings, these studies can be divided into two categories. The first group of studies reports that energy or environmental-related innovations contribute reducing CO_2 emissions (Lee & Min (2015) in Japan; Churchill et al. (2019) and Khan et al. (2020) in G7; Álvarez-Herránz et al. (2017) and Dzator & Acheampong (2020) in Organisation for Economic Co-operation and Development (OECD) economies; Carrio'n-Flores & Innes (2010) and Dinda (2004) in United States; Shahbaz et al. (2018) in France; Du et al. (2019)

in high-income countries), while the second group didn't find any relationship (Garrone & Grilli (2010) in 13 advanced economies; Weina et al. (2016) and Herring & Sorrell (2009) in Italy; Wang et al. (2012) in China; Mensah et al. (2018) in Canada, Japan, United States, and United Kingdom). Also, the studies utilize various indicators for innovation, primarily relying on R&D expenditures and patents (Carrio'n-Flores & Innes, 2010; Churchill et al., 2019; Mensah et al., 2018) in the environmental and energy-related fields, while number of researchers (Huang et al., 2018; Wu et al., 2018) and, particularly, scientific publications (de Gouveia & Inglesi-Lot, 2021) in these areas are rarely used.

Given that the examination of the relationship between scientific publications and CO_2 emissions is not sufficiently covered in the existing literature, the aim of this study is to enrich the existing knowledge in this specific field. As can be seen in the previous paragraph, through a comprehensive search of various scientific publication databases, only one study addressing this issue has been identified. de Gouveia and Inglesi-Lotz (2021) conducted a comprehensive analysis of the causality between climate change-related research output and CO_2 emissions in developed and developing countries from 1996 to 2019. The results indicate the presence of bidirectional causality between research output and CO_2 emissions in developed countries, while there is a one-directional causality running from research output to CO_2 emissions in developing countries. When individually examining the world's leading economies (G7), only Germany and Italy exhibited a one-directional causality running from CO_2 emissions to research output. This research solely examined causality, which offers evidence regarding the presence and direction of causality. However, it does not provide information about dynamic behavior of variables or whether the impact is positive or negative. To overcome the given limitations, we will utilize impulse response and variance decomposition forecast error analysis. Additionally, the authors construct the research output indicator by aggregating publications from 13 climate-related scientific fields, which undoubtedly ensures extensive coverage. Nevertheless, this approach may lead to a loss of insight into the specificity and significance of each field in reducing CO_2 emissions. For this reason, and in line with the described state of the art in research, we have decided to use two indicators of scientific output: the number of publications in the field of energy and in the field of environmental science. For the research sample, an informal grouping of seven advanced world economies known as the G7 has been selected. These are among the most industrialized countries in the world with significant influence in shaping global policies (Ajmi et al., 2015). They have established ambitious targets for reducing CO_2 emissions and have placed R&D investments at the core of their energy and environmental policies. In accordance with the available data, the research covers the time frame of 1996–2019.

2. Materials and Methods

The main goal of this chapter is to investigate the dynamic interrelationship between scientific productivity in the field of energy and environmental sciences and CO_2 emission in the G7 group of countries. As indicators of scientific productivity in the fields of energy and environmental science, the number of scientific publications was used. Environmental science encompasses scientific production in 11 subfields, while energy covers 5 subfields (Table 1.1). The required information on the number of scientific publications was retrieved from the Scopus-linked SCImago electronic database. On the other hand, the indicator of CO_2 emission is the total annual CO_2 emissions in kilotons. It covers emissions stemming from the burning of fossil fuels and the manufacture of cement. They include CO_2 produced during consumption of solid, liquid, and gas fuels and gas flaring. Data on CO_2 emission were obtained from the World Bank website. Limited by the availability of relevant data, the study covers a time frame from 1996 to 2019.

We begin our journey toward achieving the stated research aim by employing the VAR model. The VAR approach builds the model by expressing each endogenous variable in the system as a function of the lagged values of all endogenous variables within the system. This extends the univariate autoregressive model to a vector autoregressive model that consists of multiple time series variables. The general form of a VAR(m) model in terms of a mathematical expression follows:

$$y_t = \varphi_1 y_{t-1} + \ldots + \varphi_m y_{t-m} + ¥_1 x_t + \varepsilon_t \tag{a}$$

where y_t – endogenous column vector of order 2 × 1; x_t – exogenous column vector of order K × 1; *m* is the lag length for the endogenous variable; ε_t – error

Table 1.1. Scientific Subfields Included in the Analysis.

Fields	**Subfields**
Environmental science	Ecological modeling
	Ecology
	Environmental chemistry
	Environmental engineering
	Global and planetary change
	Health, toxicology, and mutagenesis
	Management, monitoring, policy, and law
	Nature and landscape conservation
	Pollution
	Waste management and disposal
	Water science and technology
Energy	Energy engineering and power technology
	Fuel technology
	Nuclear energy and engineering
	Renewable energy, sustainability, and the environment

Source: SCImago (n.d.).

column vector of order 2 × 1; φ_l, ..., φ_m are 2 × 2 order matrices; and 2 × K order matrices ¥ are the coefficient matrices to be estimated. We estimated VAR models in levels rather than in first differences. A VAR estimation in levels is considered by many to be valid even if the underlying variables have unit roots (Ashley & Verbrugge, 2009; Gospodinov et al., 2013; Hamilton, 1994; Sims, 1980). Gospodinov et al. (2013) found that the level of specification of the VAR model is generally more robust than the vector error correction model (VECM) and VAR in differences in terms of impulse response estimation when the true data generation process is unknown. Their findings align with the results of Ashley and Verbrugge (2009) who demonstrated that overdifferencing of the model leads to inaccurate estimations of impulse response functions, including inadequate coverage of confidence intervals.

In the pursuit of measuring the dynamic interrelationship among variables, the VAR analysis frequently leads to the computation of impulse response function and forecast variance decomposition error.

The impulse response function explains how a variable reacts to a one standard deviation disturbance caused by another variable in the system over short- and long-time horizons, while keeping all other variables unchanged. We employed the cumulative impulse response function to showcase the accumulation of disturbance impact on our variables over time rather than focusing on the impact at a single moment. The impulse response function is based on a moving average representation of the VAR model in Equation (a). The Cholesky decomposition is used to orthogonalize the variance–covariance matrix in the VAR framework. In this way, the problem of contemporaneous correlation among the variables is mitigated (Swanson & Granger, 1997). The variables are ordered in a specific manner, introducing a deliberate framework that guides the calculation of impulse response function and forecast variance decomposition error as explained by Sims (1980). The order of variables is set as follows: [CO_2 Env] and [CO_2 Enrg].[1] To examine impulse response parameters, it is essential to compute confidence intervals. The confidence interval of the impulse response function is calculated by estimating the standard error of the estimated VAR parameters, as they form the basis for creating the impulse response matrix. Due to the small

[1]Placing CO_2 as the first variable in a model assumes that changes in CO_2 in the current period may directly influence scientific production in the fields of Env and Enrg in the same period. However, this ordering also implies that immediate or simultaneous changes in scientific productivity in the fields of Env and Enrg do not have a direct impact on CO_2 in the same period. In other words, when there are sudden economic shocks happening right now, those shocks are not assumed to immediately affect CO_2 at the same time. Instead, this ordering suggests that any impact from publications in the Env and Enrg scientific fields on CO_2 might take some time to show up or occur with a delay. To summarize, this ordering assumes that changes in CO_2 can affect publications in the Env and Enrg scientific fields right away, but changes in scientific productivity in the fields of Env and Enrg do not immediately affect CO_2; there may be a time lag or delay for publications in the Env and Enrg scientific fields effects to influence CO_2.

sample size, we cannot rely confidently on asymptotically based confidence interval as previous research has shown that it provides adequate coverage only in sufficiently large samples (Kilian & Kim, 2011). Instead, we opted for a bootstrap approach. Nevertheless, Kilian (1998) states that the standard bootstrap interval will perform poorly in small samples, because it doesn't explicitly account for the bias and skewness of the small-sample distribution of the impulse response estimator. To address this issue, a so-called two-stage bias-adjusted approach has been developed (Kilian, 1998). Accordingly, we will obtain the standard error distribution of the impulse response function through two-stage bias-adjusted bootstrap confidence intervals with 1,000 bootstrap replications and 500 double-bootstrap replications and use the 0.5th and 99.5th, 2.5th and 97.5th, and 5th and 95th percentiles of the distribution as the lower and upper bound limits of the confidence interval of the impulse response results.

The impulse response function indicates only the direction of the impact but not its magnitude. Hence, we utilize forecast variance decomposition error to estimate the proportion of the change in a variable that can be attributed to its own disturbances and the disturbances of other variables in the system. In case that a variable explains most of its own disturbance, then it does not allow variances of other variables to contribute to it being explained and is therefore said to be relatively exogenous (Sims, 1982). Variance decompositions and associated standard errors are calculated using 1,000 Monte Carlo simulations.

3. Results

Different criteria can assist in selecting the appropriate lag length for the VAR model. The results of the Akaike information criterion (AIC), Schwarz information criterion (SIC), and Hannan and Quinn information criterion (HQIC) are provided in Table 1.2. In some cases, these three information criteria choose different lag lengths. While choosing a small number of lags can generate an omitted-variables bias problem, introducing an excessive number reduces the sample size available for estimation and, hence, increases the standard errors (Puente-Ajovín & Sanso-Navarro, 2015). Bearing in mind that our sample is relatively small, the final decision is to rely on the Schwarz information criterion, as it selects the most parsimonious model in the case of finite small samples.

In this study, the VAR models are two-way variable systems with lag specifications determined in the previous step. In all models, the values of adjusted R^2 are quite high and slightly lower than those of unadjusted R^2.[2] Therefore, the explanatory power of all equations is robust.

To check for the statistical adequacy of the established VAR models, stability, heteroscedasticity, and serial correlation tests were performed (Table 1.3). This is particularly important because if the model is not statistically adequate, the reliability of the obtained results and the derived inferences based on them can be questioned. The Lagrange multiplier test shows that the residuals are independent

[2]The results of the estimated VAR models are available upon request.

Table 1.2. Optimal Lag Length Selection Criteria.

Country	AIC				SIC				HQIC			
	Model 1	*m*	**Model 2**	*m*	**Model 1**	*m*	**Model 2**	*m*	**Model 1**	*m*	**Model 2**	*m*
Canada	−7.974	1	−6.539[a]	3	−7.675	1	−5.848[a]	1	−7.915	1	−6.404[a]	3
France	−7.459	1	−5.945[a]	1	−7.161	1	−5.647[a]	1	−7.402	1	−5.887[a]	1
Germany	−7.703	1	−6.133	3	−7.404	1	−5.515	2	−7.644	1	−5.997	3
Italy	−6.807[b]	2	−5.072[b]	2	−6.309[b]	2	−4.698[b]	1	−6.709[b]	2	−4.975[b]	2
Japan	−6.226	2	−5.405	2	−5.728	2	−5.036	1	−6.129	2	−5.307	2
The United Kingdom	−6.931	2	−5.782[b]	1	−6.433	2	−5.483[b]	1	−6.837	2	−5.724[b]	1
The United States	−7.609[b]	1	−6.083[c]	1	−7.31[b]	1	−5.785[c]	1	−7.551[b]	1	−6.025[c]	1

Source: Authors' calculation.

Note: Except for CO_2, Model 1 and Model 2 include environment and energy variables, respectively. Constant was used as an exogenous variable in each model. *m* – optimal number of lags. The maximum lag length considered was four.

[a]Two lags were selected because of heteroscedasticity.

[b]Three lags were included because of instability.

[c]Two lags were included because of instability.

Table 1.3. Residual and Stability Tests.

Equation No.	**Autocorrelation**	**Heteroscedasticity**	**Stability**
Panel a: Canada			
Env → CO_2 and CO_2 → Env	No	No	Stable
Enrg → CO_2 and CO_2 → Enrg	No	No	Stable
Panel b: France			
Env → CO_2 and CO_2 → Env	No	No	Stable
Enrg → CO_2 and CO_2 → Enrg	No	No	Stable
Panel c: Germany			
Env → CO_2 and CO_2 → Env	No	No	Stable
Enrg → CO_2 and CO_2 → Enrg	No	No	Unstable
Panel d: Italy			
Env → CO_2 and CO_2 → Env	No	No	Stable
Enrg → CO_2 and CO_2 → Enrg	No	No	Stable
Panel e: Japan			
Env → CO_2 and CO_2 → Env	No	No	Stable
Enrg → CO_2 and CO_2 → Enrg	No	No	Stable
Panel f: The United Kingdom			
Env → CO_2 and CO_2 → Env	No	No	Unstable
Enrg → CO_2 and CO_2 → Enrg	No	No	Stable
Panel g: The United States			
Env → CO_2 and CO_2 → Env	No	No	Stable
Enrg → CO_2 and CO_2 → Enrg	No	No	Stable

Source: Authors' calculation.

of each other. White test for heteroscedasticity confirms that the variance of the residuals is equal over a range of measured values. Most of the VAR models are stable as all the roots of the autoregressive characteristic polynominal have the modulus less than one, except in the case of Germany (Enrg → CO_2 and CO_2 → Enrg) and the United Kingdom (Env → CO_2 and CO_2 → Env). Hence, it is important to approach the findings of these four models with caution, viewing them as indicative.

The results of the cumulative impulse response analysis are reported in Table 1.4, with the corresponding two-stage bias-adjusted bootstrap confidence intervals presented in Tables A1–A3. We have presented a 10-year forecasting disturbance reaction horizon.

Table 1.4. Two-Stage Bias-Adjusted Bootstrap Cumulative Impulse Response Function.

β	α	$\lambda = 1$	$\lambda = 2$	$\lambda = 3$	$\lambda = 4$	$\lambda = 5$
Panel a: Canada						
CO_2	Env	/	0.002	0.004	0.007	0.01
Env	CO_2	0.012	0.036	0.068	0.104	0.142
CO_2	Enrg	/	−0.002	−0.0004	0.0004	0.002
Enrg	CO_2	0.003	0.024	0.089	0.157	0.235
Panel b: France						
CO_2	Env	/	−0.004	−0.011	−0.019	−0.029
Env	CO_2	−0.012	−0.018	−0.021	−0.023	−0.023
CO_2	Enrg	/	−0.005	−0.017	−0.03	−0.045
Enrg	CO_2	−0.024	−0.025	−0.011	0.007	0.032
Panel c: Germany						
CO_2	Env	/	−0.008	−0.016	−0.024	−0.031
Env	CO_2	−0.009	−0.029	−0.049	−0.069	−0.089
CO_2	Enrg	/	0.002	−0.005	−0.008	−0.015
Enrg	CO_2	0.01	0.026	−0.006	−0.02	−0.049
Panel d: Italy						
CO_2	Env	/	0.021	0.03	0.026	0.019
Environment	CO_2	−0.012	−0.007	0.006	0.019	0.034
CO_2	Enrg	/	−0.002	−0.009	−0.019	−0.035
Energy	CO_2	−0.026	−0.064	−0.14	−0.194	−0.253
Panel e: Japan						
CO_2	Env	/	0.001	0.001	−0.0003	−0.002
Env	CO_2	−0.019	−0.039	−0.061	−0.077	−0.091
CO_2	Enrg	/	−0.004	−0.01	−0.017	−0.024
Enrg	CO_2	−0.013	−0.005	0.015	0.04	0.067
Panel f: The United Kingdom						
CO_2	Env	/	0.006	−0.003	−0.013	−0.028
Env	CO_2	−0.014	−0.033	−0.049	−0.067	−0.087
CO_2	Enrg	/	−0.007	−0.026	−0.043	−0.067
Enrg	CO_2	−0.048	−0.072	−0.119	−0.143	−0.176

(*Continued*)

Table 1.4. (*Continued*)

β	α	$\lambda=1$	$\lambda=2$	$\lambda=3$	$\lambda=4$	$\lambda=5$
Panel g: The United States						
CO_2	Env	/	0.005	0.008	0.0001	−0.01
Env	CO_2	−0.004	−0.011	−0.021	−0.024	−0.026
CO_2	Enrg	/	−0.0002	−0.012	−0.027	−0.042
Enrg	CO_2	−0.005	−0.024	−0.032	−0.038	−0.044

β	α	$\lambda=6$	$\lambda=7$	$\lambda=8$	$\lambda=9$	$\lambda=10$
Panel a: Canada						
CO_2	Env	0.014	0.017	0.021	0.024	0.028
Env	CO_2	0.181	0.221	0.261	0.301	0.341
CO_2	Enrg	0.003	0.005	0.007	0.008	0.01
Enrg	CO_2	0.313	0.392	0.469	0.546	0.622
Panel b: France						
CO_2	Env	−0.039	−0.049	−0.059	−0.07	−0.08
Env	CO_2	−0.022	−0.022	−0.02	−0.019	−0.018
CO_2	Enrg	−0.061	−0.077	−0.092	−0.108	−0.123
Enrg	CO_2	0.058	0.085	0.113	0.141	0.168
Panel c: Germany						
CO_2	Env	−0.039	−0.046	−0.053	−0.06	−0.067
Env	CO_2	−0.108	−0.127	−0.145	−0.163	−0.181
CO_2	Enrg	−0.018	−0.024	−0.028	−0.034	−0.038
Enrg	CO_2	−0.063	−0.089	−0.106	−0.132	−0.152
Panel d: Italy						
CO_2	Env	0.009	−0.003	−0.016	−0.029	−0.044
Env	CO_2	0.048	0.063	0.079	0.096	0.113
CO_2	Enrg	−0.051	−0.069	−0.089	−0.109	−0.129
Enrg	CO_2	−0.288	−0.327	−0.349	−0.374	−0.388
Panel e: Japan						
CO_2	Env	−0.004	−0.005	−0.006	−0.007	−0.008
Env	CO_2	−0.101	−0.112	−0.124	−0.135	−0.147
CO_2	Enrg	−0.03	−0.036	−0.041	−0.044	−0.048
Enrg	CO_2	0.092	0.115	0.135	0.151	0.164

Table 1.4. (*Continued*)

β	α	$\lambda = 6$	$\lambda = 7$	$\lambda = 8$	$\lambda = 9$	$\lambda = 10$
Panel f: The United Kingdom						
CO_2	Env	−0.046	−0.068	−0.092	−0.119	−0.149
Env	CO_2	−0.107	−0.128	−0.15	−0.174	−0.198
CO_2	Enrg	−0.091	−0.119	−0.148	−0.179	−0.211
Enrg	CO_2	−0.199	−0.223	−0.242	−0.261	−0.276
Panel g: The United States						
CO_2	Env	−0.017	−0.027	−0.039	−0.053	−0.067
Env	CO_2	−0.03	−0.034	−0.036	−0.038	−0.04
CO_2	Enrg	−0.058	−0.074	−0.09	−0.106	−0.123
Enrg	CO_2	−0.05	−0.055	−0.061	−0.066	−0.071

Source: Authors' calculation.

Note: β is a variable that reacts to a disturbance in variable α. λ – forecast horizon.

A negative impact of scientific output in the field of environmental science and energy is observed in France, Germany, Italy, the United Kingdom, and the United States. Such findings suggest that an increase in scientific productivity in these fields contributes to the reduction of CO_2 emissions. When it comes to environmental science, both short- and long-term impacts are observed in France and Germany, while in the United Kingdom mid- and long-term impact are found. In Italy and the United States, only the long-term impacts are detected. When it comes to scientific research in the field of energy, both short-term and long-term impacts are observed in France, and the United States, while in the United Kingdom and Germany mid- and long-term impact are detected.

In the case of Canada, the impact goes in the opposite direction and has a positive sign. Increased CO_2 emissions stimulate scientific productivity in the fields of environmental science and energy in both the short and the long run.

No interrelationship is detected in Japan in either energy or environmental science field.

The results of forecast variance decomposition error analysis are reported in Tables 1.5 and 1.6. The tables show a 10-year-long forecasting.

In France, Germany, Italy, the United Kingdom, and the United States, approximately 6%, 16%, 20%, 6%, and 6% of the one-step forecast variance in CO_2 emissions, respectively, is attributed to disturbances in scientific productivity in the field of environmental sciences in the short term (Table 1.6). In the long run, the impact of the scientific output in the field of environmental sciences on the forecast error variance of CO_2 emissions increases by approximately 35, 24, 16, 48, and 52 percentage points in France, Germany, Italy, the United Kingdom, and the United States, respectively. The reaction of CO_2 emissions to disturbances

Table 1.5. Decomposition of the Forecast Error Variance of CO_2 (%).

Variable	λ = 1	λ = 2	λ = 3	λ = 4	λ = 5	λ = 6	λ = 7	λ = 8	λ = 9	λ = 10
Panel a: Canada										
Env	0	0.31	0.93	1.77	2.71	3.7	4.69	5.66	6.59	7.47
CO_2	100	99.69	99.07	98.23	97.29	96.29	95.31	94.34	93.42	92.53
Monte Carlo SE	0.023	0.028	0.03	0.031	0.032	0.033	0.033	0.034	0.034	0.034
Enrg	0	0.53	1.57	2.92	4.38	5.85	7.24	8.53	9.7	10.76
CO_2	100	99.47	98.43	97.09	95.62	94.15	92.76	91.47	90.29	89.24
Monte Carlo SE	0.024	0.029	0.032	0.033	0.034	0.035	0.036	0.036	0.037	0.037
Panel b: France										
Env	0	1.96	6.07	11.48	17.29	22.94	28.14	32.79	36.92	40.56
CO_2	100	98.05	93.93	88.52	82.7	77.06	71.86	67.21	63.09	59.44
Monte Carlo SE	0.027	0.031	0.034	0.035	0.036	0.038	0.039	0.04	0.042	0.043
Enrg	0	4.11	22.15	36.01	48.56	57.07	63.08	67.27	70.28	72.5
CO_2	100	95.89	77.85	63.99	51.44	42.93	36.92	32.73	29.72	27.49
Monte Carlo SE	0.023	0.025	0.028	0.031	0.034	0.038	0.041	0.044	0.047	0.049
Panel c: Germany										
Env	0	9.15	15.82	21.22	25.67	29.4	32.57	35.29	37.65	39.72
CO_2	100	90.85	84.18	78.78	74.33	70.59	67.43	64.71	62.35	60.28
Monte Carlo SE	0.026	0.027	0.029	0.029	0.031	0.032	0.033	0.034	0.035	0.036
Enrg	0	0.61	6.74	7.85	12.08	13.21	16.17	17.64	20.19	21.85
CO_2	100	99.39	93.26	92.15	87.92	86.79	83.83	82.37	79.81	78.15
Monte Carlo SE	0.026	0.028	0.029	0.029	0.03	0.03	0.031	0.031	0.032	0.032
Panel d: Italy										
Env	0	22.18	20.02	18.55	19.55	22.18	25.49	28.85	32.53	36.46
CO_2	100	77.82	79.99	81.45	80.45	77.82	74.5	71.15	67.47	63.54
Monte Carlo SE	0.026	0.044	0.051	0.054	0.055	0.056	0.057	0.059	0.06	0.062
Enrg	0	0.09	1.64	3.95	7.74	11.69	16.29	20.65	25.09	29.12

Table 1.5. (*Continued*)

Variable	λ = 1	λ = 2	λ = 3	λ = 4	λ = 5	λ = 6	λ = 7	λ = 8	λ = 9	λ = 10
CO_2	100	99.91	98.36	96.05	92.26	88.31	83.71	79.35	74.9	70.88
Monte Carlo SE	0.038	0.053	0.062	0.067	0.071	0.075	0.078	0.081	0.084	0.087
Panel e: Japan										
Env	0	0.08	0.09	0.13	0.28	0.38	0.47	0.52	0.56	0.59
CO_2	100	99.92	99.91	99.87	99.72	99.62	99.53	99.48	99.44	99.4
Monte Carlo SE	0.029	0.042	0.045	0.045	0.045	0.046	0.046	0.046	0.046	0.046
Enrg	0	1.18	3.21	5.49	7.61	9.35	10.68	11.61	12.23	12.62
CO_2	100	98.83	96.79	94.51	92.39	90.65	89.32	88.39	87.77	87.38
Monte Carlo SE	0.03	0.037	0.041	0.043	0.044	0.045	0.045	0.046	0.046	0.046
Panel f: The United Kingdom										
Env	0	2.66	6.45	11.08	18.58	27.02	35.02	42.23	48.42	53.65
CO_2	100	97.34	93.55	88.92	81.42	72.98	64.98	57.78	51.58	46.36
Monte Carlo SE	0.03	0.034	0.039	0.043	0.048	0.053	0.059	0.066	0.073	0.08
Enrg	0	3.37	20.41	27.75	37.84	45.87	53.08	58.86	63.79	67.79
CO_2	100	96.63	79.59	72.25	62.16	54.13	46.92	41.14	36.21	32.21
Monte Carlo SE	0.032	0.035	0.045	0.05	0.058	0.064	0.071	0.077	0.084	0.09
Panel g: The United States										
Env	0	4.24	6.45	15.19	24.76	29.33	36.95	45.72	52.52	58.38
CO_2	100	95.76	93.55	84.8	75.24	70.67	63.05	54.28	47.48	41.62
Monte Carlo SE	0.022	0.023	0.024	0.026	0.028	0.029	0.031	0.034	0.036	0.039
Enrg	0	0.008	19.81	37.65	49.66	58.55	64.95	69.65	73.24	76.05
CO_2	100	99.99	80.19	62.35	50.34	41.45	35.05	30.35	26.76	23.95
Monte Carlo SE	0.023	0.024	0.027	0.031	0.034	0.038	0.041	0.044	0.047	0.05

Source: Authors' calculation.

Note: λ – forecast horizon. SE – standard error.

Table 1.6. Decomposition of the Forecast Error Variance of Env and Enrg (%).

Variable	$\lambda = 1$	$\lambda = 2$	$\lambda = 3$	$\lambda = 4$	$\lambda = 5$	$\lambda = 6$	$\lambda = 7$	$\lambda = 8$	$\lambda = 9$	$\lambda = 10$
Panel a: Canada										
Env	93.79	84.33	76.53	70.72	66.45	63.3	60.93	59.1	57.67	56.53
CO_2	6.21	15.67	23.47	29.28	33.55	36.7	39.07	40.89	42.33	43.47
Monte Carlo SE	0.048	0.069	0.086	0.102	0.116	0.128	0.139	0.15	0.159	0.169
Enrg	99.21	95.84	92.07	88.63	85.71	83.31	81.37	79.79	78.51	77.46
CO_2	0.79	4.16	7.93	11.38	14.29	16.69	18.63	20.2	21.49	22.54
Monte Carlo SE	0.133	0.181	0.216	0.245	0.268	0.288	0.306	0.321	0.335	0.346
Panel b: France										
Env	94.38	96.4	97.49	98.12	98.51	98.76	98.93	99.06	99.16	99.23
CO_2	5.62	3.59	2.51	1.88	1.49	1.24	1.07	0.94	0.84	0.77
Monte Carlo SE	0.049	0.069	0.086	0.1	0.112	0.123	0.133	0.142	0.151	0.159
Enrg	95.61	96.97	97.44	97.3	96.76	96.27	95.81	95.41	95.08	94.81
CO_2	4.39	3.03	2.56	2.69	3.24	3.73	4.19	4.59	4.92	5.19
Monte Carlo SE	0.113	0.136	0.174	0.202	0.229	0.253	0.273	0.292	0.308	0.322
Panel c: Germany										
Env	96.87	89.82	87.64	86.54	85.88	85.44	85.12	84.89	84.7	84.55
CO_2	3.14	10.18	12.36	13.46	14.12	14.56	14.88	15.12	15.29	15.45
Monte Carlo SE	0.051	0.071	0.086	0.098	0.109	0.118	0.127	0.134	0.141	0.148
Enrg	98.39	95.18	87.74	87.14	84.62	84.74	83.89	83.89	83.38	83.32
CO_2	1.62	4.84	12.27	12.86	15.39	15.26	16.11	16.1	16.62	16.68
Monte Carlo SE	0.08	0.087	0.108	0.112	0.126	0.132	0.143	0.15	0.16	0.167
Panel d: Italy										
Env	96.14	97.13	95.92	95.73	95.3	94.97	94.76	94.49	94.22	93.96
CO_2	3.87	2.87	4.08	4.27	4.68	5.03	5.24	5.51	5.78	6.07
Monte Carlo SE	0.062	0.077	0.093	0.111	0.125	0.137	0.149	0.16	0.171	0.182
Enrg	92.9	84.81	73.72	71.75	73.23	74.86	77.32	79.09	81.03	82.43

Table 1.6. (*Continued*)

Variable	λ = 1	λ = 2	λ = 3	λ = 4	λ = 5	λ = 6	λ = 7	λ = 8	λ = 9	λ = 10
CO_2	7.09	15.19	26.28	28.26	26.77	25.14	22.69	20.91	18.97	17.57
Monte Carlo SE	0.098	0.118	0.174	0.196	0.231	0.249	0.274	0.289	0.309	0.323
Panel e: Japan										
Env	93.93	88.86	88.23	87.38	88.16	88.41	88.87	88.99	89.12	89.13
CO_2	6.07	11.14	11.77	12.62	11.84	11.59	11.13	11	10.88	10.87
Monte Carlo SE	0.079	0.084	0.103	0.109	0.119	0.125	0.132	0.135	0.142	0.146
Enrg	99.37	99.46	98.81	97.83	96.81	95.89	95.15	94.61	94.23	93.98
CO_2	0.63	0.54	1.19	2.17	3.19	4.11	4.85	5.39	5.77	6.02
Monte Carlo SE	0.161	0.205	0.228	0.24	0.248	0.252	0.254	0.255	0.256	0.256
Panel f: The United Kingdom										
Env	93.54	88.82	88.42	87.74	87.25	86.89	86.58	86.32	86.11	85.92
CO_2	0.46	11.18	11.58	12.26	12.76	13.11	13.42	13.68	13.89	14.08
Monte Carlo SE	0.054	0.07	0.083	0.097	0.109	0.121	0.133	0.145	0.157	0.169
Enrg	77.94	81.47	80.43	83.42	85	86.81	88.13	89.36	90.32	91.17
CO_2	22.06	18.53	19.58	16.58	14.99	13.19	11.87	10.64	9.68	8.83
Monte Carlo SE	0.102	0.125	0.161	0.184	0.212	0.234	0.257	0.278	0.298	0.316
Panel g: The United States										
Env	99.32	98.79	97.92	98.27	98.59	98.73	98.87	99.01	99.11	99.19
CO_2	0.68	1.2	2.08	1.73	1.41	1.27	1.13	0.99	0.89	0.81
Monte Carlo SE	0.048	0.073	0.089	0.1	0.112	0.125	0.136	0.147	0.157	0.167
Enrg	99.83	98.38	98.71	98.98	99.13	99.24	99.32	99.38	99.43	99.46
CO_2	0.17	1.62	1.29	1.02	0.87	0.76	0.68	0.62	0.57	0.54
Monte Carlo SE	0.112	0.156	0.189	0.221	0.249	0.274	0.297	0.318	0.337	0.356

Source: Authors' calculation.

Note: λ – forecast horizon. SE – standard error.

in the scientific output in the field of energy in France, Germany, Italy, the United Kingdom, and the United States accounts for around 22%, 7%, 2%, 20%, and 20% of the forecast error variance over the short term and 73%, 22%, 29%, 68%, and 76% in the long run, respectively.

In the case of Canada, CO_2 emissions account for 34% of the forecast error variance in scientific productivity in environmental science in the short term and 44% in the long term (Table 1.6). On the other side, around 14% of the forecast error variance in scientific output in the field of energy is attributed to CO_2 emissions in the short term, while this figure increases to 23% in the long term.

4. Conclusion

Given the devastating impact of climate change on public welfare and population health because of irresponsible and environmentally unsustainable human behavior, environmentalists, scientists, policymakers, and other stakeholders are challenged to identify the primary causes of CO_2 emissions and develop innovative mitigation solutions. Considering the importance of major advanced economies in policy discussions and coordination on a wide range of global issues such as the economy, trade, security, and the environment, as well as their significant scientific output and contributions to various fields of research, the main objective of this chapter was to investigate the dynamic interrelationship between scientific productivity in energy and environmental sciences and CO_2 emissions in the G7 countries.

This chapter's findings show that the relationship between scientific productivity in energy and environmental sciences and CO_2 emissions varies across the G7 countries. Namely, in France, Italy, the United Kingdom, the United States, and Germany, the number of scientific publications in the field of environmental science, and in the same countries, except Italy, the number of scientific publications in the field of energy influence a decrease in CO_2 emissions, whereas in Canada, an increase in CO_2 emissions influences an increase in the number of scientific publications. No interrelationship was found in Japan. Energy and environmental science publications play a positive role in addressing and mitigating CO_2 emissions by generating knowledge, identifying solutions, assessing impacts, informing policy and regulation, increasing public awareness and engagement, driving innovation, and promoting global collaboration on climate change mitigation.

Because the relationship between scientific publications and CO_2 emissions has not been thoroughly researched in the literature, this chapter contributes to the existing body of knowledge in this field. However, scientific publications alone are not sufficient to reduce CO_2 emissions. Effective research implementation, stakeholder collaboration, and strong policy and regulatory frameworks are required to transform scientific knowledge into concrete actions that result in emission reductions.

Acknowledgments

The research presented in this chapter received support from the Ministry of Science, Technological Development, and Innovation of the Republic of Serbia (Grant No. 451-03-47/2023-01/200005).

The authors extend their gratitude to the participants of the 15th International Scientific Conference "Environmental and Energy Economics: Climate Change Mitigation and Adaptation, Green Transition, Circular Economy," held on October 9–10, 2023, in Belgrade, Serbia, for their valuable comments and suggestions aimed at improving the research presented in this chapter.

References

Acheampong, A. O. (2018). Economic growth, CO_2 emissions and energy consumption: What causes what and where? *Energy Economics*, *74*, 677–692.

Ajmi, A. N., Hammoudeh, S., Nguyen, D. K., & Sat, J. R. (2015). On the relationships between CO_2 emissions, energy consumption and income: The importance of time variation. *Energy Economic*, *49*, 629–638.

Alam, M. S., Apergis, N., Paramati, S. R., & Fang, J. (2020). The impacts of R&D investment and stock markets on clean-energy consumption and CO_2 emissions in OECD economies. *International Journal of Finance & Economics*, *26*(4),1–14.

Aldieri, L., Kotsemir, K., & Vinci, C. P. (2021). Environmental innovations and productivity: Empirical evidence from Russian regions. *Resources Policy*, *74*, 101444.

Álvarez-Herránz, A., Balsalobre, D., Cantos, J. M., & Shahbaz, M. (2017). Energy innovations-GHG emissions nexus: Fresh empirical evidence from OECD countries. *Energy Policy*, *101*, 90–100.

Apergis, N., & Ozturk, I. (2015). Testing environmental Kuznets curve hypothesis in Asian countries. *Ecological Indicators*, *52*, 16–22.

Ashley, R. A., & Verbrugge, R. J. (2009). To difference or not to difference: a Monte Carlo investigation of inference in vector autoregression models. *International Journal of Data Analysis Techniques and Strategies*, *1*(3), 242–274.

Beraha, I., & Đuričin, S. (2022). *Perspektiva razvoja inovacionog sistema Republike Srbije*. Institute of Economic Sciences. ISBN: 978-86-89465-68-6.

Cai, Y., Sam, C. Y., & Chang, T. (2018). Nexus between clean energy consumption, economic growth and CO_2 emissions. *Journal of Cleaner Production*, *182*, 1001–1011.

Carrio'n-Flores C. E., & Innes, R. (2010). Environmental innovation and environmental performance. *Journal of Environmental Economics and Management*, *59*, 27–42.

Cheng, Y., Sinha, A., Ghosh, V., Sengupta, T., & Luo, H. (2021). Carbon tax and energy innovation at crossroads of carbon neutrality: Designing a sustainable decarbonization policy. *Journal of Environmental Management*, *294*, 112957.

Chiu, C. L., & Chang, T. H. (2009). What proportion of renewable energy supplies is needed to initially mitigate CO2 emissions in OECD member countries? *Renewable and Sustainable Energy Reviews*, *13*, 1669–1674.

Churchill, A., Inekwe, S., Smyth, R., & Zhang, X. (2019). R&D intensity and carbon emissions in the G7: 1870–2014. *Energy Economics*, *80*, 30–37.

de Gouveia, M., & Inglesi-Lotz, R. (2021). Examining the relationship between climate change-related research output and CO_2 emissions. *Scientometrics*, *126*, 9069–9111.

Difenbaugh, N. S. (2020). Verification of extreme event attribution: Using out-of-sample observations to assess changes in probabilities of unprecedented events. *Science Advances*, *6*(12), eaay2368.

Dinda, S. (2004). Environmental Kuznets curve hypothesis: A survey. *Ecological Economics*, *49*, 431–455.

Dong, K., Hochman, G., Zhang, Y., Sun, R., Li, H., & Liao, H. (2018). CO_2 emissions, economic and population growth, and renewable energy: Empirical evidence across regions. *Energy Economics*, *75*, 180–192.

Du, K., Li, P., & Yan, Z. (2019). Do green technology innovations contribute to carbon dioxide emission reduction? Empirical evidence from patent data. *Technological Forecasting and Social Change*, *146*, 297–303.

Đuričin, S., Beraha, I., Jovanović, O., Mosurović-Ružičić, M., Lazarević-Moravčević, M., & Paunović, M. (2022). The efficiency of national innovation policy programs: The case of Serbia. *Sustainability*, *14*(14), 8483.

Đuričin, S., Savić, S., Bodroža, D., Cvijanović, G., & Đorđević, S. (2016). Climate change impacts on agricultural water management: Challenge for increasing crop productivity in Serbia. *Economics of Agriculture*, *63*(4), 1333–1346.

Dzator, J., & Acheampong, A. O. (2020). The impact of energy innovation on carbon emission mitigation: An empirical evidence from OECD countries. In C. Hussain (Ed.), *Handbook of environmental materials management*. Springer, 1–21.

Garrone, P., & Grilli, L. (2010). Is there a relationship between public expenditures in energy R&D and carbon emissions per GDP? An empirical investigation. *Energy Policy*, *38*, 5600–5613.

Gessinger, G. (1997). Lower CO_2 emissions through better technology. *Energy Conversion and Management*, *38*, 25–30.

Gospodinov, N., Marı´a Herrera, A., & Pesavento, E. (2013). Unit roots, cointegration, and pretesting in VAR models. In T. B. Fomby, L.. Kilian, & A. Murphy (Eds.), *VAR models in macroeconomics—new developments and applications: Essays in honor of Christopher A. Sims* (pp. 81–115). Emerald Group Publishing Limited.

Hamilton, J. D. (1994). *Time series analysis*. Princeton University Press. https://doi.org/10.2307/j.ctv14jx6sm

Herring, H., & Sorrell, S. (2009). *Energy efficiency and sustainable consumption*. The Rebound Effect.

Huang, J. B., Liu, Q., Cai, X. C., Hao, Y., & Lei, H. Y. (2018). The effect of technological factors on China's carbon intensity: New evidence from a panel threshold model. *Energy Policy*, *115*, 32–42.

Khan, Z., Ali, S., Umar, M., Kirikkaleli, D., & Jiao, Z. (2020). Consumption based carbon emissions and international trade in G7 countries: The role of environmental innovation and renewable energy. *Science of the Total Environment*, *730*, 138945.

Kilian, L. (1998). Small-sample confidence intervals for impulse response functions. *The Review of Economics and Statistics*, *80*(2), 218–230.

Kilian, L., & Kim, Y. J. (2011). How reliable are local projection estimators of impulse responses? *The Review of Economics and Statistics*, *93*(4), 1460–1466.

Lee, K. H., & Min, B. (2015). Green R&D for eco-innovation and its impact on carbon emissions and firm performance. *Journal of Cleaner Production*, *108*, 534–542.

Mahmood, N., Wang, Z., & Hassan, S. T. (2019). Renewable energy, economic growth, human capital, and CO2 emission: An empirical analysis. *Environmental Science and Pollution Research*, *26*(20), 20619–20630.

Mensah, C. N., Long, X., Boamah, K. B., Bediako, I. A., Dauda, L., & Salman, M. (2018). The effect of innovation on CO_2 emissions of OCED countries from 1990 to 2014. *Environmental Science and Pollution Research*, *25*, 29678–29698.

Mongo, M., Belaid, F., & Ramdani, B. (2021). The effects of environmental innovations on CO_2 emissions: Empirical evidence from Europe. *Environmental Science & Policy, 118*, 1–9.

Montgomery, H. (2017). Preventing the progression of climate change: One drug or polypill? *Biofuel Research Journal, 13*, 536–536.

NASA. (2019). *Global warming vs. climate change*. https://climate.nasa.gov/global-warming-vs-climate-change/

Petrović, P., & Lobanov, M. M. (2020). The impact of R&D expenditures on CO_2 emissions: Evidence from sixteen OECD countries. *Journal of Cleaner Production, 248*, 119187.

Puente-Ajovín, M., & Sanso-Navarro, M. (2015). Granger causality between debt and growth: Evidence from OECD countries. *International Review of Economics & Finance, 35*, 66–77.

Raghutla, C., & Chittedi K. R. (2021). Financial development, energy consumption, technology, urbanization, economic output and carbon emissions nexus in BRICS countries: An empirical analysis. *Management of Environmental Quality: An International Journal, 32*(2), 290–307.

Romer, P. (1986). Increasing returns and long-run growth. *Journal of Political Economy, 94*(5), 1002–1037.

Sadorsky, P. (2014). The effect of urbanization on CO_2 emissions in emerging economies. *Energy Economics, 41*, 147–153.

SCImago. (n.d.). *SJR – SCImago journal & country rank* [Portal]. http://www.scimagojr.com

Shahbaz, M., Nasir, A., & Roubaud, D. (2018). Environmental degradation in France: The effects of FDI, financial development, and energy innovations. *Energy Economics, 74*, 843–857.

Sims, C. A. (1982). Policy analysis with econometric models. *Brookings Papers on Economic Activity, 1*, 107–152.

Sims, C. A. (1980). Macroeconomics and reality. *Econometrica, 48*, 1–48.

Stern, N. H. (2007). *The economics of climate change: The Stern review*. Cambridge University Press.

Swanson, N. R., & Granger, C. W. J. (1997). Impulse response functions based on a causal approach to residual orthogonalization in vector autoregressions. *Journal of the American Statistical Association, 92*, 357–367.

Többelmann, D., & Wendler, T. (2020). The impact of environmental innovation on carbon dioxide emissions. *Journal of Cleaner Production, 244*, 118787.

UNFCCC. (2015). *The Paris Agreement*. https://unfccc.int/process-and-meetings/the-paris-agreement/the-paris-agreement

Wang, Z., Yang, Z., Zhang, Y., Yin, J. (2012). Energy technology patents – CO_2 emissions nexus: An empirical analysis from China. *Energy Policy, 42*, 248–260.

Weina, D., Gilli, M., Mazzanti, M., & Nicolli, F. (2016). Green inventions and greenhouse gas emission dynamics: A close examination of provincial Italian data. *Environmental Economics and Policy Studies, 18*(2), 247–263.

World Health Organization. (2018). *COP24 special report: Health and climate change*. WHO.

Wu, Y., Zhu, Q. W., & Zhu, B. Z. (2018). Comparisons of decoupling trends of global economic growth and energy consumption between developed and developing countries. *Energy Policy, 116*, 30–38.

Zhang, G., Zhang, N., & Liao, W. (2018). How do population and land urbanization affect CO_2 emissions under gravity center change? A spatial econometric analysis. *Journal of Cleaner Production, 202*, 510–523.

Appendix

Table A1. 99% Two-Stage Bias-Adjusted Bootstrap Confidence Intervals with 1,000 Bootstrap Replications and 500 Double-Bootstrap Replications.

β	α	$\lambda = 1$	$\lambda = 2$	$\lambda = 3$	$\lambda = 4$	$\lambda = 5$
Panel a: Canada						
CO_2	Env	/	−0.001, 0.006	−0.004, 0.014	−0.007, 0.024	−0.011, 0.035
Env	CO_2	−0.01, 0.04	−0.02, 0.08	−0.02, 0.14	−0.02, 0.21	−0.03, 0.28
CO_2	Enrg	/	−0.009, 0.006	−0.012, 0.008	−0.017, 0.013	−0.02, 0.018
Enrg	CO_2	−0.04, 0.05	−0.05, 0.09	−0.03, 0.18	−0.01, 0.29	0.01, 0.43
Panel b: France						
CO_2	Env	/	−0.009, 0	−0.019, 0	−0.031, 0	−0.044, 0
Env	CO_2	−0.03, 0.02	−0.07, 0.04	−0.11, 0.08	−0.15, 0.13	−0.2, 0.2
CO_2	Enrg	/	−0.017, 0.007	−0.032, 0.002	−0.053, −0.001	−0.077, −0.005
Enrg	CO_2	−0.1, 0.03	−0.18, 0.1	−0.27, 0.2	−0.36, 0.33	−0.46, 0.48
Panel c: Germany						
CO_2	Env	/	−0.014, −0.002	−0.024, −0.004	−0.036, −0.008	−0.048, −0.011
Env	CO_2	−0.04, 0.01	−0.09, 0.02	−0.14, 0.04	−0.2, 0.06	−0.25, 0.09
CO_2	Enrg	/	−0.001, 0.04	−0.007, −0.002	−0.011, −0.004	−0.018, −0.007
Enrg	CO_2	−0.03, 0.05	−0.04, 0.09	−0.09, 0.09	−0.11, 0.1	−0.17, 0.11
Panel d: Italy						
CO_2	Env	/	0, 0.03	−0.01, 0.05	−0.03, 0.09	−0.05, 0.11
Env	CO_2	−0.04, 0.02	−0.07, 0.06	−0.11, 0.12	−0.15, 0.2	−0.2, 0.3
CO_2	Enrg	/	−0.02, 0.02	−0.05, 0.03	−0.08, 0.05	−0.13, 0.06
Enrg	CO_2	−0.1, 0	−0.2, 0.1	−0.4, 0.1	−0.5, 0.2	−0.8, 0.2
Panel e: Japan						
CO_2	Env	/	−0.013, 0.016	−0.022, 0.027	−0.033, 0.038	−0.04, 0.043
Env	CO_2	−0.06, 0.02	−0.1, 0.03	−0.17, 0.05	−0.25, 0.1	−0.34, 0.13
CO_2	Enrg	/	−0.01, 0.01	−0.03, 0.02	−0.06, 0.03	−0.08, 0.04
Enrg	CO_2	−0.09, 0.08	−0.17, 0.18	−0.25, 0.31	−0.35, 0.46	−0.45, 0.67

Table A1. (*Continued*)

β	α	λ = 1	λ = 2	λ = 3	λ = 4	λ = 5
Panel f: The United Kingdom						
CO_2	Env	/	0, 0.009	−0.006, 0	−0.019, −0.004	−0.038, −0.011
Env	CO_2	−0.04, 0.02	−0.08, 0.02	−0.11, 0.03	−0.15, 0.04	−0.2, 0.05
CO_2	Enrg	/	−0.02, 0.01	−0.05, 0	−0.08, 0.01	−0.12, 0.01
Enrg	CO_2	−0.08, 0.02	−0.15, 0.07	−0.28, 0.11	−0.41, 0.18	−0.58, 0.27
Panel g: The -United States						
CO_2	Env	/	−0.008, 0.015	−0.013, −0.024	−0.021, 0.023	−0.033, 0.022
Env	CO_2	−0.03, 0.02	−0.07, 0.05	−0.12, 0.07	−0.17, 0.12	−0.22, 0.18
CO_2	Enrg	/	−0.004, 0.003	−0.017, −0.006	−0.033, −0.013	−0.05, −0.021
Enrg	CO_2	−0.05, 0.06	−0.13, 0.11	−0.19, 0.16	−0.26, 0.22	−0.32, 0.28
β	**α**	**λ = 6**	**λ = 7**	**λ = 8**	**λ = 9**	**λ = 10**
Panel a: Canada						
CO_2	Env	−0.016, 0.046	−0.021, 0.059	−0.027, 0.072	−0.031, 0.087	−0.036, 0.102
Env	CO_2	−0.04, 0.36	−0.05, 0.45	−0.05, 0.56	−0.06, 0.67	−0.07, 0.78
CO_2	Enrg	−0.024, 0.023	−0.027, 0.029	−0.03, 0.034	−0.034, 0.04	−0.036, 0.048
Enrg	CO_2	0.03, 0.59	0.05, 0.78	0.08, 0.95	0.1, 1.14	0.12, 1.37
Panel b: France						
CO_2	Env	−0.059, 0	−0.076, 0	−0.092, 0	−0.108, 0.001	−0.129, 0.001
Env	CO_2	−0.25, 0.28	−0.3, 0.35	−0.35, 0.45	−0.4, 0.51	−0.45, 0.65
CO_2	Enrg	−0.106, −0.016	−0.141, −0.022	−0.174, −0.026	−0.208, −0.032	−0.239, −0.035
Enrg	CO_2	−0.54, 0.67	−0.63, 0.89	−0.72, 1.13	−0.83, 1.36	−0.95, 1.63
Panel c: Germany						
CO_2	Env	−0.06, −0.015	−0.072, −0.018	−0.084, −0.022	−0.097, −0.025	−0.11, −0.027
Env	CO_2	−0.31, 0.11	−0.36, 0.13	−0.42, 0.15	−0.48, 0.17	−0.54, 0.18

(*Continued*)

Table A1. (*Continued*)

β	α	$\lambda = 6$	$\lambda = 7$	$\lambda = 8$	$\lambda = 9$	$\lambda = 10$
CO_2	Enrg	−0.023, −0.009	−0.029, −0.012	−0.035, −0.014	−0.041, −0.017	−0.048, −0.019
Enrg	CO_2	−0.2, 0.12	−0.25, 0.13	−0.28, 0.14	−0.33, 0.15	−0.37, 0.16
Panel d: Italy						
CO_2	Env	−0.07, 0.13	−0.09, 0.14	−0.11, 0.15	−0.14, 0.16	−0.17, 0.17
Env	CO_2	−0.26, 0.42	−0.31, 0.54	−0.37, 0.68	−0.43, 0.85	−0.51, 1.06
CO_2	Enrg	−0.18, 0.07	−0.24, 0.08	−0.31, 0.09	−0.38, 0.1	−0.45, 0.11
Enrg	CO_2	−1.1, 0.3	−1.4, 0.4	−1.7, 0.5	−2.2, 0.6	−2.6, 0.8
Panel e: Japan						
CO_2	Env	−0.045, 0.047	−0.053, 0.052	−0.06, 0.06	−0.068, 0.067	−0.077, 0.075
Env	CO_2	−0.41, 0.17	−0.5, 0.23	−0.6, 0.27	−0.71, 0.32	−0.81, 0.37
CO_2	Enrg	−0.11, 0.05	−0.14, 0.07	−0.17, 0.08	−0.21, 0.1	−0.24, 0.11
Enrg	CO_2	−0.54, 0.89	−0.64, 1.16	−0.73, 1.44	−0.83, 1.72	−0.95, 2
Panel f: The United Kingdom						
CO_2	Env	−0.06, −0.019	−0.087, −0.028	−0.117, −0.038	−0.151, −0.05	−0.188, −0.062
Env	CO_2	−0.24, 0.06	−0.028, 0.07	−0.33, 0.09	−0.38, 0.1	−0.44, 0.11
CO_2	Enrg	−0.17, 0.01	−0.23, 0	−0.29, 0.01	−0.34, 0.01	−0.41, 0.01
Enrg	CO_2	−0.75, 0.38	−0.96, 0.49	−1.23, 0.6	−1.58, 0.74	−1.83, 0.93
Panel g: The United States						
CO_2	Env	−0.047, 0.022	−0.069, 0.018	−0.1, 0.016	−0.131, 0.014	−0.164, 0.012
Env	CO_2	−0.28, 0.26	−0.33, 0.34	−0.4, 0.42	−0.48, 0.53	−0.58, 0.53
CO_2	Enrg	−0.068, −0.029	−0.087, −0.037	−0.106, −0.046	−0.125, −0.054	−0.145, −0.062
Enrg	CO_2	−0.39, 0.34	−0.45, 0.41	−0.52, 0.47	−0.58, 0.53	−0.65, 0.59

Note: β is a variable that reacts to a disturbance in variable α. λ – forecast horizon.

Table A2. 95% Two-Stage Bias-Adjusted Bootstrap Confidence Intervals with 1,000 Bootstrap Replications and 500 Double-Bootstrap Replications.

β	α	λ = 1	λ = 2	λ = 3	λ = 4	λ = 5
Panel a: Canada						
CO_2	Env	/	−0.001, 0.004	−0.002, 0.01	−0.004, 0.016	−0.006, 0.024
Env	CO_2	−0.01, 0.03	0, 0.08	0, 0.13	0.01, 0.19	0.01, 0.26
CO_2	Enrg	/	−0.007, 0.004	−0.008, 0.006	−0.011, 0.01	−0.012, 0.014
Enrg	CO_2	−0.03, 0.04	−0.04, 0.08	−0.01, 0.15	0.02, 0.25	0.06, 0.37
Panel b: France						
CO_2	Env	/	−0.007, −0.001	−0.017, −0.003	−0.029, −0.005	−0.041, −0.008
Env	CO_2	−0.03, 0.01	−0.05, 0.02	−0.09, 0.05	−0.12, 0.09	−0.16, 0.14
CO_2	Enrg	/	−0.011, 0.005	−0.024, −0.001	−0.041, −0.007	−0.063, −0.015
Enrg	CO_2	−0.08, 0.02	−0.14, 0.06	−0.2, 0.15	−0.26, 0.25	−0.31, 0.36
Panel c: Germany						
CO_2	Env	/	−0.012, −0.003	−0.022, −0.006,	−0.033, −0.01	−0.044, −0.014
Env	CO_2	−0.03, 0.01	−0.07, 0.01	−0.11, 0.02	−0.16, 0.02	−0.2, 0.03
CO_2	Enrg	/	0, 0.004	−0.006, −0.003	−0.01, −0.004	−0.017, −0.008
Enrg	CO_2	−0.02, 0.04	−0.02, 0.02	−0.07, 0.07	−0.09, 0.07	−0.13, 0.07
Panel d: Italy						
CO_2	Env	/	0.003, 0.03	−0.006, 0.053	−0.018, 0.069	−0.032, 0.084
Env	CO_2	−0.03, 0.02	−0.06, 0.05	−0.08, 0.09	−0.11, 0.15	−0.13, 0.21
CO_2	Enrg	/	−0.02, 0.01	−0.04, 0.02	−0.07, 0.04	−0.11, 0.04
Enrg	CO_2	−0.07, 0.03	−0.15, 0.04	−0.3, 0.06	−0.45, 0.09	−0.63, 0.14
Panel e: Japan						
CO_2	Env	/	−0.009, 0.011	−0.014, 0.017	−0.021, 0.023	−0.028, 0.026
Env	CO_2	−0.05, 0.01	−0.08, 0.02	−0.14, 0.04	−0.21, 0.05	−0.28, 0.08
CO_2	Enrg	/	−0.01, 0.005	−0.025, 0.012	−0.043, 0.02	−0.064, 0.028
Enrg	CO_2	−0.07, 0.06	−0.14, 0.16	−0.2, 0.28	−0.27, 0.41	−0.34, 0.56

(*Continued*)

Table A2. (*Continued*)

β	α	λ = 1	λ = 2	λ = 3	λ = 4	λ = 5
Panel f: The United Kingdom						
CO_2	Env	/	0, 0.008	−0.005, 0	−0.017, −0.006	−0.034, −0.013
Env	CO_2	−0.03, 0.01	−0.07, 0.01	−0.1, 0.01	−0.14, 0.01	−0.17, 0.01
CO_2	Enrg	/	−0.02, 0	−0.04, 0	−0.07, −0.01	−0.1, −0.01
Enrg	CO_2	−0.07, 0	−0.13, 0.03	−0.24, 0.05	−0.33, 0.11	−0.46, 0.16
Panel g: The United States						
CO_2	Env	/	−0.006, 0.012	−0.009, 0.022	−0.018, 0.018	−0.029, 0.014
Env	CO_2	−0.02, 0.01	−0.05, 0.03	−0.09, 0.05	−0.13, 0.08	−0.17, 0.12
CO_2	Enrg	/	−0.003, 0.003	−0.015, −0.006	−0.03, −0.015	−0.045, −0.025
Enrg	CO_2	−0.04, 0.04	−0.1, 0.06	−0.15, 0.1	−0.19, 0.13	−0.24, 0.17

β	α	**λ = 6**	**λ = 7**	**λ = 8**	**λ = 9**	**λ = 10**
Panel a: Canada						
CO_2	Env	−0.009, 0.032	−0.012, 0.04	−0.015, 0.049	−0.019, 0.058	−0.023, 0.069
Env	CO_2	0.02, 0.34	0.02, 0.43	0.03, 0.52	0.04, 0.62	0.05, 0.73
CO_2	Enrg	−0.014, 0.018	−0.015, 0.022	−0.017, 0.027	−0.019, 0.032	−0.021, 0.036
Enrg	CO_2	0.08, 0.51	0.12, 0.67	0.14, 0.83	0.18, 0.99	0.21, 1.15
Panel b: France						
CO_2	Env	−0.055, −0.012	−0.069, −0.017	−0.084, −0.022	−0.1, −0.026	−0.116, −0.03
Env	CO_2	−0.19, 0.19	−0.23, 0.25	−0.27, 0.32	−0.31, 0.38	−0.35, 0.46
CO_2	Enrg	−0.088, −0.022	−0.115, −0.03	−0.145, −0.036	−0.175, −0.045	−0.206, −0.049
Enrg	CO_2	−0.37, 0.41	−0.43, 0.61	−0.5, 0.76	−0.57, 0.93	−0.62, 1.11
Panel c: Germany						
CO_2	Env	−0.056, −0.018	−0.067, −0.022	−0.079, −0.025	−0.09, −0.029	−0.101, −0.032
Env	CO_2	−0.24, 0.03	−0.29, 0.04	−0.33, 0.05	−0.37, 0.06	−0.42, 0.07

Table A2. (*Continued*)

β	α	$\lambda = 6$	$\lambda = 7$	$\lambda = 8$	$\lambda = 9$	$\lambda = 10$
CO_2	Enrg	−0.021, −0.01	−0.027, −0.013	−0.032, −0.015	−0.039, −0.019	−0.044, −0.021
Enrg	CO_2	−0.16, 0.07	−0.2, 0.07	−0.23, 0.07	−0.27, 0.08	−0.31, 0.08
Panel d: Italy						
CO_2	Env	−0.046, 0.093	−0.063, 0.099	−0.083, 0.093	−0.103, 0.092	−0.124, 0.087
Env	CO_2	−0.17, 0.31	−0.21, 0.4	−0.25, 0.49	−0.29, 0.61	−0.33, 0.72
CO_2	Enrg	−0.14, 0.05	−0.19, 0.05	−0.23, 0.05	−0.28, 0.06	−0.33, 0.06
Enrg	CO_2	−0.81, 0.2	−1, 0.27	−1.17, 0.36	−1.39, 0.45	−1.61, 0.56
Panel e: Japan						
CO_2	Env	−0.033, 0.028	−0.04, 0.031	−0.045, 0.034	−0.05, 0.037	−0.058, 0.04
Env	CO_2	−0.35, 0.1	−0.42, 0.13	−0.51, 0.15	−0.6, 0.18	−0.68, 0.2
CO_2	Enrg	−0.087, 0.036	−0.111, 0.044	−0.138, 0.053	−0.164, 0.061	−0.191, 0.068
Enrg	CO_2	−0.41, 0.73	−0.49, 0.91	−0.57, 1.09	−0.65, 1.28	−0.73, 1.49
Panel f: The United Kingdom						
CO_2	Env	−0.055, −0.022	−0.08, −0.033	−0.108, −0.044	−0.139, −0.057	−0.173, −0.071
Env	CO_2	−0.21, 0.01	−0.25, 0.02	−0.29, 0.02	−0.34, 0.02	−0.39, 0.02
CO_2	Enrg	−0.15, −0.02	−0.2, −0.03	−0.25, −0.04	−0.31, 0.05	−0.37, −0.06
Enrg	CO_2	−0.58, 0.24	−0.74, 0.32	−0.89, 0.43	−1.03, 0.55	−1.2, 0.68
Panel g: The United States						
CO_2	Env	−0.041, 0.012	−0.057, 0.007	−0.079, 0.003	−0.103, −0.001	−0.127, −0.005
Env	CO_2	−0.21, 0.16	−0.25, 0.22	−0.3 0.27	−0.35, 0.34	−0.4, 0.41
CO_2	Enrg	−0.063, −0.034	−0.081, −0.044	−0.099, −0.054	−0.118, −0.064	−0.136, −0.074
Enrg	CO_2	−0.28, 0.21	−0.33, 0.25	−0.38, 0.29	−0.43, 0.33	−0.47, 0.37

Note: β is a variable that reacts to a disturbance in variable α. λ – forecast horizon.

Table A3. 90% Two-Stage Bias-Adjusted Bootstrap Confidence Intervals with 1,000 Bootstrap Replications and 500 Double-Bootstrap Replications.

β	α	$\lambda = 1$	$\lambda = 2$	$\lambda = 3$	$\lambda = 4$	$\lambda = 5$
Panel a: Canada						
CO_2	Env	/	0, 0.004	−0.001, 0.009	−0.003, 0.015	−0.004, 0.021
Env	CO_2	0, 0.003	0, 0.007	0.01, 0.12	0.02, 0.17	0.03, 0.24
CO_2	Enrg	/	−0.006, 0.003	−0.007, 0.005	−0.01, 0.008	−0.011, 0.011
Enrg	CO_2	−0.02, 0.03	−0.02, 0.07	0.02, 0.14	0.05, 0.23	0.09, 0.35
Panel b: France						
CO_2	Env	/	−0.007, 0.001	−0.016, −0.004	−0.026, −0.007	−0.039, −0.011
Env	CO_2	−0.02, 0.01	−0.05, 0.02	−0.07, 0.04	−0.01, 0.07	−0.13, 0.11
CO_2	Enrg	/	−0.011, 0.003	−0.023, −0.004	−0.039, −0.01	−0.057, −0.018
Enrg	CO_2	−0.08, 0.02	−0.13, 0.05	−0.18, 0.12	−0.23, 0.19	−0.28, 0.3
Panel c: Germany						
CO_2	Env	/	−0.011, −0.003	−0.021, −0.008	−0.031, −0.012	−0.041, −0.016
Env	CO_2	−0.02, 0	−0.06, 0	−0.1, 0.01	−0.14, 0.01	−0.18, 0.02
CO_2	Enrg	/	0, 0.004	−0.006, −0.003	−0.01, −0.004	−0.016, −0.009
Enrg	CO_2	−0.02, 0.03	−0.02, 0.06	−0.06, 0.05	−0.08, 0.04	−0.13, 0.04
Panel d: Italy						
CO_2	Env	/	0.005, 0.027	0, 0.051	−0.011, 0.065	−0.022, 0.075
Env	CO_2	−0.03, 0.01	−0.05, 0.04	−0.04, 0.08	−0.09, 0.13	−0.11, 0.19
CO_2	Enrg	/	−0.01, 0.01	−0.04, 0.02	−0.06, 0.03	−0.09, 0.03
Enrg	CO_2	−0.03, 0.02	−0.13, 0.02	−0.26, 0.02	−0.41, 0.04	−0.58, 0.07
Panel e: Japan						
CO_2	Env	/	−0.007, 0.009	−0.012, 0.013	−0.019, 0.018	−0.024, 0.019
Env	CO_2	−0.04, 0.01	−0.08, 0.01	−0.14, 0.02	−0.18, 0.04	−0.24, 0.06
CO_2	Enrg	/	−0.009, 0.003	−0.022, 0.006	−0.038, 0.011	−0.057, 0.015
Enrg	CO_2	−0.07, 0.05	−0.12, 0.13	−0.17, 0.22	−0.22, 0.34	−0.28, 0.46

Table A3. (*Continued*)

β	α	λ = 1	λ = 2	λ = 3	λ = 4	λ = 5
Panel f: The United Kingdom						
CO_2	Env	/	0, 0.008	−0.005, 0	−0.016, −0.006	−0.032, −0.015
Env	CO_2	−0.03, 0.01	−0.06, 0.01	−0.09, 0.01	−0.12, 0.01	−0.15, 0.01
CO_2	Enrg	/	−0.01, 0	−0.04, 0	−0.06, −0.01	−0.1, −0.02
Enrg	CO_2	−0.05, −0.01	−0.12, 0.01	−0.22, 0.02	−0.31, 0.06	−0.42, 0.09
Panel g: The United States						
CO_2	Env	/	−0.004, 0.012	−0.006, 0.018	−0.014, 0.015	−0.021, 0.01
Env	CO_2	−0.02, 0.01	−0.04, 0.03	−0.08, 0.05	−0.1, 0.07	−0.13, 0.1
CO_2	Enrg	/	−0.03, 0.02	−0.014, −0.007	−0.029, −0.017	−0.045, −0.027
Enrg	CO_2	−0.04, 0.04	−0.09, 0.06	−0.13, 0.09	−0.18, 0.13	−0.22, 0.17

β	α	**λ = 6**	**λ = 7**	**λ = 8**	**λ = 9**	**λ = 10**
Panel a: Canada						
CO_2	Env	−0.006, 0.028	−0.007, 0.035	−0.009, 0.042	−0.011, 0.05	−0.013, 0.057
Env	CO_2	0.04, 0.31	0.05, 0.39	0.06, 0.47	0.07, 0.55	0.08, 0.64
CO_2	Enrg	−0.014, 0.013	−0.015, 0.017	−0.017, 0.02	−0.018, 0.023	−0.02, 0.027
Enrg	CO_2	0.12, 0.46	0.18, 0.6	0.2, 0.74	0.24, 0.89	0.27, 1.05
Panel b: France						
CO_2	Env	−0.051, −0.015	−0.064, −0.02	−0.079, −0.025	−0.095, −0.03	−0.111, −0.036
Env	CO_2	−0.16, 0.15	−0.19, 0.2	−0.22, 0.25	−0.25, 0.31	−0.29, 0.37
CO_2	Enrg	−0.078, −0.027	−0.102, −0.035	−0.128, −0.042	−0.157, −0.05	−0.185, −0.057
Enrg	CO_2	−0.33, 0.42	−0.38, 0.55	−0.43, 0.71	−0.48, 0.85	−0.52, 1
Panel c: Germany						
CO_2	Env	−0.051, −0.02	−0.06, −0.024	−0.07, −0.028	−0.081, −0.03	−0.092, −0.035
Env	CO_2	−0.22, 0.02	−0.26, 0.03	−0.3, 0.03	−0.34, 0.04	−0.37, 0.04

(*Continued*)

Table A3. (*Continued*)

β	α	$\lambda = 6$	$\lambda = 7$	$\lambda = 8$	$\lambda = 9$	$\lambda = 10$
CO_2	Enrg	−0.02, −0.011	−0.026, −0.014	−0.031, −0.017	−0.037, −0.02	−0.042, −0.023
Enrg	CO_2	−0.15, 0.04	−0.19, 0.03	−0.22, 0.03	−0.26, 0.03	−0.29, 0.02
Panel d: Italy						
CO_2	Env	−0.035, 0.079	−0.05, 0.079	−0.064, 0.072	−0.081, 0.065	−0.1, 0.055
Env	CO_2	−0.14, 0.26	−0.17, 0.34	−0.2, 0.43	−0.23, 0.52	−0.25, 0.61
CO_2	Enrg	−0.13, 0.04	−0.17, 0.04	−0.2, 0.04	−0.25, 0.04	−0.29, 0.04
Enrg	CO_2	−0.74, 0.12	−0.95, 0.18	−1.13, 0.25	−1.34, 0.34	−1.56, 0.44
Panel e: Japan						
CO_2	Env	−0.029, 0.02	−0.034, 0.021	−0.038, 0.022	−0.042, 0.023	−0.046, 0.025
Env	CO_2	−0.29, 0.08	−0.36, 0.10	−0.42, 0.11	−0.48, 0.13	−0.54, 0.15
CO_2	Enrg	−0.077, 0.02	−0.098, 0.026	−0.12, 0.032	−0.143, 0.036	−0.166, 0.041
Enrg	CO_2	−0.33, 0.6	−0.4, 0.74	−0.45, 0.89	−0.52, 1.05	−0.58, 1.21
Panel f: The United Kingdom						
CO_2	Env	−0.054, −0.025	−0.078, −0.037	−0.105, −0.05	−0.136, −0.065	−0.169, −0.081
Env	CO_2	−0.19, 0.01	−0.22, 0.01	−0.26, 0.01	−0.3, 0.01	−0.34, 0.01
CO_2	Enrg	−0.13, −0.03	−0.17, −0.04	−0.22, −0.04	−0.27, −0.05	−0.32, −0.06
Enrg	CO_2	−0.53, 0.14	−0.67, 0.20	−0.79, 0.27	−0.95, 0.34	−1.11, 0.43
Panel g: The United States						
CO_2	Env	−0.035, 0.007	−0.051, 0.003	−0.07, −0.001	−0.091, −0.008	−0.115, −0.012
Env	CO_2	−0.16, 0.14	−0.2, 0.18	−0.23, 0.23	−0.27, 0.28	−0.31, 0.33
CO_2	Enrg	−0.062, −0.038	−0.079, −0.049	−0.097, −0.06	−0.115, −0.07	−0.133, −0.081
Enrg	CO_2	−0.26, 0.21	−0.3, 0.25	−0.34, 0.29	−0.38, 0.33	−0.43, 0.36

Note: β is a variable that reacts to a disturbance in variable α. λ – forecast horizon.

Chapter 2

China's Pursuit of Carbon Neutrality: Roadblocks and Greenlights

Vasilii Erokhin and Tianming Gao

Harbin Engineering University, China

Abstract

Sustainable development is inseparable from rational and responsible use of resources and promotion of green entrepreneurship. The contemporary green development agenda encompasses climate, economic, technical, social, cultural, and political dimensions. International efforts to greening the global development are conducted by the major economies, including China as the world's largest consumer of energy and the biggest emitter of greenhouse gases. China is aware of its environmental problems, as well as of its part of the overall responsibility for the accomplishment of the sustainable development goals. By means of the decarbonization efforts, the latter are integrated both into the national development agenda (the concept of ecological civilization) and China's international initiatives (the greening narrative within the Belt and Road Initiative). Over the past decade, China has made a breakthrough on the way to promoting green entrepreneurship and greening of its development (better quality of air and water, renewable energy, electric vehicles, and organic farming). On the other hand, emissions remain high, agricultural land loses productivity, and freshwater resources degrade due to climate change. In conventional industries (oil, coal mining, and electric and thermal energy), decarbonization faces an array of impediments. In this chapter, the authors summarize fundamental provisions of China's approach to building an ecological civilization and measures to reduce emissions and achieve the carbon neutrality status within the nearest decades. The analysis of obstacles to the decarbonization of the economy and possible prospects for

Emerging Patterns and Behaviors in a Green Resilient Economy, 31–59

doi:10.1108/978-1-83549-780-720241002

the development of green entrepreneurship summarizes China's practices for possible use in other countries.

Keywords: China; decarbonization; ecological civilization; green development; renewable energy; policy

Introduction

The progressing climate change is widely recognized as one of the critical challenges to sustaining global development and growth (Bosello et al., 2018; Chisholm, 2010). Most scholars associate climate change with the greenhouse effect, i.e., with a total increase in the concentration of greenhouse gases (GHGs) in the atmosphere as a result of economic activities, emissions from industrial production, transport, and agriculture, and degradation of lands, forests, and other natural resources (Auffhammer et al., 2013; Chen, Yao, et al., 2023; Espoir et al., 2022; Tol, 2005). Thus, climate changes are anthropogenic in their nature. As a result of burning fossil fuels, the increasing concentration of GHGs in the air is warming up the lower layers of the atmosphere and the upper layers of oceans and seas (Gowdy & Julia, 2010). The rise in the average annual temperature upsets the balance of all environmental systems, including a change in the precipitation regime, temperature anomalies, melting of polar ice and glaciers, increase in the sea level, and higher acidity of seas and oceans due to the absorption of carbon dioxide (CO_2) from the atmosphere (Darwin & Tol, 2001). As a result, there increases the frequency of extreme weather events (hurricanes, floods, droughts, etc.), creating not only a deadly threat to people, flora, and fauna but also causing economic damage across industries and sectors worldwide (Botzen et al., 2010; Kelly et al., 2005; Zhilina, 2020).

The anthropogenic origin of the problem implies an anthropogenic response to this problem. In the event that GHG emissions are not radically reduced in the next two to three decades, extreme weather events related to climate change can lead to devastating economic losses to all countries (Collier et al., 2008; Dell et al., 2012; Deschenes & Greenstone, 2007; Keller et al., 2004). Nevertheless, despite the widespread recognition of the climate change issue, GHG emissions have been rising since the mid-20th century. In 2015, the Paris Agreement (United Nations, 2015) was adopted, providing for the obligations of all the countries that joined to reduce GHG emissions and work together to adapt themselves to the effects of climate change. The ultimate goal of the agreement is to keep the growth of the average temperature on the planet at least within 2.0 °C by 2100 in comparison with the pre-industrial period (mid-19th century). To stabilize the climate, the desired change of the average temperature should not exceed 1.5 °C. To achieve these targets, it is necessary to reduce to zero the balance between the volume of anthropogenic GHG emissions and the absorption capacity of the terrestrial ecosystem. The transition to zero emissions by 2050 will require a radical revision of the principles of land use and agriculture (Mendelsohn &

Dinar, 2003), urban planning and industrial development, as well as the promotion of energy efficiency, renewable energy, organic agriculture, electric vehicles and machinery, and other carbon neutral solutions (Bagheri et al., 2018; Bistline et al., 2018).

One of the most comprehensive responses of humanity to the threats of uncontrolled climate change and environmental degradation is the green economy concept. It is based on the principle of rational use of natural resources with fewer negative consequences for the environment (Reilly, 2012). It is assumed that the countries will use new opportunities for cooperation and access to cheaper technologies for the production of energy, food, housing, and other vital needs of the population while seizing control of the environmental degradation (Hassan, 2010). However, the contemporary green development agenda goes far beyond climatic and environmental dimensions. Green transformation (a.k.a. green transition) involves a whole range of political, economic, technological, social, and even cultural aspects. The United Nations (UN) and other international organizations promote the green development concept as a key to success in achieving the sustainable development goals (SDGs) and complying with the Framework Convention on Climate Change, the Paris Agreement, and other climate-related initiatives. The green development agenda includes comprehensive measures to adapt to climate change and decarbonize the economy, providing for the reduction of GHG emissions and the pursuit of carbon neutrality (Eurasian Development Bank, 2023).

Since the 2010s, China has emerged into one of the most prominent and consistent new leaders of the modern green agenda. Being one of the most populous and rapidly developing countries in the world, China has also been one of the largest polluters (Su et al., 2021). It accounts for about 30% of all global emissions – twice as much as the United States. It pollutes the atmosphere more than all European countries combined. Over the past two decades, China's CO_2 emissions have grown six times faster than those in the rest of the world (Kranina, 2021). The country's share in global GHG emissions is significantly higher than its share in global output (gross domestic product (GDP)) (about 19.35%), which indicates a strong carbon footprint. Some reduction in GHG emissions was observed in China during the COVID-19 outbreak in 2020–2021, due to which many industries temporarily suspended their activities (Le et al., 2020; Nsabimana & Foday, 2020). In 2020, output across major industries in China decreased by 15%–40%, while CO_2 emissions in February 2020 decreased by 200 million tons compared to 800 million tons in February 2019. Total CO_2 emissions in 2020 decreased by 3.15% under the impact of COVID-19 from 9.89 billion tons in 2019 (Lei et al., 2023). The interrelated dynamics of the parameters of industrial output and CO_2 discharge demonstrate the link between GHG emissions and economic growth rates.

In order to reduce its carbon footprint, China is making unprecedented efforts to decarbonize not only industrial production but also all sectors of the economy (Heggelund, 2021). Today, China accounts for about 50% of electric vehicle sales in the world and 99% of electric bus production (United Nations, 2020). China plans to receive the status of carbon neutral society by 2060 while coal consumption will be controlled and systematically reduced (Cao et al., 2009; National People's Congress, 2006). China has approved the Kigali Amendment to the Montreal Protocol on Substances that Deplete the Ozone Layer (United Nations, 2016) to strengthen control over hydrofluorocarbons (HFC) and GHGs other than CO_2. By implementing the green development agenda, China stands in solidarity with developing countries and emphasizes that there is a new model for economic growth, and China is following in the wake of its approbation. The country strives to create an image of a responsible power in achieving carbon neutrality. The country is taking steps to assist developing economies and partner countries within the Belt and Road Initiative (BRI) not only in improving industrial, energy, and transport infrastructure but also in facilitating the green transition (Pan et al., 2020; Zhuang & Zhang, 2020).

China's successes in promoting the green agenda and solving environmental problems are ambiguous. On the one hand, China has progressed in many areas in less than a decade, including in reducing air pollution in major cities (Li et al., 2019). China has made significant progress in the development of green technologies (wind and solar energy, electric transport). The integrated approach to promoting green growth includes long-term planning and development of green-focused industries, green products, green finance, green standards, and green energy. On the other hand, the environmental situation in China remains uncertain in most areas (high GHG emissions, degradation of arable land, reduced availability of freshwater, biodiversity loss). There is still a gap between the need to consume a large amount of resources and energy to maintain high rates of economic growth and the need for rational environmental management and reduction of pollutant emissions to ensure sustainable development (Bai et al., 2020; Casey & Galor, 2017; Su et al., 2021). This study aims to address this growth-sustainability dilemma by interpreting the fundamental provisions of China's approach to building an ecological civilization. The authors analyze major challenges to reducing China's carbon footprint and attempt to identify prospects for greening economic development of the country.

Major Obstacles to Greening China's Economic Development

The current intensification of the green development agenda in China is based on the fact that China's economic rise since the start of economic reforms in the 1980s has been associated with an increase in the need for energy and integration into global value chains (Zhang, Wang, et al., 2021). The increase in energy consumption and the concomitant increase in pollutant emissions were accompanied by serious environmental problems, including air and water pollution, GHG emissions, degradation of agricultural lands and natural landscaped, and biodiversity loss (Wu et al., 2020). According to estimates made by Ma et al. (2020) and Pyatachkova et al. (2022), among others, China lost from 2% to 3% of GDP per year due to environmental degradation in the late 2010s. Most studies agree that the spectrum of China's deadliest environmental problems includes the complex impact of climate change across major sectors of the economy and spheres of life, high degree of pollution of vital resources (air, water, soil, and forests), as well as the degradation of traditional plant and animal habitats and the associated loss of biodiversity (Chen et al., 2016; Wang et al., 2009).

Effects of Climate Change

The impact of climate change on the economy and ecology of China could hardly be measured explicitly by any specific set of parameters. It is far more complex and diverse (weather, extreme natural events, agriculture, and many others). Still, the climate-related factors have one common feature, which is the destabilization of the established patterns (sharper fluctuations and more frequent occurrence of extremes). Thus, climate change is recognized as the main cause of the more severe typhoon seasons in China (Tian et al., 2021). The season starts earlier, while typhoons become more and more destructive. More intense climatic and atmospheric phenomena increase the destructive power of typhoons, their frequency increases, and the number of typhoons penetrating farther in to inland territories goes up (Wood et al., 2023). Up to 20 million hectares of crops suffer to varying degrees from weather events (typhoons, floods, droughts, tornadoes, hail, frosts) annually (Table 2.1). In 2021, direct economic loss in agriculture due to natural disasters amounted to $45 billion (National Bureau of Statistics of China, 2023).

According to Zhang, Fang, et al. (2021) and Liu et al. (2022), floods may become more severe if global warming exceeds the 2 °C threshold, compared to the 1.5 °C bar. With only 1.5 °C temperature rise, direct economic losses may amount to about $33 billion per year in the case of strong floods. It may increase to $70 billion in the case of weak floods that affect most of the country. In some areas of China, the damage may be even deadlier. Climate-induced floods will have the greatest impact on the lower coastal territories in China's east and southeast. As climate warming progresses, flood risks will spread from coastal areas to the west and north of the country (Wang et al., 2021).

When one part of China suffers from typhoons, floods, and destruction they produce, the other part faces increasingly severe droughts (Yang et al., 2023). Climate change in the south of China leads to waterlogging caused by a large amount of precipitation, while in the north and west of the country, insufficient moisture is becoming more acute. Climate change is a major threat to the ecological balance of ecosystems, especially in the steppe regions of northeastern China. An increase in temperatures and a decrease in soil moisture can significantly undermine the fertility of land in China's north, the main crop-producing region in the country. The above-ground net primary production in plant communities has decreased significantly due to climate change, especially in warmer and drier years. The decrease in the productivity of plant communities has led to a change in the stability of ecosystems. On the one hand, arid ecosystems play a crucial role in the global carbon cycle. On the other hand, they are particularly sensitive to climate change processes. According to Chen et al. (2016), climate change will accelerate, which dictates the need to promote the green transition in China's agriculture to improve the resilience of the sector to climate-related shocks.

Table 2.1. Effects of Natural Disasters on Crops in China in 2011–2021, Million Hectares.

Indicator	**2011**	**2012**	**2013**	**2014**	**2015**	**2016**	**2017**	**2018**	**2019**	**2020**	**2021**
Area of farm crops	32.470	24.962	31.350	24.891	21.770	26.221	18.478	20.814	19.257	19.958	11.739
Area of crop failure, total, including	2.892	1.826	3.844	3.090	2.233	2.902	1.827	2.585	2.802	2.706	1.633
by drought	1.505	0.374	1.416	1.485	1.046	1.018	0.752	0.922	1.114	0.704	0.464
by flood, geophysical disaster, and typhoon	0.873	1.095	1.829	0.977	0.841	1.442	0.766	1.010	1.481	1.498	0.918
by wind and hail	0.302	0.213	0.412	0.458	0.309	0.269	0.225	0.197	0.171	0.291	0.206
by low temperature, freezing, and snow disaster	0.211	0.143	1.181	0.168	0.036	0.173	0.083	0.456	0.036	0.213	0.044

Source: Authors' development based on National Bureau of Statistics of China (2023).

Air Pollution

China has been facing high content of harmful PM2.5 and PM10 particles and CO_2 in the air, thick smog in large cities, and the associated negative environmental effects on public health for decades (Huang et al., 2018; Xu et al., 2013). The main sources of atmospheric pollution are industrial enterprises, especially steel smelting factories, and coal-fired thermal power plants (Pyatachkova et al., 2022; Rohde & Muller, 2015). In cities, major polluters are cars (over 360 million across the country). In 2021, the total amount of pollutant emission in waste gas, including sulfur dioxide, nitrogen oxides, and particulate matter, exceeded 18 million tons (Table 2.2). Atmospheric pollution has a detrimental effect on public health. The rate of premature mortality from diseases caused by a high content of harmful substances in the air is about 1.1 million people per year.

In 2013, China adopted the Air Pollution Prevention and Control Action Plan (Clean Air Alliance of China, 2013). It articulated measures to improve the environmental situation, such as the acceleration of the transition from coal to gas as the main resource for electricity generation, construction of new and modernization of existing facilities for desulfurization and denitrification at industrial enterprises, commissioning of new air quality control systems in large cities, and reduction of exhaust gases from public transport. In 2015, amendments to the Law on the Prevention and Control of Air Pollution set the responsibility of provincial-level and municipal-level governments for the development and implementation of plans to achieve air quality targets (Feng et al., 2019).

In 2016, the 13th Five-Year Plan for Economic and Social Development of The People's Republic of China for the first time included a goal to reduce the level of pollution by harmful small particles of PM2.5 by 25% (Central Committee of the Communist Party of China, 2016). It also stressed the need to accelerate the transition from coal to gas and renewable energy sources. In 2018, President Xi Jinping named the fight for clean air among the "three hard battles" of modern China (along with the fight against poverty and financial risks) (Xinhua, 2018). The institutional reform and the creation of the Ministry of Ecology and Environment have produced fruitful results. By 2020, the tasks set in the 13th Five-Year Plan to reduce the content of harmful particles in the air were fulfilled. The content of PM2.5 particles in the air was reduced by 36% in the Beijing–Tianjin–Hebei agglomeration, while the share of coal in the primary energy balance decreased from 63.7% in 2015 to 56.8% in 2020 (Zhao & Kim, 2022).

The 14th Five-Year Plan sets an ambitious goal to eliminate the bulk of air pollution in the country, which implies reducing the content of ozone, nitrates, and PM2.5 particles in the air (National Development and Reform Commission of the People's Republic of China, 2022). The share of coal in the country's energy balance is expected to be cut to 50%, while that of gas and non-fossil energy is projected to go up to 10% and 20%, respectively. Special attention is given to the development of solar, wind, hydrogen, and nuclear energy.

Table 2.2. Main Pollutant Emission in Waste Gas in China in 2011–2021, Million Tons.

Indicator	**2011**	**2012**	**2013**	**2014**	**2015**	**2016**	**2017**	**2018**	**2019**	**2020**	**2021**
Sulfur dioxide	22.179	21.180	20.439	19.744	18.591	8.549	6.108	5.161	4.573	3.182	2.748
Nitrogen oxides	24.043	23.378	22.274	20.780	18.510	15.033	13.484	12.884	12.338	10.197	9.884
Smoke and dust	12.788	12.358	12.781	17.407	15.380	–	–	–	–	–	–
Particulate matter	–	–	–	–	–	16.080	12.849	11.323	10.885	6.114	5.376

Source: Authors' development based on National Bureau of Statistics of China (2023).

Water Pollution

China is one of the poorest countries in the world in terms of freshwater availability per capita (2.1 thousand m^3 of freshwater per capita, 121st place in the world). The critically low water availability threshold set by the UN is 1.7 thousand m^3 per capita per year (now observed in 16 territories across China). Water scarcity degrades the efficiency of agricultural production and requires additional investments in the creation and maintenance of water supply infrastructure. However, simply increasing the parameter of water availability is not enough to solve environmental problems in this area. Over 70% of water resources are polluted, while water from 52 rivers flowing through urban settlements cannot be used for irrigation (Kranina, 2021). The main pollutants are chemical oxygen demand, nitrogen, phosphorus, petroleum, and volatile phenol (Table 2.3). Most of China's megacities are experiencing problems with water supply. Major water systems of China, such as the Yangtze River, the Yellow River, the Zhujiang River, the Heilongjiang River, and the Liaohe River, are heavily polluted.

In 2021, the Ministry of Ecology and Environment of China and the National Development and Reform Commission of China released the Basic Provisions of the Program for Environmental Protection and High-Quality Development of the Yellow River Basin and the Action Plan for the Protection and Restoration of the Yangtze River. The two plans document legal aspects of environmental protection and development of river basins, cover general land planning, water resources allocation, water pollution control, restoration, modernization, and transformation of traditional industries along the Yellow River and the Yangtze River. The water quality in over 85% of the river sections is expected to reach Level III and higher. Polluting industrial and agricultural enterprises will be relocated or reformed. The water management programs are part of China's climate program, which assumes achieving a zero carbon footprint by 2060.

In the 14th Five-Year Plan (National Development and Reform Commission of the People's Republic of China, 2022), special government bonds and bank loans are used to maximize the scale of investments in the field of water management in order to neutralize the consequences of the COVID-19 outbreak. China has launched the construction of 45 projects in the field of water management, including flood control projects and construction of reservoirs and irrigation facilities. More than 700 large companies engaged in deep water purification have been established, while 800 more facilities are planned to be created in the coming years. The government considers the protection of drinking water sources to be one of the crucial tasks of the national environmental protection campaign.

Degradation of Lands and Forests

The high content of heavy metals in land across China results in the degradation of fertile layer of soils and compromises health parameters of the population. More than 20 million hectares of arable land (20% of all agricultural lands in China) are polluted to various extent, while soil deterioration is recorded on 40% of arable land (Sun et al., 2019). The main sources of pollution are mining

Table 2.3. Main Pollutant Emission in Waste Water in China in 2011–2021.

Indicator	**2011**	**2012**	**2013**	**2014**	**2015**	**2016**	**2017**	**2018**	**2019**	**2020**	**2021**
Chemical oxygen demand, million tons	24.999	24.240	23.527	22.946	22.235	6.581	6.089	5.842	5.671	25.648	25.310
Total nitrogen, million tons	4.471	4.514	4.481	4.561	4.613	1.235	1.203	1.202	1.176	3.223	3.167
Ammonia nitrogen, million tons	2.604	2.536	2.457	2.385	2.299	0.568	0.509	0.494	0.462	0.984	0.867
Total phosphorus, million tons	0.554	0.489	0.487	0.534	0.547	0.090	0.070	0.064	0.059	0.337	0.338
Petroleum, thousand tons	21.012	17.494	18.385	16.204	15.192	11.599	7.639	7.158	6.293	3.734	2.217
Volatile phenol, tons, thousand tons	2.431	1.501	1.277	1.378	0.988	0.272	0.244	0.174	0.147	0.060	0.052

Source: Authors' development based on National Bureau of Statistics of China (2023).

and smelting of metals, heavy industry, electric power generation, agriculture (including the use of chemical fertilizers and pesticides), waste disposal, urbanization, and transport. In 2020, areas covered by natural disasters exceeded 12 million hectares (Table 2.4). Over 2.0 million hectares and 1.4 million hectares were directly affected by drought and flood, respectively. The 2016 Action Plan for the Prevention and Control of Soil Pollution allocated about $760 billion to cleaning contaminated farmlands. The portion of previously polluted land that can be used safely is projected to reach 95% by 2030. The 2018 Law on the Prevention and Control of Soil Pollution established new standards for soil quality control and shifted part of the responsibility for cleaning contaminated lands to provincial authorities.

One of the most acute climate-related issues China is facing is desertification. It spreads over 173 million hectares. Drought affects about 160 thousand km^2 of arable land every year. In some territories, losses due to drought amount to over one-fifth of the gross regional product. The National Forestry and Grassland Administration of China is taking numerous measures to combat desertification. One of the initiatives is a protective afforestation in China's northwest, north, and northeast. About 36 million hectares of new forest will be planted by 2050. Second initiative is a project to combat the sources of sandstorms around Beijing and Tianjin (Kranina, 2021). China ranks first in the world in artificial plantations using genetic modification (GMO), such as phytocomplexes of genetically modified plants capable of absorbing more CO_2 than conventional forests. On an industrial scale, with the help of special construction equipment, sand dunes are torn down and leveled, and seeds are dropped onto the prepared soil from airplanes (Zheng, 2021). The Agricultural Development Bank of China issued the country's first green bonds to finance projects on carbon uptake by forests, including afforestation and reforestation.

Biodiversity Loss

China enjoys to have one of the highest degrees of diversity of landscapes and natural resources among the countries of the world (Yu & Czarnezki, 2013). However, due to the destruction of habitats, environmental pollution, and climate change, many plant and animal species in China turn to be depleted, threatened, or endangered (Lu et al., 2020; Zheng & Cao, 2015). Since 2019, China has become the largest contributor to the core budget of the Convention on Biological Diversity (CBD) and its protocols, strongly supporting the functioning and implementation of the CBD. In recent years, China has become the largest developing donor country to the Global Environment Facility. Over the past decade, the country has adopted and revised more than 20 laws and regulations in the spheres of biodiversity, fisheries, protection of wild animals, environmental protection, and biological safety.

In 2021, State Council Information Office of the People's Republic of China (2021) released the white paper titled "Biodiversity Conservation in China." It summarizes the fundamental approaches of the country to the management and conservation of natural and biological resources. The document calls for the

Table 2.4. Land and Forest Areas Affected by Natural Disasters and Diseases in China in 2011–2021, Million Hectares.

Indicator	**2011**	**2012**	**2013**	**2014**	**2015**	**2016**	**2017**	**2018**	**2019**	**2020**	**2021**
Areas affected by natural disasters	12.440	11.470	14.300	12.680	12.380	13.670	9.200	10.570	7.910	7.990	4.682
Areas affected by flood	2.840	4.140	4.860	2.700	3.330	4.340	3.020	2.550	2.610	3.040	2.065
Areas affected by drought	6.600	3.510	5.850	5.680	5.860	6.130	4.440	2.620	3.330	2.510	1.407
Area of occurrence of forest diseases	1.197	1.312	1.392	1.373	1.390	1.389	1.331	1.769	2.295	2.951	2.847
Area of occurrence of forest pest plague	8.459	8.463	8.475	8.413	8.466	8.570	9.060	8.404	8.115	7.906	7.766
Area of occurrence of forest rat and rabbit plague	2.025	1.994	2.242	2.116	2.148	1.955	1.942	1.844	1.780	1.740	1.747

Source: Authors' development based on National Bureau of Statistics of China (2023).

promotion of the adoption and revision of laws and regulations in the field of protection of wild animals, fisheries, wetlands, nature reserves, forests, and wild plants. Also, it requires the elimination of all forms of illegal use and destruction of aquatic biological resources, landscapes, and habitats of plants and animals.

China has also stepped up the establishment of nature reserves, national parks, and protected natural areas (Cai et al., 2019). There are over 160 botanical gardens, 470 national nature reserves, and 10,000 protected natural territories across the country, in which 60% of local plant species are protected (Kranina & Liu, 2022). Due to large-scale efforts to combat desertification, China has taken the first place in the world in terms of forest fund growth; 90% of the forms of terrestrial ecosystems and vegetation, as well as 85% of the populations of key wild animals, are protected by the state. In 2023, China lowered the protected status of almost 500 species of wild plants and animals, which indicates an improvement in the physiological state of wild plants, as well as a slowdown in the deterioration of the status of endangered vertebrates. Currently, China's list of species under protection covers 39,330 species of wild plants and 4,767 species of animals.

Evolution of the Ecological Civilization Narrative

The green narrative emerged on China's development agenda after the launch of economic and social reforms in the late 20th century. Since the early 2010s, the economic development of the country has been shifting from a system dependent on a large amount of labor, investment, energy, and resources to an economy based on technologies and innovations (Hansen et al., 2018; Yan & Bocharnikov, 2022). Environmental innovations have become a tool for restoring and preserving natural resources, increasing the level of economic well-being of the people and the competitiveness of the country in the world. Such a transformation of approaches to determining the foundations and priorities of the country's development is taking place within the framework of the so-called green transition to building an ecological civilization in China (Li, Liu, et al., 2022).

The term "ecological civilization" was first used in 2007 at the XVII National Congress of the Communist Party of China. At that time, the construction of ecological civilization was understood as the creation of a model of economic growth and consumption that rationally uses resources and protects the environment. Gare (2012), Gu et al. (2020), and Huang and Westman (2021), among others, interpreted the concept as a transformation of value patterns, i.e., as a transition from extreme forms of capitalism to a more equitable sustainable development based on the principles of social equity and awareness. However, the blossoming of the ecological civilization narrative is strongly associated with the presidency of Xi Jinping. In 2016, President Xi declared the high time for the intensification of ecological and environmental protection in China. He acknowledged that "eco-environmental problems that have accumulated over years of rapid development are prominent" (Xi, 2017, p. 425). On the other hand, President Xi encouraged the nation to solve ecological destruction and pollution issues to promote sustainable development and improve public health. The vision of beautiful China encompasses the rational and responsible use of resources and protection and restoration of the natural environment in order to return to nature its inherent peace, harmony, and beauty (Xi, 2017, p. 429). To push the green development forward, China set rather ambitious goals:

1. Promote economic development by accelerating the creation of a legal system and policy settings focused on green production and consumption.
2. Improve environmental management practices by standing firmly on the position of national participation in the prevention and elimination of pollution at its very origins, as well as continuing working on the prevention and elimination of atmospheric pollution.
3. Accelerate environmental protection and restoration. It is necessary to implement the most significant projects for the protection and restoration of important ecological systems, optimize the system of ecological protective barrier, and create ecological corridors and a network for the protection of biological diversity and the quality of ecosystems.
4. Facilitate conservation and utilization of natural resources by improving the awareness of responsible consumption at all levels (government, industries, households).
5. Advocate green way of life by educating people, advertising the green development agenda, and popularizing role models in the sphere of responsible consumption.
6. Ensure ecological progress by intensifying the overall design, organization, and management in the sphere of ecological civilization and establishing bodies for the management of state natural resource assets and monitoring and control of natural ecosystems.

Therefore, the focus of China's environmental efforts is the prevention and elimination of pollution, comprehensive reorganization and technical reconstruction of resource-intensive industries that consume unjustifiably large amount of energy and raw materials, as well as the implementation of a qualitatively different approach to environmental expertise. Environmental protection in China is ensured by one of the strictest legal systems in the world. Improving the quality of legislative work is considered as one of the most challenging and important tasks.

Promising Venues for Achieving Carbon Neutrality

The sustainable development agenda incorporated all kinds of efforts to increase the resistance of all sectors of the economy to global climate change and extreme natural events (Erokhin et al., 2020). As options for responding to climate change, China has been implementing a whole range of projects and initiatives aimed at pursuing carbon neutrality (curbing emissions of pollutants and reducing the carbon footprint), green economy (organic agriculture and the use of alternative and renewable energy sources), and blue economy (aquaculture based on renewable energy sources, control of the use of marine and water resources, conservation of biodiversity).

Implications of the Circular Economy Approach for Decarbonization

Over the past years, China has developed 7 and revised 17 laws in the sphere of environmental protection, including the Circular Economy Promotion Law (Ministry of Ecology and Environment of the People's Republic of China, 2009). The most significant and promising innovative areas within the green economy framework are low-carbon energy, climate change technologies, combating pollution of the atmosphere, water, and soil, and digitalization (Mathews & Tan, 2011). The new five-year cycle that started in 2021 for the first time included a section on long-term development goals until 2035 (a decade beyond the exact period of the cycle). Five of the 20 parameters of the plan related to environmental regulation aim at forming a closed-cycle economy, an economic development pattern based on the reducing, reusing, and recycling activities conducted in the process of production, circulation, and consumption (Liu et al., 2017; Pesce et al., 2020). For the first time, the five-year plan included a clause on environmental human rights and a task to achieve carbon neutrality. In 2021, China unveiled a new development plan for the 14th five-year period to promote a circular economy (State Council of the People's Republic of China, 2021). The goal of the plan is to switch to closed-cycle production by 2025, spread the use of green technologies, and increase the efficiency of resource use. It lists three key tasks (rather, directives that provincial governments must interpret and implement in accordance with local conditions) to be completed by 2025:

1. Creation of an industry-wide resource processing system and improving the efficiency of resource use (promoting environmental friendliness of products by improving policies, guidelines, and classification of green technologies; strengthening clean production through mandatory and voluntary audits; accelerating innovation and modernization of eco-friendly production; promoting a closed-cycle economy in industrial parks by encouraging the widespread use of resources, construction of green plants, and creation of eco-industrial demonstration facilities; expanding research and development in the field of waste disposal and recycling).
2. Creation of a waste recycling system and development of a recycling-oriented society (improving the waste recycling network by integrating recycling facilities into land planning; improving recycling networks in rural areas; increasing the level of recycling and use of renewable resources by strengthening environmental supervision; standardization of recycling and disposal of electronics and automobiles; promoting the development of the recovery sector in industries such as auto parts, construction machinery, and robotics.).
3. Development of the closed-cycle agricultural economy and the creation of appropriate agricultural production (improving the use of agricultural and forest waste, such as crop straw or livestock manure, in agricultural production; processing of agricultural waste by involving farmers in the construction of waste recycling enterprises in rural areas; promoting a closed-cycle model of agricultural development by creating industrial consortia of ecological agriculture; promoting the use of renewable energy sources in agricultural processes).

The plan identifies 11 priority areas to achieve the goals and objectives of the circular economy, including the construction of a municipal waste disposal system, development of a recycling park, integrated solid waste disposal, use of construction waste, key innovations in technologies and equipment, high-quality development for the recovery sector, improvement of the processing and disposal of electrical waste and electronic products, management of life cycle of automobiles, control of plastic pollution, promotion of environmentally friendly packaging for transportation and logistics, and disposal of used batteries.

In June 2022, China's Ministry of Ecology and Environment released the National Strategy for Adaptation to Climate Change until 2035 (Center for Security and Emerging Technology, 2022), which further elaborated the key areas of circular economic development and the promising innovative aspects of the green economy narrative. Compared to the 2013 version of the climate change strategy, the 2022 edition pays more attention to climate change monitoring, early warning, and disaster prevention management and mitigation. It clarifies adaptation tasks in key areas such as water resources, terrestrial ecosystems, oceans and coastal zones, agriculture and food security, public health, infrastructure, and cities and settlements. It creates a multi-level regional model of adaptation to climate change with spatial planning and forecasting of consequences and risks of climate change across key territories of China, including major urban agglomerations and basins of the Yangtze River and the Yellow River. Also, the 2022 Climate Change Strategy prioritizes the creation of mechanisms to strengthen protective measures, such as financial, scientific and technical support, capacity-building, and international cooperation.

Green Entrepreneurship and Investment

The promotion of green entrepreneurship, green finances, and green investment is indispensable for the development of a green resilient economy (Steblyanskaya et al., 2021). In China's academic and political discourse, green entrepreneurship combines production, research, credit, and financial activities for the production of goods, performance of works, and provision of services aimed at ensuring the preservation and restoration of the environment and the protection of natural resources (Chen, Shen, et al., 2023; Li, Yue, et al., 2022; Yu & Gibbs, 2019; Zhang et al., 2019). Green finance refers to financial services provided for economic activities that support environmental protection, mitigate the effects of climate change, and promote or facilitate the efficient use of resources (Baruzzi, 2021). These activities include financing, project implementation, and risk management of activities related to environmental protection, energy conservation, clean energy, green transport, and financial services of green construction (Lee, 2020; Liu et al., 2019; Zeng et al., 2021). According to the People's Bank of China's Guiding Opinions for Further Promoting Innovative Development of Green Finance (Baruzzi, 2021), priority measures for the development of green entrepreneurship through green financing include the following:

1. Development of the green financial system. Banks, financial and leasing companies, intermediary agencies in the spheres of credit rating, information consulting, and environmental risk assessment, and trust companies are all encouraged to expand their capabilities to provide green financial services (for example, by creating green finance business units, green franchising branches, and green leasing departments) to actively expand the green entrepreneurship and provide relevant services.
2. Innovative products and services of green lending. In order to accelerate the introduction of innovative green credit products and services, China's government calls on financial institutions to improve the environmental credit management system, to actively develop energy efficiency loans, to promote innovations in green credit products in sectors such as clean production, clean energy, recycling economics, green buildings, and green consumption, to support green agricultural projects, as well as to encourage entrepreneurs to invest in urban water treatment and garbage recycling.
3. Development of the green bond market. Qualified financial institutions are supported in issuing green financial bonds and reducing capital expenditures. In addition, qualified non-financial enterprises are encouraged to issue green debt instruments. Both financial and non-financial institutions receive support in issuing secured green financial products. In addition, foreign parent companies or subsidiaries of enterprises with foreign capital are recommended to issue green debt financing instruments.
4. Development of green leasing. Financial leasing companies are recommended to strengthen the structure of the green leasing business, explore ways to conduct financial leasing of pollution control equipment, and improve the management of green leasing assets. Such companies are encouraged to issue environmental financial bonds and carry out cross-border financing.
5. Development of green supply chain finance. Financial institutions are encouraged to strengthen their business relationships with key green supply chain companies, actively develop supply chain finance as well as related financial products and services. The government calls for using the Internet, big data, blockchain, and other technologies should be used to expand risk management capabilities in supply chain financing and to reduce overall business costs.
6. Strengthening the development of green finance. Measures such as promoting the creation of a system of green financial statistics, improving the mechanism for exchanging green financial information, organizing meetings to promote projects, and improving the effectiveness of banking and business cooperation are being introduced. Entrepreneurs are encouraged to use Chinese yuan in cross-border transactions anyhow related to green development.
7. Improving mechanisms for preventing and controlling green finance risks. The following measures are being introduced: involving third-party professional agencies in assessing the use of funds to ensure that these funds are invested in green projects; improving the capabilities of banks and other risk analysis organizations that issue environmental loans and bonds; improving the assessment of environmental and social risks and related management

processes; improving internal reporting, public disclosure systems; and reporting systems across all entrepreneurs.

8. Increasing political support for the development of green finance. The development of green finance should be achieved through the implementation of policies and measures aimed at supporting the sustainable and healthy development of all types of enterprises involved in green spheres. Other policy measures include the full implementation of monetary policy instruments such as refinancing and recalculation, improved evaluation of the effectiveness of green credit, and the provision of more convenient financial services for cross-border financing.
9. Strengthening research and education in the green sector. China's government emphasizes the importance of nurturing professionals, specialists, and researchers to promote and disseminate knowledge about green development policies and projects. To this end, various measures should be taken, such as organizing seminars, deepening cooperation between financial departments, financial institutions, and research institutes, as well as investing in the education of specialists and retraining of entrepreneurs in the green sector.

With its huge financial resources, China is emerging into one of the major sources of green financing for the world. The country's savings rate is one of the highest in the world (45% of GDP), while the total assets of the banking sector are about $50 trillion. Even if a tiny part of the resources is directed to green investments, this could trigger a significant breakthrough in terms of greening economic growth – both in China and abroad. China is making rapid progress in developing its green financial system and markets as part of national efforts to achieve carbon neutrality. In 2022, the green lending amounted to $3.3 trillion (increase by 38.5% compared to 2021). In 2021, the volume of green lending increased by 33.0% compared to 2020. Therefore, the aggregated green loans portfolio of Chinese banks is the largest in the world.

At the same time, green loans account for less than 7% of China's total lending, while green bonds account for only 1% of the bond market. Despite the more than impressive growth rates in the green lending sector, a radical increase in the share of green investment in the overall investment portfolio would be rather challenging. The bulk of infrastructure investment in China is accounted for by the state (companies and banks backed up by the state). Despite the double-digit growth of green investment, the bulk of resources is still directed to conventional industries, where the carbon footprint is still substantial. The standards for green investments in China are less stringent than those in many developed countries. Thus, a bond is considered green if 95% of the funds raised go to green investment. In China, this threshold could be much lower (in some cases, down to 50%). Chinese entrepreneurs need to improve environmental risk management and disclosure requirements. Finally, it is essential to increase the green component in outgoing capital flows, not only the domestic market. Until recently, China's large-scale investments in developing countries have been concentrated in dirty sectors (mining, energy). Since recently, China has been promoting investment in renewable energy and other lower-carbon sectors.

Renewable Energy

Decarbonization efforts can hardly be separated from the development of the renewables sector. One of the vital tasks for China on its way to reducing its carbon footprint and achieving carbon neutrality is the fullest possible integration of renewable energy sources into all sectors of the economy and all spheres of public life (Khazova, 2019). The contemporary vision of China's comprehensive energy security is inspired by the Four Reforms and One Cooperation concept initiated by President Xi Jinping in 2014 (State Council Information Office of the People's Republic of China, 2020). Reforms include the improvement of the energy consumption structure by containing unnecessary consumption, development of a more diversified energy supply structure, promotion of energy technologies to upgrade the industrial sector, and optimization of the energy system for faster growth of the energy sector (State Council Information Office of the People's Republic of China, 2020). The cooperation component of the energy security agenda envisages collaboration in the energy sphere with other countries to ensure energy security in an open environment. The globalization of the energy security problem and a call to the global community to join efforts to reduce emissions are the characteristic features of China's green development policy in the new era. In 2017, President Xi recognized the green development model to be an essential requirement of China's new development concepts (Xi, 2017, p. 428). China "embraces the vision of a global community of shared future and accelerates its transformation towards green and low-carbon development in economy and society" (State Council Information Office of the People's Republic of China, 2020) and aims to "speed up the building of … an industrial system for green, circular, and low-carbon development" (Xi, 2017, p. 429).

The renewables agenda has been penetrating into the energy policy of China since the late 2000s, from China's first White Paper on Energy in 2007 (State Council Information Office of the People's Republic of China, 2007) to Energy Policy 2012 (State Council Information Office of the People's Republic of China, 2012) and the Energy Development Strategies Notice of Action Plan 2014–2020 (State Council Information Office of the People's Republic of China, 2014).

The future of renewable energy in China is seen in several aspects. The obvious goal in the short term is to reduce emissions of pollutants from conventional industries and the fossil-based energy sector. Less obvious today but not the least important goals in the long run are the structural transformation of the entire economy to radically reduce dependence on fossil fuels and a comprehensive improvement in the standards of living and public welfare through improving the quality of the environment, nutrition, and public health (Erokhin & Gao, 2022). According to Wu and Storey (2007) and Fang (2010), China's policy in the renewable sector could be divided into domestic and external dimensions. The former prioritizes the development of gas and nuclear energy to diversify renewable energy sources, promotion of energy-saving practices and improving the efficiency of fuel and energy use, establishment of the strategic reserve of oil, development of clean coal technologies for optimal use of domestic reserves of coal, advancement of infrastructure for generation, storage, and transmission of energy, and implementation of market reforms in the energy sector. The latter is about diversifying energy cooperation and search for new markets, improving the safety of transportation of imported energy resources, promoting collaboration in the sphere of advanced energy technologies, and diversifying types and sources of energy imported to China.

Some of the most promising venues for achieving carbon neutrality through implementing the renewable energy solutions include hydropower (large hydropower facilities on the largest rivers in central and southern provinces), wind power (centralized and decentralized wind power installations both onshore and offshore), and solar power (industrial and small-scale power-generation grids across the country).

Organic Agriculture

Along with India, China is the leading country in Asia in terms of the area of land allocated for organic agriculture (about 2.4 million hectares out of 6.1 million hectares in the organic sector in Asia). The government aims to reduce the use of agrochemicals and develop organic agriculture. In 2022, China's Ministry of Agriculture and Rural Affairs adopted a five-year plan to reduce the use of pesticides in agriculture. As part of the plan, restrictions on the use of 70 categories of pesticides will come into force by 2024. To ensure the quality and safety of agricultural products, the sale and use of such pesticides as phorate, isofenphos-methyl, isocarbophos, and ethoprophos will be banned from September 2024. In May 2022, the State Council of China adopted an Action Plan for Pollution Control, a roadmap for the development of an environmental risk management system in the field of chemicals. In December 2022, the Ministry of Agriculture and Rural Affairs announced its intentions to reduce the use of pesticides in the cultivation of vegetables, fruits, and tea by 10% by 2025. Also, the Ministry announced the goal of replacing 5% of pesticides used in the cultivation of grain crops with organic fertilizers.

In August 2022, the State Council of China announced the launch of the national soil survey. The need for conducting a comprehensive survey of soils across the country to be able to develop soil protection mechanisms has been stressed by many scholars, including Liao et al. (2007), Teng et al. (2014), and Zhou et al. (2022). China promotes cooperation in agricultural science and technological innovation, making an important contribution to global poverty reduction and ensuring sustainable agricultural development (Erokhin et al., 2022). In particular, Juncao technology has already been introduced in more than 100 countries for growing edible mushrooms, which are used as livestock feed and as a green barrier to combat desertification. In 2022, Nestle China and Syngenta Group China joined forces to promote the development of regenerative agriculture. In addition, Nestle China has launched Nescafe Plan 2030 to help farmers implementing regenerative coffee growing technologies. In general, the companies' project is aimed at helping consumers to nurture healthier nutrition habits and adjusting their nutrition patterns to contribute to greening of China's development.

China's agriculture loses about 50 million tons of grain crops annually due to climate change and related natural disasters. In June 2022, the Ministry of Agriculture and Rural Affairs of China together with the National Development and Reform Commission released a plan to reduce emissions and carbon sequestration in agriculture. The plan prioritizes the reduction of methane emissions in rice fields (16% of the total anthropogenic methane emissions nationally). Pilot projects on environmentally friendly rice cultivation have been launched in southwest China to reduce methane emissions into the atmosphere. Nestle China, together with Bayer Crop Science, announced the start of cooperation on low-carbon rice cultivation in northeast China in order to jointly study and implement sustainable farming methods to ensure carbon emissions reduction throughout the food chain.

The development of organic agriculture in China is due not only to the climate agenda and the country's efforts to reduce the carbon footprint of the agricultural sector. The government is systematically tightening the requirements for the quality and safety of food products, while the demand for organic products is growing. Due to the rapid economic growth in China, the number of households with incomes above the average level is increasing. As the standards of living improve, the demand for food shifts toward higher-quality, healthier, and environmentally friendlier products (Erokhin et al., 2022). Today, China is Asia's largest and the third-largest organic market in the world after the United States and the European Union (EU). Thus, it is fair to emphasize the conjugacy of the green production and green consumption trends in China, both of which make a significant contribution to the decarbonization of agricultural production and the entire economy.

Blue Economy Agenda

For such a large producer of fish and seafood as China, the development of the blue economy sector is an integral part of achieving carbon neutrality (Erokhin et al., 2021). Two hundred marine farms will be built by 2025 as part of the implementation of the plan for the construction of showpiece marine farms. A solar-powered hybrid fish farm with automatic feeding systems has been launched in Shanghai. Farms combine fish farming with energy generation. More than 300,000 photovoltaic solar panels with a total annual capacity of up to 140 million kWh are installed above the surface of ponds for breeding fish, shrimp, and shaggy crabs.

In 2022, China ceased subsidizing fuel used for fishing in order to reduce the volume of uncontrolled movement of fishing vessels in its territorial waters and reduce catch volumes. In March 2022, there was released the 14th Five-Year Plan for the Protection of Marine Ecology and the Environment. It provides for strengthening control over the pollution of water resources, taking active measures to protect and restore ecosystems, developing an effective and integrated management system in the spheres related to blue economy, as well as developing measures to minimize the effects of climate change and protect the ecology of marine systems. The 14th Five-Year Plan for Monitoring the Ecological Situation also provides for the development of the marine economy, including the optimization of the placement of marine aquaculture, the creation of marine farms, the development of sustainable catch of pelagic fish, as well as the ensurance of a sustainable marine environment. In June 2022, China introduced the first state standard in the sphere of construction of marine farms with a focus on preserving biodiversity and marine fish resources, environmental safety, as well as promoting the development of sustainable fisheries and fish farming. Within the 21st-Century Maritime Silk Road Initiative, China has developed a series of proposals to partner countries (particularly, ASEAN states) to collaborate for the sustainable development of the marine environment in the South China Sea and implement programs for the sustainable development of water areas and optimization of fishing processes (Fabinyi et al., 2021).

Conclusion

Similar to the majority of developing countries in the situation of an economic boom, China has faced two fundamental environmental problems during more than four decades of its skyrocketing growth. The first set of problems is caused by overpopulation (especially a high proportion of the rural population at the initial stage of reforms), low living standards of the population, and economically forced damage to the environment. The second type of environmental problem is caused by the rapid (and therefore poorly controlled) processes of industrialization and the increasing use of fossil fuels. Until the beginning of the 2010s, fragmented measures taken by China to protect the environment failed to radically increase the efficiency of nature management in the country. With the elaboration of a new paradigm of environmental regulation and the establishment of an integrated approach to solving environmental problems during Xi Jinping's presidency, China has succeeded to reverse the current trends of degradation of most types of natural resources. The country is now following the path of building an ecological civilization based on the principles of green development, responsible use of resources, decarbonization of all spheres of economy and public life, and sustainable development.

Obviously, the success in reducing carbon footprint achieved by China over the past decade is still too insignificant to noticeably affect the global processes of climate change. Most environmental problems have remained acute, in particular, pollution of vital resources (air, water, soil, forests), degradation of traditional plant and animal habitats, and the associated loss of biodiversity. Nevertheless, China is systematically moving toward a fundamental solution to environmental problems, aiming to maintain the growth-development dilemma of sustainability. China's government focuses on the prevention and elimination of environmental pollution and comprehensive reorganization and technical reconstruction of polluting industries. The most promising venues of the decarbonization efforts include curbing emissions of pollutants, promotion of organic practices in agriculture, use of alternative and renewable energy sources across industries, control of the use of natural resources and terrestrial and marine ecosystems, and protection of biodiversity.

China has launched one of the world's most comprehensive programs to counteract climate change and support activities that have high economic returns and low emissions of GHGs and other pollutants. In order to prevent the degradation of lands, forests, and water resources, the government encourages the establishment of protected zones, modernization of all kinds of enterprises, and promotion of green development awareness of the population. Thus, within the sustainable development, green transition, and decarbonization agendas, China is transforming its economy and society, which helps to tackle the accumulated environmental problems of development within the country as well as contributes to the global efforts to mitigate climate change effects across the world.

Acknowledgment

The study is supported by the Grant of Central Universities of the Ministry of Education of the People's Republic of China (Grant No. 3072022WK0917).

References

Auffhammer, M., Hsiang, S. M., Schlenker, W., & Sobel, A. (2013). Using weather data and climate model output in economic analyses of climate change. *Review of Environmental Economics and Policy*, *7*(2), 181–198. https://doi.org/10.1093/reep/ret016

Bagheri, M., Zeus, G., Mohammad, A., Christopher, A. K., & Ganesh, D. (2018). Green growth planning: A multi-factor energy input-output analysis of the Canadian economy. *Energy Economics*, *74*, 708–720. https://doi.org/10.1016/j.eneco.2018.07.015

Bai, C., Feng, C., Du, K., Wang, Y., & Gong, Y. (2020). Understanding spatial-temporal evolution of renewable energy technology innovation in China: Evidence from convergence analysis. *Energy Policy*, *143*, 111570. https://doi.org/10.1016/j.enpol.2020.111570

Baruzzi, S. (2021). *Developing green finance in Tianjin: 10 policy measures*. Retrieved September 11, 2023, from https://www.china-briefing.com/news/developing-green-finance-in-tianjin-10-policy-measures/?hilite=%27China-%27

Bistline, J. E., Hodson, E., Rossmann, C. G., Creason, J., Murray, B., & Barron, A. R. (2018). Electric sector policy technological change and US emissions reductions goals: Results from the EMF 32 model intercomparison project. *Energy Economics*, *73*, 307–325. https://doi.org/10.1016/j.eneco.2018.04.012

Bosello, F., Campagnolo, L., Cervigni, R., & Eboli, F. (2018). Climate change and adaptation: The case of Nigerian agriculture. *Environmental and Resource Economics*, *69*, 787–810. https://doi.org/10.1007/s10640-016-0105-4

Botzen, W. J. W., Bouwer, L. M., & van den Bergh, J. C. J. M. (2010). Climate change and hailstorm damage: Empirical evidence and implications for agriculture and insurance. *Resource and Energy Economics*, *32*(3), 341–362. https://doi.org/10.1016/j.reseneeco.2009.10.004

Cai, D., Fraedrich, K., Guan, Y., Guo, S., Zhang, C., Carvalho, L. M. V., & Zhu, X. (2019). Causality of biodiversity loss: Climate, vegetation, and urbanization in China and America. *Sensors*, *19*(20), 4499. https://doi.org/10.3390/s19204499

Cao, J., Garbaccio, R., & Ho, M. H. (2009). China's 11th five-year plan and the environment: Reducing SO_2 emissions. *Review of Environmental Economics and Policy*, *3*(2), 231–250. https://doi.org/10.1093/reep/rep006

Casey, G., & Galor, O. (2017). Is faster economic growth compatible with reductions in carbon emissions? The role of diminished population growth. *Environmental Research Letters*, *12*(1), 0114003. https://doi.org/10.1088/1748-9326/12/1/014003

Center for Security and Emerging Technology. (2022). *National climate change adaptation strategy 2035*. Retrieved September 11, 2023, from https://cset.georgetown.edu/publication /national-climate-change-adaptation-strategy-2035/

Central Committee of the Communist Party of China. (2016). *The 13th five-year plan for economic and social development of The People's Republic of China (2016–2020)*. Central Compilation & Translation Press.

Chen, S. A., Chen, X. G., & Xu, J. T. (2016). Impacts of climate change on agriculture: Evidence from China. *Journal of Environmental Economics and Management*, *76*, 105–124. https://doi.org/10.1016/j.jeem.2015.01.005

Chen, S., Shen, W., Qiu, Z., Liu, R., & Mardani, A. (2023). Who are the green entrepreneurs in China? The relationship between entrepreneurs' characteristics, green entrepreneurship orientation, and corporate financial performance. *Journal of Business Research*, *165*, 113960. https://doi.org/10.1016/j.jbusres.2023.113960

Chen, M., Yao, T., & Wang, K. (2023). The economic impact of climate change: A bibliometric analysis of research hotspots and trends. *Environmental Science and Pollution Research*, *30*, 47935–47955. https://doi.org/10.1007/s11356-023-25721-2

Chisholm, R. A. (2010). Trade-offs between ecosystem services: Water and carbon in a biodiversity hotspot. *Ecological Economics*, *69*(10), 1973–1987. https://doi.org/10.1016/j.ecolecon.2010.05.013

Clean Air Alliance of China. (2013). *Air pollution prevention and control action plan*. CAAC.

Collier, P., Conway, G., & Venables, T. (2008). Climate change and Africa. *Oxford Review of Economic Policy*, *24*(2), 337–353. https://doi.org/10.1093/oxrep/grn019

Darwin, R. F., & Tol, R. S. J. (2001). Estimates of the economic effects of sea level rise. *Environmental and Resource Economics*, *192*, 113–129. https://doi.org/10.1023/A:1011136417375

Dell, M., Jones, B. F., & Olken, B. A. (2012). Temperature shocks and economic growth: Evidence from the last half century. *American Economic Journal: Macroeconomics*, *4*(3), 66–95. https://doi.org/10.1257/mac.4.3.66

Deschenes, O., & Greenstone, M. (2007). The economic impacts of climate change: Evidence from agricultural output and random fluctuations in weather. *American Economic Review*, *97*(1), 354–385. https://doi.org/10.1257/aer.97.1.354

Erokhin, V., & Gao, T. (2022). Renewable energy as a promising venue for China-Russia collaboration. In S. A. R. Khan, M. Panait, F. Puime Guillen, & L. Raimi (Eds.), *Energy transition. Industrial ecology* (pp. 73–101). Springer. https://doi.org/10.1007/978-981-19-3540-4_3

Erokhin, V., Gao, T., & Andrei, J. V. (Eds.). (2020). *Sustainable economic development: Challenges, policies, and reforms*. MDPI. https://doi.org/10.3390/books978-3-03936-703-0

Erokhin, V., Gao, T., Chivu, L., & Andrei, J. V. (2022). Food security in a food self-sufficient economy: A review of China's ongoing transition to a zero hunger state. *Agricultural Economics – Czech*, *68*(12), 476–487. https://doi.org/10.17221/278/2022-AGRICECON

Erokhin, V., Gao, T., & Ivolga, A. (2021). Cross-country potentials and advantages in trade in fish and seafood products in the RCEP member states. *Sustainability*, *13*(7), 3668. https://doi.org/10.3390/su13073668

Espoir, D. K., Mudiangombe, B. M., Bannor, F., Sunge, R., & Tshitaka, J. L. M. (2022). CO_2 emissions and economic growth: Assessing the heterogeneous effects across climate regimes in Africa. *The Science of the Total Environment*, *804*, 150089. https://doi.org/10.1016/j.scitotenv.2021.150089

Eurasian Development Bank. (2023). *Global green agenda in the Eurasian region. Eurasian region on the global green agenda*. EDB.

Fabinyi, M., Wu, A., Lau, S., Mallory, T., Barclay, K., Walsh, K., & Dressler, W. (2021). China's blue economy: A state project of modernisation. *The Journal of Environment & Development*, *30*(2), 127–148. https://doi.org/10.1177/1070496521995872

Fang, T. (2010). Current state of China's energy policy. *Moscow University Bulletin of World Politics*, *4*, 124–134.

Feng, Y., Ning, M., Lei, Y., Sun, Y., Liu, W., & Wang, J. (2019). Defending blue sky in China: Effectiveness of the "air pollution prevention and control action plan" on air quality improvements from 2013 to 2017. *Journal of Environmental Management*, *15*(252), 109603. https://doi.org/10.1016/j.jenvman.2019.109603

Gare, A. (2012). China and the struggle for ecological civilization. *Capitalism Nature Socialism*, *23*(4), 10–26. https://doi.org/10.1080/10455752.2012.722306

Gowdy, J., & Julia, R. (2010). Global warming economics in the long run: A conceptual framework. *Land Economics*, *86*(1), 117–130. https://doi.org/10.3368/le.86.1.117

Gu, Y., Wu, Y., Liu, J., Xu, M., & Zuo, T. (2020). Ecological civilization and government administrative system reform in China. *Resources, Conservation and Recycling*, *155*, 104654. https://doi.org/10.1016/j.resconrec.2019.104654

Hansen, M. H., Li, H., & Svarverud, R. (2018). Ecological civilization: Interpreting the Chinese past, projecting the global future. *Global Environmental Change*, *53*, 195–203. https://doi.org/10.1016/j.gloenvcha.2018.09.014

Hassan, R. (2010). The double challenge of adapting to climate change while accelerating development in Sub-Saharan Africa. *Environment and Development Economics*, *15*(6), 661–685. https://doi.org/10.1017/S1355770X10000306

Heggelund, G. M. (2021). China's climate and energy policy: At a turning point? *International Environmental Agreements: Politics, Law and Economics*, *21*(1), 9–23. https://doi.org/10.1007/s10784-021-09528-5

Huang, J., Pan, X., Guo, X., & Li, G. (2018). Health impact of China's air pollution prevention and control action plan: An analysis of national air quality monitoring and mortality data. *The Lancet Planetary Health*, *2*(7), e313–e323. https://doi.org/10.1016/S2542-5196(18)30141-4

Huang, P., & Westman, L. (2021). China's imaginary of ecological civilization: A resonance between the state-led discourse and sociocultural dynamics. *Energy Research & Social Science*, *81*, 102253. https://doi.org/10.1016/j.erss.2021.102253

Keller, K., Bolker, B. M., & Bradford, D. F. (2004). Uncertain climate thresholds and optimal economic growth. *Journal of Environmental Economics and Management*, *48*(1), 723–741. https://doi.org/10.1016/j.jeem.2003.10.003

Kelly, D. L., Kolstad, C. D., & Mitchell, G. T. (2005). Adjustment costs from environmental change. *Journal of Environmental Economics and Management*, *50*(3), 468–495. https://doi.org/10.1016/j.jeem.2005.02.003

Khazova, V. (2019). Prospects for the development of renewable energy in China. *Moscow Economic Journal*, *7*, 430–441. https://doi.org/10.24411/2413-046X-2019-17009

Kranina, E. (2021). China on the way to achieving carbon neutrality. *Financial Journal*, *13*(5), 51–61. https://doi.org/10.31107/2075-1990-2021-5-51-61

Kranina, E., & Liu, X. (2022). *New horizons of China's economy in the 14th Five-Year Period (2021-2025)*. Russian Academy of Sciences. https://doi.org/10.48647/ICCA.2022.35.52.001

Le, T., Wang, Y., Liu, L., Yang, J., Yung, Y. L., Li, G., & Seinfeld, J. H. (2020). Unexpected air pollution with marked emission reductions during the COVID-19 outbreak in China. *Science*, *369*(6504), 702–706. https://doi.org/10.1126/science.abb7431

Lee, J. W. (2020). Green finance and sustainable development goals: The case of China. *The Journal of Asian Finance, Economics and Business*, *7*(7), 577–586. https://doi.org/10.13106/JAFEB.2020.VOL7.NO7.577

Lei, W., Mao, S., & Zhang, Y. (2023). Estimating China's CO_2 emissions under the influence of COVID-19 epidemic using a novel fractional multivariate nonlinear grey model. *Environment, Development and Sustainability, 2023*, 1–32. https://doi.org/10.1007/s10668-023-03325-7

Li, Y., Chiu, Y., & Lin, T. (2019). The impact of economic growth and air pollution on public health in 31 Chinese cities. *International Journal of Environmental Research and Public Health, 16*(3), 393. https://doi.org/10.3390/ijerph16030393

Li, Y., Liu, B., Zhao, P., Peng, L., & Luo, Z. (2022). Can China's ecological civilization strike a balance between economic benefits and green efficiency? A preliminary province-based quasi-natural experiment. *Frontiers in Psychology, 13*, 1027725. https://doi.org/10.3389/fpsyg.2022.1027725

Li, B., Yue, Z., & Liu, H. (2022). Factors influencing green entrepreneurship of returning migrant workers under the dual-carbon background. *Security and Communication Networks*, 2022, 7611810. https://doi.org/10.1155/2022/7611810

Liao, Q., Evans, L., Gu, X., Fan, D., Jin, Y., & Wang, H. (2007). A regional geochemical survey of soils in Jiangsu Province, China: Preliminary assessment of soil fertility and soil contamination. *Geoderma, 142*(1–2), 18–28. https://doi.org/10.1016/j.geoderma.2007.07.008

Liu, L., Gao, J., & Wu, S. (2022). Warming of 0.5 °C may cause double the economic loss and increase the population affected by floods in China. *Natural Hazards and Earth System Sciences, 22*, 1577–1590. https://doi.org/10.5194/nhess-22-1577-2022

Liu, L., Liang, Y., Song, Q., & Li, J. (2017). A review of waste prevention through 3R under the concept of circular economy in China. *Journal of Material Cycles and Waste Management, 19*, 1314–1323. https://doi.org/10.1007/s10163-017-0606-4

Liu, R., Wang, D., Zhang, L., & Zhang, L. (2019). Can green financial development promote regional ecological efficiency? A case study of China. *Natural Hazards, 95*, 325–341. https://doi.org/10.1007/s11069-018-3502-x

Lu, Y., Yang, Y., Sun, B., Yuan, Y., Yu, M., Stenseth, N., Bullock, J., & Obersteiner, M. (2020). Spatial variation in biodiversity loss across China under multiple environmental stressors. *Science Advances, 47*(6), eabd0952. https://doi.org/10.1126/sciadv.abd0952

Ma, G., Peng, F., Yang, W., Yan, G., Gao, S., Zhou, X., Qi, J., Cao, D., Zhao, Y., Pan, W., Jiang, H., Jing, H., Dong, G., Gao, M., Zhou, J., Yu, F., & Wang, J. (2020). The valuation of China's environmental degradation from 2004 to 2017. *Environmental Science and Ecotechnology, 1*, 100016. https://doi.org/10.1016/j.ese.2020.100016

Mathews, J., & Tan, H. (2011). Progress towards a circular economy in China: The drivers (and inhibitors) of eco-industrial initiative. *Journal of Industrial Ecology, 15*(3), 435–457. https://doi.org/10.1111/j.1530-9290.2011.00332.x

Mendelsohn, R., & Dinar, A. (2003). Climate, water, and agriculture. *Land Economics, 79*(3), 328–341. https://doi.org/10.2307/3147020

Ministry of Ecology and Environment of the People's Republic of China. (2009). *Circular economy promotion law*. Retrieved September 11, 2023, from https://english.mee.gov.cn/Resources/laws/envir_elatedlaws/201712/t20171212_427823.shtml

National Bureau of Statistics of China. (2023). *National data*. Retrieved September 9, 2023, from https://data.stats.gov.cn/english/easyquery.htm?cn=C01

National Development and Reform Commission of the People's Republic of China. (2022). *14th five-year plan for national economic and social development of the People's Republic of China*. Retrieved September 8, 2023, from https://en.ndrc.gov.cn/policies/index_2.html

National People's Congress. (2006). *11th five-year plan for national economic and social development of the People's Republic of China*. Retrieved September 7, 2023, from https://www.gov.cn/english/special/115y_index.htm

Nsabimana, A., & Foday, E. H. (2020). Impact of COVID-19 pandemic outbreak: CO_2 and SO_2 emission reduction over China. *Open Access Library Journal*, *7*, e6899. https://doi.org/10.4236/oalib.1106899

Pan, X. Z., Chen, W. Y., Zhou, S., Wang, L. N., Dai, J. Q., Zhang, Q., Zheng, X. Z., & Wang, H. L. (2020). Implications of near-term mitigation on China's long-term energy transitions for aligning with the Paris goals. *Energy Economics*, *90*, 104865. https://doi.org/10.1016/j.eneco.2020.104865

Pesce, M., Tamai, I., Guo, D., Critto, A., Brombal, D., Wang, X., Cheng, H., & Marcomini, A. (2020). Circular economy in China: Translating principles into practice. *Sustainability*, *12*, 832. https://doi.org/10.3390/su12030832

Pyatachkova, A., Potashev, N., & Smirnova, V. (2022). *Green agenda in China's policy*. Russian International Affairs Council.

Reilly, J. M. (2012). Green growth and the efficient use of natural resources. *Energy Economics*, *34*, S85–S93. https://doi.org/10.1016/j.eneco.2012.08.033

Rohde, R. A., & Muller, R. A. (2015). Air pollution in China: Mapping of concentrations and sources. *PLoS ONE*, *10*(8), e0135749. https://doi.org/10.1371/journal.pone.0135749

State Council Information Office of the People's Republic of China. (2007). *White paper on energy. China's energy conditions and policies*. The State Council of the People's Republic of China.

State Council Information Office of the People's Republic of China. (2012). *China's energy policy 2012*. The State Council of the People's Republic of China.

State Council Information Office of the People's Republic of China. (2014). *Energy development strategies notice of action plan (2014-2020)*. Retrieved September 7, 2023, from http://www.g ov.cn/zhengce/content/2014-11/19/content_9222.htm.

State Council Information Office of the People's Republic of China. (2020). *Energy in China's new era*. Retrieved September 11, 2023, from https://english.mee.gov.cn/Resources /publications/Whitep/202012/t20201222_814160.shtml

State Council Information Office of the People's Republic of China. (2021). *Biodiversity conservation in China*. Retrieved September 8, 2023, from http://english.scio.g ov.cn/whitepapers/2021-10/08/content_77795608.htm.

State Council of the People's Republic of China. (2021). *Circular economy gets 5-year regulator boost*. Retrieved September 11, 2023, from https://english.www.gov.cn/policies/policywatch/202107/08/content_WS60e639b0c6d0df57f98dc92b.html

Steblyanskaya, A., Ai, M, Bocharnikov, V., & Denisov, A. (2021). Strategies for green economy in China. *Foresight and STI Governance*, *15*(1), 74–85. https://doi.org/10.17323/2500-2597.2021.1.74.85

Su, Y., Liu, X., Ji, J., & Ma, X. (2021). Role of economic structural change in the peaking of China's CO_2 emissions: An input-output optimization model. *The Science of the Total Environment*, *761*, 143306. https://doi.org/10.1016/j.scitotenv.2020.143306

Sun, Y., Li, H., Guo, G., Semple, K. T., & Jones, K. C. (2019). Soil contamination in China: Current priorities, defining background levels and standards for heavy metals. *Journal of Environmental Management*, *251*, 109512. https://doi.org/10.1016/j.jenvman.2019.109512

Teng, Y., Wu, J., Lu, S., Wang, Y., Jiao, X., & Song, L. (2014). Soil and soil environmental quality monitoring in China: A review. *Environment International*, *69*, 177–199. https://doi.org/10.1016/j.envint.2014.04.014

Tian, J., Liu, R., Ding, L., Guo, L., & Zhang, B. (2021). Typhoon rainstorm simulations with radar data assimilation on the southeast coast of China. *Natural Hazards and Earth System Sciences*, *21*, 723–742. https://doi.org/10.5194/nhess-21-723-2021

Tol, R. S. J. (2005). The marginal damage costs of carbon dioxide emissions: An assessment of the uncertainties. *Energy Policy*, *33*(16), 2064–2074. https://doi.org/10.1016/j.enpol.2004.04.002

United Nations. (2015). *Paris Agreement*. Retrieved September 7, 2023, from https://www.un.org/en/climatechange/paris-agreement

United Nations. (2016). *The Montreal protocol on substances that deplete the ozone layer*. Retrieved September 10, 2023, from https://ozone.unep.org/treaties/montreal-protocol/amendments/kigali-amendment-2016-amendment-montreal-protocol-agreed

United Nations. (2020). *Secretary-General's video remarks to Tsinghua University – "Global lecture on climate change – Recover better together."* Retrieved September 7, 2023, from https://www.un.org/sg/en/content/sg/statement/2020-07-23/secretary-generals-video-remarks-tsinghua-university-global-lecture-climate-change-recover-better-together%E2%80%9D?_gl=1*qe4ugp*_ga*MTY4NTQ1NTY3Mi4xNjk0MDYzNTMx*_ga_TK9 BQL5X7Z*MTY5NDA2NjQ2MC4yLjEuMTY5NDA2NjYyMC4wLjAuMA

Wang, N., Lombardo, L., Tonini, M., Cheng, W., Guo, L., & Xiong, J. (2021). Spatiotemporal clustering of flash floods in a changing climate (China, 1950-2015). *Natural Hazards and Earth System Sciences*, *21*, 2109–2124. https://doi.org/10.5194/nhess-21-2109-2021

Wang, J., Mendelsohn, R., Dinar, A., Huang, J., Rozelle, S., & Zhang, L. (2009). The impact of climate change on China's agriculture. *Agricultural Economics*, *40*(3), 323–337. https://doi.org/10.1111/j.1574-0862.2009.00379.x

Wood, M., Haigh, I. D., Le, Q. Q., Nguyen, H. N., Tran, H. B., Darby, S. E., Marsh, R., Skliris, N., Hirschi, J. J.-M., Nicholls, R. J., & Bloemendaal, N. (2023). Climate-induced storminess forces major increases in future storm surge hazard in the South China SEA region. *Natural Hazards and Earth System Science*, *23*, 2475–2504. https://doi.org/10.5194/nhess-23-2475-2023

Wu, S., Li, S., Lei, Y., & Li, L. (2020). Temporal changes in China's production and consumption-based CO_2 emissions and the factors contributing to changes. *Energy Economics*, *89*, 104770. https://doi.org/10.1016/j.eneco.2020.104770

Wu, K., & Storey, I. (2007). Energy security in China's capitalist transition: Import dependence, oil diplomacy, and security imperatives. In C. McNally (Ed.), *China's emergent political economy: Capitalism in the dragon's lair* (pp. 190–208). Routledge. https://doi.org/10.4324/9780203940587

Xi, J. (2017). *The governance of China II*. Foreign Languages Press.

Xinhua. (2018). *Xi stresses efforts to win "three tough battles."* Retrieved September 8, 2023, from http://www. xinhuanet.com/english/2018-04/02/c_137083515.htm.

Xu, P., Chen, Y., & Ye, X. (2013). Haze, air pollution, and health in China. *Lancet*, *382*(9910), 2067. https://doi.org/10.1016/S0140-6736(13)62693-8

Yan, J., & Bocharnikov, V. (2022). Knowledge and understanding of ecological civilization: A Chinese perspective. *BRICS Journal of Economics*, *3*(4), 231–247. https://doi.org/10.3897/brics-econ.3.94450

Yang, Y., Maraun, D., Ossó, A., & Tang, J. (2023). Increased spatial extent and likelihood of compound long-duration dry and hot events in China, 1961-2014. *Natural Hazards and Earth System Sciences*, *23*, 693–709. https://doi.org/10.5194/nhess-23-693-2023

Yu, W., & Czarnezki, J. (2013). Challenges to China's natural resources conservation and biodiversity legislation. *Environmental Law*, *45*, 125–144.

Yu, Z., & Gibbs, D. (2019). Unravelling the role of green entrepreneurs in urban sustainability transitions: A case study of China's solar city. *Urban Studies*, *57*(14), 2901–2917. https://doi.org/10.1177/0042098019888144

Zeng, D. Z., Cheng, L., Shi, L., & Luetkenhorst, W. (2021). China's green transformation through eco-industrial parks. *World Development*, *140*, 105249. https://doi.org/10.1016/j.worlddev.2020.105249

Zhang, H., Fang, W., Zhang, H., & Yu, L. (2021). Assessment of direct economic losses of flood disasters based on spatial valuation of land use and quantification of vulnerabilities: A case study on the 2014 flood in Lishui City of China. *Natural Hazards and Earth System Sciences*, *21*, 3161–3174. https://doi.org/10.5194/nhess-21-3161-2021

Zhang, D., Rong, Z., & Ji, Q. (2019). Green innovation and firm performance: Evidence from listed companies in China. *Resources, Conservation and Recycling*, *144*, 48–55. https://doi.org/10.1016/j.resconrec.2019.01.023

Zhang, D., Wang, H., Loschel, A., & Zhou, P. (2021). The changing role of global value chains in CO_2 emission intensity in 2000-2014. *Energy Economics*, *93*, 105053. https://doi.org/10.1016/j.eneco.2020.105053

Zhao, Y., & Kim, B. (2022). Environmental regulation and chronic conditions: Evidence from China's air pollution prevention and control action plan. *International Journal of Environmental Research and Public Health*, *19*(19), 12584. https://doi.org/10.3390/ijerph191912584

Zheng, M. (2021). Six billion cubic meters in 25 years. *China*, *187*(5), 18–21.

Zheng, H., & Cao, S. (2015). Threats to China's biodiversity by contradictions policy. *AMBIO*, *44*, 23–33. https://doi.org/10.1007/s13280-014-0526-7

Zhilina, I. (2020). The economic consequences of climate change. *Russia and the Contemporary World*, *3*, 50–67. https://doi.org/10.31249/rsm/2020.03.04

Zhou, Y., Fan, Y., Lu, G., Zhang, A., Zhao, T., Sun, G., Sun, D., Yu, Q., & Ren, X. (2022). Assessment of soil quality for guided fertilization in 7 barley agro-ecological areas of China. *PLoS ONE*, *17*(1), e0261638. https://doi.org/10.1371/journal.pone.0261638

Zhuang, Y., & Zhang, J. (2020). Diurnal asymmetry in future temperature changes over the main belt and road regions. *Ecosystem Health and Sustainability*, *6*(1), 1749530. https://doi.org/10.1080/20964129.2020.174953

Chapter 3

CO_2 Emissions, Manufacturing Growth and Renewable Energy Consumption Relationship in OECD Countries: Empirical Evidence from ARDL Model

Mustafa Batuhan Tufaner[a] *and Ilyas Sozen*[b]

[a]*Istanbul Beykent University, Turkey*
[b]*Dokuz Eylul University, Turkey*

Abstract

Energy affects all areas of daily life. Especially with the industrial revolution, the fact that manufacturing has become the engine of economic growth has led to a rise in energy consumption. In this process, the countries of the world have increased their economic growth with traditional energy consumption, and this has increased carbon emissions. However, to fulfill the sustainable development goals, both the continuation of economic growth and the reduction of carbon emissions are required. In this context, the substitution of renewable energy consumption in place of traditional energy sources has started to be discussed. The aim of this study is to research the relationships among CO_2 emissions, manufacturing growth, and renewable energy consumption. For this aim, the relationship among carbon emissions, manufacturing growth, and renewable energy consumption is analyzed for the period 1997–2019 in 38 Organisation for Economic Co-operation and Development (OECD) countries. With respect to the findings of autoregressive distributed lag (ARDL) test results, manufacturing growth enhances CO_2 emissions both in the short and long terms. As the proportion of renewable energy consumption in total energy consumption rises, CO_2 emissions decrease both in the short and long terms. On the other hand, according to the Dumitrescu–Hurlin causality test results, there is a one-way causality relationship from carbon emissions

Emerging Patterns and Behaviors in a Green Resilient Economy, 61–75

doi:10.1108/978-1-83549-780-720241004

to manufacturing growth and from renewable energy consumption to carbon emissions. When the findings are evaluated together, it is understood that renewable energy consumption is a substantial factor in tackling the deadlock of lessening the carbon emissions without adversely impacting manufacturing growth. Therefore, policymakers need to encourage renewable energy consumption.

Keywords: CO_2 emissions; manufacturing growth; renewable energy consumption; panel ARDL; panel causality; OECD

Introduction

Energy plays a fundamental role in every aspect of our daily lives. The lighting systems of the cities, the transportation that provides the trade, and the industry, which is the engine of growth, depend on energy. Traditional energy sources, oil and natural gas, are unequally distributed across the globe. Therefore, a logistics cost arises for countries that do not have this resource (Asghar et al., 2023). In addition, governments are also important actors in energy markets. Both the energy supply security problem caused by factors such as the Russia–Ukraine crisis and environmental protection concerns are among the main reasons for this. In order for daily life to continue and the economy to run, governments must ensure that energy is uninterrupted and reasonably priced. At the same time, governments have introduced policies that limit negative energy externalities that lead to climate change, such as air pollution and carbon emissions (Tagliapietra, 2020). The Kyoto Protocol and Paris Agreement are prime examples of this.

It is observed that the global energy demand has increased almost three times in the last 50 years (1971–2021). The main reason for this increase is the growth of the global economy and population. Since developed countries have shifted their production to developing countries in recent years, energy demand is shifting toward developing countries. Looking at the data for 2020, it is seen that the share of OECD countries in world energy demand is approximately 37% (International Energy Agency, 2023). In particular, the concept of renewable energy comes to the fore in order to eliminate negative effects such as climate change and carbon emissions caused by greenhouse gases.

With the industrial revolution, the engine of economic growth has been manufacturing (Cantore et al., 2017). However, CO_2 emissions released as a result of production activities have also increased. On that account, how to tackle the deadlock between emission degradation and production increase has turned into an important matter for sustainable economic growth (Wang & Feng, 2015). In this context, interest in renewable energy sources such as bioenergy, hydropower, geothermal, wind, solar, marine and nuclear energy, which are considered almost carbon-free, intensified.

While previous studies have revealed a relationship among CO_2 emissions, renewable energy and output, these studies have mostly been analyzed with limited data (Acheampong, 2018; Antonakakis et al., 2017; Le et al., 2020). Although many studies have perused the linkage among CO_2 emissions, renewable energy and economic growth using all industry data, the number of studies addressing manufacturing is limited (Avenyo & Tregenna, 2022; Rasool et al., 2022; Yang et al., 2021). Considering manufacturing as a single sector allows taking into account the heterogeneity between carbon emissions and output.

Production level, technology level, and industrial diversity are very important in terms of the linkage between output and CO_2 emissions (Grossman & Krueger, 1995). Particular attention needs to be paid to CO_2 emissions resulting from rapid growth at the manufacturing level, as the energy mix between sectors in the economy is different. Therefore, we focus on the relationship between CO_2 emissions and manufacturing growth to further expand renewable energy in the manufacturing industry, which is the engine of economic growth.

The objective of this study is to explore the relationships among CO_2 emissions, manufacturing growth, and renewable energy consumption. For this purpose, the linkage among carbon emissions, renewable energy consumption, and manufacturing growth is analyzed for the period 1997–2019 in 38 OECD countries. The data start from 1997 because it was the year of adoption of the Kyoto Protocol. The importance of the study is that it does not suffer from the problem of heterogeneity between sectors by only analyzing manufacturing growth and reveals both short- and long-run relationships by applying the ARDL method. The advantages of the model are that it allows a group transition by handling the analyzed countries as different units steadily and considers possible inconsistencies in the coefficients of groups. Since there is a substitution effect in the measurement of energy consumption, the proportion of renewable energy consumption will be used to accurately determine the causal linkage between carbon emissions and manufacturing growth. Although the issue of renewable energy consumption is theoretically important and current, empirical studies on the place of renewable energy consumption in the manufacturing sector are insufficient. In terms of implementation, developing technology and policymakers' incentives make it possible to spread renewable energy in manufacturing. In this context, the influence of renewable energy consumption needs to be revealed to encourage the diffusion of renewable energy.

This study contributes to the related literature from various aspects. First, the impact of manufacturing growth and renewable energy consumption on CO_2 emissions is determined. Thus, the role of renewable energy consumption will be revealed, and the linkage between carbon emissions and manufacturing growth will be better understood. Also, as far as we know, our study is the pioneer to peruse the linkage among CO_2, renewable energy consumption and manufacturing growth in OECD countries. The fact that most of the manufacturing takes place in OECD countries is the reason for the selected country group.

The sections are listed as follows: "Literature Review" examines previous studies in the relevant literature; "Data" introduces the dataset; "Methodology" describes the ARDL model; "Results and Discussion" provides the empirical results from panel data analysis; and "Conclusions" review the main outcomes of the analysis and suggest relevant policy inferences.

Literature Review

The increase in carbon emissions is highly affected by economic growth activities. The basis of economic growth has been the manufacturing sector since the industrial revolution. The intensive use of fossil fuels in the manufacturing sector and the damage of fossil fuels to the environment are clearly seen. In this period, where global warming is becoming increasingly problematic, the 2030 United Nations sustainable development goals (SDGs) have been announced. In this direction, the study is positioned on the manufacturing sector (SDG 9), which is the most important elements of the renewable energy consumption and carbon emissions (SDG 7).

The starting point of studies investigating carbon emissions in the economics literature is the environmental Kuznets curve (EKC) hypothesis. While many studies on the EKC hypothesis have found that gross domestic product (GDP) encourages carbon emissions (Jaunky, 2011; Mensah et al., 2019; Rupasingha et al., 2004), some studies have found no relationship (Cai et al., 2018; Salahuddin & Gow, 2014). The reasons for the different results are the different economic levels of the countries selected and the different methods chosen in the studies.

Different results on the EKC hypothesis have led economists to the link between renewable energy and output. Yet, very different results have been obtained in this topic. While some studies found a mutual causality relationship between renewable energy consumption and output (Al-mulali et al., 2014; Apergis & Payne, 2010; Kahia et al., 2017), some studies found a unidirectional causality from output to renewable energy consumption (Bhattacharya et al., 2016; Bilgili & Öztürk, 2015; Inglesi-Lotz, 2016).

With the progress of the studies, different results have begun to be obtained in the relationship between renewable energy and carbon emissions. In addition to studies showing the influences of renewable energy on both GDP and carbon emissions (Adewuyi & Awodumi, 2017; Charfeddine & Kahia, 2019), there are also studies showing that carbon emissions are caused by GDP increases (Al-mulali et al., 2015; Pata, 2018). There are studies that show that trade openness negatively affects carbon emissions (Mutascu, 2018), and there are different studies that show it positively (Bernard & Mandal, 2016). Different results were found in studies on the influences of urbanization on CO_2. While it has been proven that urbanization causes an increase in CO_2, especially in studies on China (Wang et al., 2016), it has been shown that urbanization reduces CO_2 emissions in OECD countries (Shafiei & Salim, 2014). Though the linkage between industrialization and carbon emissions is very clear (Avenyo & Tregenna, 2022; Hocaoglu & Karanfil, 2011), it causes more pollution in the early stages of industrialization, while the emission rate decreases with the progressive industrialization (Li & Lin, 2015; Raheem & Ogebe, 2017). A summary of the literature review is given in Table 3.1.

The impacts of renewable energy and industrial production on carbon emissions generally show similar results in the literature. It can be said that the

Table 3.1. Literature Review Summary.

Authors	Countries	Period	Variables	Methodology	Main Findings
Shafiei and Salim (2014)	29 OECD	1980 to 2011	CO_2, REC, NREC, GDP, URB, POP, INA, SVA	Panel – GMM	URB, REC effect CO_2 (decrease) INA effect CO_2 (increase)
Liu and Bae (2018)	China	1970 to 2015	CO_2, EI, GDP, INA, URB, REC	ARDL – VECM	EI, GDP, INA, URB effect CO_2 (increase)
Yang et al. (2021)	38 Countries (3 income groups)	2000 to 2014	CO_2, MVA, REC, NGC, CCC, EHC, EI, INV, TRO, FDI	Panel – FMM	MVA effect CO_2 (increase) REC effect CO_2 (decrease)
Nan et al. (2022)	33 OECD countries	2000 to 2018	CO_2, REC, GI, GDP, IS, URB, EI	Panel – PSTR	REC effect CO_2 (decrease)
Rasool et al. (2022)	China	1991 to 2015	CO_2, MVA, REC, URB	ARDL	MVA, REC, URB effect CO_2 (decrease)
Du et al. (2022)	MINT (Mexico, Indonesia, Nigeria and Turkey)	1990 to 2018	CO_2, REC, HTE, GDP, FDI,	FMOLS, DOLS, FE-OLS, MMQR	GDP, HTE, FDI effect CO_2 (increase) REC effect CO_2 (decrease)
Wang et al. (2022)	G-7	1990 to 2020	EP, REC, TO, INA, TI, GDP	ARDL	REC effect EP (positive) GDP, TO, INA effect EP (negative)
Raihan et al. (2022)	Bangladesh	1990 to 2019	CO_2, GDP, REC, URB, INA, PA, FA	ARDL – DOLS	GDP, URB, INA effect CO_2 (increase)
Avenyo and Tregenna (2022)	68 Developing and emerging economies	1990 to 2016	CO_2, MVA, GDP, SNA, REC, FEC, TRO, CD, URB	Panel	MVA effect CO_2 (increase)

Notes: Variables: GMM: Generalized method of moments, FMM: Finite mixture models, VECM: Vector error correction model, PSTR: Panel smooth transition regression, FMOLS: Fully modified ordinary least squares, DOLS: Dynamic ordinary least squares, FE-OLS: Fixed effect ordinary least squares, MMQR: Method of moments quantile regression, CO_2: CO_2 emissions, REC: renewable energy consumption, MVA: manufacturing value added, INA: industrial value added, TRO: trade openness, URB: urbanization, NREC: non-renewable energy consumption, CCC: coal, coke and crude energy, CD: credit domestic, EHC: electricity and heat consumption, EI: energy intensity, EP: ecological footprints, FA: forest area, FDI: foreign direct investment, FEC: fossil energy consumption, HTE: high-tech industries, INV: investment, IS: industry structure, GI: globalization index, NGC: natural gas consumption, PA: number of patent applications, SNA: services value added, TI: technology innovation number of resident patents, POP: population, SVA: service industry value added.

proportional differences arise from the differences between the selected countries and years. While some studies took into account the manufacturing variable (Avenyo & Tregenna, 2022; Rasool et al., 2022; Yang et al., 2021), some studies took the entire industry as a variable (Liu & Bae, 2018; Raihan et al., 2022; Shafiei & Salim, 2014; Wang et al., 2022). While Du et al. (2022) took high-tech manufacturing as industrialization data, Nan et al. (2022) used a variable called industrialization structure - SVA/industry value added (IVA). Only Rasool et al. (2022), in their analysis on China, state that, unlike the literature, technological production, new urbanization and production/lifestyle based on renewable energy are effective in reducing CO_2.

In our study, we will investigate the effect of renewable energy consumption (RENEC) and manufacturing value added (MVA) variables on CO_2 emissions between 1997 and 2019 using ARDL method, taking into account the manufacturing production level, which has the highest rate in the economic production structure.

Data

All of the variables in the analysis were acquired from the World Bank dataset. Panel data of 38 OECD countries have been used in this study for the period 1997–2019. The LCO_2 variable is calculated as logarithm of CO_2 kiloton/population. LMVA variable calculated as logarithm of manufacturing value added (current US$)/population. LRENEC variable is logarithm of renewable energy consumption as a proportion of total energy consumption. LTRO variable is logarithm of the proportion of the total of export and import to GDP. And LURB variable is logarithm of the ratio of urban population on total population. The focus of this study is to peruse the linkages among CO_2 emissions, manufacturing growth, and renewable energy consumption. Table 3.2 ensures the descriptive statistics, and Table 3.3 shows the correlation between variables.

Table 3.2. Descriptive Statistics.

Variable	**LCO_2**	**LMVA**	**LRENEC**	**LTRO**	**LURB**
Observations	874	874	874	874	874
Mean	–4.954755	8.112697	2.552233	4.367534	4.3205
Standard deviation	0.5746425	0.7879096	0.9738129	0.5174334	0.1520627
Minimum	–6.724833	5.73447	–0.3908921	2.897327	3.925433
Maximum	–3.664999	10.16462	4.395313	5.934479	4.585386
Jarque-Bera	105.6	54.44	56.81	4.782	57.94

Table 3.3. Correlation Matrix.

	LCO_2	LMVA	LRENEC	LTRO	LURB
LCO_2	1.0000				
LMVA	0.5675	1.0000			
LRENEC	−0.4496	−0.1565	1.0000		
LTRO	0.1191	0.1739	−0.0026	1.0000	
LURB	0.2228	0.2551	−0.0738	−0.2269	1.0000

Methodology

The present study will empirically investigate the linkages among CO_2 emissions, manufacturing growth, and renewable energy consumption in the OECD countries. The model for this study will be as follows:

$$\mathrm{LCO}_{2_{it}} = \alpha_1 \mathrm{LMVA}_{it} + \alpha_2 \mathrm{LRENEC}_{it} + \alpha_3 \mathrm{LTRO}_{it} + \alpha_4 \mathrm{LURB}_{it} + \varepsilon_{it} \quad (1)$$

In econometric analysis, unit root tests are applied to test the stationarity of the variables. Panel cointegration tests can be used if the variables are stationary at the same level. ARDL models are frequently used when the variables to be analyzed are not stationary at the same level. Pesaran and Smith (1995) suggest a mean group (MG) estimator which allows the estimation of nonstationary heterogeneous panels. In the MG estimator, long-run coefficients are estimated jointly for the panel, while short-run coefficients are allowed to be estimated by individual countries. The ARDL model is as follows:

$$Y_t = \alpha_i + \gamma_i Y_{i,t-1} + \beta_i X_{it} + \varepsilon_{it} \quad (2)$$

i denotes the unit and t denotes the time. The long-run parameter is θ_i.

$$\theta_i = \frac{\beta_i}{1-\gamma_i} \quad (3)$$

$$\hat{\theta} = \frac{1}{N}\sum_{i=1}^{N}\theta_i \quad (4)$$

Equation (4) shows how the model predicts regressions for each country. Equation (5) refers to the calculation as the unweighted mean of the coefficients estimated for each country. The model allows heterogeneity in the estimation of short-run and long-run coefficients without restriction. In addition, the estimator must have a large time series size to be consistent and valid.

According to the pooled mean group (PMG) estimator propounded by Pesaran et al. (1999), the long-run parameters are fixed in units. Error correction parameters, constant term, and short-run parameters vary from unit to unit.

The result for the entire panel is obtained by averaging the estimates on a unit basis. The panel error correction model (ECM) is set up as follows, allowing heterogeneity except for the long-run parameter:

$$\Delta Y_{it} = \varnothing_i \left(Y_{it-1} - \theta' X_{it-1}\right) + \sum_{j=1}^{p-1} \lambda_{ij}^{*} \Delta Y_{it-j} + \sum_{j=0}^{p-1} \delta_{ij} \Delta X_{it-j} + \mu_i + e_{it} \quad (5) \qquad (5)$$

As seen in Equation (5), while the long-run parameter ($\varnothing$) is homogeneous according to units, other parameters vary according to units.

ARDL (p, q_1, ..., q_k) dynamic fixed effect (DFE) panel model can be set up as follows:

$$Y_{it} = \sum_{j=1}^{p} \lambda_j \Delta Y_{it-j} + \sum_{j=0}^{p} \delta_j \Delta X_{it-j} + \mu_i + e_{it} \qquad (6)$$

Assuming that the X and Y are first-order stationary I(1) and cointegrated, the error term is stationary I(0) at the level. Cointegrated variables tend to respond to any deviation from the long run. This attribute indicates the ECM in which the short-run acts of the series in the equation are affected by the deflection from the equilibrium.

According to Equation (5), $\varnothing = -\left(1 - \sum_{j=1}^{p} \lambda_j\right)$, $\theta = \sum_{j=0}^{p} \delta_j \Big/ \left(1 - \sum_k \lambda_k\right)$, $\lambda_j^{*} = -\sum_{m=j+1}^{p} \lambda_m$ and $\delta_j^{*} = -\sum_{m=j+1}^{p} \delta_m$.

θ is the long-run parameter, and λ and δ are the short-run parameters. $\varnothing$ is the error correction term and gives information about the error correction rate. If $\varnothing = 0$, there is no long-run linkage between Y_{it} and X_{it}; if it is significant and negative, there is a long-run linkage.

The Hausman test can be applied to obtain the most efficient and consistent estimator. First, the null hypothesis establishes that the variation between the PMG and MG estimators is not significant. If the null hypothesis cannot be rejected, the PMG estimator is used because it is more efficient. Second, the null hypothesis establishes that the difference between the DFE and PMG estimators is not significant. If the null hypothesis cannot be rejected, the PMG estimator is used because it is more efficient.

In addition to determining the long-run relationship, it is also critical to examine the causality. Dumitrescu–Hurlin panel causality test is preferred if the examined panel is heterogeneous. In order to create the test, the following model is estimated:

$$Y_{it} = \alpha_i + \sum_{k=1}^{K} \gamma_i^{(k)} \gamma_{it-k} + \sum_{k=1}^{K} \beta_i^{(k)} X_{it-k} + \varepsilon_{it} \qquad (7)$$

In Equation (7), the lag length (k) is the same for each unit of the panel, and when the panel is balanced, the slopes $\beta i^{(k)}$ and autoregressive parameters $\gamma i^{(k)}$ vary from unit to unit. In the Dumitrescu–Hurlin test, the null hypothesis is determined as $\beta_i = 0$, indicating that there is no causality from X to Y for the entire panel (Dumitrescu & Hurlin, 2012; Tatoglu, 2017, p. 155).

Results and Discussion

The concept of stationarity is very important with regard to the faithfulness of the results obtained from panel time series analysis. Stationarity is when the series approaches a value in the long run or fluctuates around a certain value. To test the stationarity of the series, Philip–Perron (PP) and augmented Dickey–Fuller (ADF) tests were applied. Unit root test results are given in Table 3.4.

When the results of both PP and ADF tests are examined, it is seen that the LCO_2, LMVA, and LRENEC variables are not stationary at the level; they turned into stationary when they are transformed to the first order. However, the LTRO and LURB variables are stationary at the level.

Since the series are not stationary in the same order, panel ARDL method was used to identify the long-run linkage (Table 3.5). The model architecture was also examined with the Hausman test, and the models obtained with the DFE, PMG, and MG estimators were compared, and the PMG model was decided. The Akaike information criterion (AIC) was chosen to identify the lag lengths in the panel ARDL model. The optimal lag structure was determined as ARDL (1, 1, 2, 0, 0).

With respect to the PMG test outcomes in Table 3.5, the increase in the manufacturing growth increases the CO_2 emissions in the long run. Increasing renewable energy consumption and urbanization reduce CO_2 emissions in the long run. In the short-term equation, the error correction coefficient was statistically significant and was calculated as –0.2458013. It is concluded that in the short run, 24.5% of the deviations from the long-run balance are adjusted within one period, and the convergence to the long-run balance is realized within four years. In the short run, it is seen that the urbanization variable is statistically insignificant,

Table 3.4. Panel Unit Root Test Results.

	PP		ADF	
	Level	**First Difference**	**Level**	**First Difference**
LCO_2	−0.4505	60.0532***	–1.2573	30.6708***
LMVA	–1.2742	45.7469***	–1.0877	23.3911***
LRENEC	–1.5685	57.3803***	−0.0507	28.1922***
LTRO	2.4393***	37.3253***	2.4019***	26.1206***
LURB	26.0017***	0.7139	6.5695***	6.7613***

Note: Significance levels: ***%1.
Source: Author's own work.

Table 3.5. Panel ARDL Test Results.

Variables	Mean Group		PMG		DFE	
	Long Run	Short Run	Long Run	Short Run	Long Run	Short Run
Error correction term		−0.7224164***		−0.2458013***		−0.07543***
ΔLMVA		0.0216252		0.0721797***		0.0964315***
ΔLRENEC		−0.0583489		−0.3077326***		−0.1645962***
ΔLTRO		0.0954075***		0.1288896***		0.1266745***
ΔLURB		−64.41472		−37.0314		−1.607456*
Constant		7.707018		3.533796***		0.1979619
LMVA	2.088826		0.0317336**		0.0968334	
LRENEC	−1.190903		−0.1716729***		−0.3287989***	
LTRO	−0.9240846		−0.0659203*		0.0608325	
LURB	19.69585		−4.273877***		−1.810619**	
Hausman test			2.08 (0.7214)		0.06 (0.9996)	

Notes: Significance levels: ***%1, **%5 and *%10. The Hausman test is remarking that PMG is a consistent and efficient estimator than DFE and MG estimators. The lag structure is ARDL (1, 1, 2, 0, 0), and the order of variables is LCO_2, LMVA, LRENEC, LTRO, and LURB.
Source: Author's own work.

while renewable energy consumption is significant and negative. However, manufacturing growth and trade openness variables are positive and significant in the short run.

The key finding of the study is to determine the linkages among CO_2 emissions, renewable energy consumption, and manufacturing growth. It is clear that manufacturing growth enhances CO_2 emissions both in the short and long terms. Our findings are consistent with the results of Yang et al. (2021). On the other hand, as the proportion of renewable energy consumption in total energy consumption increases, CO_2 emissions decrease. Our result is consistent with outcomes of Mukhtarov et al. (2023). When the findings are evaluated together, it is understood that renewable energy consumption has a substantial role to reduce carbon emissions without adversely influencing manufacturing growth. On the other hand, the impact of trade openness on CO_2 emissions varies from country to country. Increasing production for export or using industrial outsourcing can cause trade to increase CO_2 in the short run. Our findings are consistent with the results of Yi et al. (2015). On the other hand, one of the reasons why urbanization reduces CO_2 emissions in OECD countries in the long run is the efficient implementation of environmental policies by policymakers and the existence of environmental laws. Our outcome is coherent with the outcomes of Ali et al. (2016).

The appropriate causality test is selected according to whether the constant and slope parameters are homogeneous or heterogeneous according to the units. Swamy (1970) test was used for homogeneity test, and the results are given in Table 3.6. According to the test result, the null hypothesis indicating that the parameters are homogeneous was rejected.

The causal relationships between the series were examined with the Dumitrescu–Hurlin test, which takes the heterogeneity in the panel. Bayesian information criterion was chosen to specify the optimal lag length in the tests. The causality test results are given in Table 3.7. There is one-way causality from LCO_2 to LMVA at the 5% significance level. Similarly, there is one-way causality from LRENEC to LCO_2 at the 5% significance level. It is understood that there is a one-way causality from LTRO to LCO_2, and a mutual causality between LCO_2 and LURB variables at the 5% significance level.

Conclusion

Energy affects all areas of daily life. Especially with the industrial revolution, the fact that manufacturing has become the engine of economic growth has led to an acceleration in energy consumption. In this process, the countries of the world have increased their economic growth with traditional energy consumption, and this has increased carbon emissions. However, to attain the SDGs, both

Table 3.6. Homogeneity Test Results.

$Chi^2(185)$	**1.6e+05**
Probability	0.0000

Source: Author's own work.

Table 3.7. Causality Test Results.

Null Hypothesis	**W-Bar**	**Z-Bar**	**Probability**
$LMVA \underset{?}{\Rightarrow} LCO_2$.	1.4275	1.8636	0.0624
$LCO_2 \underset{?}{\Rightarrow} LMVA$	9.3625	8.5040	0.0000
$LRENEC \underset{?}{\Rightarrow} LCO_2$.	11.2266	12.1379	0.0000
$LCO_2 \underset{?}{\Rightarrow} LRENEC$	1.0376	0.1639	0.8698
$LTRO \underset{?}{\Rightarrow} LCO_2$	1.9809	4.2756	0.0000
$LCO_2 \underset{?}{\Rightarrow} LTRO$	0.9900	–0.0437	0.9652
$LURB \underset{?}{\Rightarrow} LCO_2$	10.3013	10.3342	0.0000
$LCO_2 \underset{?}{\Rightarrow} LURB$	10.2707	10.2745	0.0000

Source: Author's own work.

the continuation of economic growth and the reduction of carbon emissions are required. In this context, the substitution of renewable energy consumption in place of traditional energy sources has started to be discussed.

This study examines the effects of manufacturing growth and renewable energy consumption on CO_2 emissions; 38 OECD countries were analyzed for the period 1997–2019 with the panel data method. The purpose of selecting this sample group is that most of the manufacturing growth in the world is realized by these countries. The data start from 1997 because it was the year of adoption of the Kyoto Protocol. The importance of the study is that it does not suffer from the problem of heterogeneity between sectors by only analyzing manufacturing growth and revealing both short- and long-run relationships using ARDL method. Besides, as far as we know, this study is the pioneer to peruse the linkage among CO_2, renewable energy consumption, and manufacturing growth in OECD countries.

According to the findings of our study, manufacturing growth increases CO_2 emissions both in the short and long terms. As the proportion of renewable energy consumption in total energy consumption increases, CO_2 emissions lessen both in the short run and long run. Considering the LTRO and LURB added to the model as control variables, it is understood that while trade openness rises CO_2 emissions in the short run, urbanization lessens CO_2 emissions in the long run. Moreover, the findings of the study confirm that the panel is heterogeneous. According to the Dumitrescu–Hurlin causality test results, there is a one-way causality relationship from carbon emissions to manufacturing growth and from renewable energy consumption to carbon emissions.

When the findings are evaluated together, it is understood that renewable energy consumption is a substantial factor in tackling with the deadlock of lessening CO_2 emissions without adversely influencing manufacturing growth. Therefore, policymakers need to encourage renewable energy consumption. The technology transfer, financial support, and infrastructure integration needed in the manufacturing sector for the progression to renewable energy use can be driven by governments. On the other hand, emission taxes or taxes on traditional energy use can also encourage a shift toward renewable energy sources. The important point here is that the policies to be implemented for the promotion of renewable energy consumption should be shaped according to the economic conditions of the countries and the needs of the sectors. Countries should start the transformation from which sub-manufacturing sector they derive most of their economic growth from that sub-sector.

This study has limitations in some respects. First, due to data limitations, this study could not be analyzed for non-OECD countries. Second, since the data could not be reached, the sub-resources of renewable energy (such as hydroelectric, solar and wind) could not be examined separately. Future research may expand this analysis to cover different economic groups by income levels to provide a comparative analysis. For more robust results, future studies may analyze the sub-sources of renewable energy separately.

References

Acheampong, A. O. (2018). Economic growth, CO_2 emissions and energy consumption: What causes what and where?*Energy Economics*, *74*, 677–692.

Adewuyi, A. O., & Awodumi, O. B. (2017). Biomass energy consumption, economic growth and carbon emissions: Fresh evidence from West Africa using a simultaneous equation model. *Energy*, *119*, 453–471.

Ali, H. S., Abdul-Rahim, A. S., & Ribadu, M. B. (2016). Urbanization and carbon dioxide emissions in Singapore: Evidence from the ARDL approach. *Environmental Science and Pollution Research*, *24*, 1967–1974.

Al-mulali, U., Fereidouni, H. G., & Lee, J. Y. M. (2014). Electricity consumption from renewable and non-renewable sources and economic growth: Evidence from Latin American countries. *Renewable and Sustainable Energy Reviews*, *30*, 290–298.

Al-mulali, U., Ozturk, U., & Lean, H. H. (2015). The influence of economic growth, urbanization, trade openness, financial development, and renewable energy on pollution in Europe. *Natural Hazards*, *79*, 621–644.

Antonakakis, N., Chatziantoniou, I., & Filis, G. (2017). Energy consumption, CO_2 emissions, and economic growth: An ethical dilemma. *Renewable and Sustainable Energy Reviews*, *68*, 808–824.

Apergis, N., & Payne, J. E. (2010). Renewable energy consumption and economic growth: Evidence from a panel of OECD countries. *Energy Policy*, *38*(1), 656–660.

Asghar, N., Majeed, M. T., Khan, M. W., & Anwar, A. (2023). Biomass energy consumption and sustainable development: Empirical evidence from Asian economies. *Environmental Science and Pollution Research*, *30*, 145–160.

Avenyo, E. K., & Tregenna, F. (2022). Greening manufacturing: Technology intensity and carbon dioxide emissions in developing countries. *Applied Energy*, *324*, 1–12.

Bernard, J., & Mandal, S. K. (2016). The impact of trade openness on environmental quality: An empirical analysis of emerging and developing economies. *WIT Transactions on Ecology and the Environment*, *203*, 195–208.

Bhattacharya, M., Paramati, S. R., Ozturk, I., & Bhattacharya, S. (2016). The effect of renewable energy consumption on economic growth: Evidence from top 38 countries. *Applied Energy*, *162*, 733–741.

Bilgili, F., & Öztürk, I. (2015). Biomass energy and economic growth nexus in G7 countries: Evidence from dynamic panel data. *Renewable and Sustainable Energy Reviews*, *49*, 132–138.

Cai, Y., Sam, C. Y., & Chang, T. (2018). Nexus between clean energy consumption, economic growth and CO2 emissions. *Journal of Cleaner Production*, *182*, 1001–1011.

Cantore, N., Clara, M., Lavopa, A., & Soare, C. (2017). Manufacturing as an engine of growth: Which is the best fuel?*Structural Change and Economic Dynamics*, *42*, 56–66.

Charfeddine, L., & Kahia, M. (2019). Impact of renewable energy consumption and financial development on CO_2 emissions and economic growth in the MENA region: A panel vector autoregressive (PVAR) analysis. *Renewable Energy*, *139*, 198–213.

Du, L., Jiang, H., Adebayo, T. S., Awosusi, A. A., & Razzaq, A. (2022). Asymmetric effects of high-tech industry and renewable energy on consumption-based carbon emissions in MINT countries. *Renewable Energy*, *196*, 1269–1280.

Dumitrescu, E. I., & Hurlin, C. (2012). Testing for granger non-causality in heterogeneous panels. *Economic Modelling*, *29*(4), 1450–1460.

Grossman, G. M., & Krueger, A. B. (1995). Economic growth and the environment. *Quarterly Journal of Economics*, *110*(2), 353–377.

Hocaoglu, F. O., & Karanfil, F. (2011). Examining the link between carbon dioxide emissions and the share of industry in GDP: Modeling and testing for the G-7 countries. *Energy Policy*, *39*, 3612–3620.

Inglesi-Lotz, O. (2016). The impact of renewable energy consumption to economic growth: A panel data application. *Energy Economics*, *53*, 58–63.

International Energy Agency. (2023).

International energy report 2023.

Jaunky, V. C. (2011). The CO_2 emissions-income nexus: Evidence from rich countries. *Energy Policy*, *39*(3), 1228–1240.

Kahia, M., Aissa, M. S., & Lanouar, C. (2017). Renewable and non-renewable energy use - economic growth nexus: The case of MENA net oil importing countries. *Renewable and Sustainable Energy Reviews*, *71*, 127–140.

Le, T. H., Chang, Y., & Park, D. (2020). Renewable and nonrenewable energy consumption, economic growth, and emissions: International evidence. *The Energy Journal*, *41*(2), 73–92.

Li, K., & Lin, B. (2015). Impacts of urbanization and industrialization on energy consumption/CO_2 emissions: Does the level of development matter?*Renewable and Sustainable Energy Reviews*, *52*, 1107–1122.

Liu, X., & Bae, J. (2018). Urbanization and industrialization impact of CO_2 emissions in China. *Journal of Cleaner Production*, *172*, 178–186.

Mensah, I. A., Sun, M., Gao, C., Omari-Sasu, A. Y., Zhu, D., Ampimah, B. C., & Quarcoo, A. (2019). Analysis on the nexus of economic growth, fossil fuel energy consumption, CO_2 emissions and oil price in Africa based on a PMG panel ARDL approach. *Journal of Cleaner Production*, *228*, 161–174.

Mukhtarov, S., Aliyev, F., Aliyev, J., & Ajayi, R. (2023). Renewable energy consumption and carbon emissions: Evidence from an oil-rich economy. *Sustainability*, *15*(134), 1–12.

Mutascu, M. (2018). A time-frequency analysis of trade openness and CO_2 emissions in France. *Energy Policy*, *115*, 443–455.

Nan, S., Huang, J., Wu, J., & Li, C. (2022). Does globalization change the renewable energy consumption and CO_2 emissions nexus for OECD countries? New evidence based on the nonlinear PSTR model. *Energy Strategy Reviews*, *44*, 100995.

Pata, U. K. (2018). Renewable energy consumption, urbanization, financial development, income and CO_2 emissions in Turkey: Testing EKC hypothesis with structural breaks. *Journal of Cleaner Production*, *187*, 770–779.

Pesaran, M. H., Shin, Y., & Smith, R. P. (1999). Pooled mean group estimation of dynamic heterogeneous panels. *Journal of the American Statistical Association, 94*(446), 621–634.

Pesaran, M. H., & Smith, R. P. (1995). Estimating long-run relationships from dynamic heterogeneous panels. *Journal of Econometrics*, *68*(1), 79–113.

Raheem, I. D., & Ogebe, J. O. (2017). CO_2 emissions, urbanization and industrialization: Evidence from a direct and indirect heterogeneous panel analysis. *Management of Environmental Quality*, *28*(6), 851–867.

Raihan, A., Muhtasim, D. A., Farhana, S., Pavel, M. I., Faruk, O., Rahman, M., & Mahmood, A. (2022). Nexus between carbon emissions, economic growth, renewable energy use, urbanization, industrialization, technological innovation, and forest area towards achieving environmental sustainability in Bangladesh. *Energy and Climate Change*, *3*.

Rasool, S. F., Zaman, S., Jehan, N., Chin, T., Khan, S., & Zaman, Q. (2022). Investigating the role of the tech industry, renewable energy, and urbanization in sustainable environment: Policy directions in the context of developing economies. *Technological Forecasting and Social Change*, *183*, 1–11.

Rupasingha, A., Goetz, S. J., Debertin, D. L., & Pagoulatos, A. (2004). The environmental Kuznets curve for US counties: A spatial econometric analysis with extensions. *Papers in Regional Science*, *83*, 407–424.

Salahuddin, M., & Gow, J. (2014). Economic growth, energy consumption and CO_2 emissions in Gulf Cooperation Council countries. *Energy*, *73*, 44–58.

Shafiei, S., & Salim, R. A. (2014). Non-renewable and renewable energy consumption and CO_2 emissions in OECD countries: A comparative analysis. *Energy Policy*, *66*, 547–556.

Swamy, P. (1970). Efficient inference in a random coefficient regression model. *Econometrica*, *38*(2), 311–322.

Tagliapietra, S. (2020). *Global energy fundamentals: Economics, politics and technology*. Cambridge University Press.

Tatoglu, F. Y. (2017). *Panel Zaman Serileri Analizi*. Beta Yayinevi.

Wang, S., Fang, C., & Wang, Y. (2016). Spatiotemporal variations of energy-related CO_2 emissions in China and its influencing factors: An empirical analysis based on provincial panel data. *Renewable and Sustainable Energy Reviews*, *55*, 505–515.

Wang, Z., & Feng, C. A. (2015). A performance evaluation of the energy, environmental, and economic efficiency and productivity in China: An application of global data envelopment analysis. *Energy Economics*, *147*, 617–626.

Wang, W., Rehman, M. A., & Fahad, S. (2022). The dynamic influence of renewable energy, trade openness, and industrialization on the sustainable environment in G-7 economies. *Renewable Energy*, *198*, 484–491.

Yang, M., Wang, E. Z., & Hou, Y. (2021). The relationship between manufacturing growth and CO_2 emissions: Does renewable energy consumption matter?*Energy*, *232*, 1–12.

Yi, Y., Guan, W., & Gao, Y. (2015). Empirical research on the relationship between FDI and CO_2 emission in China: The empirical research based on ARDL. *Journal of Guizhou University of Finance and Economics*, *3*, 58–65.

Chapter 4

An Analysis of Employees in Serbian Organizations from the Point of View of Decisions on the Personnel Policy and the Management Style

Nikola Ćurčić[a], *Aleksandar Grubor*[b] *and Vuk Miletić*[c]

[a]*"Tamiš" Research and Development Institute, Pančevo, Serbia*
[b]*University of Novi Sad, Faculty of Economics, Subotica, Serbia*
[c]*The College of Academic Studies "Dositej," Belgrade, Serbia*

Abstract

Human resources (HR) are undoubtedly one of the most important factors of any organization. That is why making decisions on the HR policy is becoming a very sensitive issue, both when hiring adequate candidates for the job and during the process work, i.e., during training and development of employees who work in the organization. The purpose of this study was to investigate the importance of HR and decisions on the HR policy as the premise for generating the organization's expected business excellence. The starting assumption of this chapter is that appropriate decisions on the HR policy are predictors of engaging adequate employees and managing their potentials on the right way. The research is directed toward identifying differences in decisions on the personnel policy in organizations from Serbia that have different decision-makers and different management styles, which are directly related to their business success. Apart from the decision-maker, a significant role in profiling an organization's personnel should also be done by the Human Resource Department, who take part in recruiting, selecting for education, building, and motivating personnel. In order to confirm the starting assumption, the comparative

Emerging Patterns and Behaviors in a Green Resilient Economy, 77–103

Published under exclusive licence by Emerald Publishing Limited
doi:10.1108/978-1-83549-780-720241005

analysis method, the synthesis method, and the multiple comparison and statistical test methods are used.

Keywords: Organization; personnel; personnel policy; decision-makers; leadership style

Introduction

One of the key components of a strategically oriented policy of an organization is the organization's personnel policy that determines the philosophy and principles implemented by its decision-makers in relation to HR. Irrespective of whether they are those responsible for managerial activities or belong to the "other employees" category, all subjective strengths in an organization that enable its operation are the organization's personnel base (Bakator et al., 2019) for its advancement. As the organization's aware force in the production process and initiators of new ideas and innovations in it, its personnel (Chen et al., 2022) are those who make the business operations of the organization successful on condition that they are properly allocated. In that sense, the personnel policy must essentially ensure an optimum balance between the needed number of employees and the qualitative structure of them (Jovičić, 2009) according to the needs of the organization, the requirements imposed by the labor law and the situation on the labor market. The organization's human capital is key so as to achieve the goals connected with its digital transformation, which is implicative of the inclusion of its employees in the technology-led business processes (Hazim et al., 2023).

It appears in the Serbian business environment that the personnel policy is in the background, which certainly is devastating. The improvement of the personnel policy of national organizations is all but possible without a comprehensive analysis. It is a fact that an effective personnel policy (Eslami & Nakhaie, 2011) is first of all based upon a systematic calculation and analysis of the influence of the external business environment, as well as the adaptation of production to such influences in function of organizational sustainable performance (Chowdhury et al., 2023). The forming of such a personnel policy lies on the analysis of the personnel structure, the efficiency of the use of the working time, and the anticipation of the development of production and employment. The personnel policy refers to all procedures and policies that are developed and standardized in an organization with the aim of managing its most important resource, employees, to create a high-performing organization. As a management tool, personnel policy includes organizational activity whose goal is to unite the efforts of all employees in the company in order to solve the set tasks. This implies a holistic personnel activity that combines various forms of personnel work (Latin et al., 2022), the style of its implementation in the organization, and employee engagement plans (Miletić, 2020, pp. 36–37).

Independently of the fact who decision-makers in different organizations are or of their leadership style (Gardašević et al., 2021), the personnel policy should ensure decisions that contribute to an increase in the ability of employees and/or national company to respond to changeable requirements of the market in a near future.

If the goal is to achieve a high business result, it is necessary to harmonize the management style with the situation in which it is applied. At the same time, the problems of selecting the appropriate personnel can arise from the discrepancy between the personal goals of the manager and the goals that go with the managerial role (Andrejić et al., 2021). The analysis of the characteristics of the personnel policy of every successful organization starts from the organization's connectedness with the strategic direction of the development of the enterprise. Simultaneously, transformational leadership (Berber et al., 2022; Beugré et al., 2006; Canterino et al., 2022) directs the focus toward employees, their followers, and makes significant influence on them, through motivation, trust, change and a fair and ethical approach.

In market conditions, the efficiency of production depends to a great extent on the qualification of employed workers, how professionally trained and educated they are and their motivation, and the business qualities of the organization. The employees and managers of an organization are the backbone of a complex and controversial phenomenon (Mitsakis, 2014), where a lot of processes and relations are in place. Irrespective of the fact that an organization may as well possess financial resources, appropriate equipment, and technology, it is also a fact that the business operations carried out by the organization on the market are deprived of any perspective unless its employees are adequately motivated and trained and educated for the needed jobs (Miletić, 2020, p. 244). Without investing in their knowledge, training and development (Purcell et al., 2002), an acceptable selection (Djergović et al., 2019) and teamwork, the organization will not be able to grow and develop, nor will it be able to achieve sustainable competitiveness (Ilić & Cvjetković, 2014).

Therefore, employed personnel are the key and decisive factor in the production of goods and/or services, the first production force of the organization led by innovations (Budhwar et al., 2018) which contributes to the combination of goals and priorities in the function of achieving total business excellence. Differences between employees with respect to their professional qualifications, performances, talents, competences (Suciu et al., 2023), and demographic characteristics prevail in all organizations and are considered to be important in ensuring competitive advantage. The management function contains specific roles that, as a rule, no individual can perform all of them equally successfully. In the given context, the fact that there is a difference in the personnel policy in the Serbian organizations that have different decision-makers (Berber et al., 2019) and a different leadership style should be appreciated, which may significantly determine the results of their business operations. Decision-makers in an organization should bear in mind the mentioned differences, and they should also maximally appreciate them in the HR management process (Brebels et al., 2015). This is even more so because differences in decision-makers' emotional and social (Berber et al., 2022) competences (Strugar-Jelača, 2022) may significantly exert an influence on the appropriation of funds for employees' education and training, their motivation and innovative behavior (Zeng & Xu, 2020) as well as equitableness when selecting employees to attend training, the formation of the awareness level at which they share responsibility in the organization both with respect to the firm's success and failure.

Personnel Policy in Function of the Development of the Serbian Organization

Personnel and Organizational Development

This chapter deals with personnel management which implies the managerial process in which personnel are positioned in appropriate workplaces defined by the enterprise's organizational structure. The preoccupation of the management of each organization implies their bringing the right personnel in the right workplace. The needs for personnel are a synthetic expression of the total development of the organization, with the structure of the need for personnel simultaneously being dependent on the organization's development goals. Personnel determine the potential of every element of the organizational structure. The personnel system of an organization is made up of the totality of the qualitative and quantitative structure of its personnel (Latin et al., 2022) deployed within the framework of certain elements of the formal organizational structure.

Namely, the successful business operations and development of every organization imply meeting certain assumptions that concern the directing of personnel toward a precisely defined and achievable goal. The goal always implies the achievement of high business performances that should enable the organization to sustainably develop. The selection of a goal should be based upon available resources, first of all those related to personnel and other material resources, as well as the current competition. Only with an adequate structure and quality selection of personnel can such development-oriented organizational goals be realized. At the same time, it should never be neglected that employees behave differently, stochastically, in the organization, even if they work in seemingly the same conditions. Working with people is a delicate job in all phases of their engagement, due to which fact the personnel resource generation process exactly starts within the framework of planning and organizing. For the reason of that fact, personnel can be said to be the personality of particular socially needed and socially acknowledged physical, psychosocial, professional-educational and social characteristics suitable for their being given certain workplaces and positions and their performance of concrete activities, functions and roles in the organization.

A large number of jobs different as per their size, complexity, responsibility, and the time needed for them to be done are performed in every organization. For said jobs to be done, it is necessary that there be an appropriate number of personnel, structures, and their ability to work. The structure of the needs for personnel itself depends on numerous factors, such as sophisticated technology development, labor organization development, product and service matrices, the educational process development, unemployment components and so on.

The organizational needs for qualitative personnel unveiled by organizations are growing, and they impose themselves as a strategically significant question.

It has to be entrusted to professional managers and job performers who are simultaneously dedicated to reform. The determination of the needs for personnel implies the determination of the number of people as per their qualifications structure who need to be given a job in the organization. The selection of personnel represents one of the most complex phases in the personnel management process. Personnel selection is an effort to anticipate which of the candidates will be capable of effectively performing the planned work. Therefore, team cooperation (Ferreira et al., 2020) between and among the managers of the organization and a whole line of professionals of different profiles, such as industrial psychologists, occupational safety engineers, bachelors of law, and others, is necessary so as to ensure motivated personnel able to effectively engage themselves in business processes. Personnel training is a process of the additional acquisition and innovation of the knowledge and skills of employed personnel. All of the said presupposes a developed personnel system in the organization as an interconnected set of individuals and groups assigned certain jobs and work tasks.

The adaptation of the Serbian organization to numerous changes in modern technology, market requirements, and so forth cannot be achieved without personnel development. Investing in personnel as the bearers of organizational development pays off in practice only on condition that, conducting a correct personnel policy, personnel are given the workplaces that they should be positioned in due to their professional references. Otherwise, such personnel can only be a potential asset that would be an immeasurable asset in a different environment.

Every investment in the knowledge, training, and development of personnel is the most lucrative investment to be made. Investing in the human potential must not be a cost or burden for national organizations that they should bear, but it should rather be considered as an investment in sustainable survival. The existing manner and dynamics of education, training, and development do not ensure the needed number of efficient and professionally dedicated personnel. For that reason, planning both inflows and outflows, too, as well as the schooling, training, improvement, and development of personnel should be fully performed in compliance with the vision and strategic documents of every organization.

The fact that an ever-increasing role of information technology (IT) in organizations may lead to the lesser efficiency of the traditional factors of the workforce engagement given the changeable nature of the workplace, the type of organizational activities, interaction between business units, organizational connectedness, etc. should be highlighted.

Organizational Personnel Policy

The personnel policy represents a significant segment of organizational management and as such has an important role in organizing employees. It is noticeable that the term "personnel policy" is essentially used alternately with the term "human resource management" and covers a whole line of measures for finding, selecting, and managing organizational personnel development. In order for every organization to increase its efficiency as has been said, they should have developed systems for personnel development research, planning, and monitoring. Research in personnel development should encompass inflows – the employment, training, motivation, labor engagement, professional advancement, promotion, knowledge innovation, and employee turnover.

The efficient organizational personnel policy is related to the personnel development process and organizational economic efficiency (Janković & Golubović, 2019). The personnel policy should deal with (Jovičić & Radojčić, 2009) employee's motivation, the development of mechanisms for their compensation system, incentives and benefits, their learning and development process, career progression, etc.

The personnel policy is formed based upon the analysis of the personnel structure, the efficiency of using the working time, and the anticipations of the development of production and employment. The personnel strategy, as a part of personnel policy, as well as providing simultaneous help to the management in performing the tasks of organizational management are in the operational sphere of personnel management, simultaneously also supplying the organization with a high-quality workforce, including planning, selection and employment; it also encompasses firing employees, an analysis of employee fluctuation, the improvement of the organization itself and labor stimulation, ensuring occupational safety and social welfare payments. Therefore, the personnel policy of the organization should be so designed as to ensure a high quality of the work performed, its results, working conditions, as well as the workforce themselves.

A pragmatic personnel policy in Serbia may obviate personnel issues (Carić et al., 2022, p. 15), empower the open innovation concept (Miletić et al., 2020), and improve labor productivity. "Most innovative HRM practices have a statistically significant impact on firm performance in terms of labor productivity, product, process, and marketing innovations" (Aslam et al., 2023, p. 1). The successful business operations of every organization imply the teamwork (Miletić et al., 2023) and permanent harmonization of its material and personnel elements given the fact that they make up an inseparable unity of its further development. The right selection of people and assigning them right, appropriate jobs are considered as a successful personnel policy.

The Personnel Policy and Employees in Organizations Operating in Serbia

It is obvious that the majority of Serbian organizations are insufficiently competitive on the global market today. The low level of the successfulness of national organizations appears as a consequence of the influence of different factors, first of all the low productivity of business operations, a lack of innovations and the application of sophisticated technologies and knowledge as well as an inadequate personnel policy. The topic is the impermissible and unsustainable human resource "management" in some organizations, which has led to a serious personnel crisis and the certainty that neither quantitatively nor qualitatively the employee matches the needed profile of the engaged personnel. Decision-makers at all levels, including the company level as well, do not seriously realize (or do not want to realize) that the creation of a sustainable and simultaneously reliable business environment does not tolerate discontinuity in the personnel policy, ignoring the factual state of the matters, superficiality, inertness, unrealistic ambitions, and (self)deception. For this reason, it was possible to expect that, sooner or later, organizations would face a lack of personnel of different educational and professional profiles and difficulties in achieving their targeted goals.

So it happens that some organizations have found themselves in a situation that there are no people able to efficiently use and operate one part of the bought modern equipment and designed processes. For that reason, the personnel issue should constantly be in focus, while simultaneously the aspiration that all have to be employed and that the number of the unemployed must be reduced to a reasonable measure was overcome a long time ago. The problems of selecting adequate personnel in all types of organizations are always key and urgent, and they deserve special attention to be paid to them by decision-makers. Advantage should be given to professional and capable personnel since without them, there are no efficient business operations or any social progress at all. That is exactly what has been disrupted to a great extent in our conditions since, according to relevant assessments, a large number of people are in the places which do not match their professional references. That is first of all due to omissions in decisions on engaged HR and the planning of labor operations, only to be followed by the inadequate coordination between organizational units, logistic oversights as well as the decreasing moral and insufficiently trained engaged personnel.

The dissatisfaction of the employed in different organizations in Serbia (both in the public sector and in the private sector) is surely contributed to be a part of the managerial personnel who do not perceive (or who have no) interest in investing in personnel and their development or who yet withdraw for their personal reasons before those who have the authority arising from the positions they take. All in all, in the absence of healthy competition, the job doers who are not capable of achieving the expected results are "created" since, instead of acquiring knowledge, abilities, and skills necessary for success and advancement, individuals and organizations prepare themselves for acting in the conditions of falling criteria. Reduced interest in certain jobs has also been contributing to an ever-increasing number of vacant and inadequately filled workplaces in Serbia.

The question, "Is ad hoc 'getting to grips' with the challenges of attracting, training, developing and retaining personnel by organizations efficient and how efficient it actually is?" imposes itself. Time will show, although effects are possible to anticipate. Dominant pieces of news and presentations intended for the public are concerned with "bringing" foreign investors who, after the expiry of the period of subsidies given by the state for the purpose of their employing the domiciled population, leave the country with pockets full of an extra profit upon the expiry of a contract.

The fact that the significance of HR in the function of improving business performances of contemporary organizations is not reduced with the development of new technologies and sophisticated equipment should be pointed out. This is confirmed by numerous examples of companies from within international business/economic practice. The ever more significant application and introduction of contemporary technology and procedures impose the need for highly educated and highly trained personnel of diverse specialties, on whose quality organizational sustainable competitiveness depends. Equipping organizations with modern pieces of equipment and technique should raise the ladders and increase the number of requests for the degree of the training of their employees. Even apart from being equipped with high technology, the human factor has limited the ability of some organizations to reach the expected business excellence and to adequately position themselves on the market. Instead of engaging themselves in improving the position of and working conditions for their employees, the identification of the needs and finding out sustainable solutions to the selection, education and development, acceptance, building and also retention of personnel, which is surely one of the most profitable investments, decision-makers often opt for short-term and insufficiently purposeful solutions. In Serbia, quite a large number of workers find a job to do through casual and temporary employment mainly through agencies whose owners are close with the authorities. Those employees are deprived of almost all labor rights, simultaneously facing great existential uncertainty, and they are ideal to be blackmailed, while their training and development are hardly to be taken into consideration at all.

The problem of retaining highly educated and trained personnel in organizations, at institutes and in other organizations as a whole in the country, is also burdened with a decades-long absence of the perception of the treatment on decision-makers' part of the public interest in the meaning of support to domestic companies doing their best to fight foreign disloyal competition in the environment where the importing lobby "suffocates" national organizations. There are numerous pieces of information provided by some independent research centers, nongovernment organizations, and analysts that point to the ever more pronounced "outflow" of highly educated young people from Serbia. Although the human capital outflow data are not publicly available, it is possible to conclude on the basis of the data retrieved from the official information and the information coming from other sources that the outflow problem has been ever more pronounced in recent years. People leave both for material reasons and for the working conditions that have become more difficult, because they have become aware of the fact that allegiance and obedience are a dominant recommendation for a "career possible to envisage," as well as the betrayed expectations that achieved successes during their schooling and improved themselves. The work they have done and their personal ambitions throughout their careers will be valued adequately.

For that reason, investment in the improvement of HR is emphatically of essential importance given the fact that today it is one of the key organizational goods. The development of every organization begins with the selection of employees for a particular workplace, their assessment and adaptation, training and other necessary procedures. Organizations have a goal to create competitive advantage using available sources, simultaneously the key cause for their business success or failure lying in their personnel policy.

When realistic goals and adequate organizational strategies and the personnel profile that would successfully correspond with their achievements are set, results would almost certainly be guaranteed. However, the situation in practice is quite different. In the Serbian business milieu, the objective picture is such that state-owned firms have become political parties' employment bureaus, whereas the real sector is mainly focused on making profits and in which consequently educated personnel suffer the most because they cannot win recognition. The bad personnel policy has devalued all it had to do with and the whole of its domain. The question is how to move on from the rhetoric of political party's nepotism and the corruption that has permeated the whole society. Maybe at the moment when the working conditions at state-owned institutions become equal with the working conditions in the private sector. Then people would not be tending to be employed in state-owned firms. Relevant data retrieved from the Tax Administration showing that a large number of engaged workers were officially registered as receivers of the minimum salary irrespective of their respective professional qualifications may serve as an example of various negative oscillations of the status of the employed in Serbia. The result of such a personnel policy additionally implies the fact that individual persons with a university diploma are registered as receivers of the minimum salary under constant pressure to sign a contract for a definite period of time prior to the expiry of the legal deadline when the employer is obliged to declare him-/herself whether the career of an employee will end upon the expiry of the contract or he/she will sign the same for an indefinite period of time.

In Serbia, there is a systemic difference in the level of the salaries between those employed in the private sector and those employed in the state sector, namely in favor of those employed in the state sector. The nonexistence of the salary classes in the private sector is still obviously a bitter fact. There is no sound logic in the fact that employees receive different salaries for the same position at work, the same work description, importance, and responsibility only because one person works in a state-owned firm or institution, and another works in a privately owned one. Due to such practice in employment in the public sector has to a great extent become synonymous with safety, welfare and self-achievement for a numerous majority and at any price. To have this problem solved, investments should probably be made in education and development but not in such a way as to devalue education by having privately owned higher-education institutions award diplomas to persons with diverse titles without a possibility for them to undergo practical work only with the aim of infiltrating in safe workplaces such as those in state-owned institutions.

There is certainly no justification, either economic or moral, for the fact that someone is ensured a workplace, namely the workplace for which the bigger majority of such engaged individuals are not even capable of justifying that workplace with one single reasonable (in)competence they have, only for the reason of their genetical ties or political belongingness. For that very reason, it is all but realistic to expect that an individual who is barely subsisting will invest in their education or will be thinking of politics and the improvement of their environment when they cannot meet their subsisting needs. That is what depresses and makes today's young and educated individual lethargic or makes him/her leave this state. There is certainly no such system in the whole world that works perfectly, but there is probably at least one that would be acceptable to the majority.

Leadership Styles in Function of Business Excellence

The purpose of this chapter is to systematize the leadership styles that are present the most and to interpret their role in the creation or maintenance of business excellence inside an organization. Leadership is most frequently observed as a process of interaction between the manager and employees in which managers tend to exert an influence on their employees in order to achieve their joint goals (Northouse, 2010; Yukl, 2008). A leadership style is a special way in which managers behave in the working process that influences the results of the work done in a concrete organization. In this chapter, the authors' attention is focused on the role of the current leadership styles. Namely, the successful running of business operations requires a good knowledge of managerial activities both from the point of view of their importance to how an organization works and its development and from the point of view of the hierarchical organizational structure, i.e., the decision-making structure in the organization itself. A leadership style does not only relate to employee management but it also pertains to planning, organizing, and valuing the achieved business results.

In that sense, it is necessary that we are generally aware of the responsibility lying on some subjects – the owner and decision-makers in their working process, i.e., in the manufacturing of goods and providing services to clients and the establishment of the needed balance between them. There are no unique criteria for classifying leadership styles. Some among such criteria that help group leadership styles include an approach to job observation, the level of the manager's orientation toward and treatment of the job and employees, the level of the inclusion of junior workers/employees in the decision-making process by the manager, the manager's dominant orientation toward either his employees or the tasks, the way how the manager uses power, the determination of the goals and the decision-making cycle, and so forth.

Given the fact that leaders/managers are a very important factor in the development and advancement of an organization, it is necessary that the leadership styles that provide us with the best results and are exposed to employees' resistance the least be studied. This is even more so necessary given the fact that the leader's individual qualities determine the employees' motivation and satisfaction and their commitment to the organization and also influence the character of the total relationships between the members of the organization (Nanjundeswaraswamy & Swamy, 2014). In that sense, numerous research studies in this field have confirmed the existence of different classical leadership styles (House et al., 2004), whereas recently, transactional and transformational leadership have differentiated themselves (Bass, 2008; Jensen et al., 2019).

Difficulties in anticipating the effectiveness of the results of some leadership styles necessitate withdrawing from searching for a superior style and searching for concrete situational conditions under which leadership styles will always be efficient. A management style should certainly be harmonized with the situation in which it is applied in and with the manager who is applying it as well if there is a wish to achieve expected business excellence.

Leadership Styles

Every leadership style includes specific methods and their combination of the manners and actions characteristic of each single manager – bearer of the managerial function. A style is created as a result of a combination of one's personal characteristics, skills, knowledge, and experiences, and over time, it develops into a manager's signature of its own kind (Simović et al., 2018). This aside, a style also includes the visual component, i.e., the exact appearance of a manager and the way in which the environment perceives him. Apart from the other determinants, the foundational determinants of a style are also implicative of the manager's other attributes, such as the way he or she treats his or her associates, taking advantage of the position of an authority and the power he or she has been assigned, his or her treatment of the tasks that should be performed, and so on. It is expressed in the manner in which a manager encourages associates to purposefully, initiatively, and creatively act, i.e., perform tasks, and the way how he or she controls the results of the work done.

There is evidence of a lot of leadership styles both in theory and, even more, in practice. As has been mentioned, those styles differentiate between one another as per numerous attributes. For the reason of that fact, it is not surprising that every style establishes interpersonal relationships and the atmosphere of an organization, which is a precondition for achieving high business performances. It should be said that a leadership style is exposed to permanent assessments made by employees and significantly reflects on how the organization works and overall organizational behavior. The creation of a leadership style is a complex process requiring a lot of time given the fact that it forms gradually until a certain set of actions, methods, techniques, and assets appropriate to the structure of the manager's personality has been formed. Every manager builds his own style through a long-lasting and hard work on it (Shin et al., 2011). A style created in such a manner should ensure the realization of the leadership tasks that are not contradictory to the appropriate standards of an objective order.

As has been said, the managerial styles of work are different and primarily caused by the individual's available psychic and educational qualifications for performing this function. Even though there are certain theoretical difficulties in the identification of dominant leadership styles for managing working processes, based upon a rough classical classification of certain characteristics of the work done and behavior demonstrated by a manager, practically the following working styles are distinguished: autocratic, democratic, and liberal (Bulatović & Jokić, 2017).

The authoritarian and democratic management styles are taken as the extreme points of the continuum, in-between which there are further mixed variants of the decision-making style. These two styles differ from each other in a series of characteristics, and more recent research studies have mainly been directed toward their differences with respect to the participation of the members from within the employed in making decisions. When applying a particular style, managers step into the existential space of their employees and have an influence on modeling their lives. It is actually about the issue of maintaining the values and value assumptions that maintain the pattern of the order among the people and their interpersonal relationships within organizational operations.

An authoritarian manager makes decisions on his own, uses coercion as a means of shaping behavior, and exerts his or her influence using formal authority. Such a style of managerial conduct is mainly used in small organizations where the founder is simultaneously the owner as well. He is the one to create a strategy, structure, and behavior patterns. This leadership style relies the most on the first superior's cognitive abilities and rational management, implying that he has great unique knowledge (Jolović, 2019). Such a style may be efficient in bigger organizations as well in crisis situations.

Currently, when accelerating changes and market adaptations require close cooperation between managers and their workers, on the one hand, and a creative treatment of work by all employees, on the other hand, this leadership style is all but acceptable. Its application demotivates employees, which implicitly causes a drop in the economic and overall business performances of a particular organization.

The democratic leadership style is more favorable and more flexible because the manager prefers participative and decentralized decision-making. He trusts his employees, who on their part are to a greater extent included in business problem-solving, creating new solutions, and decision-making. In that way, a feeling of one's responsibility for the realization of the decisions made is created in employees (Erhardt et al., 2016). A manager adhering to this style renounces one part of his power in favor of his lower-level managers and specialists in particular problems. In that way, his authority is no lesser, but he only demonstrates it in a different form.

A manager encourages communications and controls them to a reasonable extent which enables him to be familiar with how the organization works. It is characteristic of both mid-size and big organizations, whereas the key reason why it is applied lies in the awareness and responsibility of his associates/workers themselves. A leadership style like this does not correspond with the requirements of market-oriented organizations (Mićović & Miletić, 2019), but it is applicable in situations when complex and creative problems should be solved.

The liberal leadership style (the so-called *laissez-faire* style) favors full involvement, trust, and absolute freedom of all employees in making decisions. The key characteristic of this style reflects the fact that employees are mainly experts in their field of work, so they set goals and resources needed for the realization of the same by themselves. Here, a manager is only a proxy between employees, on the one hand, and information and the external environment, on the other hand. This style is fully applicable in both small and big organizations structured as per teams and departments whose team members are persons with a university diploma and possessing sophisticated knowledge. It is applied in interdisciplinary projects where high expertise is required and where the employees selected are rare (or even the only) authorities in that field. This simultaneously makes it a very specific and closely applicable style, for which reason it is not frequently opted for by managers. Although seemingly liberal, correct, and extremely efficient, this leadership style has a plethora of traps. Given the fact that the manager's contribution may factually be rejected as a consequence of his or her great autonomy in making decisions, it is exactly that independence that may give rise to chaos in organizational work.

Finally, according to the current knowledge, there are a small number of research studies dedicated to the characteristics of the management of the IT sector, especially in Serbian organizations, and there are even fewer research studies focusing on employees' preferences for specific leadership styles.

Relationship Between Leadership Styles and Decision-Making Styles

The results of numerous relevant research studies have verified the assertion that there is a relationship between leadership styles and decision-making styles (Hariri et al., 2014; Kayode et al., 2014; Marković, 2011; Torlak et al., 2022). Decision-making represents one of the most important and most frequent managerial activities. Managers make a large number of different decisions significant for the survival of the business operations and development of the organization on a daily basis (Wren & Dan Voich, 1994).

Decision-making studies have pointed to numerous versions of the decision-making process that depend on internal and external (context) factors. Alker et al. (1972) see decision-making as a process based on available information. The decision-making process includes the identification of all the existing alternatives – the valuation of options according to the preferences and their potential outcomes; collecting information; replacement between preferences and outcomes; and the selection of the most favorable alternative (Phillips, 1997). Rowe et al., (1989) identifies the analytical, conceptual, directive and behavioral decision-making styles which should be compliant with the selected organizational strategy.

A decision-making style represents a combination of cognitive complexity and orientation toward values. Given the fact that the manager's strategy includes a lot of complex interdependent variables, their readiness to understand and put under control the given situation depends on their cognitive complexity. The leadership style adopted by the organization lends a note for decision-making. For that reason, the complexity of the decision-making process and leadership requires the examination of connectedness with numerous other factors (Azeska et al., 2017) such as the manager's characteristics, i.e., personality attributes, intellectual capacities, situation factors and so on. He can stimulate a positive and cooperative environment or create a toxic one, as is the case with authoritarian leadership.

Apart from the fact that they have confirmed the fact that decision-making styles and leadership styles are interconnected (Rowe et al., 1989), the outcomes of the conducted studies have also shown that they are individually also connected with other factors, such as the decision-maker's years of age, type of education, leadership line, and so forth. As far as decision-making styles are concerned, there are no significant differences between the managers of different levels. When speaking about the connectedness between the years of age of the respondents with the leadership styles, the research studies that have been carried out show the presence of significant connectedness only with the autocratic leadership style. Older managers are prone to the administrative leadership style characterized by adherence to working rules and regulations, but in its extreme form, it leads toward the introduction of bureaucratic practices in operations and the negligence of the essence of the operations due to the form. In the domain of the connectedness of the leadership style with the leadership line, the verified outcomes in theory and in practice show that there is a difference between the managers of the first and second lines of leadership in observability of the administrative and entrepreneurial styles in that both are more emphasized in the second-line managers. No differences have been found in the sense of the observability of the decision-making style in relation to the different leadership lines (Marković, 2011).

Also, the outcomes of the research studies have pointed to the existence of pieces of hard evidence that the education type is a significant factor of the decision-making styles. A positive impact of the expected organizational fairness on one's identification with the organization is also recognized (Patel et al., 2012).

Leadership Styles in Serbia

In the explanations of the leadership styles in Serbia, there are diverse approaches that can be singled out, such as the approach to the personality characteristics, which tends to provide an answer to the question, "Which attributes are those that make a difference between good managers and bad ones?"; the behavioral approach, which tends to answer the question, "How should a manager behave in order to be efficient?"; employees' expectations and conduct; as well as the characteristics of the environment and so on.

If the goal the Serbian organization tends to pursue, and it certainly is, is to achieve a high business result, it is necessary to bring into compliance the leadership style with the situation in which the same is applied and the manager applies it, aspiring as much as possible to reach a compromise in "orienting towards the performance and orienting towards the people." When searching for the optimal solution to the leadership style that would stimulate employees' performances, traps that inevitably come with the classical leadership styles should be avoided, and we should be searching for an acceptable compromise between the business result and the requirement of the working process, on the one hand, and the working atmosphere and respecting the inferior employees' interests and their personal characteristics, on the other hand. Efforts made in Serbian organizations to change the approach to human potential management range in the context of what came with the territory, complex economic, social, and other problems inseparable from that time, as well as a big impact of the global economy, so that changes in the leadership style as well take place gradually but hopefully successfully.

When the leadership styles and the abilities that the Serbian manager should possess are further spoken about, it needs to be highlighted that without the serious preparation, fundamental and continuous education of both present and future managers, no more significant work results can be expected. Among other things, every Serbian manager should surveil their own selves and manage themselves and keep on being in the positive mood before managing other people.

The national-level managerial educational content should enable the acquisition of knowledge and skills in parallel with the development of one's positive attitudes about their own selves and their environment. The final goal of their education in the Serbian conditions comprises the aspiration to increase the manager's labor effectiveness and efficiency through quality education, thus contributing to better and better organized business operations, greater labor productivity and the development of healthy and positive relationships in the organization.

The Assessment of the Personnel Policy in Serbian Organizations in the Context of the Specificity of Decision-Makers and a Different Leadership Style

Research Methodology

From a broad variety of points of view, the extensive research that was carried out confirmed the strong commitment of successful organizations to the training of their employees and the improvement of the personnel policy as a significant means for gaining a competitive edge. The research carried out in this chapter was conducted as a summary of an analytical character for the purpose of conceptualizing the significance of the personnel policy for the achievement of high performances in different organizations in light of the specificity of the business decision-makers in organizations like these in the context of a different leadership style. In order to become knowledgeable of the important aspects of the strategic significance of employees and the personnel policy for the business success of the most different organizations, the primary data started being collected, processed, and analyzed in the field.

The research was carried out by using an online questionnaire in Google form, on a sample of 123 companies from the Business Registers Agency of the Republic of Serbia. The structure of the sample regarding the size of the companies was micro-organizations (18%), small (29%), medium sized (30%) and big (23%). Regarding the industry in which they operate, the majority of companies were from the production and service sectors (over 38%), most of which were doing business for 31–40 years. In the observed sample, the largest number of the organizations operate on the international market (41%), only to be followed by those operating on the national market (29%), the organizations operating on the regional market (18%), while those operating only on the local market account for at least 12%. The data collection was focused on the determination of the influence of the personnel policy as the independent variable on the dependent variables, such as equitableness during the selection of the employees to be educated, the allocation of funds for the education and training of employees, the significance of employees in the organization as a source of creativity and new ideas and teamwork in the organizations that have different decision-makers and a different leadership style, which ultimately determines total organizational performances.

The respondents' answers were processed by means of the analysis of variance (ANOVA) test and the nonparametric χ^2 test (the existence of a statistically significant difference for the values Sig. ≤ 0.05). The obtained data were presented descriptively, tabularly, and graphically. The graphs were created using the Microsoft Excel 2020 program.

Results and Discussion

In the largest number of the Serbian organizations in the observed sample, decisions are made by the owner, only to be followed by the organizations where decisions are made by the top management and then the organizations in which decisions are made by the top management and the employees, whereas in only a small percentage of the organizations, the respondents answered they were not sure who was the one to make decisions. The percentage overview of those who make decisions in the organizations is presented in Fig. 4.1.

In the considered sample, the participative leadership style dominates, only to be followed by the democratic and autocratic leadership styles, where in a small percentage of the organizations, the respondents were not sure which leadership style in the organization it was all about. The percentage overview of the leadership styles in the organizations included in the sample is given in Fig. 4.2.

Irrespective of the fact that an organization may have funds, appropriate pieces of equipment and technology, the business operations of the organization on the market have no certain future unless its employees are adequately

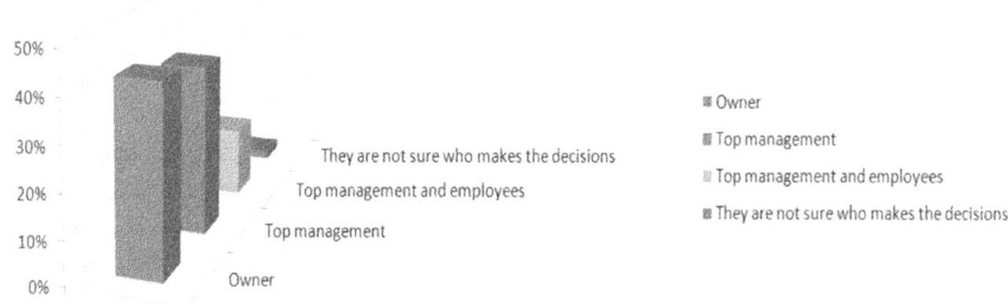

Fig. 4.1. The Decision-Makers in the Considered Organizations. *Source*: The Authors.

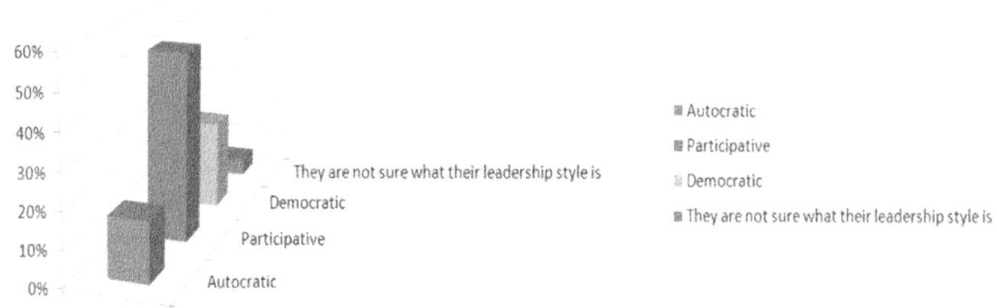

Fig. 4.2 The Leadership Style in the Analyzed Organizations. *Source*: The Authors.

motivated and trained and educated for the needed jobs. Without investing in their knowledge, education, and training, and without an acceptable selection, it is impossible for the Serbian organization to grow and develop, nor is it possible for it to achieve sustainable competitiveness and transform into a high-performance organization. The analysis of the employees in the selected sample was processed by the ANOVA test with a 0.05 probability level in relation to the independent variables:

- the decision-makers in the organization and;
- the leadership style.

The dependent variables were rated with the marks from 1 to 5, where 1 stood for the lowest, and 5 stood for the highest mark. The research study requested that the respondents should designate who is the one to make decisions in the organizations: the owner, the top management, the top management, and the employees or the recommended option "I am not sure." Table 4.1 accounts for the comparative statistics of the existence of a difference in the personnel policy in the organizations which have different decision-makers. It can be concluded that the differences in the decision-makers exert a significant influence on the following:

- the appropriation of funds for the employees' education and training, Sig. = 0.010;
- equitableness when selecting the employees to undergo education, Sig. = 0.023;
- the employees in the organization as the sources of new ideas and innovations, Sig. = 0.021, and
- teamwork in the organization, Sig. = 0.008.

The subsequent Tukey test will determine between which organizations where there are different decision-makers there is a difference observing the variables in which a significant difference in marks was identified.

In Table 4.2, it is possible to see the differences in the appropriation of the funds for the education of the employees and training that appear in some of the organizations where there are different decision-makers. It is evident that the differences especially appear in the organizations where the decision-maker is the owner and in the organizations where the decision-maker is the top management.

Table 4.3 represents the differences in equitableness when selecting employees in the organizations which have different decision-makers. It can be seen that the differences appear in the organizations where the owner and top management are the decision-maker.

The research further requested that the respondents should designate the leadership style in the organizations: autocratic, participative, democratic or the option was "I am not sure." Table 4.4 accounts for the comparative statistics of the existence of the difference in the personnel policy in the organizations in

Table 4.1. The Differences in the Personnel Policy in the Organizations Which Have Different Decision-Makers.

		Sum of Squares	df	Mean Square	*F*	Sig.
The organization's employees' work habits	Between the groups	5.806	3	1.935	2.114	0.101
	Within the groups	120.833	132	0.915		
	Total	126.640	135			
The employees' positively inclined response(s) to education and training programs, as well as their readiness for education and training	Between the groups	3. 052	3	1.017	0.758	0.519
	Within the groups	177.066	132	1.341		
	Total	180.118	135			
The appropriation of the organization's funds for its employees' education and development	Between the groups	18.478	3	6.159	3.929	0.010
	Within the groups	206.927	132	1.568		
	Total	225.404	135			
Equitableness when selecting the employees who are to undergo education	Between the groups	13.130	3	4.377	3.271	0.023
	Within the groups	176.635	132	1.338		
	Total	189.765	135			
The level at which the organization's employees share responsibility both for the firm's success and for the firm's failure	Between the groups	6.675	3	2.225	1.585	0.196
	Within the groups	185.317	132	1.404		
	Total	191.993	135			
The organization's employees as the sources of new ideas and innovations	Between the groups	11.352	3	3.784	3.355	0.021
	Within the groups	148.883	132	1.128		
	Total	160.235	135			
Teamwork in the organization	Between the groups	11.870	3	3.957	4.137	0.008
	Within the groups	126.240	132	0.956		
	Total	138.110	135			

Source: The authors.

Table 4.2 The Appropriation of the Funds for the Education of the Employees and Training in the Organizations in Which There Are Different Decision-Makers.

The Appropriation of the Organization's Funds for Its Employees' Education and Training		**Mean Value of the Difference (I – J)**	**Standard Error**	**Standard Error**	**95% Confidence Interval**	
(I) In the Organization, Decisions Are Made By	**(J) In the Organization, Decisions Are Made By**				**Lower Limit**	**Upper Limit**
The owner	Top management	0.514	0.237	0.037	–0.10	1.13
	Top management and employees	–0.278	0.318	0.819	–1.11	0.55
	I am not sure	1.627	0.741	0.130	–0.30	3.56
Top management	The owner	–0.514	0.237	0.037	–1.13	0.10
	Top management and employees	–0.792	0.323	0.073	–1.63	0.05
	I am not sure	1.113	0.743	0.442	–0.82	3.05
Top management and employees	The owner	0.278	0.318	0.819	–0.55	1.11
	Top management	0.792	0.323	0.073	–0.05	1.63
	I am not sure	1.905	0.773	0.070	–0.11	3.92
I am not sure	The owner	–1.627	0.741	0.130	–3.56	0.30
	Top management	–1.113	0.743	0.442	–3.05	0.82
	Top management and employees	–1.905	0.773	0.070	–3.92	0.11

Source: The authors.

Table 4.3 The Differences in the Equitableness When Selecting the Employees Who Will Undergo Education in the Organizations in Which There Are Different Decision-Makers.

Fairness in the Selection of Employees Who Will Be Educated		**Mean Value of Difference (I – J)**	**Standard Error**	**Error Significance (Sig.)**	**95% Confidence Interval**	
(I) The Leadership Style in the Organization	**(I) The Leadership Style in the Organization**				**Lower Limit**	**Upper Limit**
The owner	Top management	0.611	0.219	0.030	0.04	1.18
	Top management and employees	0.102	0.294	0.986	–0.66	0.87
	I am not sure	1.102	0.685	0.377	–0.68	2.88
Top management	The owner	–0.611	0.219	0.030	–1.18	–0.04
	Top management and employees	–0.509	0.298	0.324	–1.29	0.27
	I am not sure	0.491	0.687	0.891	–1.30	2.28
Top management and employees	The owner	–0.102	0.294	0.986	–0.87	0.66
	Top management	0.509	0.298	0.324	–0.2	1.29
	I am not sure	1.000	0.714	0.501	–0.86	2.86
I am not sure	The owner	–1.102	0.685	0.377	–2.88	0.68
	Top management	–0.491	0.687	0.891	–2.28	1.30
	Top management and employees	–1.000	0.714	0.501	–2.86	0.86

Source: The authors.

Table 4.4. The Differences in the Personnel Policy in the Organizations That Have a Different Leadership Style.

		Sum of Squares	df	Mean Square	*F*	Sig.
The organization's employees' work habits	Between groups	2.032	3	0.677	0.717	0.543
	Within groups	124.608	132	0.944		
	Total	126.640	135			
The employees' positively inclined response(s) to education and training programs, as well as their readiness for education and training	Between groups	1.476	3	0.492	0.364	0.779
	Within groups	178.642	132	1.353		
	Total	180.118	135			
The appropriation of the organization's funds for its employees' education and training	Between groups	7.323	3	2.441	1.478	0.224
	Within groups	218.081	132	1.652		
	Total	225.404	135			
Equitableness when selecting the employees who are to undergo education	Between Groups	19.922	3	6.641	5.161	0.002
	Within Groups	169.843	132	1.287		
	Total	189.765	135			
The level at which the organization's employees share responsibility both for the firm's success and for the firm's failure	Between Groups	11.687	3	3.896	2.852	0.040
	Within Groups	180.305	132	1.366		
	Total	191.993	135			
The organization's employees as the sources of new ideas and innovations	Between Groups	12.250	3	4.083	3.642	0.015
	Within Groups	147.985	132	1.121		
	Total	160.235	135			
Teamwork in the organization	Between Groups	17.861	3	5.954	6.536	0.000
	Within Groups	120.249	132	0.911		
	Total	138.110	135			

Source: The authors.

which there is a different leadership style. A fact can be established that the differences in the leadership style have a significant influence on the following:

- equitableness when selecting the employees who will undergo education, Sig. = 0.002;
- the level at which the organization's employees share responsibility for both the success of the organization and for the organization's failure, Sig. = 0.040, and
- the organization's employees as the sources of creativity and new ideas, Sig. = 0.015.

The subsequent Tukey test will determine between which organizations where there is a different leadership style there are differences observing the variables in which a significant difference in marks was identified.

Table 4.5 shows the differences in equitableness when selecting the employees who will undergo education in the organizations where there is a different leadership style. It can be seen that the organizations where the leadership style is autocratic and participative differ from the organizations where the leadership style is autocratic and democratic.

Conclusion

The study deals with the relationship between the decision-makers in HR and the leadership style in the Serbian organization and the personnel policy that has been discussed. The research results show that, among the largest share of companies analyzed in the sample, decisions are made by the owner, with the participative leadership style being dominant. The comparative statistics confirm the existence of a significant difference in the personnel policy in the organizations in which there are different decision-makers. Different decision-makers importantly determine how much the organization will allocate the funds for the education of the employees and training and development, the selection of the employees who will be educated, the significance of the organization's employees as a source of creativity and new ideas, and the creation of the atmosphere of teamwork in the organizations.

The comparative statistics are indicative of the fact that there is a disproportion in the decisions about personnel policy in the organizations with a different leadership style, so a fact can be established that differences in the leadership style significantly influence equitableness when selecting the employees who will undergo education, the level at which the organization's personnel share responsibility not only for the firm's success but also for the firm's failure and the significance of the organization's employees as the sources of creativity and new ideas.

Given the significance of personnel, the obtained results unambiguously reveal that without investing in knowledge, education and development, and acceptable selection for employees' education, it is impossible for the organization to grow and develop, achieve sustainable competitiveness, and transform into the organization of the desired business excellence. In order to achieve productive results and remain competitive against the players in the target market,

Table 4.5 Equitableness When Selecting the Employees Who Will Undergo Education in the Organizations Where There Is a Different Leadership Style.

Equitableness When Selecting the Employees Who Will Undergo Education		Mean Value of Difference (I – J)	Standard Error	Error Significance (Sig.)	95% Confidence Interval	
(I) The Leadership Style in the Organization	(J) The Leadership Style in the Organization				Lower Limit	Upper Limit
Autocratic	Participative	–0.767	0.260	0.020	–1.44	–0.09
	Democratic	–0.848	0.278	0.015	–1.57	–0.12
	I am not sure	0.250	0.455	0.946	–0.93	1.43
Participative	Autocratic	0.767	0.260	0.020	0.09	1.44
	Democratic	–0.081	0.231	0.985	–0.68	0.52
	I am not sure	1.017	0.427	0.086	–0.10	2.13
Democratic	Autocratic	0.848	0.278	0.015	0.12	1.57
	Participative	0.081	0.231	0.985	–0.52	0.68
	I am not sure	1.098	0.438	0.064	–0.04	2.24
I am not sure	Autocratic	–0.250	0.455	0.946	–1.43	0.93
	Participative	–1.017	0.427	0.086	–2.13	0.10
	Democratic	–1.098	0.438	0.064	–2.24	0.04

Source: The authors.

organizations should allocate significant resources for the purpose of managing innovations and contemporary technology, improving the working process, especially investing in employees' training and development so as to achieve the wanted performances.

Reports from practice unveil that human capital is key to business results in that a considerable number of organizations have not succeeded in achieving their goals because of a lack of the inclusion of employees in the technology-led business processes. In such conditions, the application of new sophisticated technologies in the organization may be resisted by the employees and cause anxiety in them, whereas consequently, it may also have an influence on their motivations and may lead to lower productivity and their reduced commitment to the job.

Due to accelerated changes and the need to adapt to new conditions of organizational operations, close cooperation between managers and employees and a creative treatment of work are required, which is also implicative of an appropriate leadership style. This is even more so since there are significant associations between the leadership styles and the decision-making styles. Apart from their interconnectedness, they are individually networked with the other factors as well, such as the years of age of the decision-makers, the leadership line, the education type, and so forth. When speaking about the decision-making styles, there are no more significant differences between the managers at different managerial levels. From the point of view of the connectedness of the leadership style with the leadership line, the verified outcomes in practice show the presence of a difference between the managers of the first- and second-line leadership, in a way that the administrative and entrepreneurial styles are more pronounced in the second-line managers. The education type is also a significant factor of the decision-making styles.

In order for the Serbian organization to achieve a high business result, it is necessary for it to bring into compliance its managerial style with the situation in which the same is being applied and the manager who is applying the selected style and making relevant decisions. The process in which such decisions are made certainly depends on numerous internal factors and the organizational context, so it is necessary to aspire as much as possible to a compromise in orienting toward employees and orienting toward performances.

Speaking in that sense, organizations can be suggested to think about investing in a manager with qualities, who would exclusively be responsible for the personnel in a manner which would allow for a reduction in the differences in the personnel policy in the organizations with different decision-makers and/or a different leadership style.

References

Alker, H. N., Rao, V. R., & Hughes, G. D. (1972). Value consistent and expedient decision making. *American Psychological Association Proceeding*, *7*, 149–150.

Andrejić, M., Ketin, S., & Čabarkapa, O. (2021). Metodi i stilovi rada menadžmenta preduzeća. *Tehnika – Menadžment*, *71*(3), 367–375.

Aslam, M., Shafi, I., Ahmed J., Garat de Marin, S. M., Flores, S. E., Rojo Gutiérrez, A. M., & Ashraf, I. (2023). Impact of innovation-oriented human resource on small and medium enterprises' performance. *Sustainability*, *15*(7), 6273.

Azeska, A., Starc, J., & Kevereski, L. J. (2017). Styles of decision making and management and dimensions of personality of school principals. *International Journal of Cognitive Research in Science, Engineering and Education*, *5*(2), 47–56.

Bakator, M., Petrović, N., Borić, S., & Đalić, N. (2019). Impact of human resource management on business performance: A review of literature. *Journal of Engineering Management and Competitiveness*, *9*, 3–13.

Bass, B. M. (2008). *The Bass handbook of leadership: Theory, research, and managerial applications* (4th ed.). Free Press.

Berber, N., Jelača, M. S., Bjekić, R., & Marić, S. (2022). Effects of social demographic factors on leadership style in Serbian banking industry. *Anali Ekonomskog fakulteta u Subotici*, *58*(47), 117–130.

Berber, N., Slavić, A., Miletić, S., Simonović, Z., & Aleksić, M. (2019). A survey on relationship between leadership styles and leadership outcomes in the banking sector in Serbia. *Acta Polytechnica Hungarica*, *16*(7), 167–184.

Beugré, C. D., Acar, W., & Braun, W. (2006). Transformational leadership in organizations: an environment-induced model. *International Journal of Manpower*, *27*(1), 52–62.

Brebels, L., De Winne, S., Marescaux, E., Sels, L., Beauregard, T. A., Dries, N., Lepak, D. P., Ortlieb, R., & Sieben, B. (2017). Managing differences between employees: Different perspectives on HR differentiation. In S. Taneja (Ed.), *Academy of management proceedings* (Vol. 2015, No. 1, p. 14325). https://doi.org/10.5465/ambpp.2015.14325symposium.

Budhwar, P. S., Do, H., & Patel, C. (2018). Relationship between innovation-led HR policy, strategy, and firm performance: A serial mediation investigation. *Human Resource Management*, *57*, 1271–1284.

Bulatović, D., & Jokić, B. (2017). Operativni menadžment u malom biznisu. *Ekonomski Izazovi*, *6*(12), 105–111.

Canterino, F., Guerci, M., Cirella, S., & Shani, A. B. R. (2022). The intertwined effect of HRM practices and transformational leadership on employees' attitudes in an M&A context: Evidence from a collaborative and mixed-methods study. *European Management Journal*, *42*(1), 46–56.

Carić, M., Prodanović, R., Khoja Amina, H. A., & Gardašević, J. (2022). Human resources management in domestic agricultural enterprises. *Ekonomija: Teorija I Praksa*, *2*, 14–32.

Chen, M., Zada, M., Khan, J., & Saba, N. U. (2022). How does servant leadership influences creativity? Enhancing employee creativity via creative process engagement and knowledge sharing. *Frontiers in Psychology*, *13*, 947092.

Chowdhury, S. R., Mendy, J., & Rahman, M. (2023). A systematic literature review of GHRM: Organizational sustainable performance reimagined using a new holistic. *Sustainability, 15*(9), 7513.

Djergović, D., Kukobat, L., & Andrejić, M. (2019). Prilog unapredjenju selektovanja, stvaranja i razvoja menadžera u velikim kompanijama, *Vojno Delo*, *71*(6), 419–440.

Erhardt, N., Martin-Rios, C., & Heckscher, C., (2016). Am I doing the right thing? Unpacking workplace rituals as mechanisms for strong organizational culture. *International Journal of Hospitality Management*, *59*, 31–41.

Eslami, N., & Nakhaie, H. (2011). Effects of human resource management activities to improve innovation in enterprises. *International Proceedings of Economics Development and Research*, *12*, 518–522.

Ferreira, J., Coelho, A., & Moutinho, L. (2020). Dynamic capabilities, creativity and innovation capability and their impact on competitive advantage and firm performance: The moderating role of entrepreneurial orientation. *Technovation*, *92*, 102061.

Gardašević, J., Ćirić, M., & Stanisavljević, I. (2021). Odnosi između savremenih stilova rukovođenja i dimenzija nacionalna kultura u savremenom poslovnom okruženju. *Ekonomika*, *67*(1), 77–89.

Hariri, H., Monypenny, R., & Prideaux, M. (2014). Leadership styles and decision-making styles in an Indonesian school context. *School Leadership & Management*, *34*(3), 284–298.

Hazim, M., Akter, H., Sentosa, I., Waqas, A., Masrek, M. N., & Ali, J. (2023). Predicting workforce engagement towards digital transformation through a multi-analytical approach. *Sustainability*, *15*(8), 6835.

Ilić, D., & Cvjetković, M. (2014). Uloga znanja u kreiranju konkurentske prednosti. *Ekonomski Izazovi*, *3*(5), 32–42.

Janković, G., & Golubović, M. (2019). Open innovation in small and medium-sized enterprises. *Ekonomika*, *65*(3), 89–101.

Jensen, U. T., Andersen, L. B., Bro, L. L., Bøllingtoft, A., Eriksen, T. L. M., Holten, A. L., Jacobsen, C. B., Ladenburg, J., Nielsen, P. A., Salomonsen, H. H., Westergård-Nielsen, N., & Würtz, A. (2019). Conceptualizing and measuring transformational and transactional leadership. *Administration & Society*, *51*(1), 3–33.

Jovičić, D. (2009). Kadrovanje – Kadrovska politika. 1. Naučni skup sa međunarodnim učešćem Sinergija (pp. 162–167).

Jolović, N. (2019). Menadžment ljudskih resursa u funkciji sticanja konkurentske prednosti u bankarstvu.*Oditor*, *5*(3), 65–78.

Jovičić, M., & Radojčić, B. (2009). Značaj i uloga kadrovske politike u upravljanju preduzećima. *Poslovni Konsultant*, *1*(3/4), 32.

Kayode, B. K., Mojeed, A. Q., & Fatai, I. A. (2014). Leadership and decision-making: A study on reflexive relationship between leadership style and decision-making approach. *Journal of Education, Society and Behavioural Science*, *4*(4), 473–484.

Latin, R., Jevtić, P., & Živanović, N. (2022). Organizovanje preduzeća u globalnom poslovanju. *FBIM Transactions*, *10*(1), 45–52.

Marković, Z. (2011). Povezanost stilova rukovođenja i stilova odlučivanja. *Godišnjak za Psihologiju*, *7*(9), 167–183.

Mićović, S., & Miletić, J. (2019). Poslovni subjekt kao osnova održivosti razvoja.*Održivi Razvoj*, *1*(1), 43–51.

Miletić, V. (2020). Leadership in a modern organization. *Ekonomika*. ISBN-978-86-901918-2-6.

Miletić, V., Ćurčić, N., & Kostić, Z. (2020). Openness of companies in Serbia to creativity, new ideas and innovation. *The Annals of the Faculty of Economics in Subotica*, *57*(46), 021–034.

Miletić, V., Ćurčić, N., & Simonović, Z. (2023). Teamwork valotization in Serbian textile organizations of a different length and level of operations. *Industria Textila Journal*, *4*, 388–396. https://doi.org/10.35530/IT.074.04.2022109

Mitsakis, F. (2014). Ljudski resursi (HR) kao strateški biznis partner: Kapacitet za stvaranje vrednosti i smanjenje rizika. *International Časopis za studije ljudskih resursa. 4*, 154.

Nanjundeswaraswamy, T. S., & Swamy, D. R. (2014). Leadership styles. *Advances in Management*, *7*, 57–62.

Northouse, F. G. (2010). *Leadership theory and practice* (5th ed.). Sage.

Patel, C., Budhwar, P., & Varma, A. (2012). Overall justice, work group identification and work outcomes: Test of moderated mediation process. *Journal of Word Business*, *47*(2), 213–222.

Phillips, S. D. (1997). Toward an expanded definition of adaptive decision making. *The Career Development Quarterly*, *45*, 275–287. http://dx.doi.org/10.1002/j.2161-0045.1997.tb00471.x

Pundt, A., House, R. J., Hanges, P. J., Javidan, M., Dorfman, P. W., & Gupta, V. (2006). Culture, leadership, and organizations: The GLOBE study of 62 societies. *Zeitschrift für Arbeits- und Organisationspsychologie A&O*, *50*(3), 167–169.

Purcell, J., Kinnie, N., Hutchinson, S., Rayton, B., & Swart, J. (2002). *Understanding the people and performance link: Unlocking the black box*. Chartered Institute of Personnel and Development.

Rowe, A., Mason, O., Dickel, K., & Snyder, N. (1989). *Strategic management – A methodological approach*.Wesley.

Shin, J., Heath, R. L., & Lee, J. (2011). A contingency explanation of public relations practitioner leadership styles: Situation and culture. *Journal of Public Relations Research*, *23*(2), 167–190.

Simović, O., Raičević, M., & Kovačević, M. (2018). Uticaj stila liderstva na organizacionu kulturu turističkih preduzeća u Crnoj Gori.*Ekonomski Izazovi*, *7*(14), 14–27.

Strugar-Jelača, M., Bjekić, R., Berber, N., Aleksić, M., Slavić, A., & Marić, S. (2022). Impact of managers' emotional competencies on organizational performance. *Sustainability, 14*(14), 8800.

Suciu, C. M., Alexandru-Plesea, D., Petre, A., Simion, A., Ovidiu, M. M., Dumitrescu, D., Bocaneala, A. M., Moroianu, M. R., & Nasulea, F. D. (2023). Competence – As a key factor for a sustainable, innovative and resilient development model based on industry 5.0. *Sustainability*, *15*(9), 7472.https://doi.org/10.3390/su15097472

Torlak, N. G., Demir, A., & Budur, T. (2022). Decision-making, leadership and performance links in private education institutes. *Rajagiri Management Journal*, *16*(1), 63–85.

Wren, A. D., & Dan Voich, J. R. (1994). *Menadžment, proces, struktura i ponašanje*. Privredni pregled.

Yukl, G. (2008). How leaders influence organizational effectiveness. *The Leadership Quarterly*, *19*, 708–722.

Zeng, J., & Xu, G. (2020). How servant leadership motivates innovative behavior: A moderated mediation model. *International Journal of Environmental Research and Public Health*, *17*, 4753.

Chapter 5

Challenges and Constraints of Female Entrepreneurship in Contemporary Economies: Empirical Insights from Romanian Business Environment

Gheorghe Dan Isbășoiu[a], *Dana Volosevici*[a] *and Jean Vasile Andrei*[a,b]

[a]*Petroleum-Gas University, Ploiești, Romania*
[b]*National Institute for Economic Research "Costin C. Kirițescu," Romanian Academy, Romania*

Abstract

This chapter addresses the intricacies and hurdles in female entrepreneurship within Romania, scrutinizing the often-indistinct lines among authentic entrepreneurship, self-employment, and fraudulent self-employment. It notably spotlights the unique challenges faced by women, stressing the necessity of educational initiatives, legislative backing, and precise policy development. Emphasizing the importance of thorough data gathering and research, the study seeks to deepen the understanding of the specific obstacles and opportunities present for female entrepreneurs. It provides a thorough overview of the status quo of women's entrepreneurship, outlines the systemic challenges, and discusses potential empowerment and development strategies in this domain.

Keywords: Entrepreneurship; gender gap; business; self-employment; stereotypes

Emerging Patterns and Behaviors in a Green Resilient Economy, 105–127

doi:10.1108/978-1-83549-780-720241006

Introduction

The opening of a business by an entrepreneur can be caused and favored by a diversity of elements, which, most often, relate to both the qualities of the person and the context, "important for understanding when, how, and why entrepreneurship happens and who becomes involved" (Welter, 2011, p. 166). The conceptualization of entrepreneurship has been centered around two major concepts, opportunity recognition and process definition. The first concept was introduced by Shane and Venkataraman (2000, p. 218) in one of the most-cited definitions of entrepreneurship: "how, by whom and with what effects opportunities to create future goods and services are discovered, evaluated and exploited." Elia et al. (2020, p. 3) offer an example of the process perspective, defining it as "the process of recognizing potential business opportunities and capitalizing on them by rearranging existing resources or creating new ones to develop and market new products and services." In terms of the personal aspect of the entrepreneurial process, the frameworks used to analyze entrepreneurial behavior typically encompass three broad categories of variables: behavioral, attitudinal, and personality based (Cuesta et al., 2018; Gielnik et al., 2021; Muniz et al., 2014). To these are added studies related to entrepreneurial competencies, evaluating the impact of entrepreneurship education. A large number of studies have indicated that entrepreneurship education is raising the positive perception of entrepreneurship, such as attitudes and intentions (Kolvereid & Moen, 1997). Peterlin (2021) undertook a study of the governance of entrepreneurship education in the European Union (EU). In line with these, Loi et al. (2022) synthesized debates on assumptions and challenges in entrepreneurship education arising from development workshops organized to increase research salience in the field. Manzoor (2019) discussed women's entrepreneurship, various challenges, and specific recommendations for the promotion of women's entrepreneurial activities in the MENA region. On the other perceptive, Rugina (2018) investigated the field of entrepreneurial activities by explaining the link between the scale of entrepreneurial activities and their social background.

On the other hand, Roos (2021) argues that women's entrepreneurial networks can challenge gender structures through a process of contextualization. In addition, Nadin et al. (2020) analyze the representations of women entrepreneurs in the media in *The Times* newspaper.

Sustainable entrepreneurship in resource-rich Gulf countries such as Oman remains under-researched, although it has received increased attention from researchers in recent years. Arslan et al.'s work (2023) is one of the first attempts, to the authors' knowledge, to assess the status of sustainable entrepreneurship development in Oman from a multi-stakeholder perspective and aims to fill this gap in the literature. Schweickart et al. (2023) examine a program to develop biomedical entrepreneurship skills, specifically the Foundations of Biomedical Start-ups course, its metrics and impact. Meanwhile, Blank et al. (2023) link the widely used Lean Start-up approach to selected academic theories of entrepreneurship and propose potential areas for future research.

Using women's solidarity as a motivational resource has become popular in leadership studies, and it can be a supportive resource for current and aspiring female leaders to progress in underrepresented environments. A study on seeking support through solidarity: female leaders' experiences of workplace solidarity in male-dominated professions was conducted by Pillay-Naidoo et al. (2023). Guo and Zhu (2023) investigated the role of female workers and entrepreneurs in the establishment and management of co-working centers (CSCs) for improving work and family balance through flexible scheduling and location. A detailed conceptual analysis and model of self-efficacy in the context of the nurse entrepreneur role were presented by Thepna et al. (2023). Cheng and Wang (2023) analyzed the phenomenon of the glass ceiling that women face when they aspire to be promoted to partner positions. By highlighting the unique obstacles faced by female officers in Turkey, Yildirim et al. (2023) improve understanding of the underlying challenges and lay the groundwork for implementing effective policies and practices that promote women's empowerment in the maritime industry in Europe. Polychronopoulos and Nguyen-Duc (2024) analyzed 91 peer-reviewed papers focusing on supporting migrant entrepreneurship in Europe, covering the characteristics, challenges, and support policies related to the issue.

Entrepreneurial activity starts with an individual's aspiration to become an entrepreneur, followed by the generation of a business idea (Ratten, 2023). This process involves seeking opportunities within the business landscape. When such an opportunity is identified, action is undertaken to transform the idea into a tangible business venture, as indicated by Baručić and Umihanić (2016).

Thus, economic action is generated and linked to the desires and ideals of the entrepreneur, themselves created on a preexisting background of personality attributes, competencies, and theoretical knowledge. This mix will determine not only the object of the enterprise's activity but also its values, highlighted in possible associations, the choice of staff or type of consultancy, as well as elements that influence the type of clients or suppliers. Experts and academics in the field propose that choosing self-employment is often not a matter of preference but rather a necessary step to evade unemployment and economic inactivity. Thus, the alleged entrepreneur is not motivated or incited into action by the desire to create a business but is compelled to find solutions to manage obstacles that prevent him from entering the labor market, taking the risk of being deprived of the rights and guarantees granted to employees, as well as the social protection attached to this status. In this regard, the responses to the Total Entrepreneurial Activity and Motivations Annex (GEM, 2023) for Romania are as follows: to make a difference (87.3% women, 77.9% men), to build wealth (74.2% women, 74.2% men), to continue family tradition (38.1% women, 43.2% men), because jobs are scarce (83.9% women, 62.9% men), showing that for women, the motivational component of "necessity" for starting a company is significantly higher than for men. Indeed, this trend is also observed in the global average, with 72.9% women and 67.2% men.

Another form of self-employment that deviates from the idea of entrepreneurship is that of "bogus self-employment," which refers to a situation where an individual is classified as self-employed for legal or tax purposes but, in reality, operates more like an employee. If in legitimate self-employment, individuals have greater control over their work, including when and how they perform their tasks, in cases of bogus self-employment, the work relationship may have more characteristics of traditional employment, such as the employer exercising significant control over the worker's duties and working conditions. Therefore, the analysis of entrepreneurship figures must also take into account the identification of those forms of self-employment that may derive from other volitional nuances than the creation of a business.

The entrepreneur's own skills, desires, and aspirations, as well as the chosen way to achieve them, lead to the definition of the organization's goals. Also, competencies related to innovation in one's own business are closely linked to the ability to develop the company. Therefore, one of the elements to be analyzed is related to the environment in which an entrepreneur has developed personally and to what extent this has determined the level of performance achieved in their education.

Another element that will be followed is the future entrepreneur's placement in the social and economic context in which they will operate, as well as the extent to which the level of education they have achieved determines the success of the activity. On the other hand, from the type of specialization carried out by an entrepreneur, it is clear that it largely influences the type of business approached, referring here to the economic sector in which the activity takes place but also to the secondary activities that they can access.

We believe that this is the general motivational framework in which an entrepreneur will start their activity and will carry it out successfully or not. On this plane, the analysis regarding the gender difference in the field of entrepreneurship must also be carried out, as only by following the process of becoming an entrepreneur can we identify those aspects in which differences in evolution occur between men and women. If the educational system does not ensure the development of competencies and the promotion of the idea of performance, then the negative influence of a predominantly traditionalist society still marked by gender stereotypes will be even greater. Moreover, the promotion of an entrepreneur-influencer image by some of today's male entrepreneurs deepens the stereotypical approach to this theme. In reality, scientific studies in the field of entrepreneurship have revealed that the category of entrepreneurs is heterogeneous (Alsos et al., 2016), with variations concerning race, gender, age, personality, background, and experience (Hamilton, 2013; Jones, 2014).

The general legal framework in which both the formation of the future entrepreneur and the establishment and operation of the business take place is governed by the principle of gender equality. The Constitution of Romania guarantees in Article 45 economic freedom, defined as free access of the person to an economic activity, free initiative, and their exercise under the law, without any distinction based on the person's gender. In the same sense, according to the Government Emergency Ordinance (GEO) No. 44/2008, an entrepreneur is identified as an individual who establishes an economic enterprise. This is described as conducting economic activities in an organized, continuous, and systematic way. It involves the amalgamation of financial resources, labor, raw materials, logistics, and information, all undertaken at the entrepreneur's own risk, under circumstances and conditions stipulated by law (Article 2 letters e and f).

Law No. 202/2002 prohibits any form of discrimination based on the criterion of sex concerning access to all levels of training and professional formation, including apprenticeship at the workplace, improvement, and, generally, continuing education. Moreover, to promote gender equality, the law obliges educational institutions of all grades, social factors involved in instructive-educational processes, as well as all other providers of training and improvement services, authorized according to the law, to include in the national education programs themes and activities related to equality of opportunities and treatment between women and men.

Regarding entrepreneurial initiative, Law No. 202/2002 emphasizes the importance of equality in labor relations, while also defining that equal opportunities and treatment for women and men in these relations include non-discriminatory access. This encompasses not only the freedom to choose and practice a profession but also to engage in any activity.

Women, Business, and the Law 2023 (WBL2023) of the World Bank revealed that in Romania, there are no legal obstacles for women in entrepreneurship concerning access to credit, the ability to enter into contracts, register a business, or the right to open a bank account, confirming that there is a consistent and coherent legal framework regarding equality between men and women. Given the existence of a significant gap between female and male entrepreneurs, 40%–60%, the analysis of the legislative framework must also aim at the existence of legal provisions or official mechanisms that not only ensure equality between the sexes but also encourage women's access to entrepreneurship.

However, at the legislative level, there are no legal provisions that directly regulate female entrepreneurship or establish measures of protection or facilities for female entrepreneurs or entrepreneurial mothers. Nevertheless, there are several programs created at the level of the Ministry of Economy, Entrepreneurship, and Tourism that encourage, either directly or indirectly, the development of female entrepreneurship. Consequently, with Order No. 1314/2022, the Ministry of Entrepreneurship and Tourism sanctioned the execution procedure for the National Multiannual Program aimed at cultivating entrepreneurial culture among female leaders in the small- and medium-sized enterprise (SME) sector. The program's foremost objective is to promote and support enterprises led and owned by women. This initiative is designed to enhance economic efficiency and promote intelligent, sustainable, and inclusive growth. It focuses on key areas vital to contemporary entrepreneurship, such as digital transformation, innovation, and education in finance and entrepreneurship, to achieve these goals. Additionally, the program addresses challenges associated with balancing family and work responsibilities and overcoming local prejudices. At least one of the associates must be a woman and own at least 50% of the social parts/shares of the company in the case of applicant SMEs. For companies established under Law No. 1/2005, the condition is considered fulfilled if the majority of the cooperative members of the Board of Directors are women.

Therefore, all forms of "simple" entrepreneurship, such as those regulated by GEO No. 44/2008, namely authorized physical person, individual enterprise, and family enterprise, are excluded, which means, as the data below show, a number of 195,202 women.

An additional requirement of the program, which restricts eligibility, pertains to the status of the business as an SME. To qualify, a company must collectively satisfy these conditions: employ no more than 249 individuals, have an annual net turnover not exceeding 50 million euros, and possess total assets up to 43 million euros, converted to lei. The program's budget is around 200 million euros for 2022–2027, aiming to support 5,000 beneficiaries. As of the end of 2023, Romania recorded 608,537 female associates in commercial companies. The budget allocated to the de minimis scheme for the fiscal year 2023 was 4 million euros. However, at this time, there is no public data regarding the amounts actually allocated during the year 2023.

The Start-up Nation program primarily aims to foster the creation and growth of SMEs and enhance their economic performance. As per insights from the World Bank team in April 2023 (WB2023), start-ups participating in the program were granted additional points if they employed women or if the applicant was a woman. This preferential treatment is provided even though it is not explicitly outlined in the procedure established by Order No. 1111/2022.

However, the issue of access to credit applies to all types of entrepreneurships. Data on the obstacles that female entrepreneurs have in obtaining financing for large-scale businesses creates an image of the stereotypes that significantly mark the business field. The State of European Tech Report 2023 highlights a rather discouraging state of affairs for the industry in question. The progress in the share of capital investment and fundraising rounds led by women remains notably sluggish. In 2023, a mere 7% of fundraising rounds were secured by exclusively female founding teams, reflecting an increase of only two percentage points over the last five years. Similarly, companies with at least one woman founder or co-founder claimed only 18% of the rounds raised in 2023, marking a meager one percentage point rise over the same five-year period. Consequently, a staggering 75% of all rounds raised in 2023 were directed toward founding teams composed entirely of men.

In terms of absolute figures, the outlook is even less optimistic. In 2023, all-women founding teams managed to secure only 3% of the total investment dollars for the year. Mixed gender founding teams fared slightly better, capturing 15%, leaving a substantial 82% of the investment dollars to be dominated by all-male founding teams. This represents a marginal one percentage point increase since 2019 (Atomico, 2023). Only 8% of start-ups in Europe are founded by all-women teams and three-quarters by all-men teams (IDC, 2022).

Another obstacle in the development of female entrepreneurship is the lack of networking opportunities for women entrepreneurs. To eliminate barriers, a series of support tools and networks for women have been created at the level of the EU, such as the WEgate platform. Inaugurated in September 2016, this platform offers a wealth of resources including information and links for training, mentorship, consulting, and opportunities for business networking. A dedicated team within the Enterprise Europe Network (EEN) is devoted to women's entrepreneurship. This team collaborates with a multitude of partner organizations spread across different European nations and beyond. They play a crucial role in linking women entrepreneurs to the network's initiatives for business and innovation support. The services provided include assistance in finding business partners, penetrating international markets, collaborating with regional networks, and accessing funding opportunities provided by the EU. Such initiatives also exist at the national level, either as non-profit organizations, for example, Femei-in-afaceri.ro, or as an employers' association organized under the law for social dialogue, for example, the Employers' Confederation for Women's Entrepreneurship.

In the following, this chapter aims to establish, through statistical data analysis, the main characteristics of the entrepreneurial situation in Romania, highlighting those aspects that have an impact on female entrepreneurship, including those regarding the reality of data and the tendency to hide employment relationships under entrepreneurial appearances.

Methodology

For establishing data on the volume of entrepreneurship in Romania and its distribution across types of entrepreneurship and genders, statistical data provided by the National Trade Register Office, the National Institute of Statistics, and Eurostat were used.

Regarding the categories of entrepreneurship, these have been divided into two main categories, namely legal entities and physical persons with professional status. Thus, according to Law No. 31/1990 on companies, for the purpose of conducting profitable activities, individuals and legal entities can associate and constitute companies with legal personality, which, unless otherwise provided by law, are established in one of the following forms: (a) collective name company, (b) simple limited partnership, (c) joint-stock company, (d) partnership limited by shares, and (e) limited liability company. GEO No. 44/2008, in turn, stipulates that under the principles of free initiative, free association, and the right of establishment, any individual, whether a Romanian citizen or a citizen of another European Union or European Economic Area member state, is permitted to engage in economic activities within Romania. Economic activities are permissible across various fields, trades, professions, or occupations, provided they are not explicitly forbidden by law for free initiative. The law outlines three modes of operation: (a) as an authorized individual acting independently, (b) as entrepreneurs owning individual enterprises, and (c) as members of a family enterprise. Legally, an authorized individual can conduct their authorized activities alone or with up to three employees under an individual employment contract that is concluded and legally registered. An individual enterprise is allowed to have up to eight employees under similar contracts. However, a family enterprise is not permitted to employ third parties under a work contract.

The data obtained were broken down by the Development Regions of Romania to be corroborated in the first phase with statistical data on the total volume of the population of Romania corresponding to the year 2023. The method of aggregation by Development Regions was chosen also considering that financing programs are dedicated to these regions.

The Entrepreneurial Situation in Romania

The analysis of data from which the situation of entrepreneurship in Romania can be inferred can be done both in relation to the actual records made and by comparison with other relevant indicators as a basis for reporting, which are not necessarily directly related to the entrepreneurial field but which contribute to establishing some of its characteristics. To begin with, we will establish the volume of entrepreneurship in Romania. Thus, Tables 5.1 and 5.2 present the number of people in Romania who carry out economic activities as associates or shareholders in companies or individually and independently, as authorized physical persons (PFA), as entrepreneurs holding an individual enterprise, or as members of a family enterprise. The data correspond to the registration moment of November 30, 2023.

As can be seen from the values recorded in the case of associates or shareholders in companies, the situation regarding the distribution by gender of the holders is overall relatively homogeneous for the Development Regions, indicating a level for Romania of 36.5% women and 63.5% men. It should be noted that in the South-West Oltenia and South-East regions, there is an improvement in the presence of women who hold the status of shareholder or associate, the value exceeding 38.0%–38.5%, with the North-West and Bucharest-Ilfov regions at the opposite end, here recording one percentage point less than the national level. We particularly mention the Bucharest-Ilfov region as here there is a large concentration of shareholders/associates, namely 27.8% of the total number of associates in Romania.

In the field of basic entrepreneurship, which does not presuppose a complex level of activities and neither the establishment of a legal entity, the gender

Table 5.1 The Number and Distribution of the Number of Associates/Shareholders Who Are Physical Persons by Development Regions (Nov. 2023).

Region	**Total**	**Women**		**Men**	
		Persons	**Percentage**	**Persons**	**Percentage**
North-East	174,278	64,103	36.78	110,175	63.22
South-East	163,330	63,604	38.94	99,726	61.06
South-Muntenia	178,862	66,683	37.28	112,179	62.72
South-West Oltenia	112,820	43,063	38.17	69,757	61.83
West	152,740	55,595	36.40	97,145	63.60
North-West	238,018	84,433	35.47	153,585	64.53
Center	182,388	64,452	35.34	117,936	64.66
Bucuresti-Ilfov	463,900	166,604	35.91	297,296	64.09
Total	1,666,336	608,537	36.52	1,057,799	63.48

Source: Authors based on ONRC (2023).

Table 5.2 The Gender Distribution of Holders/Members of Authorized Physical Persons/Individual Enterprises/Family Enterprises Active by Development Regions (Nov. 2023).

PFA	Total	Women		Men	
		Persons	Percentage	Persons	Percentage
North-East	68,077	26,765	39.32	41,312	60.68
South-East	51,001	19,709	38.64	31,292	61.36
South-Muntenia	65,226	26,135	40.07	39,091	59.93
South-West Oltenia	46,746	18,459	39.49	28,287	60.51
West	47,086	18,925	40.19	28,161	59.81
North-West	91,899	38,510	41.90	53,389	58.10
Center	69,913	28,116	40.22	41,797	59.78
Bucuresti-Ilfov	47,775	18,583	38.90	29,192	61.10
Total	487,723	195,202	40.02	292,521	59.98

Source: Authors based on ONRC (2023).

difference is smaller. Given the same homogeneity of data for all Development Regions, we can state that the proportion of women in this type is 40% and that of men is 60%. However, it should be noted that the 1% difference against women in the North-West region is compensated here with 1.5 percentage points.

Moreover, it cannot be established that a certain region out of the eight can be considered an example of good practices in the field of gender equality and more that the Bucharest-Ilfov region, which has the highest share as a number of entrepreneurs, is below the national average in both situations. To get an overall picture, the proportion of entrepreneurship in the total population was determined, taking into account the distribution by gender and by the Development Regions of Romania (Fig. 5.1). This reporting ensures comparability between the Development Regions, visualizing much more clearly the significant differences that exist between regions.

Considering the obtained values and the differences that exist between regions, the programs initiated for entrepreneurs must take into account the population's inclination in the region for involvement in entrepreneurial activities. For areas where the proportion is already high, the programs should encourage the development of entrepreneurship, both female and male, and for areas with a small percentage, the programs should be primarily focused on popularizing the idea of entrepreneurship, entrepreneurial education, and the implementation of good practices. Regarding the situation of newly created enterprises, the distribution by the gender of the founder/manager, by development regions, presented in Table 5.3, maintains the general trend of gender equality in Romania. Special situations appear in the Central region and Bucharest-Ilfov where there is a tendency toward gender equality for this type of enterprises.

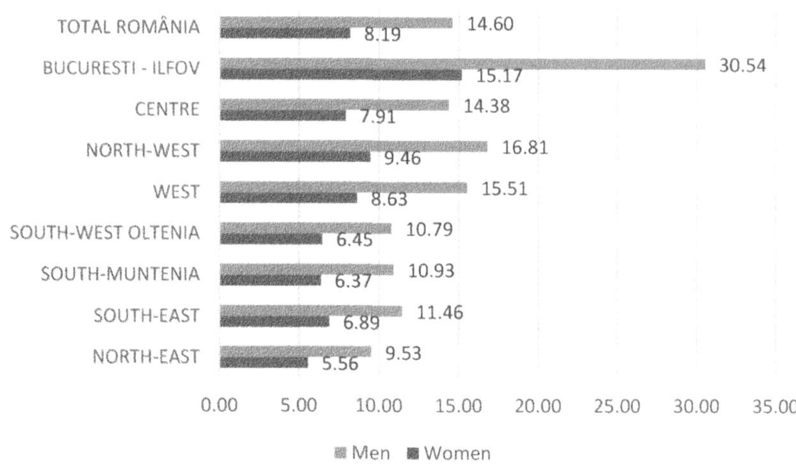

Fig. 5.1 Proportion of Entrepreneurs by Development Regions and the National Level (Nov. 2023). *Source*: Authors based on INSSE (2023).

Table 5.3 Distribution in Percent of Newly Created Active Enterprises, by the Gender of the Founder/Manager, by Development Regions, 2021.

	Men	**Women**
Total	61.6	38.4
North-East	60.1	39.9
South-East	62.9	37.1
South-Muntenia	64.2	35.8
South-West Oltenia	60.8	39.2
West	68.1	31.9
North-West	66.9	33.1
Center	55.5	44.5
Bucuresti-Ilfov	56	44

Source: Authors based on INSSE (2023).

We have analyzed whether this convergence toward gender equality could be a consequence of the founder's level of education. However, the data do not allow such a conclusion since there are major differences in the level of education of entrepreneurs between these regions. Thus, if for the Bucharest-Ilfov region only 14.3% of entrepreneurs have a lower level of education, this cannot be said about the Central region where 45.5% of entrepreneurs have a lower level of education (Table 5.4).

The data presented in Table 5.4 show that, for newly created enterprises, with the exception of the Bucharest-Ilfov region, a significant proportion of

Table 5.4 Distribution in Percentage of Newly Created Active Enterprises, by the Level of Education of the Founder/Manager, by Development Regions, 2021.

Region	Primary	Vocational	Middle School	Highschool and University
Total	0.2	9.2	33.9	56.7
North-East	0.3	8.9	40.9	49.9
South-East	0	8.8	43.7	47.5
South-Muntenia	0	14.4	36.1	49.5
South-West Oltenia	0	12.7	27.7	59.6
West	0	6.7	37.4	55.9
North-West	0.4	5.7	35.6	58.3
Center	0.6	11.1	33.8	54.5
Bucuresti-Ilfov	0	6.7	7.6	85.7

Source: Authors based on INSSE (2023).

entrepreneurs have primary, vocational, and middle-school education. However, the lack of formal education cannot remain without consequences in terms of entrepreneurial vision, the chosen field for business development, or development strategies. Even entrepreneurial education will be more effective when it intervenes at a higher level of general education. On the other hand, education also contributes to the elimination of stereotypes and traditional flaws that mark Romanian society.

The data provided by EUROSTAT – living conditions – labor market and housing – as shown in Table 5.5 have allowed for analyses regarding the volume and gender distribution of the "basic" category of entrepreneurs – self-employment.

According to the data recorded and presented in Table 5.5, initial conclusions can be drawn regarding the types of activities carried out in the category of self-employer. Thus, at the European level, there is a relatively uniform distribution of the activities undertaken with an advantage for activities in the field of social services. Relative to the situation in Europe, it should be noted the consistent presence in activities that require higher education, as here we find at least 50% of self-employers. The gender difference in favor of men is found in the agricultural sectors (about 4%) and construction (about 18%). Overall, in Europe, 29.5% of activities carried out in the self-employer category are in construction and agriculture.

In Romania, it's notable that 71% of self-employed individuals are engaged in the construction and agriculture sectors. Additionally, there is a smaller proportion of service and sales workers, at 7.1%, which is below the European average of 15.8%. However, it must be emphasized as a negative element the very small share of activities that require a high level of competencies and more of the necessity of higher education. As can be seen at the European level, these

Table 5.5 Number of Self-Employed Individuals in Romania and Europe by Gender and Activity Classes (Thousands of Persons), 2022.

Self-Employment	EU – Total	Romania – Total	EU – Males	Romania – Males	EU – Females	Romania – Females
Total	25,854.4	842.7	17,170.1	648.7	8,684.3	194
Managers	2,994.3	45.8	2,211.5	41.4	782.8	0
Professionals	5,995.7	44.7	3,303.5	20.3	2,692.2	24.4
Technicians and associate professionals	3,391.8	11.2	2,199.9	7	1,191.9	0
Clerical support workers	355.1	0	132.6	0	222.5	0
Service and sales workers	4,094.8	59.8	1,839.6	30.1	2,255.2	29.8
Skilled agricultural, forestry and fishery workers	3,546.3	459.5	2,578.7	343.5	967.6	116
Craft and related trades workers	3,976.1	138	3,683.9	133.3	292.1	0
Plant and machine operators and assemblers	881.9	32	815.7	31.6	66.2	0
Elementary occupations	554.3	49.6	365.4	39.6	188.9	10

Source: Authors based on Eurostat (2023).

categories of activities are carried out by just over 50% of them, while in Romania only 5%. The extremely small proportion of self-employers in these sectors of activity must necessarily attract measures that lead to raising the level of competencies and respectively lead to much higher involvement of this category in complex fields.

In addition, it is also necessary for future statistical records to include the basic level of training that people have when they start an activity. Also, given the speed of technological development, it is necessary to collect data that contains the level of training and the level of competencies developed in the last 5–10 years.

Analyzing the local gender ratio in Romania and in comparison with Europe, the situation can be summarized briefly: at least worrisome. First, the main field of activity for women is agriculture, with a proportion of 59.8% of the total self-employers. In comparison, in Europe, at the same level, 15% of women are found. It is clear in these conditions that in Romania in the agricultural sector, four times more people are active, at least referring to the professional status of self-employer, both in the case of women and in the case of men (Robayo-Abril & Rude, 2023).

As can be seen both from the values recorded in Table 5.6, it can be said that in Romania, the main activities approached by self-employed workers are construction and agriculture. In addition, in the case of women, the fields in which they act as independent workers are agriculture (about 60%), social services, and various (about 25%), the rest of about 5% being in various elementary occupations. It is clear that women in Romania, referring to the category of self-employed workers, have generally approached poorly remunerated activities and generally without requiring specialized higher education.

The data presented in Table 5.6 refer to self-employed workers who also have employees for achieving the objectives of their own organizations. To draw relevant conclusions in line with the purpose of the research, the values recorded here have been compared with those of the total volume of independent workers. Thus, comparability is ensured both at the specific level of Romania and at the level of the EU.

First, it must be mentioned that, globally, if in the EU independent entrepreneurs who have employees in the activities they carry out represent a share of 31.2% of the total class, in the case of Romania, this is only 9.9%. Regarding gender equality at the European level, the balance is still in favor of men, with a greater share of 9 percentage points (34.2% males compared to 25.3% females). In the case of Romania, a smaller gender difference can be considered 10.6% males compared to 7.9% females, but in this case, we must take into account the much smaller proportion of self-employed workers who have employees in turn. On the other hand, the data recorded in Table 5.6 reflect to some extent the size of entrepreneurship at the European level and, respectively, in Romania. Because here are presented data referring to workers who have their own employees, not at all to a self-employed worker without employees who can easily be considered as an employee under such a form in another independent activity of his creation. From a first glance at the data, it can be considered that the statistical data

Table 5.6 Distribution of Self-Employed Individuals with Employees, in EU and Romania (in Thousands), 2022.

Self-Employed Individuals with Employees (Employers)	EU – Total	Romania – Total	EU – Males	Romania – Males	EU – Females	Romania – Females
Total	8,057.8	83.8	5,863.9	68.5	2,193.9	15.4
Managers	2,258.7	40.8	1,703.5	37.6	555.2	0
Professionals	1,459	16.4	930.8	10.1	528.2	6.2
Technicians and associate professionals	841.7	0	630.4	0	211.3	0
Clerical support workers	110.9	0	0	0	65.6	0
Service and sales workers	1,351	16.4	759.5	12.5	591.5	3.9
Skilled agricultural, forestry and fishery workers	622.4	0	496.9	0	125.5	0.3
Craft and related trades workers	1,122.3	0	1,045.8	0	76.6	0
Plant and machine operators and assemblers	187.1	0	173.3	0	0	0
Elementary occupations	87.2	0	66.4	0	0	0

Source: Authors based on Eurostat (2023).

collected in Romania are hardly credible to correspond to reality. For instance, it is hard to believe that from about 460,000 people involved in this type of activities in agriculture, we can meet 0% without employees, but, nevertheless, there are 0.3% women self-employer with employees. As well as in the case of women managers. It is unlikely to have even 0% women managers with a proportion of men of 90.8%, of course, from the total of self-employers.

Certainly, a serious analysis must be carried out on how entrepreneurship in the field of social services in Romania is largely under the auspices of men (49.8%) compared to women (25.4%), this statement being based on traditions and culture, fundamental elements in the daily behavior of the vast majority of Romanians. This can also be easily proven, considering entrepreneurship in the field of global services and sales where men hold 41.5% of the activity and women 13.1%. Of course, the values that have been presented refer to the total number of independent workers, but even this situation reflects the desired image of having a clear radiography of entrepreneurship in Romania, first in relation to all sectors of the economy and second to make a comparison with the level and trend in Europe. As in the general case of the ensemble of independent workers and in this case of those who also have their own employees, at the European level, a relatively uniform distribution of these can be seen for all professions executed, which is not also the situation in Romania, where only social services and sales would be accessible to female entrepreneurship for development with employees.

From the data presented in Table 5.7, it appears that a large number of women fall into the category of self-employment without employees, predominantly in the sector of skilled agricultural, forestry, and fishery workers, indicating a high risk that, in reality, the activity is not independent but rather conceals an employment relationship.

As noted in scholarly works (Wiliam & Horodnic, 2018), the prevalence of so-called bogus self-employment is notably high in sectors like agriculture, forestry, and fishing. Although there's no widely agreed-upon definition of bogus self-employment (Fehringer, 2014; Thörnquist, 2014), common interpretations tend to focus on the legal and economic characteristics of employment situations that blur the lines between traditional waged employment and authentic self-employment (Jorens, 2009; Kautonen et al., 2010). When evaluating the legitimacy of self-employed individuals without employees, the assessment revolves around their economic and personal dependence. This includes examining whether they are dependent on a single or primary client and/or if they possess complete economic and personal independence.

Case law from the European Court of Justice (ECJ) indicates that identifying a subordination relationship requires examining several factors: the specific duties assigned to the individual, the environment in which these duties are performed, the level of oversight in the organization, and the terms under which the person can be terminated. In the Allonby case (C-256/01), the ECJ adopted a broad interpretation of the term "worker," encompassing those formally classified as self-employed. As a result, even if someone is officially recognized as self-employed under national law, they may still be deemed a worker under gender equality regulations, particularly if their supposed independence masks an actual employment

Table 5.7 Distribution of Self-Employed Individuals Without Employees in EU and Romania (By Thousands), 2022.

Self-Employed Individuals Without Employees (Own Account Workers)	**EU – Total**	**Romania – Total**	**EU – Males**	**Romania – Males**	**EU – Females**	**Romania – Females**
Total	1,7796.6	758.9	11,306.2	580.2	6,490.4	178.7
Managers	735.6	0	508	0	227.6	0
Professionals	4,536.6	28.3	2,372.7	10.2	2,164	18.2
Technicians and associate professionals	2,550.1	9.4	1,569.5	0	980.6	0
Clerical support workers	244.2	0	87.4	0	156.8	0
Service and sales workers	2,743.8	43.4	1,080.1	17.5	1,663.7	25.9
Skilled agricultural, forestry and fishery workers	2,923.9	458.2	2,081.8	342.5	842.2	115.7
Craft and related trades workers	2,853.7	133	2,638.1	129.2	215.6	
Plant and machine operators and assemblers	694.8	30.9	642.5	30.4	52.3	0
Elementary occupations	467.2	49.4	299	39.4	168.1	10

Source: Authors based on Eurostat (2023).

relationship. This interpretation broadens the scope of pension rights and gender-related protections to include instances of disguised employment. Furthermore, in Petersen (C-544/11), the ECJ reiterated the importance of considering the nature of duties, the context of performance, supervision level, and dismissal conditions in determining the presence of a subordinate relationship.

This leads to a distinct separation between true self-employment and dependent employment. While Romanian legislation doesn't explicitly address bogus self-employment, the Romanian Fiscal Code clearly delineates "dependent activity" and sets out criteria to determine if an activity is conducted independently. "Dependent activity" is described as any work performed by an individual in an employment relationship that generates income. In contrast, "independent activity" is characterized as any work undertaken by an individual to earn income, fulfilling at least four of the following conditions:

- The individual has autonomy in deciding the location, method, and schedule of their work.
- The individual is allowed to serve multiple clients.
- The individual bears the business's inherent risks.
- The work is executed using the individual's own assets.
- The work is performed through the individual's intellectual and/or physical abilities, depending on the type of activity.
- The individual is part of a professional organization that offers representation, regulation, and oversight of the profession, in accordance with the specific laws governing that profession.
- The individual has the liberty to conduct the activity directly, either independently, with employees, or in collaboration with third parties, as per legal provisions.

The situation of women working in rural Romania is far from portraying them as entrepreneurs independently managing small agricultural businesses. If women represent 33% of workers in the agricultural sector, this percentage reaches 66% among unpaid family workers. Therefore, intervention by tax and labor authorities is necessary to determine the reality of qualification as self-employed for entrepreneurs in agriculture, especially for women who, as statistical data show, are in a more vulnerable situation. Determining the real situation is complicated by the legal provision in GEO No. 44/2008, which states that an authorized individual will not be considered an employee of any third parties they collaborate with, even if the collaboration is exclusive (Article 17, Para. 3).

Conclusion

One of the first conclusions from the data analyzed above is that there is a major difficulty in examining and measuring entrepreneurship due to the blurred boundaries separating it from self-employment. Moreover, the data related to entrepreneurship, which come from various sources (the National Trade Register Office, the National Institute of Statistics, Eurostat), only target certain categories of entrepreneurship and are not correlated with information such as the entrepreneur's professional training and education, previous entrepreneurial experiences, or the number of businesses run concurrently. Regarding the challenges faced in entrepreneurship, most of them are identified from scholarly literature, though there is a lack of significant statistical data to quantify them. Broadly, these challenges encompass issues like limited access to financing, restrictive business regulations, cultural obstacles, restrictions in choosing business types and sectors, along with gaps in information and training. The data specific to the economic environment in Romania are presented in Table 5.8.

For women, the situation is even more challenging, as gender inequalities compound the general obstacles. Despite efforts at the European level to promote gender equality, 44% of Europeans believe that the primary role of a woman is to take care of her home and family, and 43% believe that the primary role of a man is to earn money (EC, 2020). Moreover, the entrepreneurial environment is marked by horizontal gender segregation distinct patterns where men and women tend to engage in different types of entrepreneurial activities and sectors. Thus, women entrepreneurs in the EU are more likely to start and manage businesses in sectors like retail, personal services, and health care. In contrast, men are more inclined to start businesses in sectors such as construction, manufacturing, and high-tech industries. This fact is influenced by traditional gender roles and societal expectations in some EU countries that influence the entrepreneurial journey of women. This includes expectations related to family responsibilities and societal views on women in leadership roles.

The Member States of the EU have adopted the 1989 United Nations Convention on the Rights of the Child, which asserts that both parents share responsibilities for their child's upbringing and development, with the child's best interests as their primary concern (Article 18(1)). EU policies on work-life balance aim to advance gender equality by encouraging women's participation in the workforce and promoting equal caregiving responsibilities between men and women. Despite these policies, achieving work-life balance is a significant hurdle for many female entrepreneurs with caregiving duties. This challenge is exacerbated by the growing trend of extended working hours and fluctuating work schedules, adversely affecting women's employment opportunities. A critical barrier to women's greater presence in the labor market is the struggle to balance work and family commitments, especially since female entrepreneurs do not benefit from the legal protections for maternity that are available in traditional employment, due to their non-employee status. Moreover, the specifics of entrepreneurial activity require flexibility in the work schedule, frequent travel, working more than eight hours a day, and on weekends. The absence of supportive infrastructures, such as affordable childcare services, flexible working hours, and parental leave policies for entrepreneurs, makes it difficult for women to balance work and family life. This is particularly challenging for single mothers and those without a supportive partner or family network. For example, only persons who, in the last two years prior to the child's birth, have earned income for at least 12 months from salaries and salary-equivalent incomes, incomes from independent activities, intellectual property rights, incomes from agricultural, forestry, and fishery

Table 5.8 The Distribution of Newly Established Enterprises Facing Supply-Related Challenges, by Type of Difficulty and Development Regions, 2021.

Region	Lack of Resources	Limited Access to Credit	No Customers or Customers Who Pay Late	Limited Access to Well-Paying Employees	Lack of Technology	Lack of Raw Materials
Total	80.1	36.5	37.1	37.6	27.5	14.4
North-East	83.1	23.8	30.4	37.6	13.8	8.8
South-East	90.5	52.3	48.3	33.3	46.4	18.5
South-Muntenia	83.0	52.6	55.3	50.2	31.9	24.0
South-West Oltenia	84.6	61.5	49.2	37.2	35.0	13.5
West	79.8	51.6	70.4	39.5	60.5	10.7
North-West	79.1	17.0	36.4	35.2	9.0	10.3
Center	69.3	38.6	20.0	37.0	25.3	20.7
Bucuresti-Ilfov	68.7	13.0	10.4	29.9	27.5	7.7

Source: Authors based on INSSE (2023).

activities subject to income tax according to the provisions of Law No. 227/2015 regarding the Fiscal Code, are eligible for child-rearing leave for a child up to the age of two years, or three years in the case of a child with disabilities, as well as a monthly allowance. Mothers who are associates or shareholders in a commercial company do not enjoy this measure of maternity protection, which has negative consequences on the development of female entrepreneurship.

Female entrepreneurs, therefore, must fight against both gender stereotypes and the difficulties arising from fulfilling roles that are still linked to their social role, especially those related to raising children, household chores, or caring for the elderly. As mentioned above, there have been legislative advances to ensure a balance between professional life and personal life, but these do not cover the situation of female entrepreneurs who establish commercial companies. Offering childcare services or subsidies to help women balance business development with family responsibilities, creating partnerships with local childcare providers or implementing on-site childcare facilities could contribute to reducing the obstacle in this field.

Furthermore, the time spent on roles tied to their social status prevents women from completing their education, resulting in a lower level of training, as indicated by the figures shown in this chapter. This lower level of education forms a barrier in the development of complex businesses or in obtaining funds for starting and developing businesses. Additionally, the presented data revealed that a portion of what we call female entrepreneurship runs the risk of being, in fact, bogus self-employment, which may cover the extremely vulnerable legal situation of women working in agricultural activities. Possible solutions to this problem could include offering targeted educational programs and workshops focused on business skills, financial literacy, digital technology, and leadership. These programs should be tailored to address the specific challenges and needs of women entrepreneurs. Moreover, schools and universities should aim to introduce entrepreneurship education early and encourage young women to consider entrepreneurship as a career path. In order to mitigate the horizontal gender stereotype, women should be encouraged and supported in STEM (Science, Technology, Engineering, and Mathematics) fields, where they are traditionally underrepresented, to venture into tech entrepreneurship.

The presence of women in complex entrepreneurship remains extremely low, and despite a few programs aimed at creating networks for female entrepreneurs, women's involvement seems to be more driven by individual success stories than by the establishment of a strong category of entrepreneurs.

It is considered essential to create databases dedicated to the issue of entrepreneurship, where all categories of entrepreneurship can be gathered in a single database. Combining information from the Trade Register with labor market data results in a picture that lacks clarity and precision. A more in-depth establishment of the characteristics of entrepreneurs is necessary, as well as identifying the obstacles they face in setting up and running their businesses. Conducting more targeted research will allow to better understand the barriers and opportunities for female entrepreneurs, and these data can be used to inform policy and program development and advocate for and implement policies that support women entrepreneurs, such as tax incentives, streamlined business registration processes, and laws that promote gender equality in business. While there are notable challenges for women in entrepreneurship, targeted strategies and supportive policies can significantly enhance their participation and success in this field. Further research and measures should rely on the importance of a multifaceted approach, encompassing education, policy, support systems, and societal change, to promote female entrepreneurship effectively.

References

Alsos, G. A., Clausen, T. H., Hytti, U., & Solvoll, S. (2016). Entrepreneurs' social identity and the preference of causal and effectual behaviours in start-up processes. *Entrepreneurship & Regional Development*, *28*, 234–258.

Arslan, A., Al Kharusi, S., Hussain, S. M., & Alo, O. (2023). Sustainable entrepreneurship development in Oman: A multi-stakeholder qualitative study. *International Journal of Organizational Analysis*, *31*(8), 35–59.

Atomico. (2023). *State of European tech 2023*. https://stateofeuropeantech.com/

Baručić, A., & Umihanić, B. (2016). Entrepreneurship education as a factor of entrepreneurial opportunity recognition for starting a new business. *Management: Journal of Contemporary Management Issues*, *21*, 27–44.

Blank, S., & Eckhardt, J. T. (2023). The lean startup as an actionable theory of entrepreneurship. *Journal of Management*. https://doi.org/10.1177/01492063231168095

Cheng, H., & Wang, J. (2023). What's in store for females after breaking the glass ceiling? Evidence from the Chinese audit. *Frontiers in Psychology*, *14*, 1321391.

Cuesta, M., Suarez-Alvarez, J., Lozano, L. M., García-Cueto, E., & Muniz, J. (2018). Assessment of eight entrepreneurial personality dimensions: Validity evidence of the BEPE battery. *Frontiers in Psychology*, *9*, 2352. https://doi.org/10.3389/fpsyg.2018.02352

Elia, G., Margherita, A., & Passiante, G. (2020). Digital entrepreneurship ecosystem: How digital technologies and collective intelligence are reshaping the entrepreneurial process. *Technological Forecasting and Social Change*, *150*, 119791.

European Commission. (2020). *A union of equality: Gender equality strategy 2020-2025* (p. 152). EC.

European Court of Justice. (C-256/01). Judgment of the Court of 13 January 2004. Debra Allonby v Accrington & Rossendale College, Education Lecturing Services, trading as Protocol Professional and Secretary of State for Education and Employment, ECLI:EU:C:2004:18.

European Court of Justice. (C-544/11). Judgment of the Court (First Chamber), 28 February 2013. Case law: Helga Petersen and Peter Petersen v Finanzamt Ludwigshafen, ECLI:EU:C:2013:124.

Eurostat. (2023). *Business demography by size class and NACE Rev. 2 activity*. Retrieved August 5, 2023, from https://ec.europa.eu/eurostat/ databrowser/explore/all/icts?lang=en&subtheme=bsd. bd&display=list&sort=category&extractionId=bd_size

Fehringer, E. (2014). *Tackling false (bogus) self-employment*. ec. europa.eu/social/BlobServlet?docId=13032&langId=en

GEM (Global Entrepreneurship Monitor). (2023). *Global Entrepreneurship Monitor 2022/23 women's entrepreneurship report*. GEM.

Gielnik, M. M., Cardon, M. S., & Frese, M. (Eds.). (2021). *The psychology of entrepreneurship: New perspectives*. Routledge.

Government Emergency Ordinance No. 44/2008 on the conduct of economic activities by authorized individuals, individual enterprises, and family enterprises, published in the Official Gazette of Romania, Part I, No. 328, April 25, 2008.

Government Emergency Ordinance No. 6/2011 for stimulating the establishment and development of microenterprises by business start-up entrepreneurs, published in the Official Gazette of Romania, Part I, No. 103, February 9, 2011.

Guo, X., & Zhu, X. (2023). Redefining work-life balance: Women at the helm of the post-pandemic coworking revolution. *Archives of Women's Mental Health*, *26*(6), 755–766.

Hamilton, E. (2013). The discourse of entrepreneurial masculinities (and femininities). *Entrepreneurship & Regional Development*, *25*, 90–99.

IDC. (2022). *European women in VC*. IDC European Woman in Venture Capital (idcinteractive.net).

INSSE. (2023). National Institute of Statistics, Tempo online database. Retrieved November 9, 2023, from http://statistici.ins se.ro:8077/tempo-online/#/pages/tables/insse-table

Jones, S. (2014). Gendered discourses of entrepreneurship in UK higher education: The fictive entrepreneur and the fictive student. *International Small Business Journal*, *32*, 237–258.

Jorens, Y. (2009). *Self-employment and bogus self-employment in the European construction industry. Summary of a comparative study of 11 member states*. EFBWW, FIEC, European Commission. www.fiec.eu/en/themes -72/self-employment-and-bogus-self-employment.aspx

Kautonen, T., Down, S, Welter, F., Vainio, P., Palmroos, J., Althoff, K., & Kolb, S. (2010). 'Involuntary self-employment' as a public policy issue: A cross-country European review. *International Journal of Entrepreneurial Behavior and Research*, *16*(2), 112–129.

Kolvereid, L., & Moen, Ø. (1997). Entrepreneurship among business graduates: Does a major in entrepreneurship make a difference? *Journal of European Industrial Training*, *21*(4), 154–160.

Law No. 31/1990 on companies, republished in the Official Gazette of Romania, Part I, No. 1066, November 17, 2004.

Law No. 1/2005 on the organization and functioning of cooperation, republished in the Official Gazette of Romania, Part I, No. 368, May 20, 2014.

Law No. 202/2002 on equal opportunities and treatment between women and men, republished in the Official Gazette of Romania, Part I, No. 326, June 5, 2013.

Law No. 227/2015 regarding the Fiscal Code, published in the Official Gazette of Romania, Part I, No. 688, September 10, 2015.

Loi, M., Fayolle, A., van Gelderen, M., Riot, E., Refai, D., Higgins, D., Haloub, R., Salusse, M., Lamy, E., Verzat, C., & Cavarretta, F. (2022). Entrepreneurship education at the crossroads: Challenging taken-for-granted assumptions and opening new perspectives. *Journal of Management Inquiry*, *31*(2), 123–134.

Manzoor, A. (2019). Womenpreneurs in MENA region. In *Gender and diversity: Concepts, methodologies, tools, and applications* (pp. 1144–1158). IGI Global.

Muniz, J., Su´arez-Alvarez, J., Pedrosa, I., Fonseca-Pedrero, E., & García-Cueto, E. (2014). Enterprising personality profile in youth: Components and assessment. *Psicothema*, *26*(4), 545–553. https://doi.org/10.7334/psicothema2014.182

Nadin, S., Smith, R., & Jones, S. (2020). Heroines of enterprise: Post-recession media representations of women and entrepreneurship in a UK newspaper 2008–2016. *International Small Business Journal*, *38*(6), 557–577. https://doi.org/10.1177/0266242620913209

ONRC. (2023). National trade registry. *Statistics*. Retrieved November 9, 2023, from https://www.onrc.ro/index.php/ro/statistici

Order No. 1111/2022 of the Ministry of Entrepreneurship and Tourism on the approval of the procedure for implementing the program for stimulating the establishment of small and medium enterprises "start-up nation – Romania."

Order No. 1314/2022 of the Ministry of Entrepreneurship and Tourism on the approval of the procedure for implementing the national multiannual program for the development of entrepreneurial culture among women managers in the SME sector, published in the Official Gazette of Romania, Part I, No. 799, August 11, 2022.

Peterlin, J. (2021). Entrepreneurship education management in the EU. In *Entrepreneurship, institutional framework and support mechanisms in the EU* (pp. 27–38). Emerald Publishing Limited.

Pillay-Naidoo, D., & Vermeulen, C. (2023). Seeking support through solidarity: Female leader's experiences of workplace solidarity in male-dominated professions. *Frontiers in Psychology*, *14*.

Polychronopoulos, D., & Nguyen-Duc, A. (2024). Migrant entrepreneurship support in Europe: A PRISMA systematic literature review. *F1000Research*, *12*, 1300.

Ratten, V. (2023). Entrepreneurship: Definitions, opportunities, challenges, and future directions. *Global Business and Organizational Excellence*, *42*(5), 79–90. https://doi.org/10.1002/joe.22217

Robayo-Abril, M., & Rude, B. (2023). *The gender gap in entrepreneurship in Romania: Background study for the Romania gender assessment*. World Bank Group.

Roos, A. (2021). Embeddedness in context: Understanding gender in a female entrepreneurship network. In *Understanding women's entrepreneurship in a gendered context* (pp. 113–126). Routledge.

Rugina, S. (2018). Women entrepreneurship in Estonia: Formal and informal institutional context. In S. Birkner, K. Ettl, F. Welter, & I. Ebbers, (Eds.), *Women's entrepreneurship in Europe: FGF Studies in Small Business and Entrepreneurship* (pp. 105–135). Springer.

Schweickart, T., Hill-Whilton, Z., Chitale, S., Cobos, D., Gilon-Yanai, M., Achuonjei, J., Vizgan, G., Gillespie, C., & Gold-von Simson, G. (2023). The biomedical entrepreneurship skills development program for the advancement of research translation: Foundations of biomedical startups course, metrics, and impact. *Journal of Clinical and Translational Science*, *7*(1), e77.

Shane, S., & Venkataraman, S. (2000). The promise of entrepreneurship as a field of research. *The Academy of Management Review*, *25*(1), 217–226. https://doi.org/10.2307/259271

Thepna, A., Cochrane, B. B., & Salmon, M. E. (2023). Self-efficacy in nurse entrepreneurs: A concept analysis. *Nursing Outlook*, *71*(6), 102053.

Thörnquist, C. (2014). Bogus self-employment in the European Union. Paper for the UACES panel 'Vulnerabilities of regular labour migration in the EU', Cork, Ireland, September 1–3.

Welter, F. (2011). Contextualizing entrepreneurship: Conceptual challenges and ways forward. *Entrepreneurship Theory and Practice*, *35*(1), 165–184.

Williams, C., & Horodnic, A. (2018). *Tackling undeclared work in the agricultural sector*. European Platform Undeclared Work.

Yildirim, U., Nart, S., Akar, S., Sarialioğlu, S., Toygar, A., Vardar, B., Kaya, S. C., & Sari, M. (2023). In-depth exploration of challenges faced by women in the Turkish maritime industry: A qualitative study. *Work*, 1–13.

Chapter 6

Current Challenges Facing Women Entrepreneurs in Contemporary Economics

Cristina Gafu, Ileana Georgiana Gheorghe and Violeta Sima

Petroleum-Gas University of Ploiesti, Romania

Abstract

This chapter aims to identify the current challenges facing women entrepreneurs. Female entrepreneurship must be analyzed from a binary perspective: the position of women in society and the role of entrepreneurship in society. The study focused on women entrepreneurs in the European Union (EU). Considering the social-economic diversity in the EU, we evaluated the five economic systems. To highlight how these differences are manifested in the different systems, we considered for analysis one country belonging to each model, namely, Denmark for the Scandinavian system, Germany for the Continental system, Ireland for the Anglo-Saxon system, Spain for the Mediterranean System, and Romania, for the Catching-up system. The analysis considered women entrepreneurs in the labor market, female employment/management in the labor market, female entrepreneurs in the labor market, and female mentality regarding work and entrepreneurship.

Keywords: Female entrepreneurs; labor market; female employment; culture; entrepreneurial mindset

Introduction

The impact of the successive crisis on the labor market is a common concern to all European countries. The unemployment rates are continuously increasing,

Emerging Patterns and Behaviors in a Green Resilient Economy, 129–151

doi:10.1108/978-1-83549-780-720241007

and certain groups (unskilled people) are especially affected by unemployment. Entrepreneurship and self-employment help to create jobs, develop new skills, and provide disadvantaged people and unemployed an opportunity to fully participate in the economy and the society.

The impact of the COVID-19 crisis and the economic crisis that followed it on the labor market, which means increasing poverty and widening inequalities, has become a common concern to all European countries. Certain groups, including women, are particularly affected. In this increasingly complex and complicated economic-social context, more and more women are becoming entrepreneurs. According to the GEM survey (A. Elam et al., 2023), about 274 million women were involved in businesses and startups, and 139 million managers and business owners worldwide were involved in 2020. Entrepreneurship and self-employment help create jobs, develop new skills, and allow disadvantaged and unemployed people to participate fully in the economy and society.

The world is still dependent on conservative social paradigms, and it has not eliminated stereotypes. According to Doherty and Eagly (1989), because individual skills and capabilities are not always considered in some fields believed to be men related, women are not given the same opportunities for specific roles. Such predispositions usually prevent the gender inequality gap from narrowing, giving rise to many academic discussions. These prejudiced patterns are encountered in many fields; however, they seem to be affecting women wishing to enter entrepreneurship. This chapter analyzes which factors are more challenging for women to start their own businesses. Sullivan and Meek (2012) stated that female business ownership could be a starting point in breaking the preconceptions and stereotypes about gender roles encountered in organizational professions.

Targeted and engaging education and training are the most effective ways to address this challenge. Today's existing education and training offer for entrepreneurs focuses mainly on the "hard-core" elements such as finance, marketing, and sales. Other factors influencing women's choice of an entrepreneurial career, such as motivation, life planning/purpose, and setting, are less present in such programs.

This is why there is a real need for new initiatives that respond to the characteristics and needs of potential women entrepreneurs and help them overcome the barriers that can prevent them from starting their businesses. This analysis aims to identify, adapt, and transfer some models of best practices for women entrepreneurs from different countries of the EU. The ultimate goal is to develop the skills of potential female entrepreneurs. In this sense, it is essential to collect information about entrepreneurs' mentality and the characteristics and motivations of female entrepreneurs.

Literature Review

Entrepreneurship, being intrinsically linked to evolutionary economic, demographic, and social trends, but also technological, has as social objectives the creation of new jobs, the reduction of social inequalities, and the protection of the environment. Globalization and successive crises have determined essential societal changes; these changes are also manifested in entrepreneurship. Barreto et al. (2009) seek to explain and find solutions for gender inequality in the upper echelons of organizations. They showed that although women have much more access to leadership in Western countries than at any other time in history, equal representation of the sexes has yet to be present. Although there has been a significant increase in women in leadership roles, these women are predominantly present at lower levels of leadership. Burke (2009) took into account the cultural dimension of the phenomenon, as defined by Hofstede (1984), showing differences between male and female societies regarding the approach to the role of women in the economy, respectively, on the labor market and entrepreneurship. The results published in the 2021 report The Index of Women-Entrepreneurs show that female entrepreneurship is developing. Still, although they account for 37% of global gross domestic product (GDP), they have been more severely affected by the pandemic and still face barriers to achieving their full potential (Mastercard, 2022).

Women have fewer entrepreneurial opportunities than men, as shown by Doherty and Eagly (1989). Prejudices that place women closer to housework and childcare are still strong around the globe, especially in countries where traditions are essential in organizational culture. Rubio-Bañón and Esteban-Lloret (2016) show that higher entrepreneurial activity rates tend to be observed in cultures based on stereotypically masculine values, while in more feminine cultures, employment in companies is more prevalent. The literature has substantial debate, starting with the theory of Doherty and Eagly about social norms regarding gender inequality and women's entrepreneurial opportunities (Doherty & Eagly, 1989). Differences related to gender-specific perceptions could explain the difference in entrepreneurial drive between men and women. Ascher argues that female business ownership is essential for economic development because it is a source of new job creation and ideas (Ascher, 2012). He emphasizes the importance of creating women-owned businesses in emerging economies such as Romania, Poland, or Hungary to promote faster development. Minniti and Arenius also support this hypothesis, showing that lower-income countries can benefit more from female entrepreneurship (Minniti & Arenius, 2003). Another important aspect of this issue in less developed countries is the higher birth rate and fewer years spent in education. Surprisingly, Minniti and Arenius (2003) showed that lower levels of education can promote entrepreneurship because fewer people see the opportunities that can be exploited. Competition in the business market is less tight, especially for women. Cardella et al. (2020) reinforced the theory that less developed economies promote entrepreneurship. There are fewer opportunities for women to find a suitable job, and they are also more prone to hostile work environments and gender stereotypes. The model proposed by Ascher (2012) in his paper also suggests that women in a mothering role see entrepreneurship as a tool to balance work and family life. Rembulan et al. (2016) showed that a traditional daily job can put considerable pressure on women, causing stress and fatigue, affecting the mother–child relationship and the woman's marital status. Most women in the survey by Rembulan et al. (2016) cited the lack of time and energy to engage in both roles: working individual and wife and mother in a family. In their study, the women interviewed reported an unbalanced life and intense work–family conflicts, mainly due to the inflexible working hours that today's corporations impose. Thus, economies with higher birth rates will show a greater predisposition of women to business ownership. Grilo and Thurik (2004) show that women's chances of starting a business are lower than men's. Their study addresses the factors responsible for women's lack of entrepreneurial drive and the obstacles women face when they want to start a business. Their results show that women face a more significant lack of support than men when entering entrepreneurship, an observation also supported by Langowitz and Minniti (2007).

In this case, a study by Dawson and Henley (2015) showed that the lower number of women willing to start their businesses is due to their relatively high-risk aversion. Ascher (2012) pointed out that women need more access to networking opportunities.

They also face "double burden syndrome," struggling to balance work with family responsibilities, resulting in a lack of time to develop skills and continuously update knowledge, an essential feature in today's business environment. According to European Commission Statistics, on average, European women spend twice as much time as men on household tasks, spending more than four hours a day fulfilling household responsibilities (Desvaux et al., 2017). The differential opportunities for men and women are confirmed by the Global Gender Gap Report 2023 published by the *World Economic Forum* (2023), which showed that women in leadership positions were only 32%.

A study performed in 2021 (Bastida, 2021) summarizes the most relevant factors identified in the literature as inhibitors of female entrepreneurship. These factors are:

1. Market – Market access/opportunity entrepreneurship;
2. Money – Access to financial resources;
3. Management – Human and organizational capital;
4. Motherhood – Familiar responsibilities/household context;
5. Macro/meso-level factors – National policies/environment/strategies and policy-supporting processes.

Women Entrepreneurs in EU

In today's economy, women entrepreneurs play an essential role. In this context, there is a significant increase in women-run businesses. At the same time, female entrepreneurship in the EU correlates with the economic model, representing a critical success factor.

The specialized literature identifies five capitalist economic systems in Europe (Aiginger & Guger, 2005; Aiginger & Leoni, 2009; Guger et al., 2007). The Scandinavian system, which includes the Nordic countries – Denmark, Finland, Sweden, Iceland, is based on social democratic principles. The Continental system is based on conservative principles and is present in Western European countries – Austria, Belgium,

French, Germany, Luxembourg, Netherlands. The Anglo-Saxon system, also called the liberal welfare model, includes the countries beyond the English Channel – Ireland, United Kingdom. The Mediterranean system consists of the countries of the south – Greece, Italy, Portugal, Spain, Cyprus, Malta. The "Catching-up" system includes former communist countries – Czech Republic, Hungary, Slovakia, Poland, Bulgaria, Estonia, Latvia, Lithuania, Romania, Slovenia.

Regarding female entrepreneurship, in each of the five systems stated above, specific characteristics can be highlighted:

- It represents a family tradition – especially in Mediterranean countries.
- It is strongly supported from a legislative point of view – in the Nordic countries.
- It develops within social entrepreneurship – mainly in the Nordic countries, the Anglo-Saxon ones, or those belonging to the continental model.

As a general feature, it can be stated that the development of female entrepreneurship is correlated with the evolution of the image of women in society against the background of the changes in society in general and the mentality of people in particular.

To highlight how these differences are manifested in the five economic systems, we considered for analysis one country belonging to each model, namely, Denmark for the Scandinavian system, Germany for the Continental system, Ireland for the Anglo-Saxon system, Spain for the Mediterranean System, and Romania for the Catching-up system.

Women Entrepreneurs on the Labor Market

Many unemployed women already have ideas and want to start their businesses but need more confidence, knowledge, and skills. Women represent more than half of the total population of the EU. Still, only a little over a third of them are self-employed, and only 30% of first-time entrepreneurs are women.

The decrease in the unemployment rate among women is a major concern for political decision-makers in the EU. The target for the EU is for 78% of the population aged 20–64 to be employed by 2030. The analysis of statistical data, highlighted by Eurostat, reveals a discrepancy between the employment rate of men and that of women, as seen in Fig. 6.1.

At the same time, entrepreneurship is a significant concern of the EU. Thus, at the level of thematic objectives financed by the European Social Fund, priorities are formulated that directly target Small and medium-sized enterprises (SMEs). Among these priorities are self-employment, entrepreneurship, and the creation of new businesses (Alessandrin et al., 2019). In turn, female entrepreneurship remains a priority, as it is considered a means of economic independence for women and a lever for development, growth, and innovation. However, the gender gap persists (OECD, 2023), although recent results from several OECD countries suggest that reducing this gap could positively affect the economy.

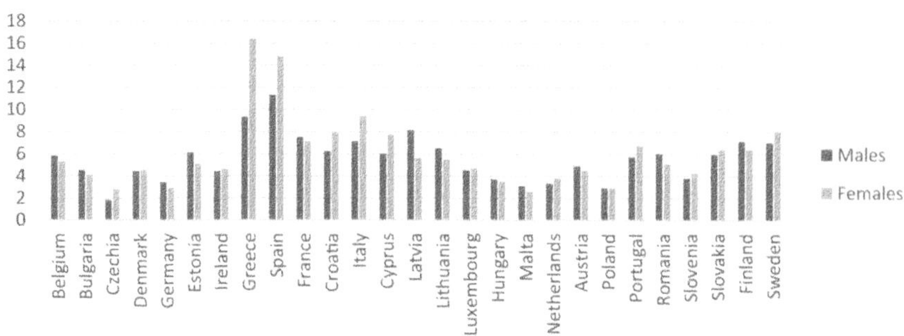

Fig. 6.1. Unemployment by Sex, in 2022 (Percentage of Population in the Labor Force). *Source*: Eurostat (online data code: une_rt_a__custom_9462632).

Female Employment/Management on the Labor Market

Regarding the registered unemployment rate, taking into account gender, in the period 2013–2022, a general downward trend can be observed until 2019. The year 2020, marked by the COVID crisis, determined the increase in the unemployment rate, which affected practically the entire Europe, and it manifested itself among both sexes. After 2020, the downward trend of the unemployment rate among the whole population has resumed. Analyzing Fig. 6.2, it can be seen that the highest level of unemployment was manifested in Spain at the beginning

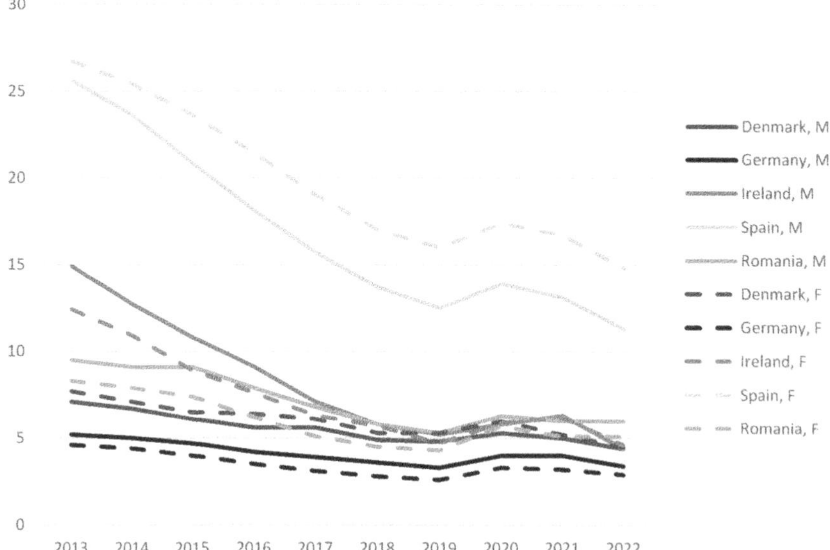

Fig. 6.2. Unemployment by Sex, During 2013–2022 (Percentage of Population in the Labor Force). *Source*: Eurostat (online data code: une_rt_a__custom_9462632).

of the analyzed period, affecting more than a quarter of the country's population. Germany has an unemployment rate of around 5%, at the opposite extreme. Denmark, Romania, and Ireland follow in the hierarchy.

Specific differences can be observed in how unemployment affects the two sexes. Thus, in Spain and Denmark, women are more affected by this phenomenon, unlike in Ireland, Romania, and Germany, where higher unemployment rates are recorded among men. Another interesting aspect is how the differences between the sexes evolve regarding unemployment. Spain stands out again, where the gap between the sexes has tripled, from approximately 1.1% in 2013 to 3.5% in 2022. At the opposite pole is Ireland, where the difference between the sexes has decreased about 10 times, from 2.5% to 0.2%. However, things have not evolved in favor of women in this country but the opposite. Also, it decreased continuously in Denmark, where the difference was minimal anyway.

See in Fig. 6.2 the evolution of the registered unemployment rate and the unemployment rates divided by sex during 2013–2022.

Several factors may explain the narrowing of the gender gap in self-employment. Thus, a study performed by OECD in 2021 (European Commission Directorate-General for Justice, 2014, p. 17) identified four major factors, namely, the implementation of specific policies to support women entrepreneurs, the position in the economic cycle, the decrease in the share of men who carry out independent activities in the last decade, or the aging of the population of entrepreneurs, because the gender differences tend to be a little smaller among younger cohorts.

It has been consistently observed that men hold the vast majority of leadership/top management positions in companies worldwide. A study published in September 2010 by the European Commission (2014, p. 6) highlighted the under-representation of women in management positions in business, showing that between 2003 and 2010, the presence of women on boards of directors. However, increasing on average by 0.5% annually, it failed to reach even 12%.

While the highest levels of female representation in management were recorded in Finland (29.1%), Latvia (29%), France (26.8%), and Sweden (26.5%) and in the Netherlands, Denmark, Germany, and Slovenia, at least 20% women are represented on boards, in Romania women occupy less than 1 in 10 positions.

Things improved during the analyzed period, 2013–2020, but not spectacularly. Thus, according to Eurostat, women are under-represented in management positions in companies in the EU. Only one manager in three is a woman, although half of the employees are men and half are women.

Analyzing Fig. 6.3, it can be seen that among the five analyzed countries, in Ireland, women are best represented in leadership positions, without reaching, however, even 40%. At the other extreme are Denmark and Germany, where less than 30% of employed women hold management positions.

Most women in management positions have a university degree and are in their prime (30–45). They have management experience and are available because they are ready to take on new challenges (changing jobs or changing jobs and even locations to get promoted).

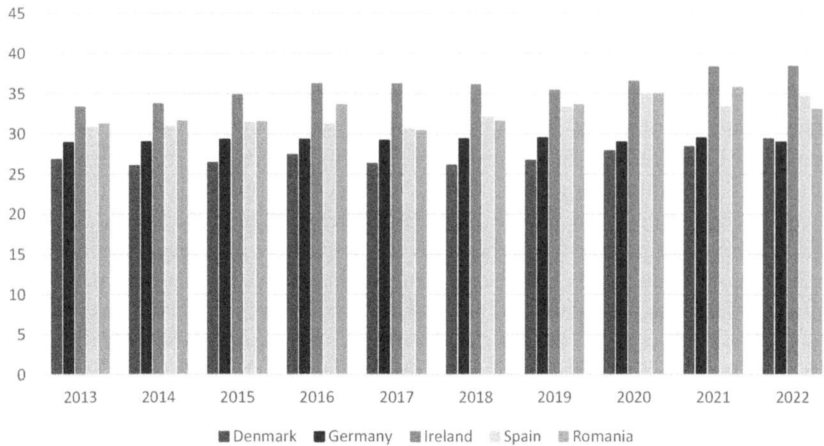

Fig. 6.3. Employed Women Being in Managerial Positions (Percentage of Total Employed Population). *Source*: Eurostat (online data code: tqoe1c2).

Female Entrepreneurs on the Labor Market

In the last years, female business medium at a global level but also at the Romanian level has developed in an accelerated rhythm. Business women have become much more visible and active and have become more interested in the business tendencies identified at an international level and in what leadership in the new economy means. They founded firms, family business, or they effectively involved themselves in the corporate competitions. The EU encourages and supports women entrepreneurship from an organizational and financial point of view.

Men and women have different motives when starting their businesses (Redmond et al., 2017). Men are more interested in earning money, while women are more motivated by schedule flexibility to balance work and family (Craig et al., 2012; Loscocco & Bird, 2012).

According to A. Elam et al. (2023), in 2022, globally, the share of women who initiated a startup was 10.1%, compared to 12.7% for men. In proportional terms, women represent approximately four out of every nine new business owners, representing 80% of the number of men who have initiated a business. In 2022, the global activity rate of startups in (TEA) for women was 10.4%, very close to that of 2021, showing a high degree of stability. Average startup activity rates for women vary significantly by country and regional income level. Thus, the highest female startup rates are found in countries with the lowest incomes (12%–13%). Also, they vary at the regional level. The lowest starting rates for women are found in Europe (6.1%). The gender differences are the biggest in Europe, the ratio between women and men being 0.73.

Denmark

Since 2009, the policymakers in Denmark are paying increased attention toward female entrepreneurship. As part of the multiple initiatives for entrepreneurship promotion, the Danish Enterprise and Construction Authority launched "Action Plan for Women Entrepreneurs." One of the initiatives in the action plan was the creation of a web platform for female entrepreneurs where women can find relevant information regarding business establishment and growth.

According to a recent survey, the need for a steady income as well as the lack of the right skills are the most important reasons why women in Denmark do not want to start a company.

Germany

According to the reports prepared by GEM, TEA increased in Germany, from 6.9% in 2021 to 9.1% in 2022; this is the highest level since 1999–2022, since GEM (IOM, 2013) has been doing analyses in Germany. Overall, Germany's growth is 1.8 percentage points above the global average. In the entire analyzed period, 2013–2022, women's entrepreneurial activity was below that of men. Thus, at the end of the period, in 2022, only 7.1% of companies were founded by women, a significantly lower percentage than that of men (11%).

In 2022, women's startup activity in Germany was 7.1%, with the ratio between women and men being in favor of men, namely 0.65 (Fig. 6.4). This situation is under the global women's startup activity, 10.1%.

Regarding the motivations of the total entrepreneurial activity in Germany in 2022, there are differences between men and women. Thus, analyzing Fig. 6.5, it

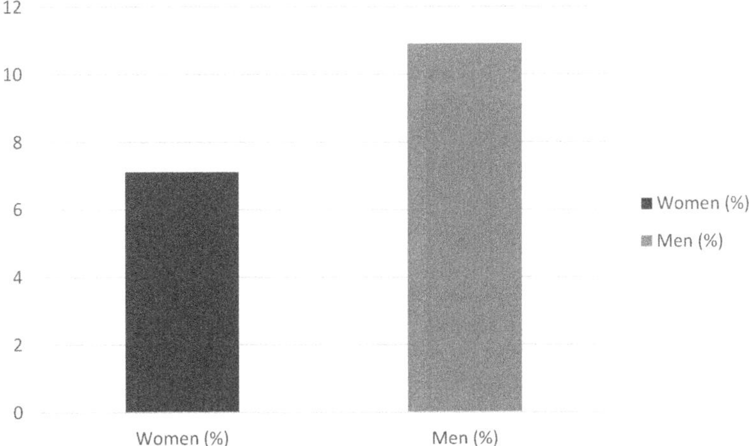

Fig. 6.4. Total Early-Stage Entrepreneurial Activity in Germany, 2022.
Source: Authors' own computations, based on GEM 2022/23 data.

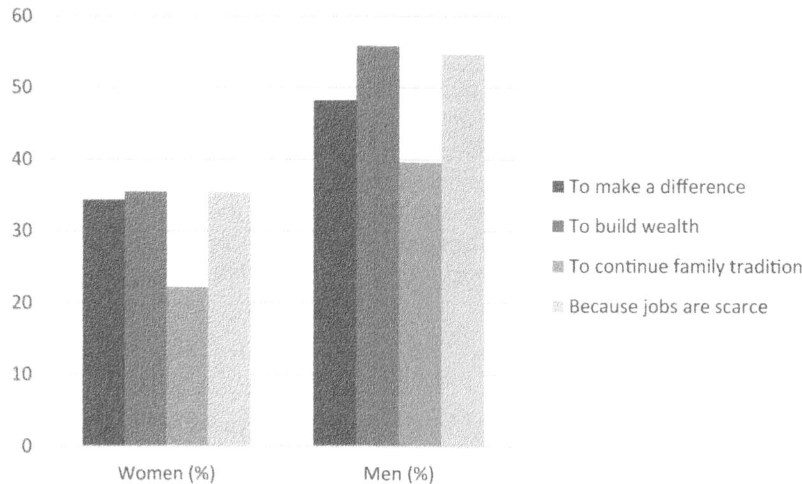

Fig. 6.5. Total Entrepreneurial Motivations, Gender Rates, Germany, 2022.
Source: Authors' own computations, based on GEM 2022/23 data.

is found that women are the least motivated by the desire to continue a family tradition; the other three factors considered, respectively, are to make a difference, to build well-being, and because the jobs available on the market are not enough, they are approximately at the same level.

In Germany, the image of the entrepreneur continues to be male dominated. This explains the difficult identification of women with this image and with entrepreneurship in general.

They rarely consider this possibility for their careers. Female entrepreneurs are an exception, and they often have a reputation as wonder women, what frightens lots of women.

Many women starting up a company have been inspired by female entrepreneurs in their direct environment, their family, and their circle of friends. They use less social networks than men (more strong ties than weak ties) and focus on women networks. There are insufficient incentives in Germany for female companies and raising the profile of such female entrepreneurial role models in order to stimulate the interest of other women in becoming entrepreneurs generally is recommended.

Female entrepreneurs often pursue different strategies and goals than their male counterparts. A high degree of transparency, consensus and team spirit are parts of their leadership. Women tend to place greater importance on independence, flexibility, and a good work–life balance. Female entrepreneurs often consider it important that their work also makes a social contribution. While their companies tend to grow slower than companies managed by men, their business policy demonstrates particular stability and risk awareness. Female entrepreneurs tend to show a higher acceptance for risks than female employees, but when compared to male entrepreneurs, they usually are more conservative in their actions, and they plan and act in longer terms. This is especially relevant in all questions of investment: Women tend to invest their own money as startup capital or to borrow money from friends and relatives rather than taking credits from a bank. Their business volumes and their growth in sale rates are smaller than the ones of their male counterparts. Success means for them to control their company, to satisfy their employees and customers, to have a serious reputation, and to offer good products or services.

Ireland

Ireland as a key source of innovation and new jobs, contributing, at the same time, to reducing income inequality and social exclusion.

According to the GEM 2019 report (Bosma et al., 2020), the rate of early-stage entrepreneurship in Ireland increased significantly in 2019. This was the effect of the increase in the rate at which both men and women were early-stage entrepreneurs, although the rate for men increased more strongly. The share of women who aspire to start a business is 15%, lower than that of men (23%).

Policymakers in Ireland have initiated a wide range of programs to encourage, support, and train women in both entrepreneurship and business management. They believe that the reasons why women are still under-represented in entrepreneurship are complex and interconnected, including factors such as an under-representation of women in senior management positions in industry, a greater fear of failure and risk aversion, design-oriented men of ecosystem supports, and the lack of visible patterns. To solve these problems, starting in 2013, they implemented specific measures aimed at women. These measures have resulted in a continued increase of the number of women setting up their businesses. Thus, if in 2012, only 8 out of 97 participating high-potential startups (HPSU) were led by women (8%), following the introduction of these measures, the share increased to 37% in 2022, when women ran 34 out of the 91 enterprises participating in the program.

Spain

Measured by number of employees, Spanish companies are characteristically small: 8 out of 10 companies have a maximum of two employees. Counting only companies with workers, 4.7% employ 20 or more people. The highest number of small businesses are concentrated in the services sector. By contrast, the lion's share of large companies is to be found in the industrial sector, where 7.7% have more than 20 employees.

Many Spanish companies are present on the international market in sectors related to infrastructure development, renewable energy, tourism, banking, textiles, healthcare and aerospace technology, the food industry, and the automotive industry. It ranks second worldwide in desalination and water treatment technologies. Five of the main European fashion companies are Spanish, including the world leader. Two of the key global financial institutions are Spanish, and two companies are among the leading insurers in their respective subsectors. This international activity necessarily entails international mobility of the workforce.

About 30% of Spanish businesses are started by women. The necessity to control their professional and personal lives leads women to become entrepreneurs. Courage, initiative, and perseverance to move forward with a project are the facts that define the Spanish woman entrepreneur.

The role of women in entrepreneurial activity increased slowly, but the benefits do not seem to follow the same trend. The female entrepreneur should ideally be brave, with a lot of initiative, perseverance, and tenacity and will to carry out the project. It is considered essential to have enthusiasm for the idea and willing to make your dream come true with professional energy and patience to accept setbacks without losing hope.

According to GEM 2022/23 data (A. Elam et al., 2023), the startup activity of women in Spain was low, with only 5.9% of women starting a new business. It should be noted that even in the case of men, Spain did not fare better, with only 6% of them involved in a new business (Fig. 6.6). Thus, from this perspective, the two sexes have no significant differences.

Starting a business because jobs are scarce is the main reason for both women and men in Spain in 2022, and continuing a family tradition is the least influential reason. Differences between the sexes appear in the desire to make a difference, which is more important than building wealth for women, unlike men who consider the opposite (Fig. 6.7).

In style of leadership, women entrepreneurs tend to be more collaborative than men, including situations where they have to receive suggestions from their employees. For them, the most important to create an enterprise quality is self-confidence and persistence in your project.

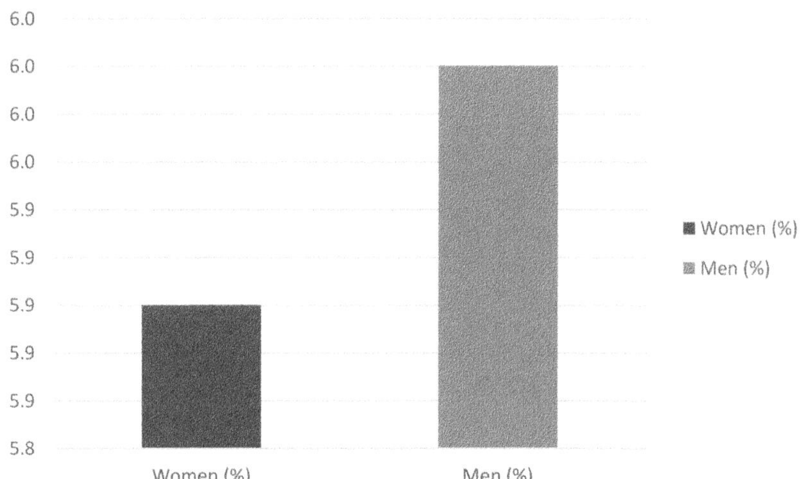

Fig. 6.6. Total Early-Stage Entrepreneurial Activity in Spain, 2022.
Source: Authors' own computations, based on GEM 2022/23 data.

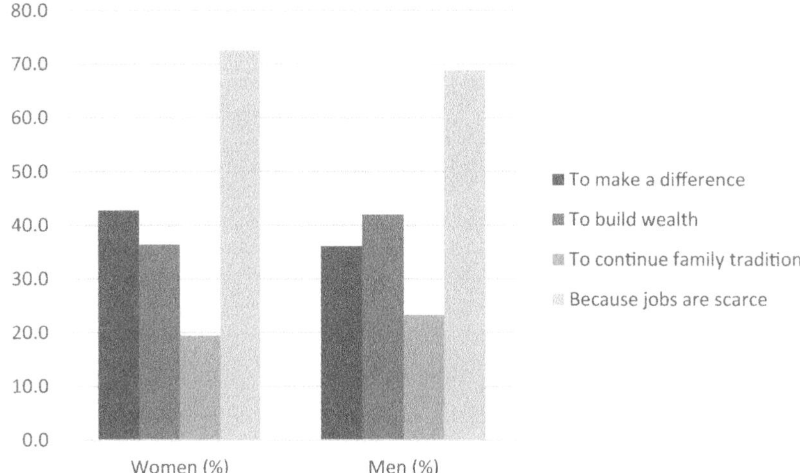

Fig. 6.7. Total Entrepreneurial Motivations, Gender Rates, Spain, 2022.
Source: Authors' own computations, based on GEM 2022/23 data.

Romania

In 2022, almost 600,000 women were shareholders or associates in companies active on the Romanian market, 11% above the level of 2019 and 46% more than in 2013. Thus, in 2021, approximately 20% of all local companies were controlled mainly by women. The turnover of these companies constitutes about 9% of the total in 2021.

The companies where Romanians work as shareholders or majority partners have, on average, three employees.

In 2021, Romania recorded the second-lowest gender pay gap in the EU, at a rate of only 3.6%.

According to data from the GEM 2020/21 Women's Entrepreneurship Report (A. B. Elam et al., 2021), 31.2% of management positions in Romania are occupied by women, a percentage above the global average (29%) but slightly below the European average of 37%. At the end of 2021, data from the Romanian National Trade Register Office showed that the number of female shareholders (or associates) in Romanian companies held a share of over 37% of the total shareholders/associates.

However, in 2022, the startup activity of women in Spain was relatively low, with only 6.6% of women starting a new business, significantly lower than the percentage of men, which was 10% (Fig. 6.8).

Regarding the motivation for starting a business in 2022 in Romania, the most influential reason is the desire to make a difference. The situation is similar to that in Spain and Germany for the least considered reason: the desire to continue a family tradition. There are differences between the two sexes regarding the other two reasons. Thus, women consider the lack of jobs more critical, unlike men, who consider it more important to build well-being (Fig. 6.9).

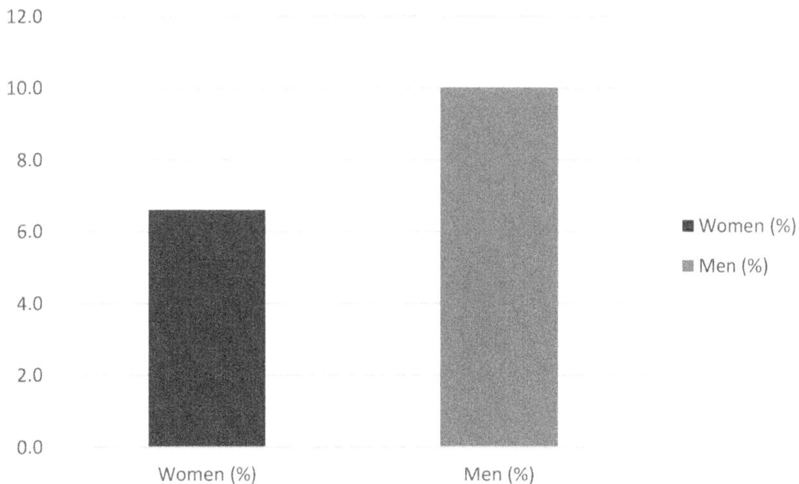

Fig. 6.8. Total Early-Stage Entrepreneurial Activity in Romania, 2022.
Source: Authors' own computations, based on GEM 2022/23 data.

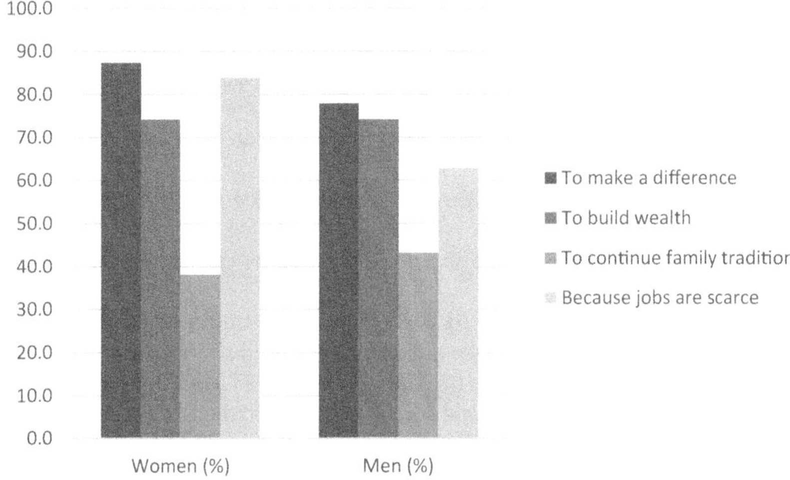

Fig. 6.9. Total Entrepreneurial Motivations, Gender Rates, Romania, 2022.
Source: Authors' own computations, based on GEM 2022/23 data.

Female Mentality with Regard to Work and Entrepreneurship

The concept which might seem a cliche in 2024, "economic sustainability," due to its frequently inadequate use (especially within public communication channel such as mass media), incorporates, in fact (if put in practice), the genuine opportunity to save not only certain labor markets sectors but also to contribute to the development of a series of socio-economic breach network.

Female self-employment, after the economic crisis (which has been resented from 2008) and the coronavirus pandemic crisis, may be an alternative solution which cannot be neglected, even if there are still considerable gender disparities as concerns the initiation of new business projects and business ownership: issues related to perceptions about gender equality in the field of entrepreneurship; issues related to the existence of certain gender disparities in the field of entrepreneurship; issues related to the characteristics, motivations, and difficulties of the women entrepreneurs and women potential entrepreneurs.

A series of research projects have been focused on the complex issue of the entrepreneurial characteristics (the profile of male/woman entrepreneur): self-control, emotional stability, self-confidence, sense of urgency, comprehensive awareness, conceptual ability, realism, capability to manage interpersonal relationships, commercial mindset, the courage to expose yourself to financially risk, the endurance to struggle in the competitive climate of a corporatist world, the possession of a certain "know-how" concerning the control over personal and other people finances, competences to deal with professional roles, the strength to face stress and adversity in order to be successful in overcoming obstacles, constructive communication and strategic planning, etc.

Some of these features are recognizable within the different profiles of the potential female entrepreneurs. Women have natural skills to work in a team, on the one hand, and to coordinate others' work, on the other hand. They are easily adaptable to environmental conditions and to develop networks, being good negotiators and decision-makers. Managing the demands of work and family is an ongoing challenge. Several empirical studies show that women experience more conflict between work and family than men, and that they have a greater motivation to balance both aspects. Since women are socially defined as family care providers, they are more likely than men to have strong negative sanctions for not fulfilling this role.

In 2008, a study in Romania included a profile of women entrepreneurs in Romania. According to this study, Romanian entrepreneur woman is:

- a very ambitious person;
- higher education, trained;
- devoted to her business;
- works more than 60 hours a week, very high resistance to effort;
- pretty perseverant, succeeding in overcoming the obstacles;
- independent (independence being the main motivation to start a business);
- the desire for self-improvement (lack of time is a barrier);
- not interested in participating in decision-making structures. It is worth noting that 81.8% of female entrepreneurs in Romania were married, and 77.8% were married with children (Eurochambers – The Association of European Chambers of Commerce and Industry, 2008).

As concerns the equality of chances between men and women in Romania, the modern mentality and the specific political, social, and cultural ideology allow women an open access to education, freedom of choice, freedom of expressing themselves, possibility to choose a wide range of professions, opportunities to access public positions, etc. It should be mentioned that, at the institutional level, gender equality is established in Romania. However, situations were identified in which certain differences in remuneration were noticed between women and men at the same qualification level. Also, we can still find companies that prefer to give men management positions more than women. At the same time, women are under-represented in business, especially in managerial positions or small entrepreneurs, and men still dominating this field.

There is almost an axiom that "creativity" is one of the main features of a future entrepreneur ("creative viewpoint," "creative perspective," and "creative aspirations" are syntagms widespread used). Creativity may be decoded in a broad meaning: inventiveness, pioneering spirit, thinking beyond the others, visionary approach, the ability of seeing the worth of taking measured risks, the gift of disseminating inspirational ideas, the instinct of seizing opportunities to optimize available resources, the so-called proactive search of new possibilities, problem-solving capacity, even the courage to stand up for your own feelings of autonomy and independence.

There have been developed theories and studies/case studies around the concept of creative mentality/creativity mindset.

The entrepreneurial mindset is not a common personality trait. The entrepreneur is willing to take risks, experiment with novelty, be creative, implement innovations, and work hard. The secret of success in entrepreneurship is not only in coming up with new ideas but rather in finding new opportunities where most people cannot do this. Moreover, the entrepreneur is able to find innovative solutions and prepare several scenarios from which to identify the optimal solution (Aslam Malik et al., 2022).

However, not only creativity stimulates women's decision to become an entrepreneur. This choice is stimulated, among others, by specific features, such as the desire to have access to an independent job and to ensure long-term financial stability for oneself.

More recent studies have highlighted several interrelated factors that stimulate the development of entrepreneurial activity among women: intention, psychological and social capital: social, psychological, and attitudinal factors all influence entrepreneurial intentions. Women entrepreneurs show a positive psychological state characterized by effectiveness, optimism, hope, and resilience. Also, they have substantial social capital, being very active in society. At the same time, they have optimistic entrepreneurial attitudes, and by being more pragmatic, they can better pursue their business objectives (Jalil et al., 2023).

The studies developed during the last decades (modernist studies of women entrepreneur/entrepreneurship) have emphasized approaches examining social (mentality, behavioral patterns, roles and stereotypes assigned by groups/community, the way women position themselves on the labor market/the way women are positioned within the business environment) and cultural determinants.

The real possibilities to increase women's entrepreneurship depend not only on individual/inner factors (such as, for example, the choice of becoming self-employed) but also on the situation of women in society and the role of entrepreneurship in that same society.

Female entrepreneurship must be viewed from a double perspective: the position of women in society and the role of entrepreneurship in society. In some countries, women are restricted from owning property and entering into contracts. The first step to improving the position of women in society is active participation in the labor market, followed by self-employment (OECD, 2004).

There are also some important external factors connected to the economic (i.e., labor market resources, access to financial resources), political, and institutional (i.e., family policy, female social protection system) framework which may influence (affect in some cases) women's decision to start a business on their own.

There has been a trend within different scientific domains to approach the social factors from the perspective of gender roles and hegemonic theory, starting from the existence of a social reality in many countries: there are still considerable gender disparities as concerns the initiation of new business projects and business ownership: issues related to perceptions about gender equality in the field of entrepreneurship, issues related to the existence of certain gender disparities in the field of entrepreneurship (the so-called gender gap in entrepreneurship).

The gender gap has been a permanent point on the labor market policy agenda, being also present in the documents stipulating the national strategies all over the world. In this respect, the issue was approached not only by the official papers, records provided by the European Commission, but also by studies and reports, different research projects or scientific conferences (2008).

The actual labor market is still segregated in either horizontal or vertical direction. The segregation of the labor market implies the fact that women and men typically work in different sectors or industries, while vertical gender segregation means that the men and women have different work functions. In conservative societies, the preconceived ideas that associate the two sexes with specific roles remain. Thus, the role of women in society is reduced to the family dimension. In this respect, Rubio-Bañón and Esteban-Lloret (2016) showed that the prevailing gender roles in a country determine the entrepreneurial behavior of its population and in particular, the differences between male and female entrepreneurship.

More recent scientific studies approaching the contemporary business environment suggest that the process of "importing" new ideas, theories, and strategies and implementing them into a new country/region should be complementary to adapting them to the values (social, cultural) context specific to that specific area. The influence of the cultural values upon the behavior and economic practices within the business environment and upon the prospects of that business environment is also emphasized.

There are significant differences as concerns the business culture characteristic to the European countries, differences which sometimes may be explained by aspects connected to the mentality and the cultural values.

From the moment when it first started to circulate among the scientific communities at a worldwide level a few decades ago, Geert Hofstede's cultural dimension theory has been applied to support the development of various research themes in domains from sociology, anthropology, to economy.

The cultural dimensions last brought up to date in 2000 (Hofstede, 2011) might function also for a theoretical attempt to identify-by comparison-cultural peculiarities which determine the entrepreneurial profile for distinct countries.

In Hofstede's framework (The 6-D Model of National Culture, n.d.), a 90% power distance value for Romania – compared to Denmark (18%), Germany (35%), Spain (57%), United Kingdom (35%), Ireland (28%) – may suggest a socio-cultural model which implies Romanians' more easily acceptance of the existence of leadership within groups, communities, and implicitly within the entire society (Fig. 6.10). With respect to a possible entrepreneurial profile emerging from this awareness of the necessity of certain hierarchies and transparent distribution of power roles, the percentage could be interpreted as a positive index in the sense that it might conduct to reaching a good rate of business success due to the fact that entrepreneurs/potential entrepreneurs, on the one hand, understand the importance of power division and assume themselves the

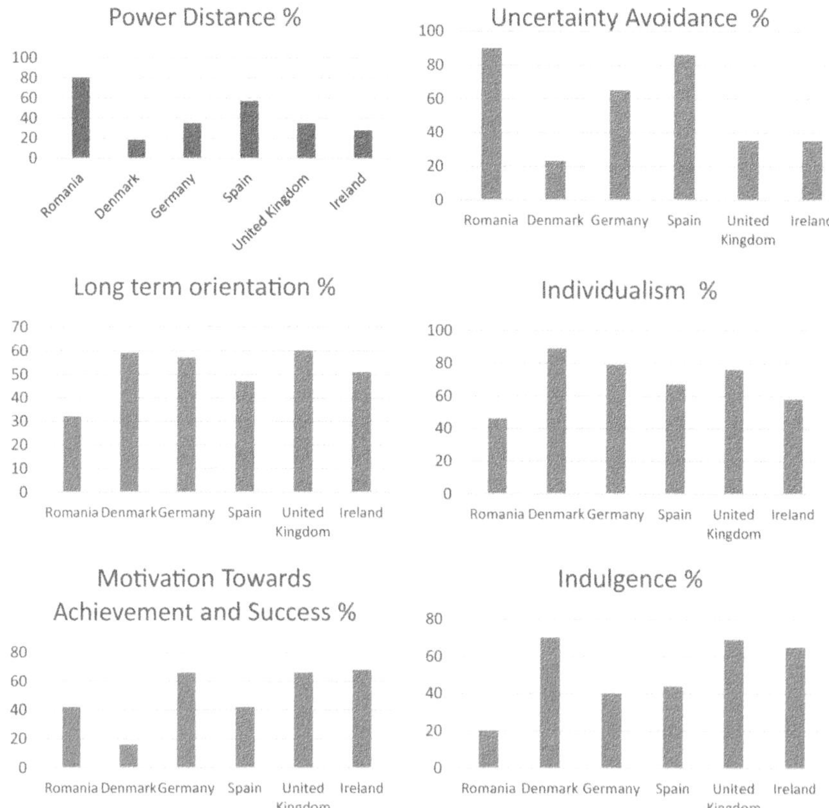

Fig. 6.10. Cultural Dimensions – Comparison Among Countries. *Source of the compared data*: https://www.hofstede-insights.com/country-comparison-tool

role of a leader within the company/firm and, on the other hand, the employed persons agree to the organizational chart, their secondary, subordinate role, and their inferior professional and financial position.

In terms of uncertainty avoidance, the high score obtained by Romania mirrors certain characteristics of Romanian economy realities and, subsequently, the Romanian entrepreneurial environment: the fact that, after over three decades from the transition to a socialist/communist economy to a capitalist one, there still exists a struggle to insert and stabilize practices, there is still need of good economic strategies, there is still uncertainty, and labor market still provides anxiety and distrust to people. Of course, it may also reflect certain remnants from the economic crisis period at a mental level.

Regarding entrepreneurial initiatives, the tendency for "fixed customs and rituals" shows people's need to feel secure with money and jobs. This behaviour can lead to a lower involvement in risky economic activities.

Following a logical mental scheme, Romania's 30% result, indicating "a short-time-oriented culture" emphasizes a possible interconnection with the highest point obtained for uncertainty avoidance. Adhering in a good measure to past values and manifesting less affinity with change, with accessing a more dynamic projection of life, "in flux and preparing for the future" (according to the findings of Hofstede's country comparison tool), Romanian entrepreneurial environment could be prejudiced (as entrepreneurship is almost a synonym to innovation, novelty).

The lowest Romania's percentage associated with individualism versus collectivism may be interpreted not necessarily as the reflection of a cultural mentality specific to Romanian people or the manifestation of Romanians – as a nation-psychological profile but rather as a remnant of the communist economic system in which "individual choices and decisions" were hardly accepted and valued; collectivism, working in collectivity, collective labor, collective ownership of the means of production, omogenity in thinking, and behaving were agreed instead. This means that entrepreneurial proposals or attempts in Romania could be influenced in a negative manner.

Similar to Spain, Romania's chart shows a quite low score (however not the lowest, which is the Denmark case). A study initiated and developed by CEBR (Centre for Entrepreneurship & Business Research, a consulting and business research company) in 2007, on a target group of 1449 people, identified the factors considered the most motivating for starting a new business. In the first place is the desire to increase family income and financial independence. Then follows the desire to achieve a higher social status, respect and success in business. Besides these, the existence of models and examples can constitute, in turn, motivating factors (Lafuente & Driga, 2007). From this point of view, social construction of different profiles of entrepreneur women-social stereotypes reflected in the public space (e.g., contemporary media expended to the virtual space/cybernetic space) and the so-called "entrepreneur-mentality" (Bruni et al., 2004) may have a positive or a negative impact on women decision to access the idea of launching their own business. The term "entrepreneur-mentality" (entrepreneurial mindset) has been introduced quite recently

> to signal the existence of a discourse on the art of being an entrepreneur and the nature of entrepreneurial practice. An entrepreneur-mentality is constructed through the discursive practices of entrepreneurs, the media that represent their achievements, and the scientific texts that expound theories of entrepreneurship, and in turn itself serves as the plot and set of constraints on entrepreneurial action and discourse.

The lowest percentage on the graph configuring a restrained culture points out a reduced sense of freedom and also a less optimistic image on life in general. After 1989, Romania placed itself (politically, economically, and socio-culturally) in a new paradigm in which freedom of choice, freedom of speaking, or expressing yourself is considered one of the most valuable and valued existence dimensions. According to World Happiness Report for 2023, Romania is ranked in the 24th position, being far behind Denmark (2nd position), Ireland (14th position), Germany (16th position), Great Britain (19th position), but higher on the ratings' list than Spain and Italy (Helliwell et al., 2023).

Conclusion

Women are under-represented as business owners or self-employed compared with men. Parenthood especially affects women's employment given that women are more often involved in childcare duties when care services are lacking or not meeting the needs of – full-time – working parents.

Programs aimed at stimulating entrepreneurial activity among women must take into account the social and cultural challenges of women and be based on their needs to mix career and family. Another important factor is strengthening women's business knowledge, equipping them with entrepreneurial skills and helping them expand their network. The research also shows that working to enhance self-confidence is an important issue, considering the characteristics of women entrepreneurs in the countries analyzed.

The entrepreneurial issues have been dealt from a binary perspective for a few decades due to the fact that gender gap still represents a reality on the labor market, and there may be still noticed concerning the female/male entrepreneurship patterns (conditioned by economic, socio-cultural, political, and also psychological determining factors).

However, researchers affiliated to different scientific domains have started to embrace, in more recent studies and articles a "gender neutral" approach, appropriated to the projections and aspirations of the contemporary societies.

References

Aiginger, K., & Guger, A. (2005). Model : From obstruction to advantage. *Journal of Progressive Politics*, *4*(3), 40–47.

Aiginger, K., & Leoni, T. (2009). *Typologies of social models in Europe* (pp. 1–27). Institute of Economic Research WIFO.

Alessandrin, M., Valenza, A., Gramillano, A., Zingaretti, C., Zillmer, S., Holsteln, F., & Salvatori, G. (2019). *EU policy framework on SMEs: State of play and challenges*. Commission for Economic Policy.European Committee of the Regions. https://doi.org/10.2863/612657

Ascher, J. (2012). Female entrepreneurship – An appropriate response to gender discrimination. *Journal of Entrepreneurship, Management and Innovation (JEMI)*, *8*(4), 97–114. http://ssrn.com/abstract=2203475

Aslam Malik, R., Batool, H., & Afzal, M. (2022). Determinants of women entrepreneurship mindset in achieving sustainable development: A case study of Lahore, Pakistan. *Journal of Positive School Psychology*, *2022*(12), 1665–1688. http://journalppw.com

Barreto, M., Ryan, M., & Schmitt, M. (2009). The glass ceiling in the 21st century: Understanding barriers to gender equality. https://psycnet.apa.org/books/TOC/11863

Bastida, M. (2021, May). *Women's entrepreneurship and self-employment, including aspects of gendered corporate social responsibility* (p. 88). European Parliament's Committee on Women's Rights and Gender Equality. http://www.europarl.europa.eu/supporting-analyses

Bosma, N., Hill, S., Ionescu-Somers, A., Kelly, D., Levie, J., & Tarnawa, A. (2020). Global Entrepreneurship Monitor 2019/2020: Global report. https://www.gemconsortium.org/report/gem-20202021-global-report

Bruni, A., Gherardi, S., & Poggio, B. (2004). Entrepreneur-mentality, gender and the study of women entrepreneurs. *Journal of Organizational Change Management*, *17*(3), 257. https://doi.org/10.1108/09534810410538315

Burke, R. J. (2009). Cultural values and women's work and career experiences. In R. S. Bhagat & R. M. Steers (Eds.), *Cambridge handbook of culture, organizations, and work* (pp. 442–461). Cambridge University Press.

Cardella, G. M., Hernández-Sánchez, B. R., & Sánchez-García, J. C. (2020). Women entrepreneurship: A systematic review to outline the boundaries of scientific literature. *Frontiers in Psychology*, *11*, 536630. https://doi.org/10.3389/fpsyg.2020.01557

Craig, L., Abigail, P., & Cortis, N. (2012). Self-employment, work-family time and the gender division of labour. *Work, Employment and Society*, *26*(5), 716–734. https://doi.org/10.1177/095001701245164

Dawson, C., & Henley, A. (2015). Gender, risk, and venture creation intentions. *Journal of Small Business Management*, *53*(2), 501–515. https://doi.org/10.1111/JSBM.12080

Desvaux, G., Devillard, S., Zelicourt, A., Kossoff, C., Labaye, E., & Sancier-Sultan, S. (2017). Time to accelerate – Ten years of insights on gender diversity. *Women Matter*, October, p. 84. https://www.mckinsey.com/featured-insights/gender-equality/women-matter-ten-years-of-insights-on-gender-diversity

Doherty, E. G., & Eagly, A. H. (1989). Sex differences in social behavior: A social-role interpretation. *Contemporary Sociology*, *18*(3). https://doi.org/10.2307/2073813

Elam, A. B., Hughes, K. D., Guerrero, M., Hill, S., Nawangpalupi, C., Fuentes, M. del M., González, J. P. D., Laviada, A. F., Martínez, C. N., Rubio Bañón, A., Chabrak, N., Brush, C., & Heavlow, R. (2021). *Women's entrepreneurship 2020/21*. https://www.gemconsortium.org/report/gem-202021-womens-entrepreneurship-report-thriving-through-crisis

Elam, A., Hughes, K. D., Samsami, M., Boutaleb, F., Guerrero, M., Meyer, N., Mohamed Alshukaili, A., & Guelich, U. (2023). *GEM 2022/23 women's entrepreneurship report: Challenging bias and stereotypes*. https://gemconsortium.org/report/20222023-global-entrepreneurship-monitor-global-report-adapting-to-a-new-normal-2

Eurochambers – The Association of European Chambers of Commerce and Industry. (2008). *Women in business and decision*. http://centru.cempres.ro/femeia si antreprenoriatul/

index.php/component/k2/item/50-antreprenoriatul-feminin-in-romania#/femeia si antreprenoriatul/in.php/compo

European Commission. (2008). No title. http://ec.europa.eu/enterprise/policies/sme/promoting-entrepreneurship/women/index

European Commission Directorate-General for Justice. (2014). *Women and men in leadership positions in the European Union, 2013: A review of the situation and recent progress*. https://doi.org/10.2838/50821

Grilo, I., & Thurik, R. (2004). *Determinants of entrepreneurship in Europe*. Erasmus Research Institute of Management Report Series.

Guger, A., Leoni, T., & Walterskirchen, E. (2007). European socio-economic models : Experiences and reform perspectives. *Society*. http://www.euroframe.org/fileadmin/user_upload/euroframe/efn/autumn2007/Annex3_WIFO.pdf

Helliwell, J. F., Layard, R., & Sachs, J. D. (2023). *The happiness agenda: The next 10 years*. World Happiness Report.

Hofstede, G. (1984). *Culture's consequences: International differences in work-related values* (Vol. 5). Sage.

Hofstede, G. (2011). Dimensionalizing cultures. *Online Readings in Psychology and Culture, 2*(1), 1–26. https://doi.org/10.9707/2307-0919.1014

IOM. (2013). *Improving access to labour market information for migrants and employers*. http://ec.europa.eu/social/BlobServlet?docId=9926&langId=en%0Apapers3://publication/uuid/5670AC7B-F784-443E-A2AE-949A9CAA33C3

Jalil, M. F., Ali, A., & Kamarulzaman, R. (2023). The influence of psychological capital and social capital on women entrepreneurs' intentions: The mediating role of attitude. *Humanities and Social Sciences Communications, 10*(1), 1–14. https://doi.org/10.1057/s41599-023-01908-3

Lafuente, E., & Driga, O. (2007). *1st report on entrepreneurial activities in Romania*. Centre for Entrepreneurship & Business Research (Issue December).

Langowitz, N., & Minniti, M. (2007). The entrepreneurial propensity of women. *Entrepreneurship Theory and Practice, 31*(3), 341–364. https://doi.org/10.1111/J.1540-6520.2007.00177.X

Loscocco, K., & Bird, S. R. (2012). Gendered paths: Why women lag behind men in small business success. *Work and Occupations, 39*(2), 183–219. https://doi.org/10.1177/07308884124442

Mastercard. (2022). *The Mastercard index of women entrepreneurs*. Mastercard. https://www.mastercard.com/news/media/phwevxcc/the-mastercard-index-of-women-entrepreneurs.pdf

Minniti, M., & Arenius, P. (2003). *Women in entrepreneurship*. https://www.researchgate.net/publication/230681247

OECD. (2004). *INAG economy: Women's entrepreneurship: Issues and policies*. OECD.

OECD. (2023). *Joining forces for gender equality*. OECD. https://doi.org/10.1787/67d48024-en

Redmond, J., Walker, E. A., & Hutchinson, J. (2017). Self-employment: Is it a long-term financial strategy for women? *Equality, Diversity and Inclusion: An International Journal, 36*(4), 362–375.

Rembulan, C. L., Ratna Indudewi, F. Y., & Rahmawati, K. D. (2016). View of work-family conflict of women entrepreneurs and women employees. *Anima Indonesian Psychological Journal, 31*(3), 111–113. https://journal.ubaya.ac.id/index.php/jpa/article/view/Work Family Conflict/428

Rubio-Bañón, A., & Esteban-Lloret, N. (2016). Cultural factors and gender role in female entrepreneurship. *Suma de Negocios, 7*(15), 9–17. https://doi.org/10.1016/j.sumneg.2015.12.002

Sullivan, D. M., & Meek, W. R. (2012). Gender and entrepreneurship: A review and process model. *Journal of Managerial Psychology*, *27*(5). https://doi.org/10.1108/02683941211235373

The 6-D Model of National Culture. (n.d.). geerthofstede.com/culture-geert-hofstede-gert-jan-fostede/6D-model-of-national-culture

World Economic Forum. (2023). Insight report. *World Economic Forum*, Issue June. https://www3.weforum.org/docs/WEF_GGGR_2023.pdf

Chapter 7

Patterns and Trends in Developing Green Energy Paradigms

Răzvan Vasile[a] *and Adriana Grigorescu*[a,b,c]

[a]*National Institute for Economic Research "Costin C. Kiritescu" – Romanian Academy, Romania*
[b]*National University of Political Studies and Public Administration, Romania*
[c]*Academy of Romanian Scientists, Bucharest, Romania*

Abstract

The global economy has been subjected to systemic shocks that have disrupted the global energy transition strategy. A paradigm of shifting in address the issue of green energy in a multidimensional context is facing now. This work aims to highlight the experts' opinions regarding energy management in the context of sustainable development approaches and the extent to which the strategic orientation toward green energy and the energy transition can be considered as economic, social, and environmental efficiency objectives. Based on the specialized literature found in the Web of Science (WoS) database, a qualitative analysis was performed to identify the development directions of the economic policies, emphasizing the specific aspects of the transition to green energy. The findings reveal that specialists, through scientific research carried out in the various fields of science, can offer solutions and identify risks in the development, but the essential role remains for decision-makers, responsible for maintaining the balance between expectations and possibilities in building policies that facilitate a sustainable energy transition, for the benefit of all.

Keywords: Green energy; patterns; trends; paradigms; bibliometric analysis

Emerging Patterns and Behaviors in a Green Resilient Economy, 153–168

doi:10.1108/978-1-83549-780-720241008

Introduction

The topic of energy has aroused the interest of experts from different fields of science for centuries, but in the last decades, the discourse of problems associated with existence as a natural source, production as a consumer good, or as a factor of production has been increasingly associated with the principles of sustainable development. Moreover, the typology of energy forms, economic efficiency, social impact, and energy transition were concerns of economic experts and politicians. In fact, we are facing a paradigm shift in addressing the issue of green energy in a multidimensional context – resource scarcity, the economic efficiency of the production of different energy sources, the optimal use of energy as a factor of production, the cost of energy as a consumer product, energy inclusion, externalities on sustainable development is in place now. Moreover, energy availability has become an important factor of national security, energy independence, and the globalized energy market, representing topics of debate for experts and politicians.

This work aims to highlight the concerns of experts regarding energy management in the context of sustainable development approaches and the extent to which the strategic orientation toward green energy and the energy transition can be considered as objectives of economic, social, and environmental efficiency. Based on the specialized literature found in the WoS database, it was performed a scientometric analysis to identify the development directions of the economic policies incident to the exploitation and management of the effects of energy use, with an emphasis on the specific aspects of the transition to green energy.

Method and Database

In the bibliometric research, it was analyzed the temporal distribution of the publications from the WoS database, the structure of the publications selected by keywords, fields of science, countries where the works were published, and structure by the Sustainable Development Goals (SDGs) theme. A clustering of the areas of interest will allow us to identify the changes in strategic orientation for better adequacy of the management of the green energy issue in the context of the medium- and long-term effects generated by the recent turbulences in the business environment, as a result of the increase in regional insecurity, and of the redefinition of policies for intelligent management of the effects of energy use on the environment and quality of life.

The data extracted from WoS concern the entire indexing period of the publications, with an emphasis on works published in recent years, using the "topic" and "all fields" search alternatives. The bibliometric processing will be done with the VOSviewer software. Similar articles will also be taken into account, which analyze from a bibliometric perspective the various aspects related to the topic of energy. Our approach is to complete the specialized literature with the bibliometric analysis of the binomial green energy – sustainable development, as an important component of the green transition.

A Historical Approach to Energy and Energy Transition Research in the Context of Sustainable Development

The research on energy is extremely vast; it includes all fields of science, from the identification of energy resources and its characteristics, from specific technologies for the extraction of energy resources and energy production, in its various forms, to economic aspects (such as energy efficiency, cost, price, and market) and social (access, affordability, etc.) to effects on the environment (changing the geographical landscape or changing ecosystems, pollution, etc.), on the work and life model of individuals, households, the business environment, and the community. A simple query of the topic "energy" only in the WoS database shows us about 4.4 million works carried out between 1975 and now, with over 100,000 scientific works annually, after 2007. If we only refer to the topic "green energy," the number of scientific works is about 9,200 works, since 1980, with about 500 works per year in the years 2017–2020 and over 1,000 after 2021. For "energy transition," it was find almost 11,500 works starting a little earlier, respectively from 1976, with an accentuation of the concerns of specialists after 2017 and especially in the last two years (44% of works were published in the period 2022–2024 – January).

Regarding the "sustainable development" topic, we find about 145,000 works in WoS, the distribution by year being associated, of course, with the evolution of environmental policy, respectively, with the UN Brundland Commission Report (UN-WCED, 1987). Defining for the first time the concept of sustainable development is also associated with several challenges, namely resources (human, energy, species, and ecosystems), production (efficient industrial development and food security), urbanization, and international cooperation. With regard to energy, it is worth noting that, on the classic theme of the analysis of fossil resources, the exploitation of forests, and nuclear energy, the problem of renewable energy as "the untapped potential" was raised, but the assurance of energy efficiency and energy conservation was also included as challenges.

Suppose we also associate "sustainability" from the perspective of the mechanisms for ensuring sustainable development and managing the effects. In that case, the number of works increased to 420,000, especially after the crisis of 2009 (with over 10,000 works per year), and in 2022–2023 with over 50,000.

Natural resources available to produce energy such as fossil, mineral, forest, are limited in time, while renewable resources as water, solar, wind, geothermal, biomass, are having geographical and climatic distribution and limits. That is why when we refer to green energy (or clean), it is primarily associated with the technologies used for energy production in the context of the principles of sustainable development, namely with the reduction of greenhouse gas emissions, the improvement of energy security, and the provision of access to energy. Not just any renewable energy is also green, and not every energy source is clean, respectively, the burning of organic materials, mining, or drilling operations produce not only CO_2 emissions but also the destruction or damage of ecosystems. Therefore, the issue of energy in the context of sustainable development is approached by experts in a complex, inter-, and multidisciplinary way, and hence, a significant number of works is carried out by experts.

An analysis of the temporal distribution of publications on energy and sustainable development shows us an evolution closely related to the dynamics of specific technologies and the concerns of experts related in particular to the effects on the environment and economic-social development in general. (Fig. 7.1).

After the financial crisis of 2009, the concerns for the analysis of solutions to solve the energy crisis were focused on the diversification of energy sources, with an emphasis on renewable energy, and the accentuation of the effects of pollution on the environment intensified the political discourse and experts analyzes regarding the energy transition with respect principles of sustainable development Fig. 7.1. It is also worth noting that the risks associated with climate change, the failure to comply with international commitments regarding pollution (the Paris Agreement), and the need to ensure energy independence, as a security factor (after the outbreak of the Russian-Ukrainian conflict), require redefining/ correcting directions and the content of the energy transition.

The scenarios for reaching the net zero objective, the concerns for the generation and use of more expensive green energy, as well as the technological and financial restrictions call into question the applicability of the established scenarios, the uncertainty being accentuated by geopolitical insecurity, the deceleration of economic development, and the weak resilience of investments in energy resources. On the one hand, decarbonization and the need to redefine expectations regarding economic return and, on the other hand, the different potential of countries to generate green energy and to manage the negative externalities from energy production and consumption, according to the current model, are

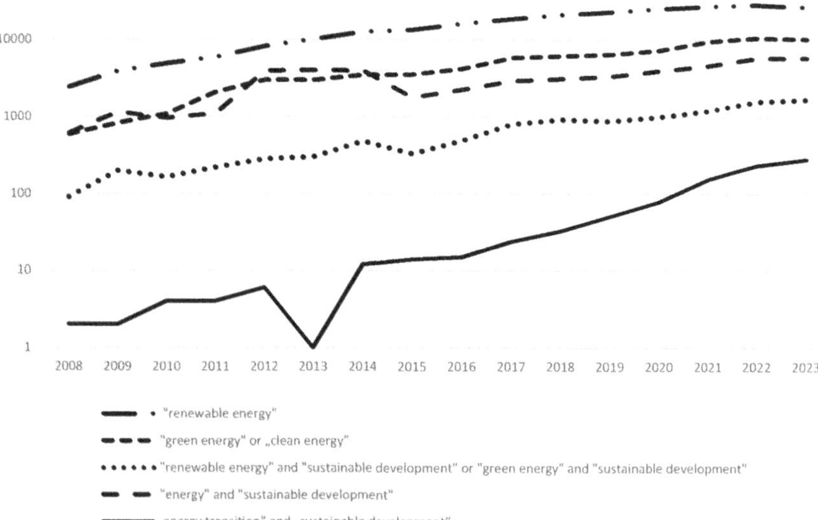

Fig. 7.1. Annual Distribution of Works Published in WoS, Bibliometric Query Based on the Keywords Energy and Sustainable Development. *Source*: Data extracted from WoS, February 1, 2024.

increasingly necessary to rethink the development strategy of green companies, based on power mix.

Practically, in recent years, it was witnessed global energy landscape transformation, bottom-up, with the tripling of the demand for sustainable fuels demand until 2050 (McKinsey & Company, 2023).

Recent Developments Related to the Issue of Energy, Respectively Green Energy

In the last decades, works on green energy increasingly take into account, on the one hand, the impact on the environment, in all its aspects, but also, on the other hand, the creation of a culture of energy use and the acceptance by economic agents of the principle total profit. That means considering the combination of economic efficiency on the value chain (from the production and use of energy but also of associated waste) with social efficiency (inclusion, at least on the components of accessibility and affordability), to which is added the energy management culture (responsibility in consumption, wise investment based on the cost–benefit ratio in the medium and long terms).

In recent years, the global economy has been subjected to a series of systemic shocks that have disrupted the global energy transition strategy and efforts to manage the effects of pollution, climate change, and externalities generated by increased energy consumption in all its forms. Energy efficiency and saving have become topics of debate and have been found in public, regional, national, and local strategies and policies. Similarly, monitoring the implementation of the SDGs, and especially Goal 7 – "affordable and clean energy," has intensified the concerns of decision-makers to achieve the assumed objectives – the diversification of clean energy sources, the price of energy, responsibility in consumption, and the reduction of negative effects.

However, during the pandemic, the global energy demand has reduced, and the immediate adverse effects on the environment from energy consumption have been highlighted. The trend of a faster transition to the use of green energy in the post-pandemic has been reconsidered from another perspective, namely geopolitical security and the need to reduce the state's dependence on Russia's energy sources. Russia's invasion of Ukraine and the policy of conditioning access to its energy resources forced the energy-dependent states to reconsider their options in this direction, redefining "a new normal" in their energy development and consumption strategies. The positions of the leading players in the globalized energy market have been redefined. Just as the pandemic hastened the digital transition, the conflict in Ukraine redefined the energy transition but in a double sense. On the one hand, the need for energy independence from Russia's resources has slowed down the process of decarbonizing the economy and liquidating fossil fuel exploitations. On the other hand, the state's potential for accelerating the transition to alternative energy sources was reanalyzed. Moreover, the deceleration of efforts to reduce gas emissions from energy consumption has redefined the importance of increasing the share of clean energy in total energy resources, to counterbalance the impossibility, in the short and medium terms, of reducing CO_2 emissions from energy production and consumption.

The effects of the energy transition are found not only in the specific production sector but, in particular, are distributed in different proportions in all human activities, generating significant changes in infrastructure, economy, and international relations, having the potential to redefine the model in which society produces and consumes energy. Thus, the need to accelerate the transition from fossil fuels to renewable sources is undoubtedly the driver of the paradigm shift in how the energy sector and society approach its energy needs.

The previous clarifications led us to the selection for a detailed bibliometric analysis of two groups of keywords, namely (a) renewable or green energy in association with sustainable development and (b) energy transition and sustainable development.

Renewable Energy and Sustainable Development or Green Energy and Sustainable Development

Although as it was previously mentioned the differences between alternative sources of energy and green energy, in our analysis, it was associated the two concepts because, in the last decades, the discourse of providing energy for development included them as a strategic alternative to the use of fossil fuel, polluting, and limited resources.

Querying the WoS database (all fields) identified almost 11,300 scientific papers, with about 400 of increased interest for the scientific community being the most cited.

These works are incidental to almost all SDGs (16 out of the 17), but they focus on Goals 7 and 13, respectively, 61% of the publications (Fig. 7.2).

The first 10 countries of authors' institutional affiliation are China, India, United States, United Kingdom, Pakistan, Italy, Turkey, Australia, Malaysia, and Poland. Germany ranks 11th and Japan 15th. It can be seen that most of them

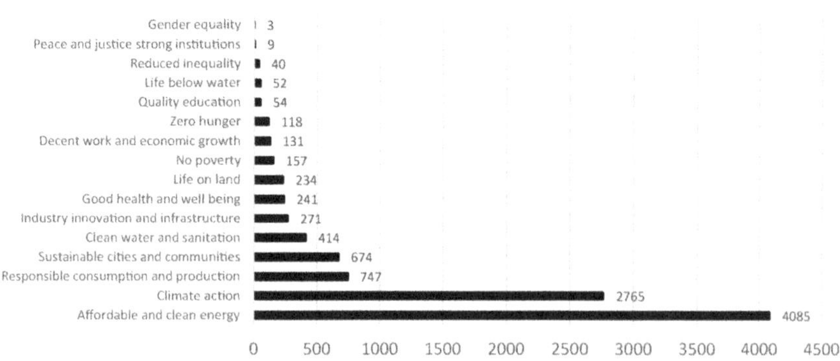

Fig. 7.2. Theme of the Works Published in WoS Regarding Renewable Energy or Green Energy and Sustainable Development, According to the 17 SDGs. *Source*: Database extraction from WoS, February 1, 2024.

are developed countries, with very good institutions in university education or research activities but also with environmental problems. Romania is on the 19th place, and other European Union (EU) countries found in the list of the first 30 are Spain, France, Sweden, and Greece (Fig. 7.3).

The scientometric analysis indicates four important sub-thematic clusters (Fig. 7.4):

The first important cluster (the green one) stands out as the one that considers the analysis of renewable energy, with the determinative chain from sustainable development and renewable energy to sustainability, electricity, and policy.

Closely related to this is the red cluster, which considers optimization technologies and systems in the production and consumption of energy, the chain starting from performance optimization and system, followed by technologies and models.

The blue cluster includes environmental issues, namely the link between energy, biomass, and hydrogen as renewable sources of interest and up to the effects on the environment – emissions – and highlights the issue of the circular economy.

The yellow cluster associates research that focuses on the economic and financial sphere, on the impact of CO_2 emissions, and the consumption model.

By research areas, have been identified a concentration on four technical fields – energy fuels, science technology and other topics, environmental sciences and ecology, and engineering being followed by papers in business economics (Fig. 7.5).

Energy Transition and Sustainable Development

In the case of limiting the research area to the keywords energy transition and sustainable development, the number of papers falls below 1,000, which are distributed on research areas and also on the first five subfields previously identified,

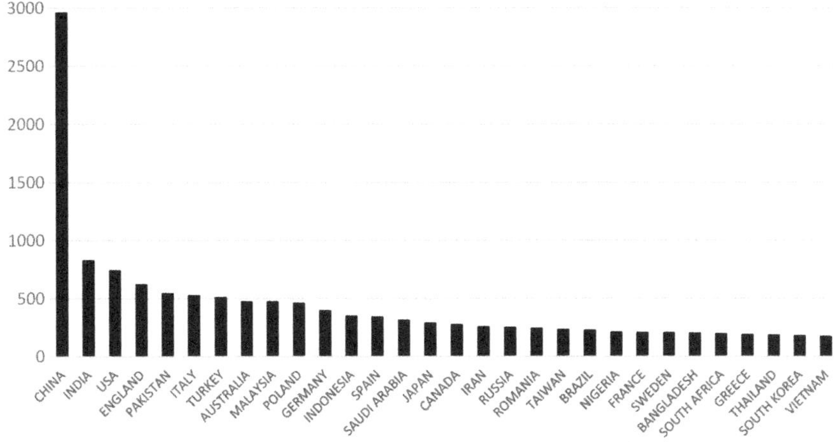

Fig. 7.3. The First 30 Countries That Support, Through Their Staff, the Scientific Publications Indexed in WoS, the Dissemination of Research on Renewable Energy, and Green Energy in the Context of Sustainable Development. *Source*: Database extraction from WoS, February 1, 2024.

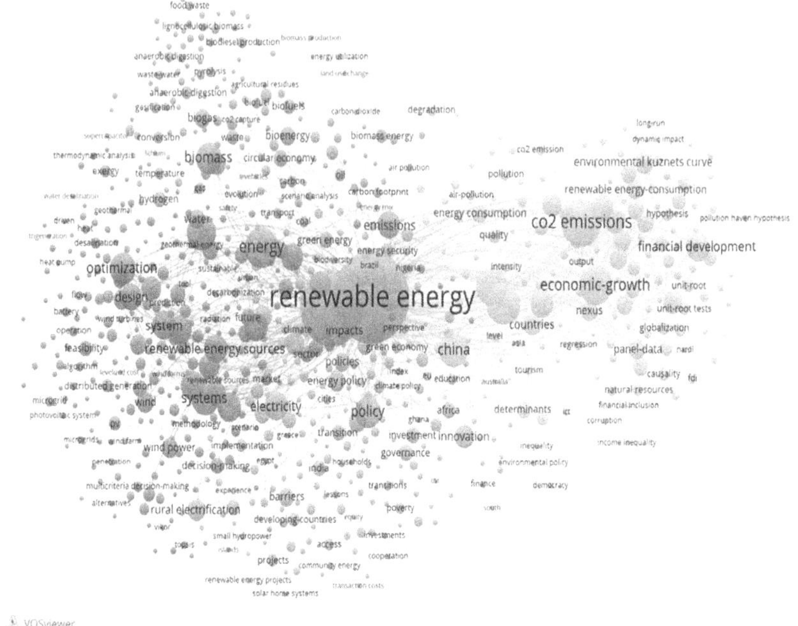

Fig. 7.4. Thematic Distribution of Works Published in WoS Based on the Keywords Renewable Energy or Green Energy and Sustainable Development. *Source*: Database extraction from WoS, February 1, 2024, VOSviewer (with 15).

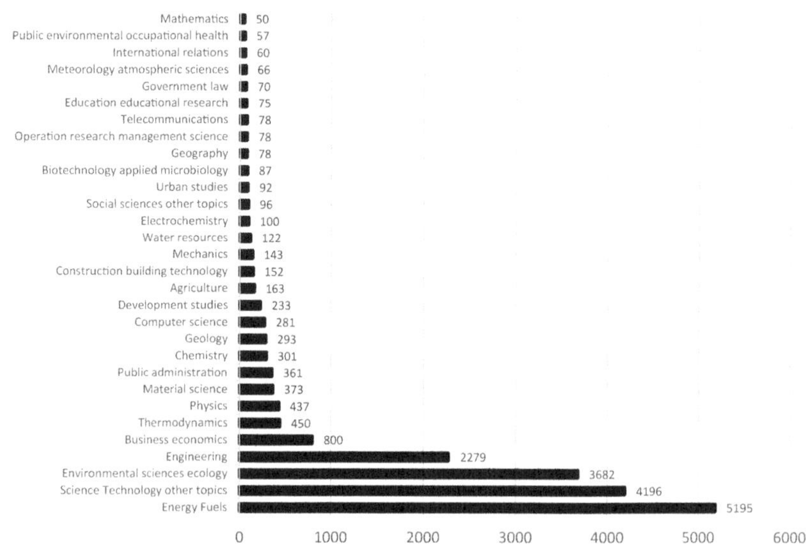

Fig. 7.5. Papers Published, By Research Areas. *Source*: Database extraction from WoS, February 1, 2024.

with the mention that about 80% of them were published during the last three years (2021–2023).

The addressability of the SDGs is narrower, namely Objectives 7 and 13 are targeted, followed by Objectives 11 and 12, respectively, targeting accessibility, climate effects, local sustainability, and responsible consumption. It is worth noting that SDG 1 is in the fifth place and SDG 3 is in the seventh place, which highlights the concerns about citizens' quality of life (Fig. 7.6).

The same strongly asymmetric distribution on the left is also found among the countries, but this time, after China, which is once again in the first place, there are mainly developed countries from the EU, respectively, 7 of the first 10 places are held by Germany, the United Kingdom, Poland, France, Italy, Netherlands, and Spain (Fig. 7.7).

About 42% of the works were published in journals with Elsevier as publisher and 8% belonging to Springer Nature.

The thematic cluster analysis of the links between the keywords indicates a thematic distribution close to the previously identified link chains but with a higher frequency of the first three clusters: (a) the red one, with sustainable development – energy – climate change – technologies – electricity; (b) the green one, with energy transition – renewable energy – sustainability – SDGs – policy; and (c) the blue one, focused on economic aspects and impact measured by pollution factors, respectively, consumption – economic growth – impact – CO_2 emissions – emissions. The last cluster, the yellow one, considers the technological side and innovation to facilitate the energy transition and comply with the requirements of sustainable development (Fig. 7.8).

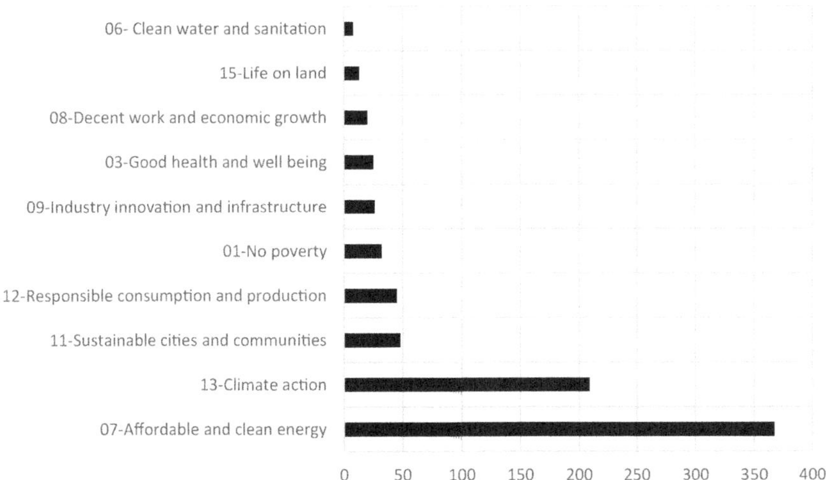

Fig. 7.6. The First 10 SDGs Considered in the Research Published in WoS Regarding the Energy Transition in the Context of Sustainable Development. *Source*: Database extraction from WoS, February 1, 2024.

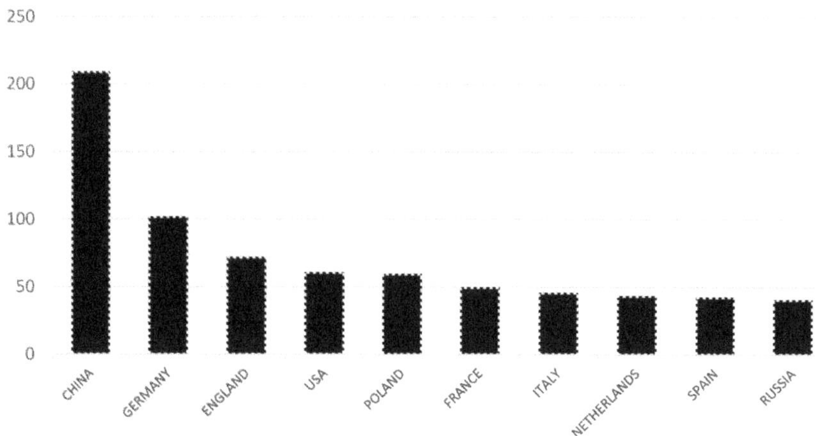

Fig. 7.7. Articles Published in WoS Magazines, According to the Country of the Author's Affiliation. *Source*: Database extraction from WoS, February 1, 2024.

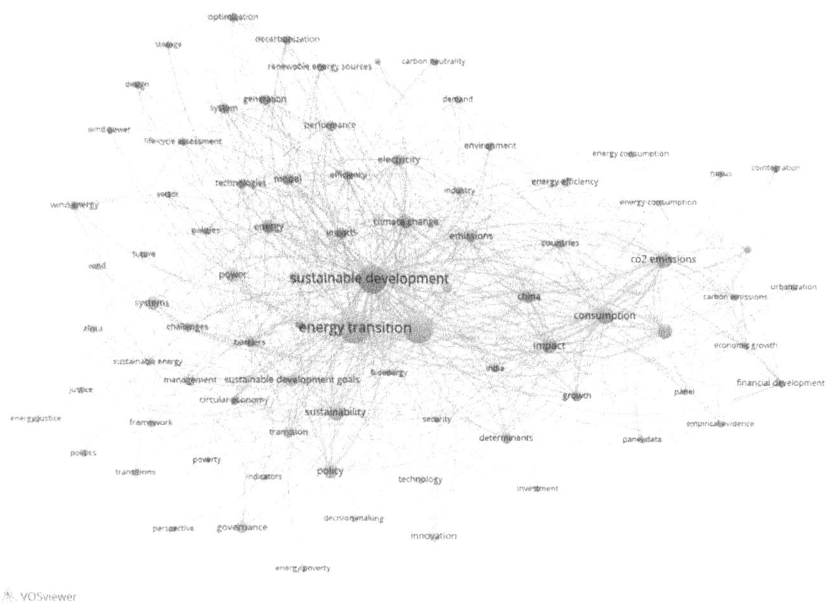

Fig. 7.8. Thematic Distribution of Works Published in WoS Based on the Keywords Energy Transition and Sustainable Development. *Source*: Database extraction from WoS, February 1, 2024, VOSviewer (with 15).

Current and Future Challenges Regarding Energy Strategy and Support Policies

The main challenge of the energy transition for the future is not only to focus on green energy as the main driver but also to consider the paradigm shift by including the "just transition," which includes not only technological reorientation of the whole activities and processing new products but also a social transformation. A just transition includes not only honesty in communication regarding the need to switch to clean energy (Stevis & Felli, 2020) but also equity, meaning access, inclusiveness, and strong correlation with accountability, as Newell and Mulvaney mentioned in 2013 referring to "climate justice" (McCauley & Heffron, 2018; Newell & Mulvaney, 2013). Achieving the targets defined by the SDGs is not always correlated with the needs associated with the just energy transition or with the ethics of applying the "in the benefit for all" principle, an objective recently highlighted as a direction in development, to reduce inequalities of any kind, for individuals and communities. Experts have analyzed the effects of decarbonization and asymmetric financing for areas in energy transition, evident in not only multiple inequities, accentuated or multiplied by an inadequate policy of implementing strategies regarding the energy transition (Ciplet & Harrison, 2019; Weller, 2019). Also, some experts have pointed out the deficiencies in the strategic documents and public policy recommendations (Le Billon & Kristoffersen, 2020; Pianta & Lucchese, 2020), such as the lack of vision regarding the equity of the post-carbon economy (i.e., The European Green Deal, EC-fit for 55, COP28).

The previous bibliometric analysis indicated policy as a keyword with a high frequency of appearance in specialists' works. It is natural because any approach to scientific analysis, regardless of the field of research, ultimately leads to policy recommendations – from, for example, the reorientation of technological transfer to economic agents for the production of clean/green products or/and investments in technological processes environmental friendliness, up to the remodeling of consumer behavior toward energy consumption, and investments for household energy efficiency and responsible consumption.

It is also why, in this chapter, the last bibliometric analysis approach followed the binomial energy policy and sustainable development. The content analysis of the published works highlighted that the focus on sustainable energy policies, which meet the SDGs, was a permanent concern after 2002 and intensified after 2017, a fact also highlighted by the double number of works published annually (from an average of approximately 60 per year in the period 2010–2016 to approximately 130 per year in the last analyzed years).

In fields of science, the focus was on energy fuels and environmental sciences ecology, followed by policies addressed to the business environment (business economics and, to a lesser extent, public administration). As countries of affiliation of the authors, China and the United States are positioned in the first place this time, followed by the United Kingdom, Poland, India, and Germany, a fact that proves the concerns of universities and research centers not only for the development of technologies that meet the requirements of energy production and sustainable energy consumption but also for the promotion at the micro, local, national, and regional levels of support policies for the green, responsible, and affordable energy transition.

From the perspective of the SDGs pursued through the analysis of the implemented policies or the policy proposals, and in this area of thematic analysis, Goals 7 –affordable and clean energy and 13 – climate action were targeted with priority (Fig. 7.9). It should be mentioned that in this case, the transversal nature of the SDGs of the energy transition requires integrated policies that facilitate not only the change of the energy management model but also the reconfiguration of the life model of individuals and the non-financial responsibility of companies.

It is also the argument for which, as a trend, there is a need for all companies, regardless of their size and field of activity, to build their sustainability strategy, respectively to remodel their own business for a future based on a green economy, energy inclusion, energy efficiency, and responsible consumption.

The thematic clustering shows us a different picture, although the large domains remain the same, it is, on the one hand, a greater diffusion between clusters, with multiple intra-cluster connections but also between them, and, on the other hand, the appearance of new nodal keywords and differently positioned dependency chains, which is what shows us the specifics of the approach to policy analyses, either on the construction, adjustment, updating component or on the implementation and monitoring component. Thus, (a) in the central cluster, which remains the red one, the chain of dependency on keywords is to the general objective of sustainable development toward energy policy – energy – limited change and power; (b) for the green cluster, closely related to the green and the blue, the chain of keywords starts from renewable energy, as a strategic objective, and aims at the theme of electricity associated with generation – biomass, and system, as policy priorities; (c) the blue cluster focuses on several nodal themes, essential for building sustainable policies, referring to the policy – sustainability – performance – emissions – systems dependency; (d) the last cluster is predominantly associated with the theme and keywords from the red one and considers the chain of links between consumption – energy efficient – economic growth – CO_2 emissions – impact (Fig. 7.10).

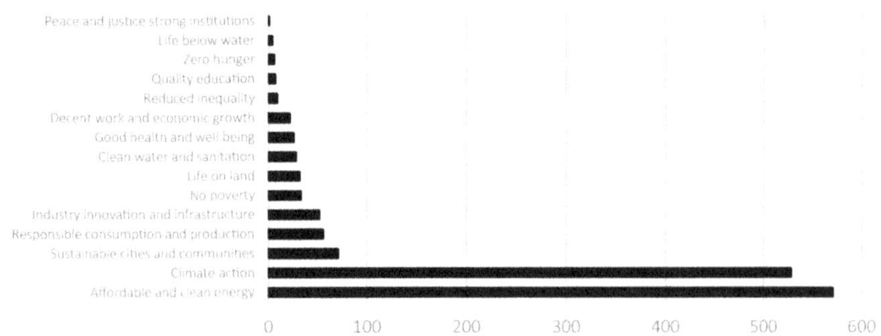

Fig. 7.9. Number of Papers Published in WoS Regarding Energy Policy and Sustainable Development, According to the 17 SDGs. *Source*: Database extraction from WoS, February 1, 2024.

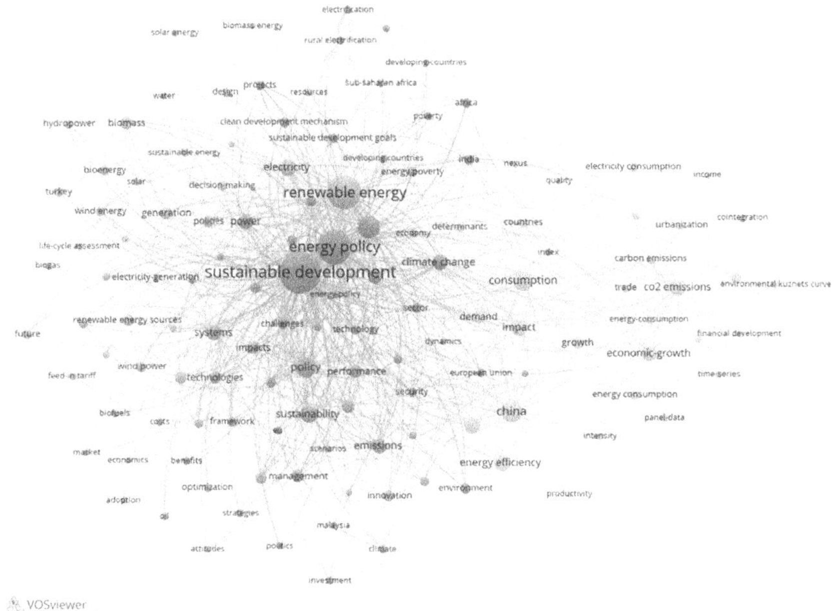

Fig. 7.10. Thematic Distribution of Papers Published in WoS Based on the Keywords Energy Policy and Sustainable Development. *Source*: Database extraction from WoS, February 1, 2024, VOSviewer (with 15).

Conclusion

Green energy for sustainable development is a topic of controversial debate among specialists. Their opinions regarding energy transition are varied, even divergent. On the one hand, there is the position of some specialists according to which greenhouse gas emissions produce negative externalities on the environment and accentuate the significant climate changes of the last decades, underlining the necessity of reaching a worldwide goal of "net zero carbon" by 2050 (The United Nations and Davos World Economic Forum are among the promoters of this orientation). Also, the EU adopted the strategy of reducing CO_2 emissions and increasing the share of renewable energy in total energy sources as a sustainable solution to cover the increase in energy demand. On the other hand, part of experts (MacKay, 2008) consider that climate warming is a long-term process caused by numerous anthropogenic factors and that the replacement of fossil fuels, hydrocarbons, natural gas, and even nuclear energy with renewable sources is not possible and damages the environment (through the resulting waste, such as, for example, electric batteries, the replacement of windmills, etc.), but also through the mining activity of extracting rare metals used in the electric car industry, other equipment and components. Energy Returned on Energy Invested is much too low, the cost of producing wind and solar energy is currently much higher than that of energy produced from traditional sources, we are witnessing the increase in energy prices with effects on the cost of living for almost all consumer goods, etc.).

In our opinion, but not only, an intelligent energy mix adapted to the specific natural conditions and the industrial development profile of each country can be a viable alternative to cover the energy demand. Also, limiting the increase in greenhouse gas emissions generated by industrial processes must be a permanent concern of the business environment and policymakers to reduce the climate footprint (Alam & Murad, 2020; Akram et al., 2021; Apostu et al., 2022; Aydin, 2019; Bozkurt & Destek, 2015; Panait et al., 2022; Simionescu et al., 2023; Tutak & Brodny, 2022).

Although there are other bibliometric analyses related to the energy transition in the specialized literature (Harichandan et al., 2022; Kar et al., 2022; Kemeç & Altınay, 2023; Toska et al., 2023; WEF, 2021; Xu et al., 2024, etc.), as well as outlook type documents that present detailed analyses on energy perspectives (EIU, 2024; IEA, 2023; OIES, 2024, for example), The present chapter highlights, in another view, the connection between green energy, energy transition, energy policy, and SDGs. On the other hand, we appreciate that a correct approach to the substantiation of the management policies of the future energy sector and the emerging changes in the range of consumer products, as well as those related to energy, must take into account the multiple approaches of risks and effects changing the energy transition paradigm. The availability of energy resources is no longer the main argument for the production and consumption of energy at the national level. To this is added the need for energy security and independence from the large exporters of energy resources but also the change in the energy consumption model of the business sector and households and other categories of consumers. Energy efficiency has become the main challenge not only for economic agents but also for domestic consumers. The present research has highlighted the complexity of the effects and the transversal character of the change in the structure of energy sources and the transition to green energy, as well as the technological, infrastructure, organizational, and policy mix barriers for achieving not only the environmental protection objectives (discussed at COP28 or, recently, at the last summit in Davos), or of achieving the previously assumed objectives, through the Paris Agreement, etc. The analysis of the studies carried out in recent years highlighted the concerns of specialists for innovation and technological transfer on the entire value chain of energy production and consumption, but also those related to the limits of economic efficiency and energy inclusion, with the complex problems of ensuring the financing of the transition, access, and affordability of energy consumption. The present work is an additional argument for the need for economic and social accountability in strategy and policies designed for a sustainable energy offer but also for the need for education for responsible consumption of energy (as a factor in maintaining the balance of ecosystems in which the man is not only a component but also an active factor of transformation). The message is that specialists, through scientific research carried out in the various fields of science, can offer solutions and identify risks in the development, but the essential role remains for decision-makers, responsible for maintaining the balance between expectations and possibilities in building policies that facilitate the energy transition, for the benefit of all. The previous bibliometric studies, to which the present chapter is added, can support initiatives to consult the results of specialized studies published in scientific databases such as WoS and to substantiate realistic policy measures to promote the benefits of green energy.

References

Akram, R., Chen, F., Khalid, F., Huang, G., & Irfan, M. (2021). Heterogeneous effects of energy efficiency and renewable energy on economic growth of BRICS countries: A fixed effect panel quantile regression analysis. *Energy*, *215*, 119019.

Alam, M. M., & Murad, M. W. (2020). The impacts of economic growth, trade openness and technological progress on renewable energy use in organization for economic co-operation and development countries. *Renewable Energy*, *145*, 382–390. https://doi.org/10.1016/j.energy.2020.119019

Apostu, S. A., Panait, M., & Vasile, V. (2022). The energy transition in Europe – A solution for net zero carbon?*Environmental Science and Pollution Research*, *29*, 71358–71379.

Aydin, M. (2019). Renewable and non-renewable electricity consumption–economic growth nexus: Evidence from OECD countries. *Renewable Energy*, *136*, 599–606. https://doi.org/10.1016/j.renene.2019.01.008

Bozkurt, C., & Destek, M. A. (2015). Renewable energy and sustainable development nexus in selected OECD countries. *International Journal of Energy Economics and Policy*, *5*(2), 507–514.

Ciplet, D., & Harrison, J. L. (2019). Transition tensions: Mapping conflicts in movements for a just and sustainable transition. *Environmental Politics*, *29*(3), 435–456.

EIU. (2024). Energy outlook 2024. Surging demand defies wars and high prices. https://www.eiu.com/n/wp-content/uploads/2023/10/Energy-report-2023.pdf

Harichandan, S., Kar, S. K., Bansal, R., Mishra, S. K., Balathanigaimani, M. S., & Dash, M. (2022). Energy transition research: A bibliometric mapping of current findings and direction for future research. *Cleaner Production Letters*, *3*, 100026. ISSN 2666-7916. https://doi.org/10.1016/j.clpl.2022.100026

IEA. (2023). *World energy outlook*. Retrieved February 2, 2024, from https://iea.blob.core.windows.net/assets/66b8f989-971c-4a8d-82b0-4735834de594/WorldEnergyOutlook2023.pdf

Kar, S., Harichandan, S., & Roy, B. (2022). Bibliometric analysis of the research on hydrogen economy: An analysis of current findings and roadmap ahead. *International Journal of Hydrogen Energy*, *47*(20), 1–22. https://doi.org/10.1016/j.ijhydene.2022.01.137

Kemeç, A., & Altınay, A. T. (2023). Sustainable energy research trend: A bibliometric analysis using VOSviewer, RStudio Bibliometrix, and CiteSpace software tools. *Sustainability*, *15*(4), 3618. https://doi.org/10.3390/su15043618

Le Billon, P., & Kristoffersen, B. (2020). Just cuts for fossil fuels? Supply-side carbon constraints and energy transition. *Environment and Planning A: Economy and Space*, *52*(6), 1072–1092. https://doi.org/10.1177/0308518X18816702

MacKay, D. (2008). *Sustainable energy without hot air*. UIT Cambridge. https://withouthotair.com/, https://www.inference.org.uk/sustainable/book/tex/sewtha.pdf

McCauley, D., & Heffron, R. (2018). Just transition: Integrating climate, energy and environmental justice. *Energy Policy*, *119*(C), 1–7.

McKinsey & Company. (2023). Global energy perspective. https://www.mckinsey.com/industries/oil-and-gas/our-insights/global-energy-perspective-2023

Newell, P., & Mulvaney, D. (2013). The political economy of the 'just transition'. *Geographical Journal*, *179*(2), 132–140. https://doi.org/10.1111/geoj.12008

OIES. (2024). *Key themes for the global energy economy in 2024*. The Oxford Institute for Energy Studies. https://www.oxfordenergy.org/wpcms/wp-content/uploads/2024/01/2024-Key-Themes-Global-Energy-Economy-in-2024.pdf

Panait, M. C., Apostu, S. A., Vasile, V., & Vasile, R. (2022). Is energy efficiency a robust driver for the new normal development model? A Granger causality analysis. *Energy Policy*, *169*, 113162. ISSN 0301-4215, EISSN 1873-6777. https://doi.org/10.1016/j.enpol.2022.113162

Pianta, M., & Lucchese, M. (2020). Rethinking the European Green Deal: An industrial policy for a just transition in Europe. *Review of Radical Political Economics*, *52*(4), 633–641.

Simionescu, M., Rădulescu, M., & Cifuentes-Faura, J. (2023). Renewable energy consumption-growth nexus in European countries: A sectoral approach. *Evaluation Review*, *47*(2), 287–319. https://doi.org/10.1177/0193841X221125982

Stevis, D., & Felli, R. (2020). Planetary just transition? How inclusive and how just? *Earth System Governance*, *6*, 100065. ISSN 2589-8116. https://doi.org/10.1016/j.esg.2020.100065

Tutak, M., & Brodny, J. (2022). Renewable energy consumption in economic sectors in the EU-27. The impact on economics, environment and conventional energy sources. A 20-year perspective. *Journal of Cleaner Production*, *345*, Article 131076. https://doi.org/10.1016/j.jclepro.2022.131076

Toska, E., Chatzitheodoridis, F., Loizou, E., & Kontogeorgos, A. (2023). A bibliometric analysis on energy transition with emphasis on decarbonization of lignite towards a post-lignite era. In N. Persiani, I. E. Vannini, M. Giusti, A. Karasavvoglou, & P. Polychronidou (Eds.), *Global, regional and local perspectives on the economies of Southeastern Europe* (pp. 223–235). EBEEC 2022. Springer Proceedings in Business and Economics. Springer. https://doi.org/10.1007/978-3-031-34059-8_11

UN-WCED. (1987). Report of the World Commission on Environment and Development: Our common future. https://sustainabledevelopment.un.org/content/documents/5987our-common-future.pdf

WEF. (2021). *Fostering effective energy transition* (2021 edition). WEF. https://www3.weforum.org/docs/WEF_Fostering_Effective_Energy_Transition_2021.pdf

Weller, S. A. (2019). Just transition? Strategic framing and the challenges facing coal dependent communities. *Environment and Planning C: Politics and Space*, *37*(2), 298–316.

Xu, J., Liu, Q., Wider, W., Zhang, S., Fauzi, M. A., Jiang, L., Udang, L. N., & An, Z. (2024). Research landscape of energy transition and green finance: A bibliometric analysis. *Heliyon*, *10*(3), e24783. ISSN 2405-8440. https://doi.org/10.1016/j.heliyon.2024.e24783

Chapter 8

Possibilities of Sustainable Business Operations of Economic Entities in Conditions of Extraordinary External Influences

Ljiljana Rajnović[a] and Snežana Cico[b]

[a]*Institute of Agricultural Economics, Belgrade, Serbia*
[b]*Public Communal Company Prostor Sombor, Sombor, Serbia*

Abstract

The author's interest in studying this topic was inspired by new extraordinary external influences, such as the COVID-19 pandemic and war operations in Europe, which have a direct impact on economic entities and therefore on the economies of many countries in the surrounding area and beyond. The aforementioned external, unpredictable factors appeared unexpectedly. As soon as they appeared, they caused major disruptions in business operations and a crisis on the market, which could not be influenced beforehand, nor could its occurrence be prevented. The impact of external shocks on economies will vary depending on individual countries' exposure to Russian energy sources, food security, as well as their own economic structure, geographic location, and the degree of flexibility of their public finances. Empirical findings show that there are relatively significant differences in the reactions to the resulting conditions, between large companies that still take into account the durability and publicity of development indicators and others, which are characterized by the absence of a long-term perspective and its reduction to a set of short-term goals that are sought to be achieved in the framework of the visible future. In addition to the standard theoretical analysis, the authors conducted research by surveying selected business entities in Serbia, which provided an insight into the current state of the company and indicated the

Emerging Patterns and Behaviors in a Green Resilient Economy, 169–186

doi:10.1108/978-1-83549-780-720241009

necessary directions for changes both at the level of business entities and at the level of the entire economy. Based on the conducted research, the authors came to the knowledge that economic entities can solve economic instability by implementing one or more reorganization models.

Keywords: Adverse impact of external conditions; economic instability; disruption of business entities operations; sustainable business; crisis resolution; restructuring

Introduction

The current operations of business entities in the world are characterized by exposure to major economic and geopolitical risks, which in various ways affect economic trends in the world, regions, companies, and the lives of individuals. Companies and entrepreneurs perform a very important function for every state and other persons interested in their business, including a great influence on the social community. That is why business entities have an obligation to act in the general social interest.

A crisis as a serious negative deviation that can generally endanger the business operations of companies and other persons, including the state, does not arise all at once but gradually over a shorter or longer period of time, mainly in certain territories, in certain activities of the company, and if it is not resolved in a shorter period of time period, the negative impacts of the crisis increase over time. External conditions, COVID-19 and war actions in Europe, caused a crisis that immediately caused a major disruption in the business operations of companies, entrepreneurs, and other economic entities, which could not be avoided or predicted that it could happen at all (Cico et al., 2021). It hit many economic activities with great intensity.

The economic recovery from the pandemic crisis, which was expected in 2021, was abruptly interrupted by the hostilities in Europe. The war triggered a deep energy crisis affecting not only energy prices but also food and all other prices, production value chains, trade flows, consumer welfare, investor's confidence, financial markets, and exchange rate stability. Already in 2022, this phenomenon produced a significantly lower level of economic activity, which further slowed down in 2023 due to delayed adaptation to the new global energy reality and inflationary pressures. This time, the consequences of the war in Europe and the environment/surroundings are the most affected advanced economies, especially the countries of the Eurozone.

The effects of the war have so far been reflected in various countries and regions of the world, as they have contributed to the growth of the inflation rate with a significant increase in the prices of products and services. This caused strong interventions by major central banks around the world, such as the US Federal Reserve Bank and the European Central Bank. These institutions play new roles, which puts them in a very difficult position. All this was accompanied by great pressure on central banks in order to raise interest rates, in order to face the rise in the inflation rate. At the same time, there is a danger that high interest rates will cause a decline in development and slow down economic activity.

Inflationary movements really caused a shock on the world market, and there is almost no country that was not affected, because they arose as a consequence of events on the world political and economic scene. As such, they have brought many challenges for business operations, such as difficult access to energy sources at a certain price, an increase in the number of suppliers, prolongation of the procurement time of components to maintain the business cycle, and the impossibility of entering certain markets (Ruta, 2022). As the war events in the east of Europe do not calm down, it is difficult to say with precision when this state of market and price destabilization will stop. Some analysts claim that the peak can be expected in the summer of 2023.

There are numerous industries on which the conflict in Ukraine and the pandemic have had a major negative impact:

- The field of energy: due to the outbreak of conflict in Ukraine, energy prices are increasing significantly. The crisis caused by the armed conflict affects many buyers of Russian energy products, not only the countries of the European Union (EU), which are highly energy dependent on the purchase of energy products from Russia but also other European countries (Ruta, 2022), including the economy of Serbia.
- When taking into account the entire exchange of goods and services of the Republic of Serbia (Serbia) with other countries, Russia ranks fourth. However, more than 65% of the exchange of goods and services with Russia is the import of energy products, which is why Serbia is highly dependent on these goods, especially on the import of gas.
- In this situation, it is a good circumstance that the regular delivery of the oil industry of Serbia to Serbia has not been interrupted, which was ensured by changing the relevant EU regulations.
- Natural gas prices have risen, starting with the outbreak of riots in Ukraine, which had a significant impact on slowing down global growth and increasing inflation. Russia is the second producer of natural gas in the world (https://investingnews.com/top-natural-gas-producers/), and EU countries import about 40% of natural gas from Russia.
- When it comes to food, the value of food increases from month to month, so that in March 2022, the value of food was higher by one-third in accordance with the same month in 2021 (https://www.fao.org/worldfoodsituation/foodpricesindex/en/).
- There has been a high increase in grain prices as Russia and Ukraine export about one-third of the total exports.
- Russia is the global leader in the export of fertilizers used in agriculture to protect crops, including nutrients that significantly enable the growth of plants and other crops, whose prices have also significantly increased (https://www.fao.org/worldfoodsituation/foodpricesindex/en/).

- In addition, the question arises as to whether part of the agricultural products from those countries will be brought to the market at all, due to problems in the supply chains in Europe and the surrounding area.
- With the start of hostilities in Ukraine, neighboring countries are particularly exposed to trade, supply chain, and remittance disruptions that accompany trade. The goods have been delayed or the delivery has been stopped and the transport costs have increased significantly.
- There was an increase in the prices of several metals, of which Russia and Ukraine are significant producers (https://www.alumeco.com/news/2022/faq-how-does-the-situation-in-ukraine-affect-metal-production-and-supply/).
- A large amount of neon is produced in Ukraine and supplied to numerous economic subjects throughout Europe, Japan, China, Korea, and Taiwan, and most of it is sold to companies in the United States (Ruta, 2022), whose prices have also increased.
- In addition, numerous European countries are faced with additional, unplanned financial expenses due to the citizens of Ukraine who left the country as a result of the war operations.

The current economic situation in Serbia and the region is quite similar. Politics and economics are intertwined more than is desirable, and often economic decisions are conditioned by political convictions. Partly, it is a consequence of what is happening on world markets, but partly it is also our specific geopolitical milieu. Events on the world stage, such as the fall in the value of currencies, the growth of inflationary trends, the increase in unemployment, sudden changes in priorities in the energy agenda, and the return of some countries to nuclear energy sources, as well as layoffs in the financial and information technology (IT) industry, liquidity problems, and the lack of investment havens, will certainly influence both our country and the countries of the region.

When talking about the milieu in which the Serbian economy operates, Serbia has long relied on the projections of major world economies and their economists, which indicate that the peak of inflation is expected during the summer. This is particularly pointed out by the risk sectors of large international companies operating both in Serbia and in the region. This means that economic developments in Serbia are expecting an extremely challenging period, both for the economy and for the citizens.

It can be said that for now, Serbia is coping well with the new situation, but the recovery of the Serbian economy depends a lot on the developments on the European market. The reports of the International Monetary Fund from March 2023 indicate that inflation in Serbia amounted to 16.2%, that is, it was at the level of January 2008 (International Monetary Fund, 2023).

Also, war can lead to a growing negative attitude toward the idea of globalization, global economic integration and free trade that benefit everyone. The war will lead to the adoption of more protectionist policies, especially with the return of the supply chain crisis, the impact of which has intensified after the imposition of many sanctions on Russia and threats of sanctions on other countries. This is accompanied by increased suspicion of international financial institutions as well as recognized mechanisms such as the SWIFT mechanism. This can increase the chances of electing political leaders who support trade wars and protectionist policies, which have a negative impact on all participants in the international market.

In particular, it is assumed that the economic growth of the entire EU and Serbia will be seriously affected by the disruptions resulting from the war in Ukraine. Rising energy prices, the threat of rising food prices, disruption of international trade, and weakening confidence threaten to spoil the second year of Europe's expected strong economic recovery from the COVID-19 pandemic. That event, in the coming period, could determine whether Europe faces the additional costs of mass migration that have the potential to reshape the economic landscape.

The impact of external shocks on economies will vary depending on the exposure of individual countries to Russian energy sources, as well as on their own economic structure, geographic location, and the degree of flexibility of their public finances.

In this regard, in the conditions caused by the COVID-19 pandemic (the "new normal"), perceptions are spreading about reducing the necessity of (long-term) planning in companies. The events that immediately followed - the war conflict in Ukraine, and the related energy crisis and, in perspective, the food crisis, as by all accounts a prelude to an all-out economic crisis, narrowing the perspectives of many companies to the shortest possible terms, bringing them dangerously close to simple daily survival.

Empirical findings (surveys in Serbia, public data of international bodies, professional literature, etc.) show that the above characterizes not only the companies and the economy of Serbia but also a much wider area, but that at the same time, there are relatively significant differences in the reactions to the resulting conditions, primarily between large companies and other business entities. While, in the former, the totality and connection of goals, tasks, instructions, as well as the durability and publicity of development indicators are still taken into account, the latter is characterized by the aforementioned absence of a long-term perspective and its reduction to a set of short-term goals, the achievement of which is sought within the framework of the visible future. To that should certainly be added problems more or less specific to the Serbian economy, which arise from the consequences of the privatization process and unregulated or non-transparent ownership relations, as well as inadequate or inconsistent regulations in many areas, etc. On the other hand, unfavorable and unpredictable external influences are reflected differently on various economic activities and companies that operate in them, which indicates the need for a differentiated approach to achieving sustainable business in current conditions.

The mentioned external influences particularly affect the field of agriculture, because food production is one of the most important branches of the economy of every country, and it depends on the available resources for agricultural production. Beside these factors, unpredictable factors that have occupied the entire world population for the last two years, such as the coronavirus pandemic and war events in Ukraine, also have a strong influence.

Economic security is one of the pillars of the national security for every country. The business represents the backbone of the economy and financial flows and, above all, the income side of the state budget. Sudden and in most cases unplanned risks, such as pandemics or outbreaks of armed conflict, have shown that business companies, in order to operate sustainably and work in different circumstances, must also take into account such external dangers, which have transnational consequences.

Adaptation of Companies to External Influences

Causes have their effects. When we look at the causes of the crisis, it can be concluded that there are new causes of the crisis: COVID-19 and war actions in Europe. As a consequence of those causes, some other types of crisis appeared, because one cause causes another and so on until the crisis somehow stops or companies fail to find a solution when bankruptcy occurs. As a result, other types of crisis appear: the crisis of the management of economic entities, which does not manage well in the new circumstances, the impossibility of adequate management of funds, the started projects that become unsustainable for the company must be changed, the necessity of major or minor organizational changes is indicated, and other models of restructuring of economic entities, and then there are negative trends in the supply and demand of goods and services, which are reflected differently in various economic activities of companies, because the crisis has different effects on activities and economic entities (Cico et al., 2021). That is why it is necessary to create models of adaptation of economic entities to new external effects.

The authors believe that in such conditions, the standard assumptions of successful business must be supported by well-thought-out planning, based above all on the analysis of external influences (production and financial markets, technological progress, etc.). Also, it is necessary to ensure a good foundation of corporate governance, not only in business entities but also in the domain of state regulation.

In such a situation, business entities can implement appropriate restructuring models in order to give favorable results in the shortest possible time, in order to achieve the goal of companies adapted to new phenomena on the market, that is, to achieve a more favorable economic position of the company. In this way, companies could find a way to solve the crisis in business due to the drop in economic activities caused by external influences. Restructuring is not an option that contributes only and exclusively to the growth of the company, but in such cases, it has the function of recovering the company from unfavorable influences due to which the business was brought to a crisis, and the management was unable to manage the company as planned. One of the possible ways, which in the short term can lead to some positive effects in business, is organizational restructuring (Rajnović et al., 2016). Which restructuring model will be applied depends on each specific case, i.e., how much the business entity is affected by external influences, company activities, opportunities and intentions of buyers and sellers, etc.

Therefore, companies not only have to fight for survival but at the same time continuously work on introducing new sophisticated ways of working, establishing automation and digitization, taking into account sustainable development, the environment, and safety. All these are activities that, in addition to professional staff, require significant knowledge and investments and therefore must establish new types of traffic and accept the recommendations of the scientific and professional public.

The mission of the project is to contribute to the social and economic discourse and enable the political and business decisions of economic entities to be based on the best possible available scientific knowledge, as well as to encourage research in order to fill gaps in knowledge and provide answers to open questions at this matter, especially at the level of the national economy.

The goal of this chapter is to find conceptual solutions for the organization of business entities and the economy of Serbia which can contribute to overcoming of the last effects of the crisis and, in the future, for recognizing external influences and timely adaptation on them. This would certainly contribute to the development of business entities and the economy of Serbia as a whole, having the fact that there is no comprehensive research in Serbia.

Based on the results of theoretical and empirical research, the affirmation of long-term aspects of planning within the framework of economic entities, as well as at the regional and macro level, which are under the influence of unpredictable external factors in current conditions, is to a large extent compromised and endangered. Business entities will pay more attention at their future development and business activities to scientific knowledge about the assumptions and conditions for achieving sustainable development (West, 2000). In this sense, the strengthening of analytical and planning functions in companies is expected, primarily in smaller and more exposed subjects.

Given that the rules of corporate governance, corporate security, and restructuring models in the Serbian economy are still unexplored and not applied in practice, there is not enough research by domestic scientists in this area, the contribution of the project in scientific work is original and manifold useful for further scientific research.

In this chapter, the authors show the possibilities of companies, that is, what measures they can take in order to solve the crisis caused by external influences, which has multiple negative effects on many aspects of the life and work of people and other economic entities, on the external environment and on a significant part of the globe (Malinić, 2002), including the policy of states, toward their economic subjects and toward the outside world.

The subject of the research was chosen precisely for the reason that it indicates the necessity of restructuring the company as soon as the occurrence of circumstances that can threaten the good business of the company is foreseen, which ensures the continuity of the business of the company, not only for companies with perceived or foreseeable problems in business but also for other companies, because over time the asset and capital structures become dysfunctional, which is why it is necessary to make changes in order to maintain the stability of the business.

Materials and Methods

The following methods were used for objective research results: detailed review of the literature, descriptive statistics, and comparative analysis. As part of the research, historical material, available scientific works, statistical reviews, and reports of relevant state institutions, as well as the economic entities themselves, were used and analyzed, which were selected according to a defined methodology, which includes the size of companies, activities, etc.

During the research, case studies were used as a descriptive method, which show that the observed cases within the same or different economic branches can be taken as a typical case. Within the presented cases, authors started from specific indicators from financial reports and reorganization plans of companies in Serbia, pointing out the importance of timely implementation of possible reorganization of companies and negative consequences of not adapting to external influences.

The application of the comparative method allowed the authors to draw a conclusion by analyzing the observed cases in practice. A model for better restructuring will be established.

The authors conducted research by surveying selected business entities, which provided an insight into the current state of the company and indicated the necessary directions for changes at the level of the company and the entire economy.

For the purposes of this work, the authors investigated the impact of unpredictable external factors, primarily war in the environment, on a large company engaged in the pharmaceutical industry and on agricultural companies and agricultural farms, as well as any measures taken by the surveyed business entities in order to adapt to external influences.

The authors collected data by interviewing directors and owners of companies and agricultural holdings. A total of 150 representatives of business entities on the territory of Serbia in the municipality of Ruma were surveyed. In order to research this topic, the authors used domestic and foreign literature, regulations adopted by Serbia in this area and financial reports of business entities that were the subject of research, which are publicly available.

In order to research this topic, the authors examined the economic activities of selected subjects in the period from January 2022 to April 2023.

Respondents are engaged in agricultural production, of which 80% are small economic entities and 20% are large agricultural entities according to the standards in the Republic of Serbia. All business entities had at least one decade of successful business, and some even more decades, with significant experience and knowledge in agriculture.

In accordance with the research plan, the author's goal was to determine the following facts: whether business entities could foresee the occurrence of facts that could affect their business, COVID-19 and war actions in the environment; whether and how the mentioned factors affected the operations of business entities; whether they have taken consolidation measures; and what do they expect in the near future?

According to the conducted research, the authors believe that the largest number of economic entities saw the risky consequences of external influences and immediately started implementing possible restructuring measures. Most often, various forms of organizational restructuring were applied.

Numerous economic entities were in a situation of lack of sufficient financial resources due to the increase in the price of energy and raw materials, so they also applied measures of financial restructuring, through various grants from the state, and a smaller number of economic entities received a loan from the bank. When it comes to models of organizational restructuring, the model of downsizing the corporation as the transfer of some tasks to external legal and natural persons is most often applied. To some extent, all this had favorable effects on the business operations of economic entities, but the price growth continued so that the adjustment to external influences has not yet been completed.

Based on the investigated cases and other examples in practice, the authors concluded that by applying adequate restructuring measures, it is possible to find a solution for the survival of economic entities.

Results and Discussion

The authors analyzed the changes in the operations of one large company headquartered in Serbia that deals with the pharmaceutical industry and 150 micro, small- and medium-sized, and large business entities that deal with agricultural production and processing of agricultural products whose seat is in the municipality of Ruma in Serbia, in order to study the impact of the crisis in the business operations of the largest number of economic entities due to the consequences of the pandemic and war operations, as well as the measures they may have taken in order to recover their business.

In general, the pharmaceutical industry in Serbia experienced growth during this period. The observed company is engaged in the production of consumer health products, generics, and pharmaceutical specialties. The company markets its products on the territory of Serbia and other countries of the world. In 2022, the company had double-digit sales and profit growth. That trend continued in 2023. Consumer health products represent the company's largest business organizational unit by sales, and prescription pharmaceutical specialty brands account for one-fifth of turnover.

Despite the challenging geopolitical and economic environment, in 2022, the company managed to stay on its strong growth path that it has been on in recent years. In that year, the company expanded its offer for users by launching new products and expanding the lines of existing products, further improving its position on the market and ensuring a reliable supply of products. The company continues to benefit from a broad geographic presence, with all major markets contributing to growth in 2022. As a reliable partner, the company remains committed to providing access to essential and affordable medicines in all countries in which it operates.

The company continued to grow in 2023 and remained the regional pharmaceutical leader, as well as number one in the segment of generic, CHC and OTC products. It has expanded its portfolio and increased production efficiency with the aim of being the main partner to its users in key segments.

Therefore, despite numerous geopolitical and macroeconomic turbulences, which disrupted global supply chains and increased inflationary pressures, the observed company managed to increase production and deliver 1.2 billion packages of medicines to around 120 countries around the world in the mentioned period. New product launches during the observed period strengthened the company's position as the fourth largest supplier of generic drugs in Europe, by value.

In order to research this topic, the authors interviewed representatives of 150 micro, small, medium and large economic entities engaged in agricultural production and processing of agricultural products. The subject of the research was changes in business operations, production/processing costs, terms of procurement of raw materials, product sales, possible loss of the market, the state of the workforce, as well as what measures were taken in order to ensure continued operations of business entities, etc.

In the case of economic entities, companies, and agricultural farms in the Republic of Serbia, whose activity is agricultural production and processing of agricultural products, the results of the research showed that the impact of the war on the environment on the agricultural sector of Serbia is reflected in the following: increase in the prices of energy sources, raw materials for production, processing equipment, final products, and agricultural land:

- due to the increase in the prices of energy, raw materials, and transport, many manufacturers have raised the prices of finished products;
- there was an increase in inflation;
- falling purchasing power of consumers, longer payment terms for sold goods;
- reductions in income, lack of own financial resources;
- due to the changed circumstances, in many cases, the already contracted obligations could not be fulfilled, so there were numerous court disputes;
- in the reduction of sales, less inflow of money, which caused a lack of labor force;
- about 4%–5% of smaller companies have changed their activity;
- businessmen do not expect a reduction in the number of employees, which is good for the Serbian economy;
- employees' wages have increased but not realistically;
- the Republic of Serbia, like all other countries in the region, provided part of the financial resources to help the economy but not enough;
- many business entities are unable to reduce some costs, e.g., fixed costs, because the reduction of those costs requires a longer period (Hörcher et al., 2020).

The research showed that due to external influences, small companies are most affected, followed by medium ones, while medium-sized and large ones are the least or not at all affected and are already approaching the possibility of increasing profits. Also, through the research, it was found out that the most numerous are those business entities that started the rehabilitation process in a timely manner, by applying the model of organizational changes, mainly by reducing the corporation, status, and contractual connections in order to reduce business costs and work together on some projects. Agricultural farms joined cooperatives and made various contractual connections. In this way, they reduced their own costs and created greater financial potential for the procurement of raw materials and materials for the maintenance of agricultural land.

There has been a change in the market in purchasing products. In periods of crisis, consumers do not buy luxury goods but only basic foodstuffs that are necessary for life. Increase in earnings of the population does not follow the growth of product prices, so the requirements for the purchase of goods and services are low, which negatively affects the financial potential of economic entities (Hörcher et al., 2020).

Agricultural production is a complicated process with numerous participants. These are business entities that provide material for agricultural production, such as producers of seeds, fertilizers, means for maintaining and preserving plants, then direct agricultural producers, agricultural devices used for tillage, sowing and other tasks, logistics, accommodation facilities, refrigeration equipment, then the processing industry, and, when all this is successfully realized, the sales of goods, of various forms, which sell goods to the end user. In that long chain of participants, the occurrence of any problem slows down or stops the delivery of the product to the consumer and the payment of the product (Cico et al., 2021). Stable agriculture is a very important activity for people's existence, especially in Serbia, which is an agricultural country.

Subsidies provided by the Government of the Republic of Serbia, with the aim of consolidating the business of business entities whose operations were affected by the crisis caused by the aforementioned external factors, have helped the survival of the largest number of business entities, but they are not sufficient for the establishment of sustainable business in the long term.

The agriculture of the Republic of Serbia needed material and non-material aid even before the emergence of the above-mentioned external conditions because it was burdened with numerous problems, insufficient financial resources, outdated equipment for carrying out activities, high expenses for energy and other duties, leaving the village by the young workforce, labor shortage, etc.

Considering the number of people engaged in agriculture in Serbia, the percentage of participation in GDP, the general importance of agriculture for the healthy nutrition of people, and the preservation of the environment, the agriculture sector in the Republic of Serbia is very important. That is why it is necessary to attach greater importance to this sector and provide additional financial and non-financial assistance, especially to small companies and agricultural farms (Subić et al., 2012).

Consolidation of Business Entities Through the Application of Restructuring Measures

External influences created in the company's environment are phenomena whose origin is beyond the influence and will of commercial business entities. Their impact on the operation of the commercial sector can be different, and it can be desirable or undesirable and even very negative. Knowing the external factors (of course also internal) that affect business gives companies the knowledge they need to be able to effectively address their priorities. If companies solve problems caused by external influences, they gain experience and knowledge about the importance of timely detection of external influences and the possibility of preparing plans for future business in order to ensure the survival and/or development of the company (Sherman, 2018).

It is very important to assess the impact of external factors on the company's operations in order to determine the order in which to solve them, which ones to prioritize and which can be postponed or ignored for a certain period of time (Rajnović, 2021). Timely identification of external factors that can affect the company's operations has become an indispensable part of business tasks and a way of protecting business operations of economic entities for a long time (Gleeson, 2018).

Media, blogs and newsletters, scientific research, unfinished negotiations between states or interest groups within states, political issues, historical events, geopolitical changes in the world, etc. are only some of the sources of knowledge about possible political and commercial trends in the wider or narrower environment, in the immediate or distant future. Knowledge of this information can help responsible persons, primarily managers and owners of business entities, to be aware of potential market trends and, in this connection, to adapt business to possible new circumstances and needs of business entities (Rajnović, 2021).

Numerous, globally significant products originate from Russia and Ukraine. Both countries are major world producers of various goods and raw materials, including agriculture. As a result of the war operations on the territory of Ukraine, there was an increase in the prices of goods originating from those regions, which caused other disturbances and significant uncertainty in a large part of the world market:

- Russia exports the largest amount of natural gas in the world, in terms of oil production it ranks third in the world, so it is considered a world power in the field of energy,
- Due to the events in Ukraine, the prices of oil and natural gas have increased sharply and caused other disturbances in the market,
- As a consequence of external influences, which affected a large part of the world, including Serbia, inflation was caused by the increase in the price of energy and, as a consequence, other goods and services,
- Both countries are large producers and exporters of agricultural products, for numerous companies around the world,
- Ukraine is a significant producer of neon, globally, etc. (https://www.oecd.org/economic-outlook/).

In the face of market disturbances caused by unpredictable external conditions and other environmental changes, companies try to find effective organizational models in order to survive in the market and improve their business (Burke & Litwin, 1992).

By analyzing the external cause and their consequences, it has been shown in practice that many companies have set new rules and goals in their business:

- preparation of feasible business plans in the future, including plans related to sales;
- education related to assessment and monitoring of potential risks;
- reduction of expenses;
- market analysis, monitoring the situation and events not only in the country but in the broader or narrower environment;
- monitoring the business of suppliers, customers, competitors;
- finding new partners from surrounding, closer markets;
- investing in the country where companies have their headquarters.

In practice, it has been shown that a large number of economic entities most often opt for organizational restructuring, which implies significant changes in the organizational structure of the company, such as reducing production diversification, reducing costs and workforce, expanding the scope of control, streamlining processes, and improving management (Zakić et al., 2015).

Organizational restructuring is a predictable response of the company to radical changes that occur in the environment (Zajac & Kraaty, 1993). Due to the influence of external factors, organizational restructuring is a frequent organizational change that business entities opt for in order to increase business efficiency, greater market participation, and profit growth. Faced with market conditions and greater demands for cost control, companies undertake significant downsizing, reorganize their operations, improve operations, and close unprofitable parts of the company (Bowman & Singh, 1993). Distressed companies often attribute such a situation to inefficient processes and as a means of these inefficiencies they seek to implement restructuring, increase productivity, and reduce costs (Cascio, 1993). Internal problems in companies and crises caused by environmental influences make organizational restructuring accepted as a way of increasing the organizational effectiveness and performance of companies, although organizational restructuring is not a remedy for all organizational problems (Hannan & Freeman, 1984). Certainly, the choice of an adequate model of organizational restructuring can help solve the problem or part of the problem in a shorter period of time.

The essential goal of any company is to operate for an indefinite period of time and to make money for the owner. This goal is the basis of all other goals (Gross, 1968) and is described in the literature as the iron law of survival of every company and is an absolute prerequisite for satisfying the interests of its stakeholders. Otherwise, as the environment becomes more and more turbulent, changes in the environment accelerate, and the need for companies to adapt increases (Lawrence & Lorsch, 1967). All this means that companies have to adapt to the environment faster and find adequate solutions for future business. However, many organizations have the problem of changing at the pace with which the environment is changing and are increasingly late in following changes in the environment, which is why they can put their survival into question (Kralj, 1975).

Companies behave differently in adapting to changes in the environment. Most companies react to changes in the environment since they have already appeared, and it is also important to note how much time passed from the change to the taking of certain measures by the company. Some organizations are able to anticipate changes in the environment and provide adequate responses before a threat or opportunity arises (Rasmunsen, 2010).

In theory and practice, there are three approaches that companies can apply:

- An anticipatory (proactive) approach implies that companies prepare and implement the necessary changes before the appearance of changes in the environment that can negatively affect business. In Serbia, mostly medium-sized and larger companies have the potential to permanently monitor the external environment and adapt their internal situation to the new situation in a timely manner.
  In this way, they have more opportunities to turn external threats into opportunities. Applying anticipatory changes really contributes to increasing competitiveness (Black & Gregersen, 2008).
- A reactive approach to change is generally applied by companies that react when it becomes obvious that change is inevitable. Such companies are usually able to weather the change, but recovery costs are higher and may weaken their ability to compete in the market.
  If companies prolong the taking of certain measures, their position may become more and more difficult.
- In the case of a crisis approach, companies ignore the acceptance of change even though all parameters show that change is necessary. Managers of such organizations do nothing (Slatter & Lovett, 2004). Organizations that fail to respond to changes in the environment until entering a state of deep crisis often lose significant market share, and some fail to overcome the crisis and cease to exist.

In practice, when implementing organizational restructuring, companies should apply an anticipatory or reactive approach. The latter two approaches require significantly higher switching costs. As previously stated, crisis changes may involve significant reductions in the workforce, cost reductions, and the closing of unprofitable or less profitable plants or the sale of parts of the company but may result in a loss of reputation (Kralj, 1975).

Energy price increases are inevitable in Serbia, because energy sector reforms are not cheap, just like modernization and building new capacities. It is also true that the price of electricity was one of the factors that protected the economy sector in the previous period. But with the latest suggestions of the International Monetary Fund, it is certain that Serbia must approach the reforms of this sector and the state-owned company Elektroprivreda Srbije, as the largest producer of electricity in Serbia. This will be one of the challenges and inflationary shocks in the financial system of Serbia and will affect the Serbian economy as well as the quality of life of the citizens.

What is happening in the world's major economies cannot fail to affect the Serbian economy. Serbia is too small an economy to be able to bypass the events on the world, especially the European stage. Turbulences occurring in the world's leading economies are also reflected in the economic and financial system of Serbia. Investments in Serbia primarily come from Europe, the largest export is to European countries (especially regional countries), Serbia's currency system is tied to the currency of the EU countries, so it is obvious that events in the region are also reflected in our country. To what extent – it depends on several key risks, especially political ones.

The banking system of Serbia is not part of the banking system of the European Central Bank, but financial operations are, because they are linked to the euro as a currency and to the policies of that bank, so changes in key interest rates will be reflected in the monetary system of Serbia, including the arrangements that are related to doing business with third countries, which are expressed in euros.

Competent institutions in Serbia regularly have information about phenomena on the international market, and in this regard, the Republic of Serbia adjusts its reference interest rate, given that the growth of inflation affects the increase in the value of capital, which is significant for every business entity. Therefore, it can be expected that this trend will continue in the coming period. This is certainly not favorable or stimulating for the economy, because the price of capital competes with inflation and certainly leads to reduced economic activity. All of the above indicates that the most favorable models for adapting companies to external changes are an anticipatory or reactive approach.

Challenges in Pursuing Resilient Economy

The realism of these projections crucially depends on the short-term policy mix aimed at taming inflation, sustaining economic growth, and protecting the poor and the vulnerable. In the medium run, the challenges are to initiate reforms and structural policies to successfully move Serbia to a positive economic outlook based on a more productive and resilient economy.

Additional potential sources of inflationary pressures may come from open and hidden contingent liabilities of public energy and utility companies, as has been demonstrated already in the revisions of the 2022 budget and new 2023 budget. This sector may be further loaded with future energy sector losses and direct fiscal losses if energy prices are controlled. Sound advice to policy is to combine tight monetary policy with well-targeted and time-bound fiscal support for the low-income groups, while allowing energy prices to provide sound signals for restructuring the energy sector and achieving resilience in this very important area (Probst, 2003).

Quick stabilization policies are also critical to prevent the formation of wage-inflation spirals which proved to be one of the most difficult aspects of inflation persistence in the past.

Once short-term policy objectives have been accomplished, the main task for Serbia is to raise economic growth potential by resuming structural reforms needed to reignite productivity growth, accelerate income convergence with the EU, and fully embrace digital agenda, improved governance, and green transition. It is important to stress that these reforms represent a necessary basis for better performance and economic prosperity, a basis for sustainable green growth and true resilience to a major future.

Conclusion

The last two years have been very turbulent and burdened by the costs incurred during the pandemic, then by the sudden growth of inflation, the consequences of war events on the world and regional stage, high prices and availability of energy sources, and, finally, the decline in economic activity as a result of all of the above. For financial institutions, this meant more difficult access to financial resources and, consequently, an increase in the price of capital on the European and world financial markets.

For the economy and citizens of Serbia and other countries affected by the crisis, this meant reduced access to credit and lower purchasing power, especially in the second quarter of the previous year. Nevertheless, in the previous year, Serbia achieved an uninterrupted investment cycle and a high level of capital investments. With all that in mind, it is not expected that the data showing the results of economic activity in 2023 will be bad.

In 2023, the growth of the world economy is expected to slow down, especially the growth of the Eurozone. However, what is good and what experts from foreign and domestic financial institutions have assessed is that the persistence of the economic zone is significantly higher than expected, which is good information. Serbia started the year 2023 with satisfactory macroeconomic parameters, so stability continues, but this means that economic reforms in the country should definitely be continued. They relate first of all to more specific restructuring and reforming of large public companies and then to further investment and development of the economic environment, in order to encourage the level of domestic private investments, because it was estimated that domestic private investments from year to year are all less.

It is also expected that inflation in Serbia will return to the target limits by the end of 2024, if it continues to decrease in the countries of the EU.

The research that was conducted showed that business entities believe that economic instability caused by the mentioned external influences will negatively affect macroeconomic performance on the domestic market, due to the increase in the value of energy sources, materials for agricultural production and then those products, the increase in inflationary trends on the market, and the decrease in volume of economic operations. A good circumstance is the fact that representatives of business entities believe that there will be no significant reduction in the number of employees.

External changes in the environment represent a very influential initiator of organizational changes in economic entities, because in this way negative influences can be avoided in the shortest possible time. They encourage the creation of new worldviews, new organizations, changes in mission and strategy, company plans, values, etc. External changes make fundamental changes in the behavior of companies. Changes in structure, systems and management practices affect relationships in the working environment, employer requirements, individual needs and values that affect motivation, individual and organizational performance.

On the basis of the conducted research, it was determined that companies should apply certain reorganization measures on their own initiative and those that give results in shorter terms. On the other hand, in order to preserve the business continuity of business entities, especially in agriculture, the authors believe that considering the generally known role of agriculture in society and in Serbia, the state would have to provide additional long-term measures of financial and non-financial assistance to agricultural entities, through more favorable loans, financial loans without compensation, contracting favorable financing from international funds, all with the aim of reducing the consequences of negative external influences.

Acknowledgment

This work was financially supported by the Ministry of Science of the Republic of Serbia, based on Contract Number 451-03-47/2023-01/200009, which was concluded on February 3, 2003, between MSTDI and Institute of Agricultural Economics.

References

Black, J. S., & Gregersen, B. H. (2008). *It starts with one: Changing individuals changes organizations*. Prentice Hall.

Bowman, E. H., & Singh, H. (1993). Corporate restructuring: Reconfiguring the firm. *Strategic Management Journal*, *14*(S1), 5–14.

Burke, W. W., & Litwin G. H. (1992). A causal model of organizational performance and change. *Journal of Management*, *18*(3), 532–545.

Cascio, W. F. (1993). Downsizing: What do we know? What have we learned? *Academy of Management Executive*, *7*(1), 95–104.

Cico, S., Rajnović, L., & Bošnjak, I. (2021). Organizational restructuring as a way to resolve the crisis caused by Covid 19, in agriculture sector. *Economics of Agriculture*, *68*(3), 573–856. http://bsaae.bg.ac.rs/images/Ekonomika%20kompletna/2021/EP%203-2021%20lq.pdf

Gleeson, P. (2018). *Internal and external factors affecting the organization*. smallbusiness.chron.com.

Gross, B. (1968). *Organizations and their managing*. Free Press.

Hannan, M. T., & Freeman, J. (1984). Structural inertia and organizational change. *American Sociological Review, American Sociological Association*, *49*(3), 149–164. https://doi.org/10.2307/2095567

Hörcher, D., Singh, R., & Graham, D. J. (2020). Social distancing in public transport: Mobilising new technologies for demand management under the COVID-19 crisis. *Transportation Letters*, London.

International Monetary Fund. (2023). *Staff concluding statement of the first review under the stand-by arrangement and the 2023 IV mission*. https://www.imf.org/en/News/Articles/2023/04/05/serbia-staff-concluding-statement-first-review-under-stand-by-arrangement-2023-article-iv-mission

Kralj, J. (1975). *Financial management*. Professional Book, Belgrade.

Lawrence, P. R., & Lorsch, J. W. (1967). Differentiation and integration in complex organizations. *Administrative Science Quarterly*, *12*(1), 1–47.

Malinić, S. (2002). *Basics of accounting management*. Kragujevac, Faculty of Economics.

Probst, T. (2003). Exploring employee outcomes of organizational restructuring: A Solomon four-group study. *Group & Organizational Management*, *28*(3), 416–439.

Rajnović, L. (2021). *Contracts in the economy with reference to external influences on the contractual relationship*. Institute of Agricultural Economics. ISBN 978-86-6269-106-4. eISBN 978-86-6269-107-1.

Rajnović, L., Subić J., & Zakić, N. (2016). *Organizational and financial restructuring of companies in the function of improving the economic environment in the Republic of Serbia*. Institute for Agricultural Economics. ISBN 978-86-6269-051-5.

Rasmunsen, L. B. (2010). From reactive to proactive approach of interactive leadership. In F. Garibaldo & V. Telljohann (Eds.), *The ambivalent character of participation: New tendencies in worker participation in Europe* (pp. 585–612). Peter Lang, Frankfurt am Main.

Ruta, M. (2022). *The impact of the war in Ukraine on global trade and investment*. http://hdl.handle.net/10986/37359

Sherman, F. (2018). *What are the internal and external environmental factors that affect business?* Mala preduzeća – Chron.com.

Slatter, S., & Lovett, D. (2004). *Corporate recovery managing companies in distress* (pp 13–53). Beard Books.

Subić, J., Jeločnik, M., & Ivanović, L. (2012). Evaluation of economic sustainability on the agricultural husbandries in the Upper Danube region. *Rural Areas and Development*, *9*, 305–324.

West, G. (2000). *The effects downsizing on survivors: A meta-analysis*. Virginia Politechnic Institute and State University.

Zajac, E. J., & Kraaty, M. S. (1993). A diametric forces model of strategic change: Assessing the antecedents and consequences of restructuring in the higher education industry.*Strategic Management Journal*, *14*(S1), 83–102.

Zakić, N., Grozdanić, R., & Kovačević, V. (2015). Evolution of organizations – From hierarchical to network organization. *Military Deed*, *67*(1), 232–249.

Chapter 9

Marketing Strategies in Historical Tourism Based on Tourist Motivation and Needs

Mahta Saremi, Hassan Darabi, Mohammad Javad Amiri, Gholamreza Nabi Bidhendi and Homa Irani Behbahani

University of Tehran, Iran

Abstract

Marketing tourism is essential for long-term tourism development which requires gaining knowledge about the motivation and needs of tourists. In order to help tourists gain a hospitable experience, information regarding the needs, perception, and their behavior while on site is important. This research attempts to explore the priority of tourists' needs in visiting historical sites. It also tries to conceptualize new forms of hospitality strategies for smart tourism development. Based on grounded theory, Maslow's hierarchy of needs is conceptualized for historical tourists and used as the main framework for this work. The Persepolis-Pasargadae Historical Range (PPHR) is chosen as the case study of the research because of the historical and cultural attractions located in this historical range. Results indicate that tourists interested in visiting this destination are looking to fulfill their growth needs. These growth needs can be complemented by new technologies while on site such as virtual reality (VR) goggles that help tourists gain knowledge about the reality of these destinations. The research concludes with findings and suggestions that can contribute to the planning of an effective marketing plan based on tourists' motivation and needs for visiting historical destinations.

Keywords: Marketing; motivation; needs; Maslow hierarchy of needs; historical sites; tourist behavior

Emerging Patterns and Behaviors in a Green Resilient Economy, 187–203

Published under exclusive licence by Emerald Publishing Limited
doi:10.1108/978-1-83549-780-720241010

Introduction

The tourism industry has become one of the fast-growing industries bringing revenue to its society and income for its local residents. Being able to develop this industry for the long term requires gaining knowledge about the needs of its visitors as well as its local residents. One of the main indicators in planning strategies for marketing tourism is understanding the behavioral patterns of tourists (Woodside & Martin, 2008). In order to help visitors gain a hospitable experience while visiting tourism sites, knowledge about the perceptions of tourists, their needs, and what they want to experience while on site is essential. Tourist motivation to travel to specific sites and engage in specific activities requires knowledge about their needs and behavior.

Tourists are motivated to travel and visit specific areas because of personal reasons or internal motivations (push factors) and the site attractions based on their characteristics (pull factors) that draw them toward these destinations (Crompton, 1979; Dann, 1977, 1981). Park and Yoon (2009) claim that "need" is the key driver of motivation. Therefore, tourist's demands can vary based on their needs and create difficulties for planners in order to build them a hospitable experience. Bowen and Shoemaker (2003) mention emotional or nostalgia attachments as components in tourism marketing and highlight them for future research in customer loyalty for tourism companies.

There are several reasons that explain why people are motivated to travel and help marketing strategies for tourism development. Site attractions are important motivation factors for tourists and the reason that people decide to visit a destination. According to "The Meaning of Place" written by Relph (1976), some travel because of their emotional bonds toward a destination or their so-called place attachment. Social exchange theory and the principles of this theory talk about the motivation to maximize rewards and minimize costs in social relationships (Homan, 1958). Critical tourism theory highlights the needs for more sustainable and responsible tourism practices and critically tries to analyze the social, cultural, and political implications of tourism in less developed countries (Harrison, 1992). Cognitive dissonance theory provides an in-depth explanation of the theory and its implications for human behavior. Several empirical studies have supported the predictions of cognitive dissonance theory in the context of destination marketing, such as the study by Wang and Li (2018) on the effect of cognitive dissonance on travel satisfaction. Service-dominant logic, although new in marketing, tries to analyze the perspectives in this logic and its implication for marketing and business strategy (Vargo & Lusch, 2008).

Marketing tourism based on the needs of tourists can ensure that they can have a hospitable experience while traveling. For effective marketing, it is important that we first identify our target audience to find out about their needs and wants. Then, we need to develop targeted messaging that can directly speak the needs of the tourists. This should help us provide a variety of options for tourists with their needs and their desired experience. Then, we should emphasize the value of what we want to offer and use visual content to showcase the experience that they are going to expect. Overall, marketing tourism based on the needs of tourism requires a deep understanding of what drives tourists behavior when they decide to travel.

Among the different types of tourists, cultural and historical tourists mainly seek to gain knowledge about a historical destination. McKercher (2002) defines and classifies cultural tourists, and Saremi et al. (2022) try to analyze the perceptional patterns of historical tourists by studying travelogues about historical destinations. Based on the research of Saremi et al., historical tourists are claimed to be the type of visitors who are interested in gaining knowledge about the history of a site, sensing the place, era of the site, and place identity. Their experience of travel and tourism is mainly based on the historical remains and the story behind these remains (Saremi et al., 2022).

In 1943, Maslow's hierarchy of needs was proposed as an idea in psychology, but today, this theory has been developed in other sectors such as the tourism sector to find out the needs and motivation factors of tourists who decide to visit tourism sites. Based on Maslow's hierarchy of needs, people are motivated to gain their basic needs before moving on to others. Maslow talks about this hierarchy of needs as: 1 – biological and physiological needs, 2 – safety needs, 3 – belongingness and love needs, 4 – esteem needs, 5 – cognitive needs, 6 – esthetic needs, 7 – self-actualization, and 8 – transcendence (Maslow, 1943). Maslow's theory has not been seen as a pyramid by himself (Bridgman et al., 2019) but is represented as a pyramid in some tourism researches such as Ştefan (2019), Häfner et al. (2020), Kataya (2021), Dehdar et al. (2022), Panagiotopoulos et al. (2022), to name a few. This can create vagueness and ambiguity of data for planning tourism based on tourists' needs. Maslow (1943) in part of his research divides the hierarchy of needs to deficiency needs and growth needs which can be more applicable for the needs of tourists visiting different tourism sites.

Now in the case of historical tourists, should Maslow's hierarchy of needs be seen as a pyramid to fulfill their needs while visiting historical destinations, or should the needs of historical tourists be prioritized by the growth needs that Maslow mentions in his research? This chapter tries to point out the needs of historical tourists as well as their motivation to visit historical destinations.

The Motivation to Travel

Different theories of tourism motivation can help better understand the behavior of tourists and plan for hospitality in tourism sites such as the push and pull factors (Crompton, 1979; Dann, 1977, 1981), the escape and seeking dichotomy (Iso-Ahola, 1982), and Maslow's hierarchy of needs (1954).

Tourists are driven to a site based on the push–pull factors that are internal motivations for traveling and destination characteristics that draw tourists to the site (Crompton, 1979; Dann, 1977, 1981). Yoon and Uysal (2005) believe that pull factors are the external, situational, or cognitive aspects of motivation.

Iso-Ahola (1982) maintains that there are two major motivation forces that impact the behavior of tourists, namely escapism from their daily routine and seeking psychological rewards by experiencing new things like new places, tastes, etc.

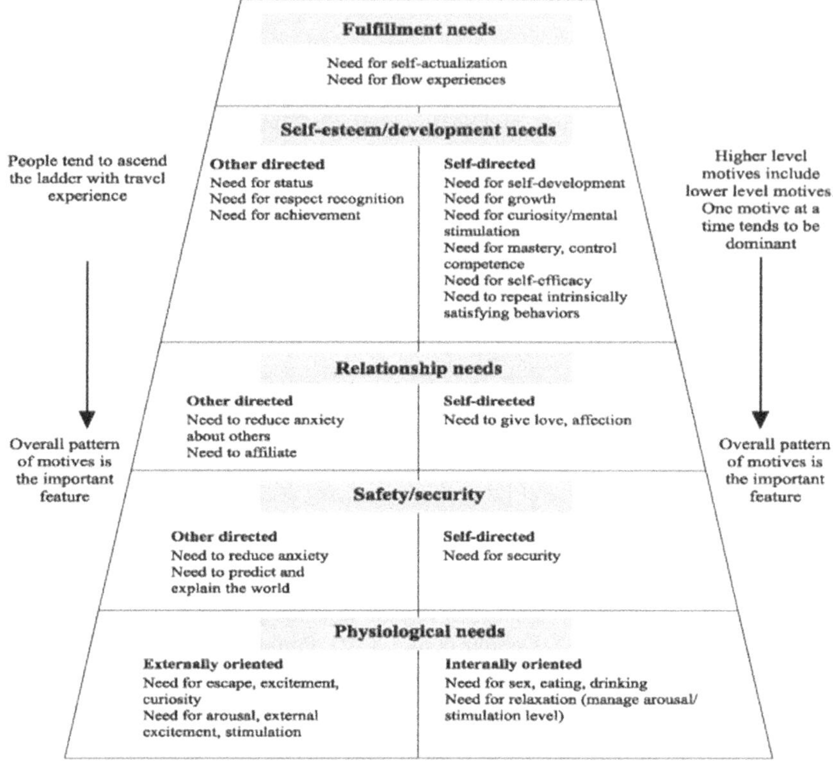

Source: Pearce (1991)

Illustration of Travel Career Ladder (TCL)

Fig. 9.1. Pearce's TCL Model (Wong & Musa, 2014).

Chon (1989) maintains that the motivation to travel is dependent on Maslow's five hierarchy of needs, namely physiological, safety, belonging, self-esteem, and self-actualization but does not mention the cognitive, esthetic, and spiritual needs. Mill and Morrison (1985) classify the hierarchy of needs as the human needs (physiological, safety, belonging) that are tension reducing, and the rest (self-esteem, self-actualization, esthetic, knowledge) as inductive arousal-seeking motives.

Pearce's travel career ladder (TCL) model[1] (Pearce, 1988; 1996) is with regard to Maslow's work (Fig. 9.1). He hypothesized that the more that the tourist is experienced, the more he seeks for higher-order needs such as esteem or affiliation, while the less experienced tourists look for lower-order needs such as safety or food.

[1]The Pearce's TCL model illustrates the different levels of career in the travel industry. The model includes five levels: entry level, first-level management, second-level management, senior management, and executive management.

Tanrisever et al. (2016) talk about the aspects that impact tourist motivations in the TCL model as the psychological, technological, socioeconomic, and demographic factors.

Chuang et al. (2014) believe that a destinations' attractiveness factors may motivate tourists to choose a particular destination. These factors are the location, infrastructure, services, and their cultural and natural attractions. McIntosh et al. (1995) highlight four basic motivation in tourism as the physical motivation, the cultural motivation, interpersonal motivations and motivations regarding status and prestige. In the case of historical sites, even though research has been done on the motivation of travel for cultural and historical tourism (Chuang et al., 2014; Dey et al., 2020), the literature related to cultural tourist's motivation and their preferences based on the hierarchy of needs remains vague.

Maslow's Hierarchy of Needs

Maslow's hierarchy of needs is a theory in psychology proposed by Abraham Maslow in his 1943 paper "A Theory of Human Motivation." The theory states that there is a hierarchy of needs that motivates people, starting with the most basic needs and progressing to the most complex (Fig. 9.2). The most basic needs are physiological needs, such as the need for food, water, and sleep. The next level of needs is safety needs, such as the need for security and protection. After that come love and belonging needs, such as the need for friends, family, and social acceptance. The next levels of needs that are categorized as growth needs

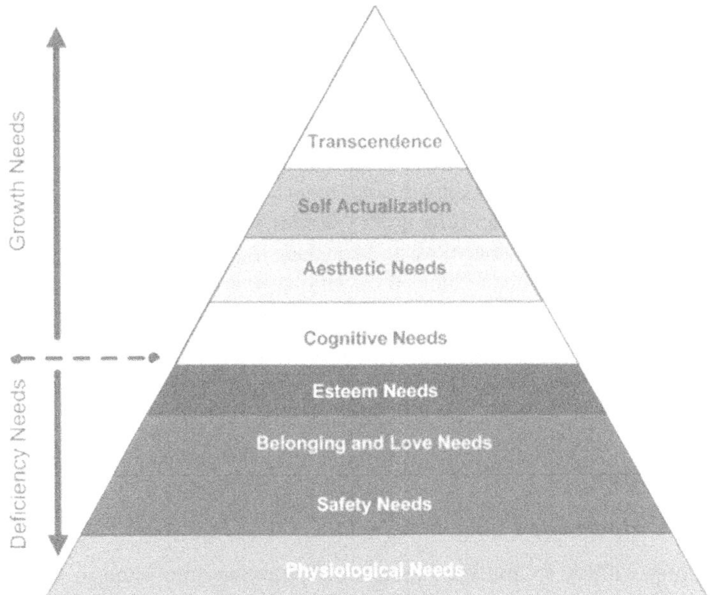

Fig. 9.2. Maslow's Hierarchy of Needs (Maslow, 1943).

are cognitive needs, such as creativity and meaning, and esthetic needs, such as beautiful imagery and esthetically pleasing experience, and then esteem needs, such as the need for self-respect and respect from others. The next level is self-actualization needs, such as the need for creativity, independence, and fulfillment. The highest level is the transcendence needs or spiritual needs (Maslow, 1943).

Maslow's Hierarchy of Needs in Connection with Tourism

One of the most prominent theories is Maslow's hierarchy of needs, which suggests that travel is a way for individuals to satisfy their higher-order needs, such as self-actualization and personal growth. This theory argues that once an individual's basic needs for food, shelter, and safety have been met, they seek experiences that will help travel in a way for individuals to fulfill their self-actualization needs. According to this theory, once an individual has satisfied their basic physiological and safety needs, they begin to seek out experiences that give them a sense of purpose and fulfillment. Travel can provide individuals with opportunities for personal growth, new experiences, and cultural immersion, which all contribute to fulfilling their self-actualization needs.

The deficiency needs are the physiological needs, such as the need for food, water, and sleep (place to stay); safety needs, such as the need for survival, security, and protection; their love and belonging needs, such as the social acceptance and perception; and esteem needs, such as the need for self-respect and respect from others and independence. The growth needs are the cognitive needs such as curiosity and searching meaning on site; esthetic needs, such as seeking an esthetically pleasing experience; self-actualization needs, such as the need for creativity, independence, and fulfillment; and transcendence needs such as spiritual needs.

Maslow's hierarchy of needs has been used in tourism researches, and some represent it as Maslow's pyramid (Dehdar et al., 2022; Häfner et al., 2020; Kataya, 2021; Panagiotopoulos et al., 2022; Ştefan, 2019), while others believe that the needs may not be in the order of the hierarchy of needs (Yousaf et al., 2018).

Adina and Medet (2012) maintain that based on Maslow's hierarchy of needs, when a need is satisfied for the tourists, it will not remain a motivator anymore, and they will try to satisfy the next most important need. Whereas Yousaf et al. (2018) try to analyze the motivation of travel among youth and conclude that even though the hierarchy of needs is validated by the cited author's proposition, some groups of travelers may have needs that are not prioritized in the same order that Maslow suggests.

This research will try to find out the motivation of travel among cultural and historical tourists and seek if their needs are based on the same order of Maslow's hierarchy of needs.

Methodology

Framework Method and Case Study

This chapter will try to analyze the needs of travelers interested in visiting historical sites and their motivation to visit these sites. In this qualitative research, grounded theory will be used as the framework method based on Maslow's hierarchy of needs. Data will be gathered from internet sources about the experience of tourists while traveling to historical destinations and their needs that have been mentioned in the Internet sources. This research will try to seek the similarities of historical tourists' needs while visiting historical destinations.

In order to find out the needs of historical travelers in historical sites, a case study is chosen that is nominated in the World Heritage List with remains of an ancient era that represent its glory. The PPHR is chosen as the case study with five distinctive sites that most have been designated in the World Heritage List of the United Nations Educational, Scientific, and Cultural Organization (UNESCO).

Statistics used in this research belonged to statistics before the COVID-19 pandemic in order to be able to evaluate the sequence of travel in the area without the influence of global outbreaks. It should be noted that based on the latest annual research of the World Travel and Tourism Council (WTTC, 2023), after the COVID-19 pandemic, in 2022, there has been a 22% increase from 2021, but the gross domestic product (GDP) global contribution from the Travel and Tourism Sector is still 23% below the level in 2019. The next phase of this research will be on the impact of outbreaks such as the COVID-19 on tourists' needs and motivation to travel to historical sites.

PPHR

Nowadays, many universities have conducted studies on Persepolis and other sites in the PPHR, such as The Oriental Institute of the University of Chicago, and research is perused in order to solve the questions and mysteries regarding this ancient destination. But in spite of all information in hand and films and documentations that picture the image of this destination, this site still remains an important place that attracts historical tourists who are eager to feel the history and the glory of the era and explore the intangible aspects that are hidden beneath the remains of this destination. Tourists who visit the historical sites in the PPHR are eager to step back into history and picture the Achaemenid Dynasty with its powerful and influential rulers. They are interested to walk on the steps that once the Achaemenid Kings walked on and feel the power and the glory of the area and the palaces. For this aim, they travel to the destination and visit the site to sense the tangible and intangible features that the historical sites in the PPHR represent and learn more about the story behind them.

The PPHR was chosen as the area of study, and five historical destinations located in this range, belonging to the Achaemenid Empire, were selected. These distinctive sites included *Persepolis*, *Naghsh-e-Rajab*, *Estakhr*, *Naghsh-e-Rostam*, and *Pasargadae*, located in Fars Province, in southwestern Iran. Some sites in this historical range have already been designated World Heritage Sites, and some are on the tentative list of the UNESCO (Fig. 9.3).

Based on the eight-year statistics (2011–2018) of the Cultural Heritage, Handicrafts, and Tourism Organization of Fars Province (2019), these sites have witnessed an upward trend in terms of international tourism visits, even though an overall decrease is being observed at some sites (Table 9.1).

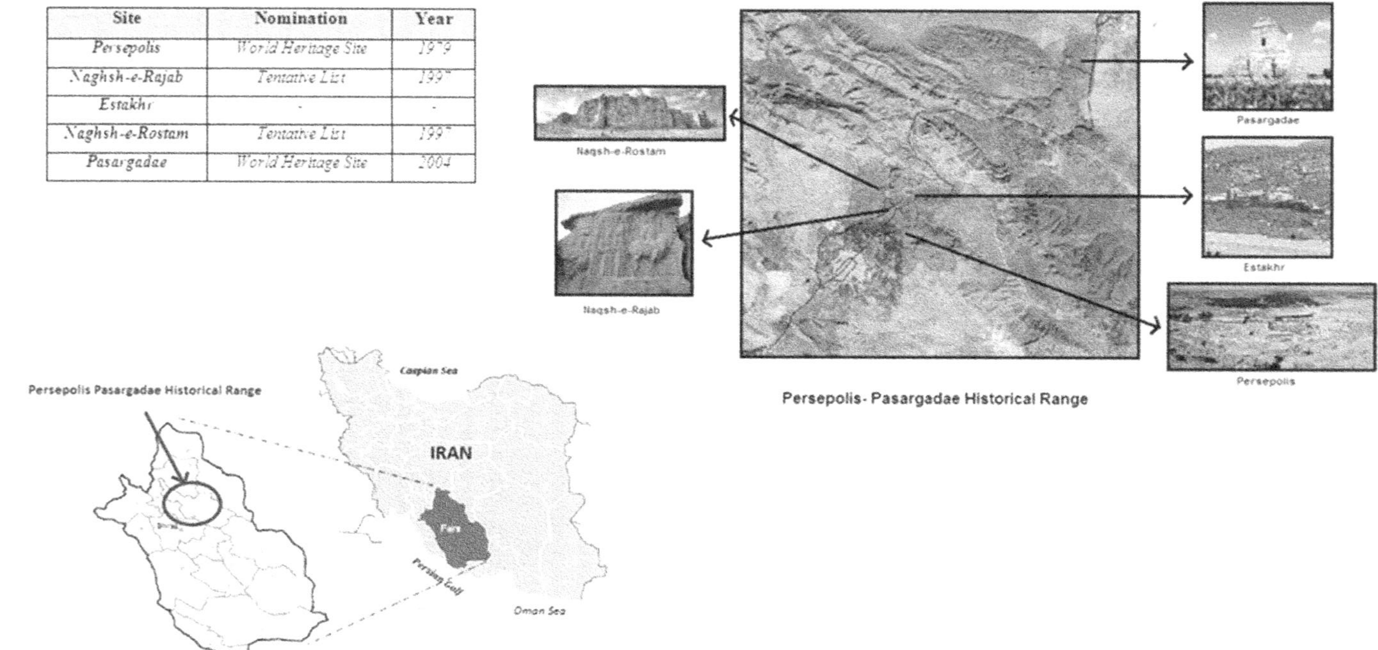

Site	Nomination	Year
Persepolis	*World Heritage Site*	*1979*
Naghsh-e-Rajab	*Tentative List*	*1997*
Estakhr	-	-
Naghsh-e-Rostam	*Tentative List*	*1997*
Pasargadae	*World Heritage Site*	*2004*

Fig. 9.3. Historical Sites Located in the PPHR (Saremi, 2022).

Table 9.1. Total Tourists (International and National) Visiting the PPHR.

Site	2011	2012	2013	2014	2015	2016	2017	2018
Persepolis	1,164,349	1,205,105	1,200,866	1,085,382	1,148,690	1,136,219	918,167	913,515
Naqsh-e-Rajab	32,555	23,757	23,391	19,497	27,961	21,792	18,878	19,790
Naqsh-e-Rostam	226,676	215,755	200,176	176,174	226,032	243,176	201,229	214,863
Pasargadae	349,699	413,426	424,204	392,951	374,823	392,112	391,935	405,612

Source: Ministry of Cultural Heritage, Tourism, and Handicrafts, 2019.

Now, this chapter aims to find what motivates tourists to visit these sites and the needs that they consider important while on site. For these reasons, the PPHR was selected for this case study.

The Hierarchy of Needs Among Tourists Visiting the PPHR

Research Context

In order to explore the needs of tourists in the PPHR, visitors were selected for the case study who had visited the PPHR from 2010 to 2019. The main aim was to reflect on the experiences of contemporary tourists who had just visited the PPHR and to assess their viewpoints regarding the aspects representing these historical sites. Since conducting interviews on site was time-consuming for tourists, their willingness to participate in the study was limited, and they did not feel comfortable answering the questions on site. After several attempts asking visitors to participate on site or reply when returning home, fewer than five interviews were conducted, so it was decided to study and analyze tourists' viewpoints and experiences about the PPHR from common tourism websites that were accessible for all and were well known and had a high participation rate among tourists.

Google, Facebook, and Instagram were used as the search engine for this research because of the common usage of these websites and pages among people worldwide. The next step was to search each website and see if comments have been recorded about the PPHR in their site.

For Facebook and Instagram, travel pages that people had written about their travel experience were searched, and among them, pages that had written about Iran and more specifically the PPHR were chosen for further research.

At the next step, surveys were obtained from the selected tourism websites in which the tourists had written about their experiences visiting the PPHR in websites such as www.tripadvisor.com, www.trip.com, www.lonelyplanet.com, www.serioustraveler.com, and www.irandestination.com as well as travel and tourism pages in Facebook and Instagram such as Solo Women Travelers and Travel Concepts International Inc. (TCI) and bloggers such as www.backpackadventures.org and www.theplanet.com. It should be noted that the survey research method was based on the grounded theory for qualitative research (Corbin & Strauss, 2008).

Based on the derived results and for the validity of this research Trip Advisor and Lonely Planet were chosen for further work. The chosen websites had the most participation among tourists which prevented being biased, had written about all the historical sites in the PPHR, were relatively up to date with less gap periods, and were well known among people interested to travel.

The data were accordingly retrieved from these websites in which individuals were able to express their experiences about their visits to the study area. Information was further gathered from a 10-year period (2010–2019) in distinction to tourists who had participated in the survey from tourism websites and had written about their experiences of travel to the PPHR. In total, 1,578 tourists were selected who had written comments about the PPHR.

All tourists' writings about the site were considered as a data source, and the main cores were coded accordingly. This process continued until saturation was achieved. In this process, more expressions became definite through the similarities mentioned by many of the tourists. At that point, the study reached the phase where no new ideas emerged, and coding of the expressions was discontinued. As a result, the number of the samples reached 401 respondents.

The components derived from each of the respondents were first coded using open coding to identify the primary subjects. Then, subjects were rearranged into new and more classified codes using axial coding in order to achieve the main basis of image formation. Finally, all the results were repositioned to finalize the definition of the concept. The results which emerged were ultimately utilized to restructure the components, helping form the hierarchy of tourist's needs visiting the PPHR.

In order to code the components from these data sources, the type of needs among tourists was derived based on Maslow's hierarchy of needs, and eight levels of needs emerged accordingly (Table 9.2).

Results

Tourists' Experiences

In this part of the research, tourists' comments about the PPHR were derived from tourism websites. These travelers were from 61 countries. They visited the site within a 10-year period and posted their experiences of visiting the PPHR on tourism websites.

All the statements were extracted and coded with reference to the grounded theory as follows:

Open coding: In accordance with open coding, 19 variables were specified as primary subjects and their frequency percentage was subsequently measured (Table 9.1). These variables were extracted from the travelers' responses regarding their perceptions toward these sites.

Axial coding: In the next step, six subcategories were derived from 19 variables with regard to axial coding (Table 9.3). The subjects extracted included the following, categorized into six groups, i.e., cognitive, affective, conative, sense of place, sense of era, and place identity. Each axis is described in this table.

Table 9.2. Tourists' Needs Based on Maslow's Hierarchy of Needs.

Spiritual needs	Transcendence needs
Self-actualization	Completeness, sustainability
Esthetic needs	Beautiful imagery, esthetically pleasing experience
Cognitive needs	Creativity, curiosity, meaning
Esteem needs	Self-respect, self-confidence, independence
Belonging needs	Social needs, perception, awareness, expectancy
Safety needs, stability	Health, personal security, emotional security, financial security
Physiological needs	Survival, basic needs

Table 9.3. Tourist's Experience in the PPHR (Derived from Saremi, 2022).

Responses	Variables (Open Coding) With Percentage	Percentage	Category (Axial Coding)	Core Category (Aspects)
Responses regarding the atmosphere of the destination, feelings toward exploring the surroundings and belonging toward the area	• Feeling and place attachment • Visual light specification (function) • Impression toward a site	52.88	Sense of place	Intangible
Responses related to the era when the site had its glory The ability to feel and sense the history in mind	• Historical background • Distinction/glory • Power	78.45	Sense of era	Intangible
Responses related to clusters of idea about the identity of the site in fields of architecture, sociology, environment (geography), planning	• Space recognition • Grandeur • Preservation and protection • Myths	90.91	Place identity	Intangible
Perceptual responses: verbal statements of beliefs opinion, beliefs	• History • Knowledge • Culture and civilization • Myths and stories	95.01	Cognitive – awareness and beliefs of the visitor toward the site	Influential
Sympathetic nervous responses: verbal statements of affects, feelings, evaluation	• Environmental conditions • Art and architecture • Sense of fun (joyfulness, leisure) • Amazing, impressing, glory (impression toward a site)	87.03	Affective – visitor's feelings toward the site	Influential
Overt actions: verbal statements concerning behavior (behavioral intentions)	• Distinction/value (appraise)	43.14	Conative – practical trends with respect toward the site	Influential

Based on the results derived from the experience of tourists visiting the PPHR and with regard to Maslow's hierarchy of needs, the priority of tourists visiting this historical range can be categorized as below:

The physiological needs were less mentioned in the reviews. The availability of hotels, restaurants, and souvenir shops was mentioned by some visitors but not considered as a main necessity.

The safety needs were considered as a need, and visiting in the cooler weather or having a hat and water while on site was mentioned. Visiting early in the morning was suggested. The lack of routes for the wheelchairs for people with less mobility was mentioned in the reviews.

The belonging needs were considered as needs such as visiting the site with tour guides or local residents for a better understanding of the site as well as gaining knowledge about the hidden stories of the destination.

The esteem needs were considered as the hospitality that was sensed in the cities and while on sites which was sensed in the culture of people in Iran and appreciated by the visitors.

The cognitive needs were considered as needs of gaining knowledge about the story and myths behind the carvings with their beliefs. These stories were gained from pre-readings, on-site information, and information gained from tour guides.

The esthetic needs were considered as the place identity and their appreciation because of the glory of the site, the architecture and carvings in the site, and their overall pleasing experience while visitation. These needs were gained based on the remains in the site and complemented by the stories said or by VR goggles that helped gain a better sense of the place and era.

The self-actualization and spiritual needs were seen together as the impression that tourists had gained toward the site after visiting the destination and gaining knowledge about the history of the site as well as knowledge about the myths and beliefs that the era represented. These needs which are also considered as their growth needs continued by gaining more knowledge after visitation. These needs were mainly mentioned by more than 90% of visitors and considered as the main reason for visiting these sites (Fig. 9.4).

Discussions and Implications

In today's competitive tourism market, being able to give service based on tourist's needs is essential. The patterns and preferences of tourists for visiting a tourism site can be considered as an information database for planners and managers in the tourism industry. Therefore, gaining knowledge about tourists' deficiency and growth needs can form a database for planners and help them build their marketing scenarios based on this information. Information is often used to minimize the perceived risk and the uncertainty that is associated with the destinations that travelers do not know (Beerli & Martin, 2004). Tourism motivation is a variable that explains their behavior and is considered one of the important factors in this industry (Crompton, 1979). Maslow's motivation theory (1970), namely the hierarchy of needs, is applied in tourist literature and in marketing scenarios. But mostly it is used as a pyramid of needs which may not be applicable for all

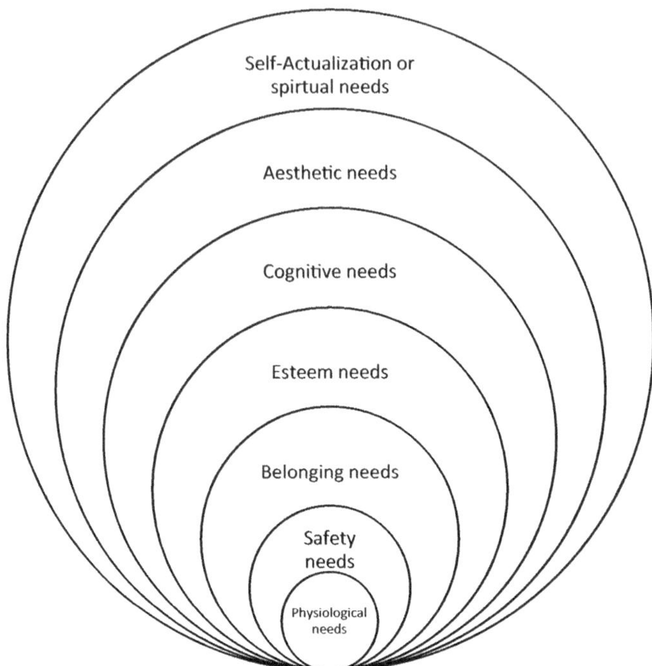

Fig. 9.4. The Priority of Needs Among the Tourists of the PPHR (Derived From Saremi, 2022, and Based on Maslow's Hierarchy of Needs).

types of tourists such as historical tourists. This research tried to gather data on the motivation of historical tourists interested in visiting historical sites and their needs while on site. Their motivation to visit these destinations can be considered as important information sources in tourism studies and a database for planners and managers in the tourism industry for marketing these sites and long-term development.

Based on the results, tourists visiting the historical sites of the case study did consider the basic needs essential for their reason to travel to these sites. Their reason for travel was more for the fulfillment of their growth needs. Their motivation was more to gain knowledge about the history behind these remains with their hidden stories. They were seeking to find an emotional connection with the site and to improve their perception toward the site. Therefore, as Meng and Uysal (2019) maintain, storytelling can enhance the authenticity of the site and give an emotional connection toward these destinations. Some needs overlapped with others in the growth needs. Based on the results, the visitors of the PPHR were interested in discovering the myths and stories of the Achaemenid era. Consequently, the use of VR gadgets complemented their experience and helped them sense this historical era. So, VR as Xiang et al. (2017) point out can enhance the emotional aspects of their tourism experience and improve their intention to visit these destinations. Virtual Tours can help enhance the value and intention to visit a destination and provide a more immersive and authentic tourism experience (Choi & Lehto, 2016). Tourists were exploring the identity of the site with their cognition and beliefs which they had toward these destinations. Most of them had gained knowledge prior to their visitation and were looking forward to feel the sense of place and era from the remains left while on site. Therefore, information sectors such as social media can help tourists gain knowledge prior to their decision to visit a site (Xiang et al., 2017).

Conclusion

Historical sites attract tourists from across the world, eager to feel the history and the splendor of the era and to explore the reality within the remains. Marketing strategies for historical tourism should be based on the needs of tourists and their motivation to visit a site. Planners and marketers in the tourism industry should be able to understand what drives a tourist to visit a tourism destination in order to plan strategies to promote these destinations. Historical sites are considered as important attraction sources. The stories of these ancient destinations are replete with myths, mysteries, and glories. There is a plethora of data sources, films, and documentation picturing these sites; however, nothing can replace the historical site itself. People are motivated to visit these sites because of sensing the place and era while on site. Additionally, incorporating new technologies like VR can enhance tourists,' experience of historical sites which may have limited remains that represent the glory of the site. These smart gadgets can help visitors experience a dynamic journey through history and sense the era of the historical destination. From highlighting the educational value of a particular location to emphasizing the sensory experience that tourists can gain for cultural immersion, marketers should be able to create a compelling narrative that resonates with each tourist. Moreover, the use of smart technology and innovative marketing techniques can help tourists experience a memorable trip. Ultimately, successful marketing strategies for historical destinations require a deep understanding of the needs of tourists interested in visiting these destinations.

References

Adina, N., & Medet, Y. (2012). Cultural tourism motivation- The case of Romanian youths. *Annals of Faculty of Economics, University of Oradea. 1*(1), 548–553.

Beerli, A., & Martin, J. D. (2004). Factors influencing destination image. *Annals of Tourism Research, 31*, 657–681.

Bowen, J. T., & Shoemaker, S. (2003). Loyalty: A strategic commitment. *Cornell Hotel and Restaurant Administration Quarterly, 44*(5–6), 31–46.

Bridgman, T., Cummings, S., & Ballard, J. (2019). Who built Maslow's pyramid? A history of the creation of management studies' most famous symbol and its implications for management education. *Academy of Management Learning & Education, 18*(1), 81–98.

Choi, H. S., & Lehto, X. Y. (2016). Virtual reality and destination marketing: A study of visitors' perception. *Journal of Travel Research*, *55*(2), 182–195.
Chon, K. S. (1990). The role of destination image in tourism: a review and discussion. *Tourism Review*. *45*, 2–9. doi: 10.1108/eb058040
Chuang, Y., Hwang, S., Wong, J., & Chen, C. (2014). The attractiveness of tourist night markets in Taiwan – A supply-side view. *International Journal of Culture, Tourism and Hospitality Research*, *8*(3), 333–344.
Corbin, J., & Strauss, A. (2008). *Basics of qualitative research: Techniques and procedures for developing grounded theory* (3rd Ed.). Sage Publications, Inc. https://doi.org/10.4135/9781452230153
Crompton, J. L. (1979). Motivations for pleasure vacation. *Annals of Tourism Research*, *6*(4), 408–424.
Cultural Heritage, Handicrafts, and Tourism Organization of Fars Province (2019). Yearly statistical data of Fars Province tourism. Cultural Heritage, Handicrafts, and Tourism Organization of Fars Province.
Dann, G. (1977). Anomie, ego-enhancement and tourism. *Annals of Tourism Research*, *4*(4), 184–194.
Dann, G. M. S. (1981). Tourism motivations: An appraisal. *Annals of Tourism Research*, *8*(2), 189–219.
Dehdar, M., Aminibehbahani, F., Karoubi, M., & Gohar, F. Y. (2022). Model of relation between temperament and travel motivation in tourism. *Journal of Positive School Psychology*, *6*(7), 231–245.
Dey, B., Mathew, J., & Chee-Hua, C. (2020). Influence of destination attractiveness factors and travel motivations on rural homestay choice: The moderating role of need for uniqueness. *International Journal of Culture, Tourism and Hospitality Research*, *14*(4), 639–666.
Häfner, F., Härting, R. C., & Kaim, R. (2020, September). Potentials of digital approaches in a tourism industry with changing customer needs – A quantitative study. In *2020 15th conference on computer science and information systems (FedCSIS)* (pp. 553–557). IEEE.
Harrison, D. (Ed.). (1992). *Tourism and the less developed world: Issues and case studies*. CAB International.
Homans, G. C. (1958). *Social exchange theory*. Wiley.
Iso-Ahola, E. (1982). Towards a social psychology theory of tourism motivation: A rejoinder. *Annals of Tourism Research*, *9*(2), 256–262.
Kataya, A. (2021). Current trends and issues of luxury tourism. Empirical research on supply and demand effects of Covid-19 pandemic. *Annals of the University Dunarea de Jos of Galati: Fascicle: I, Economics & Applied Informatics*, *27*(2), 46–54.
Maslow, A. H. (1943). A theory of human motivation. *Psychological Review*, *50*(4), 370–396.
Maslow, A. H. (1954). *Motivation and personality*. New York: Harper.
Maslow, A. H. (1970). *Motivation and personality* (2nd ed.).Harper & Row.
Maslow, A. H. (1996). Critique of self-actualization theory. In E. Hoffman (Ed.), *Future visions: The unpublished papers of Abraham Maslow* (pp. 26–32). Thousand Oaks, CA: Sage
McIntosh, R. W., Goeldner, C. R., & Ritchie, J. B. (1995). *Tourism: principles, practices, philosophies* (7 ed.). John Wiley and Sons.
McKercher, B., & Cros, H. (2002). *Cultural tourism: the partnership between tourism and cultural heritage management*. New York: Haworth Hospitality Press.
Meng, F., & Uysal, M. (2019). Storytelling as a destination marketing tool: A comparative study of U.S. and China. *Journal of Travel Research*, *58*(2), 216–229.
Mill, R. C., & Morrison, A. M. (1985). *The tourism system: An introductory text*. Prentice Hall.
Ministry of Cultural Heritage, Handicrafts, and Tourism Organization. (2019). Yearly statistical data of Fars Province tourism, Cultural Heritage, Handicrafts, and Tourism Organization.

Panagiotopoulos, P., Mitoula, R., Georgitsogianni, E., & Theodoropoulou, E. (2022). The contribution of sports tourism to sustainable development based on sustainable development indicators – The case of Greece. *International Journal of Multidisciplinary Research and Analysis*, *5*, 1666–1678.

Park, D.-B., & Yoon, Y.-S. (2009). Segmentation by motivation in rural tourism: A Korean case study. *Tourism Management*, *30*, 99–108.

Pearce, P. (1988). *The Ulysses factor: Evaluating visitors in tourist settings*. Springer.

Pearce, P. (1996). Recent research in tourist behavior. *Asia-Pacific Journal of Tourism Research*, *1*, 7–17.

Relph, E. (1976). *Place and placelessness*. Pion.

Saremi, M. (2022). Environmental planning based on modeling cultural tourist behavior case study: Persepolis-Pasargadae Range. [Doctoral dissertation, Alborz Campus, Tehran University].

Saremi, M., Darabi, H., Amiri, M. J., Nabi Bidhendi, G., & Irani Behbahani, H. (2022). Analyzing the perceptional pattern of historical tourists regarding historical sites case study: The Persepolis-Pasargadae Historical Range. *Journal of Geographic Space*, *79*, 133–156.

Ştefan, A. (2019). Development of Romanian Balneo tourism. *Ovidius University Annals. Economic Sciences Series*, *19*, 316–320.

Tanrisever, C., Pamukçu, H., & Batman, O. (2016), New tourism trends in the world and their adaptations to Turkey. *Gümüşhane Üniversitesi Sosyal Bilimler Enstitüsü Elektronik Dergisi*, *7*, 55–72.

Vargo, S. L., & Lusch, R. F. (2008). Service-dominant logic: Continuing the evolution. *Journal of the Academy of Marketing Science*, *36*(1), 1–10.

Wang, D., & Li, X. (2018). The impact of cognitive dissonance on travel satisfaction: Evidence from Chinese outbound tourists. *Journal of Destination Marketing & Management*, *8*, 62–70.

Wong, K. M., & Musa, G. (2014). Retirement motivation among 'Malaysia My Second Home' participants. *Tourism Management*, *40*, 141–154.

Woodside, A. G., & Martin, D. (2008). *Tourism management: Analysis, behaviour and strategy*. CABI.

World Travel and Tourism Council. (2023). https://wttc.org/research/economic-impact

Xiang, Z., Du, Q., Ma, Y., & Fan, W. (2017). A comparative analysis of major online review platforms: Implications for social media analytics in hospitality and tourism. *Journal of Travel Research*, *56*(8), 959–969.

Yoon, Y., & Uysal, M. (2005). An examination of the effects of motivation and satisfaction on destination loyalty: A structural model. *Tourism Management*, *26*(1), 45–56.

Yousaf, A., Amin, I., & Santos, J. A. (2018). Tourist's motivations to travel: A theoretical perspective on the existing literature. *Tourism and Hospitality Management*, *24*(1), 197–211.

Chapter 10

Salience of Corporate Sustainability: Proposed Operationalization

Hiranya Dissanayake[a,b], *Hareendra Dissabandara*[a], *Roshan Ajward*[a], *Wasantha Perera*[a], *Catalin Popescu*[c] *and Irina Gabriela Radulescu*[c]

[a]*University of Sri Jayewardenepura, Sri Lanka*
[b]*Wayamba University of Sri Lanka, Sri Lanka*
[c]*Petroleum-Gas University of Ploiesti, Romania*

Abstract

This bibliometric analysis underscores the increasing importance of corporate sustainability in the post-COVID-19 era. Despite existing confusion and a dearth of studies on measuring corporate sustainability, the study identifies a significant methodological gap and endeavors to address it by proposing a comprehensive measure. The primary goal is to bridge this gap by conducting a bibliometric analysis on the scale of corporate sustainability, examining 126 documents spanning from 2001 to 2022. The study employs an expert opinion survey to identify and finalize dimensions and sub-dimensions of corporate sustainability, followed by a literature mapping process to formulate questionnaire items. A pilot survey is then conducted to ensure the reliability of the questionnaire. The study proposes utilizing the Organisation for Economic Co-operation and Development (OECD) index construction methodology to establish the Corporate Sustainability Index (CSI). The key findings reveal that corporate sustainability comprises economic, environmental, and social sustainability. Environmental sustainability encompasses aspects such as air, water, land, biodiversity, ocean preservation, waste prevention, and environmental management. Social sustainability involves the satisfaction of various stakeholders, including employees, shareholders, customers, community, government, nongovernmental organizations (NGOs), and suppliers. Economic sustainability is characterized by long-term profits, cost efficiency,

Emerging Patterns and Behaviors in a Green Resilient Economy, 205–231

doi:10.1108/978-1-83549-780-720241011

trade-offs, sustainable investments, and spin-offs. Rooted in stakeholder theory, the proposed scale holds theoretical significance for researchers and is pertinent to policymakers striving to achieve sustainable development goals (SDGs) by 2030. Additionally, it serves as a crucial tool for practitioners and companies to assess their level of corporate sustainability.

Keywords: Corporate sustainability; operationalization; stakeholder theory; bibliometric analysis; environmental sustainability; index construction

Introduction

Corporate sustainability has become increasingly important in response to pressing global challenges such as climate change, social inequality, and resource depletion. It seeks to create a positive impact on society and the environment while ensuring economic viability (Carroll, 2015). The United Nations Global Compact defines corporate sustainability as a company's commitment to delivering long-term value in financial, social, environmental, and ethical terms (UNGC, 2015, p. 10). This concept involves integrating environmental, social, and economic considerations into business strategies and operations, acknowledging that organizations have a responsibility to balance their economic goals with the well-being of society and the preservation of the environment (Elkington, 1997). Sustainable practices are vital for addressing societal challenges, reducing environmental impact, and ensuring long-term viability.

Interestingly, the COVID-19 pandemic, originating in China in December 2019 and spreading globally in 2020 (World Health Organisation (WHO), 2020), coincided with a heightened focus on corporate sustainability issues worldwide (World Economic Forum (WEF), 2020). With lockdowns affecting cities worldwide, countries faced survival challenges for businesses.

In emerging markets and developing countries (excluding China), cumulative per capita income losses from 2020 to 2022 were projected to be equivalent to 20% of 2019 per capita gross domestic product (GDP), whereas losses in advanced economies were expected to be relatively smaller, at 11% (WEF, 2020). According to current projections, the global GDP was estimated to be approximately \$84.54 trillion in 2020, meaning that a 4.5% decline in economic growth would cost the world economy nearly \$2.961 trillion (Szmigiera, 2022). Similar dynamics affected various industries, such as declining demand for oil and new vehicles due to restrictions on daily commutes, gatherings, and events (Statista, 2020). South Asia, comprising developing countries, faced significant sustainability challenges during the COVID-19 pandemic (World Bank, 2020). South Asian Economic Focus forecasted regional growth to fall between 1.8% and 2.8% in 2020, down from the 6.3% projected six months prior (World Bank, 2020). The worst-case scenario involved prolonged and widespread national lockdowns resulting in negative growth for the entire region (World Bank, 2020). Currently, the world confronts major sustainability challenges, including climate change, stratospheric ozone depletion, loss of biodiversity, deforestation, air pollution, inequity, child labor, and human rights violations, exacerbated by the spread of COVID-19 (Rosen, 2018). Consequently, sustainability issues have gained global prominence and are expected to remain essential over the next 30 years. Hesse and Olsen (2017) anticipate a Green World in 2030 that is collective, integrated, and driven by a strong social conscience.

In this world, companies prioritize ethical and ecological agendas, responding to public opinion, dwindling natural resources, and stringent international regulations. Berger (2017) identifies sustainability and global responsibility as the seventh mega-trend (Berger, 2017). In 2022, corporate governance reports published by leading companies such as Russel Reynolds and Deloitte emphasize the importance of sustainability issues in corporate governance (Field et al., 2022).

In the wake of the COVID-19 pandemic, corporate sustainability has ascended to a position of unprecedented importance in academic discourse and the global business landscape. Organizations are under increasing scrutiny to align their operations with sustainable practices, driven by both environmental imperatives and societal expectations. However, despite the intensifying focus on corporate sustainability, a notable research gap persists – a deficiency in robust methodologies for measuring and evaluating corporate sustainability comprehensively. This deficiency is compounded by the limited availability of empirical studies addressing this pivotal issue, thus impeding our ability to enact effective and sustainable corporate practices.

This research gap finds resonance in the seminal work of Waddock (1997), who laid the foundation for contemporary discussions on corporate sustainability. They astutely observed the dearth of comprehensive metrics and advocated for a more holistic approach. Yet, despite decades of scholarly engagement, including the comprehensive bibliometric analysis conducted by Tseng et al. (2020), the confusion surrounding the measurement of corporate sustainability remains. The complexity of the post-COVID-19 era has introduced new dimensions and urgencies to the sustainability discourse, further underscoring the necessity for an updated and all-encompassing framework.

In light of these challenges, this study undertakes a dual mission: first, to bridge the existing methodological gap in the measurement of corporate sustainability and, second, to respond effectively to the evolving dimensions of sustainability in the post-COVID-19 landscape. Our research journey commences with rigorous bibliometric analysis, synthesizing insights from a comprehensive dataset comprising 126 scholarly documents published from 2001 to 2022. Through this analysis, we not only identify the core dimensions but also unveil the intricate sub-dimensions that constitute the multifaceted concept of corporate sustainability.

Our efforts are fortified by the call for comprehensiveness found in the work of Tseng et al. (2020), who emphasize the imperative of a unified framework that incorporates environmental, social, and economic aspects of sustainability. Our study resonates with this call by exploring the intricate facets of corporate sustainability, categorizing them into three fundamental dimensions: economic, environmental, and social sustainability.

Our research holds theoretical significance, rooted in stakeholder theory and building upon prior work such as (Freeman, 1999) seminal work on stakeholder theory. Moreover, it is highly relevant to policymakers who aspire to achieve the SDGs by 2030, offering a practical tool to align corporate practices with global sustainability objectives.

In this chapter, we embark on a comprehensive exploration of corporate sustainability, addressing its increasing significance in response to global challenges, especially amid the COVID-19 pandemic. We begin by highlighting the critical importance of corporate sustainability and the pressing need for a robust measurement framework. Our research journey encompasses a thorough literature review to contextualize the field, a meticulous methodology section detailing our approach, and the presentation of key findings and outcomes.

Through our research, we bridge the existing methodological gap in corporate sustainability measurement while responding adeptly to the evolving dimensions of sustainability in the post-COVID-19 landscape. Our ultimate goal is to contribute to both academic discourse and practical applications in corporate sustainability, providing stakeholders with a comprehensive tool to align business practices with global sustainability objectives.

Methodology

The discussion on corporate sustainability, its growing importance in response to global challenges, and the impact of the COVID-19 pandemic serves as the backdrop for the research methodology employed in this study. The introduction highlights the significance of corporate sustainability and the need for a comprehensive measurement framework. It also underscores the evolving nature of sustainability in the post-COVID-19 landscape. The "Methodology" section outlines the research approach taken to address the challenges associated with measuring corporate sustainability comprehensively. This approach is a response to the gaps and complexities highlighted in the earlier discussion.

Bibliometric Analysis

The study commences with a meticulous bibliometric analysis. This analysis encompasses an exhaustive review of 126 relevant documents related to corporate sustainability, spanning the years 2001–2022 using biblioshiny software (Aria & Cuccurullo, 2017). Through this extensive literature review, we gain valuable insights into the historical development, key themes, and prominent trends within the field. Moreover, this analysis helps identify critical gaps and areas of confusion surrounding the measurement of corporate sustainability, laying the groundwork for subsequent research.

Table 10.1 provides essential details about the dataset used in the study, spanning the years 2001–2022 and comprising 126 documents sourced from 84 different publications. It reveals an annual growth rate of 16.34%, signifying the

Table 10.1. Main Research Information.

Description	**Results**
Timespan	2001:2022
Sources (journals, books, etc.)	84
Documents	126
Annual growth rate (%)	16.34
Document average age	5.21
Average citations per doc	20.6
References	7,457
Document contents	
Keywords plus (ID)	382
Author's keywords (DE)	450
Authors	
Authors	365
Authors of single-authored docs	12
Authors collaboration	
Single-authored docs	12
Co-authors per doc	3.02
International co-authorships (%)	23.81
Document types	
Article	113
Book chapter	5
Conference paper	6
Review	2

Source: *Constructed by the authors with biblioshiny software.*

increasing relevance of corporate sustainability in the post-COVID-19 era. The documents have an average age of 5.21 years, with each document cited an average of 20.6 times, indicating their impact on the field. The dataset encompasses 365 unique authors, including 12 who authored single-authored documents and reflects a collaborative environment, with an average of 3.02 co-authors per document and 23.81% of co-authorships being international. Document types vary, with the majority being articles (113), followed by book chapters (5), conference papers (6), and reviews (2). Additionally, there are 382 unique keywords plus (ID) and 450 unique author's keywords (DE) within the dataset, enhancing its searchability and relevance. This comprehensive dataset forms the foundation for the study's robust analysis and findings regarding the measurement and importance of corporate sustainability.

Dimension Identification

Building on the insights gleaned from the bibliometric analysis, the study proceeds to identify the fundamental dimensions and sub-dimensions constituting the core framework for evaluating corporate sustainability. These dimensions are pivotal in capturing the multidimensional nature of sustainability effectively. Their identification draws upon a synthesis of existing literature and expert opinions.

Expert Opinion Survey

To enhance the credibility and relevance of the identified dimensions, an expert opinion survey is conducted. Esteemed experts in the field of sustainability are engaged to provide critical insights and validation. Their expertise and feedback serve as a crucial validation mechanism, ensuring that the selected dimensions align with the complexities and nuances of corporate sustainability. This expert input also aids in prioritizing and weighting the dimensions appropriately.

Literature Mapping: Subsequently, a comprehensive literature mapping process ensues. This iterative step involves a meticulous review of existing research to delineate sub-dimensions and formulate specific questionnaire items under each dimension. This process is indispensable in capturing the richness and diversity of corporate sustainability aspects, ensuring that the measurement tool remains in tune with the latest research findings and industry developments.

Questionnaire Development: Building upon the refined dimensions and sub-dimensions, a comprehensive questionnaire is meticulously crafted. This instrument becomes the primary means by which corporate sustainability is assessed across the identified dimensions. The questionnaire design ensures that it is practical, clear, and capable of capturing both quantitative and qualitative data, making it a valuable tool for researchers, policymakers, and practitioners alike.

Pilot Survey

To evaluate the reliability and effectiveness of the questionnaire, a pilot survey is meticulously administered. A representative sample participates in this phase, providing valuable feedback and data. The findings from the pilot survey enable iterative refinements to the questionnaire, ensuring that it is a robust and dependable tool for assessing corporate sustainability.

Index Construction

Finally, the study proposed the OECD index construction methodology, a well-established and recognized framework (OECD, 2020). This methodology integrates data from the refined questionnaire responses, enabling the construction of the CSI. This index provides a holistic and standardized assessment of corporate sustainability performance, encompassing economic, environmental, and social dimensions.

These steps collectively form a comprehensive methodology designed to develop a robust measure for evaluating corporate sustainability. It ensures that the measure is research driven, expert validated, aligned with contemporary trends, and practical for various stakeholders. This methodology bridges the gap in measuring corporate sustainability comprehensively and contributes to addressing the evolving dimensions of sustainability in the post-COVID-19 landscape.

Results

In this section, we delve into the analysis of the outcomes generated by our research methodology. This phase encompasses the examination and interpretation of the findings across each stage of our study, beginning with the bibliometric analysis and culminating in the development of the CSI.

Insights from Bibliometric Analysis

The bibliometric analysis conducted in this study provided valuable insights into the dynamics of corporate sustainability research. It unearthed a notable surge in the significance of corporate sustainability in the post-COVID-19 landscape, confirming the urgency of sustainability concerns. Importantly, the analysis also unveiled a perplexing landscape characterized by diverse methodologies employed to measure corporate sustainability across the literature. This finding underscores the necessity of a standardized measurement framework, the absence of which had previously created confusion within the field.

Table 10.2 presents a comprehensive trend analysis of the corporate sustainability questionnaire over a span of two decades, from 2001 to 2022. It showcases the evolving research interest and engagement with corporate sustainability, particularly in the context of questionnaire-based studies. The data reveal noteworthy trends: a gradual emergence in the early 2000s, followed by a consistent increase in the number of articles incorporating corporate sustainability questionnaires from 2010 onward.

The year 2022 stands out as a pinnacle, with 24 articles, signifying a substantial surge in research activity in this field. This trend analysis underscores the growing recognition of corporate sustainability's significance and the corresponding academic interest, reflecting the dynamic and evolving nature of sustainability research over time.

Table 10.3 provides a concise overview of country-based involvement in corporate sustainability questionnaire research, shedding light on the global distribution of academic and corporate engagement in this critical field. China leads the pack with 41 instances, showcasing its strong commitment to sustainability assessment, followed closely by the United States and Indonesia, each with 26 instances. Notably, Brazil, Malaysia, and Thailand also exhibit significant participation, indicating the growing importance of sustainability practices in these regions. This table underscores the worldwide recognition of corporate sustainability's significance, as countries from diverse continents, including Europe, Asia, and the Americas, actively contribute to research and development in the realm of sustainability measurement and assessment.

Table 10.2. Trend Analysis.

Year	Articles
2001	1
2002	0
2003	0
2004	0
2005	1
2006	1
2007	1
2008	1
2009	0
2010	3
2011	3
2012	5
2013	3
2014	3
2015	9
2016	7
2017	6
2018	10
2019	17
2020	20
2021	11
2022	24

Source: *Constructed by the authors with biblioshiny software.*

Table 10.4 provides a comprehensive author analysis related to corporate sustainability questionnaires, offering valuable insights into the scholarly impact and productivity of each author in the field. Notably, all authors, including K. Ely and E. Stanny, possess an h-index and g-index of 1, denoting that they have at least one highly cited publication, underscoring their individual contributions to the field's body of knowledge. The varying m-index values reflect differences in sustained impact since their initial publications, while the total citations (TC) reveal the cumulative recognition of their work. Additionally, the number of publications (NP) demonstrates their research output within the domain of corporate sustainability questionnaires. The year of the first publication (PY_start), which ranges from 2001 for I. Knoepfel to 2018 for W. Cong, offers insights into their experience and engagement in this area of study. These statistics collectively

Table 10.3. Country Analysis.

Country	Frequency
China	41
Indonesia	26
USA	26
Brazil	22
Malaysia	18
Thailand	17
Australia	16
UK	16
Czech Republic	15
Spain	14
India	11
Slovakia	11
Germany	10
Nigeria	10
Pakistan	10
Portugal	9
Romania	7
Switzerland	7
Turkey	7
Italy	6

Source: *Constructed by the authors with biblioshiny software.*

illuminate the authors' scholarly influence and their significant roles in advancing the understanding and practice of corporate sustainability assessment.

This source analysis table (Table 10.5) provides valuable insights into the scholarly impact and productivity of various journals within the domain of corporate sustainability questionnaire research. Notably, the *Journal of Cleaner Production* emerges as a standout source with a high h-index and g-index of 7, indicating its significant contributions and sustained impact since 2012. *Sustainability (Switzerland)* also shines with a remarkable h-index of 9 and a high g-index of 12, signifying a substantial and well-distributed influence since its inception in 2016. While other journals such as *Corporate Social Responsibility and Environmental Management* and *Business Strategy and the Environment* have made meaningful contributions, this table aids researchers in identifying influential journals in the field, considering their impact, longevity, and total citations, thereby assisting scholars and practitioners in selecting reliable sources for their corporate sustainability research endeavors.

Table 10.4. Author Analysis.

Authors	h_index	g_index	m_index	TC	NP	PY_start
K. Ely	1	1	0.0625	300	1	2008
E. Stanny	1	1	0.0625	300	1	2008
E. Hession	1	1	0.0526	164	1	2005
B. O'dwyer	1	1	0.0526	164	1	2005
J. Unerman	1	1	0.0526	164	1	2005
D. Elkhawas	1	1	0.0833	157	1	2012
C. Searcy	1	1	0.0833	157	1	2012
A. Al-Ghassani	1	1	0.0556	142	1	2006
C. Anumba	1	1	0.0556	142	1	2006
P. Carrillo	1	1	0.0556	142	1	2006
P. Hąbek	1	1	0.1250	142	1	2016
H. Robinson	1	1	0.0556	142	1	2006
R. Wolniak	1	1	0.1250	142	1	2016
I. Knoepfel	1	1	0.0435	115	1	2001
T. Angus-Leppan	1	1	0.0714	97	1	2010
S. Benn	1	1	0.0714	97	1	2010
L. Young	1	1	0.0714	97	1	2010
W. Cong	1	1	0.1667	84	1	2018
Q. Jiang	1	1	0.1667	84	1	2018
T. Li	1	1	0.1667	84	1	2018

Source: Constructed by the authors with biblioshiny software.

This frequency analysis table (Table 10.6) provides valuable insights into the core themes and concepts within the realm of corporate sustainability questionnaire research. First, the prominence of "corporate sustainability" as the most frequently occurring phrase underscores its central position in the field. It reflects a concentrated effort to assess and measure the sustainability practices of corporations, indicating a dedicated inquiry into how businesses contribute to sustainable development. Additionally, the recurring appearance of "sustainability" independently further reinforces the overarching focus on sustainability-related topics and considerations, illustrating the comprehensive nature of the questionnaire's exploration.

Second, the presence of "corporate social responsibility (CSR)" as a substantial keyword reaffirms the close relationship between CSR practices and corporate sustainability, suggesting that a significant portion of the research pertains to the social dimensions of sustainability.

Table 10.5. Source Analysis.

Source	h_index	g_index	m_index	TC	NP	PY_start
Journal of Cleaner Production	7	7	0.583	403	7	2012
Corporate Social Responsibility and Environmental Management	3	3	0.188	361	3	2008
Business Strategy and the Environment	4	4	0.286	197	4	2010
Sustainability (Switzerland)	9	12	1.125	186	21	2016
European Accounting Review	1	1	0.053	164	1	2005
Business Process Management Journal	1	1	0.056	142	1	2006
Quality and Quantity	1	1	0.125	142	1	2016
Corporate Environmental Strategy	1	1	0.043	115	1	2001
Amfiteatru Economic	1	1	0.083	64	1	2012
Corporate Governance	1	1	0.059	61	1	2007

Source: Constructed by the authors with biblioshiny software.

The emergence of "sustainable development goals" emphasizes a commitment to aligning corporate actions with global sustainability targets, highlighting the growing importance of international sustainability agendas within corporate strategies. Furthermore, the inclusion of leadership-related terms such as "leadership," "sustainable leadership," and "transformational leadership" indicates a recognition of the pivotal role that leadership plays in driving sustainability initiatives within organizations. This suggests that the questionnaire not only assesses sustainability practices but also delves into leadership approaches that promote sustainable development.

Overall, this analysis provides a glimpse into the multifaceted nature of corporate sustainability research, spanning environmental, social, and leadership dimensions, and its alignment with global sustainability aspirations.

This word cloud figure (Fig. 10.1) visually represents the frequency of specific terms and phrases within the corporate sustainability questionnaire research, offering a concise and engaging overview of the most prevalent themes and concepts.

Table 10.6. Keywords Analysis.

Words	Occurrences
Corporate sustainability	67
Sustainability	18
Corporate social responsibility	12
Sustainable development	9
Leadership	5
Performance	4
Sustainable development goals	4
Sustainable leadership	4
Triple bottom line	4
Corporate sustainability performance	3
CSR	3
Environmental management	3
Job satisfaction	3
Knowledge management	3
Organizational culture	3
Servant leadership	3
Small and medium enterprises	3
Sufficiency economy	3
Transformational leadership	3
Accountability	2

Source: Constructed by the authors with biblioshiny software.

The size of each term in the word cloud corresponds to its frequency, with larger terms indicating higher occurrence. At the center of this word cloud is the term "corporate sustainability," which dominates the landscape, highlighting its central focus in the research. Surrounding it are related terms such as "sustainability," "corporate social responsibility," "sustainable development," "leadership," and "performance," indicating the multidimensional nature of corporate sustainability assessment.

The word cloud also features terms like "sustainable development goals," "triple bottom line," "environmental management," "job satisfaction," "knowledge management," and "organizational culture," emphasizing the diverse facets that are explored in the questionnaire. Additionally, there are terms related to specific regions and concepts, including "Taiwan," "China," "climate change," "competitiveness," "cooperatives," and "sufficiency economy," reflecting the global scope and contextual nuances of corporate sustainability research. Overall, this word

Fig. 10.1. Research WordCloud. *Source*: Constructed by the authors with biblioshiny software.

cloud provides an immediate and visually compelling snapshot of the key topics and areas of interest within the corporate sustainability questionnaire domain, aiding in quickly grasping the research's thematic landscape.

Questionnaire Development

In the pursuit of assessing and comprehensively understanding corporate sustainability, the development of a sound measurement framework is paramount. This section delves into the methodological approach employed to construct a robust and comprehensive measurement tool for corporate sustainability. It unfolds through a series of interconnected steps, each meticulously designed to ensure the reliability, validity, and relevance of the framework. From the foundational literature mapping process to the engagement of domain experts, a rigorous pilot survey, and thorough content validation, each step contributes to the development of a measurement framework that aligns with the dynamic nature of contemporary corporate sustainability practices. The attention to detail in this methodological journey underscores the commitment to delivering a credible and practical instrument for evaluating corporate sustainability across its multifaceted dimensions.

Literature Mapping: Foundation for Comprehensive Measurement

The research embarked on an extensive literature mapping process as its initial phase. This involved a systematic review of existing literature on corporate sustainability, with the primary objective of identifying relevant dimensions, sub-dimensions, and specific questionnaire items within each primary dimension, namely environmental, social, and economic sustainability. The thoroughness of this process was critical as it laid the groundwork for constructing a well-rounded and comprehensive measurement framework. It ensured that no critical aspects of corporate sustainability were overlooked, aligning the sub-dimensions with emerging research trends to capture the evolving landscape effectively.

Expert Validation and Refinement: Elevating Credibility

Expert validation played a pivotal role in refining and validating the dimensions identified in the literature mapping phase. Domain experts, possessing extensive experience and deep knowledge in corporate sustainability, were engaged to add credibility and authenticity to the measurement framework. These experts contributed critical insights and feedback, aligning the selected dimensions with the complex and nuanced facets of corporate sustainability, ensuring that they accurately represented contemporary practices. Furthermore, experts' input facilitated the prioritization and weighting of dimensions, drawing from their profound expertise and strengthening the foundation of the measurement framework.

Pilot Survey for Reliability Enhancement

The pilot survey was a critical step in assessing the reliability and effectiveness of the questionnaire. By collecting valuable feedback and data during this phase, the research team was able to iteratively refine the measurement tool. This iterative approach ensured that the questionnaire was not only robust but also user-friendly, making it conducive to collecting high-quality data. The pilot survey involved distributing online questionnaires to a targeted sample, and the adequate response rate provided confidence in the researchers' ability to collect data effectively. The pilot survey involved distributing online questionnaires to a targeted sample of 17 individuals including chief executive officers, compliance officers, executives, and academics. Table 10.7 depicts the responses to the pilot survey.

Table 10.7. Response Rate of Pilot Study.

Respondent Group	Sample	Response	Response (%)
Chief risk officers	5	3	80
Compliance officer	5	3	80
Executives	5	5	100
Academics	2	2	100

Source: Constructed by the authors.

Cronbach's Alpha for Reliability

To evaluate the reliability of the questionnaire items, Cronbach's alpha, a widely accepted measure of internal consistency, was employed. The fact that Cronbach's alpha for each of the five dimensions exceeded the threshold of 0.7 demonstrated the questionnaire's reliability. This statistical analysis confirmed that the questionnaire consistently measured the intended constructs related to corporate sustainability, which is crucial for obtaining trustworthy research results.

Content Validity

A strong emphasis was placed on content validity, an essential aspect of questionnaire development. A systematic six-step process was followed to establish content validity, including the preparation of a content validation form and the selection of a panel of content experts. These experts participated in multiple Zoom meetings where they provided scores and feedback on each questionnaire item. The calculation of the Content Validity Index (CVI) ensured that the items were not only relevant but also representative of the targeted construct. Subsequently, the questionnaire underwent revisions based on expert feedback, enhancing its clarity and precision. This rigorous content validation process guaranteed that the questionnaire effectively measured the intended constructs related to corporate sustainability.

Feedback Integration: Finalizing the Measurement Tool

The feedback obtained from the pilot survey, as summarized in Table 10.8, was thoughtfully considered in the finalization of the questionnaire. These collective efforts in literature mapping, expert validation, and pilot testing ensured that the measurement tool was robust, reliable, and content valid. It positioned the questionnaire as a valuable instrument for assessing corporate sustainability comprehensively and accurately.

This methodological approach reflects the meticulousness and rigor applied to develop a high-quality measurement framework for corporate sustainability, contributing significantly to the credibility and significance of the research findings.

Establishment of the CSI

The culmination of this study was the construction of the CSI, following the well-established OECD index construction methodology. This comprehensive index synthesized and consolidated data from the refined questionnaire responses. It represents the ultimate distillation of the comprehensive measurement framework, offering a standardized and holistic evaluation of corporate sustainability performance. Importantly, this index facilitates comparative assessments across economic, environmental, and social dimensions, allowing for a comprehensive overview of corporate sustainability efforts.

Table 10.8. Feedback Survey Report-Pilot Survey.

Questions	**Response Rate**	**Response Rate**
	Yes	**No**
Were the instructions clear and easy to understand?	100%	
Were there any major factual errors?		100%
Was the design clear and appealing?	100%	
Which questions, if any, were unclear or ambiguous? Please leave your thoughts and explain the reasons.		
Which questions, if any, did you find challenging to answer? Please leave your thoughts and explain the reasons.		
Do you have any other thoughts?		
How much time did it take to complete the questionnaire? (in minutes)	Average 30 minutes	

Source: *Constructed by the authors.*

Data Quality Dimensions

In line with the European Statistics Code of Practice, the methodology emphasizes six key dimensions of data quality:

1. *Relevance*: Data are collected through a carefully constructed questionnaire, drawing from systematic literature, expert opinions, and a pilot test. This comprehensive approach ensures the data's relevance and alignment with the objectives.
2. *Accuracy*: To ensure precision, data are gathered using a representative sample selected through proportional random sampling. Additional measures, such as email and phone reminders, are employed to minimize non-response rates and enhance data accuracy.
3. *Timeliness*: In the dynamic landscape of corporate sustainability, timeliness is critical. Data collection is conducted in 2022 as cross-sectional data, ensuring its relevance and currency.
4. *Accessibility*: The research aims to share its findings with a broader audience by publishing them in reputable journals and media outlets, enhancing data accessibility.
5. *Interpretability*: To facilitate understanding, the research provides clear definitions of corporate governance and sustainability, outlines target populations, variables, terminology, and acknowledges any limitations, ensuring interpretability.

6. *Coherence*: Data are meticulously connected and mutually consistent. Weighting and aggregation methods align with empirical findings, ensuring coherence throughout the analysis.

Dimensions of Corporate Sustainability and Governance

The foundation of the CSI lies in defining the key dimensions related to corporate sustainability and governance. Table 10.9 illustrates these central dimensions, serving as a blueprint for the development of the index. Accordingly, 10 steps are to be followed to construct the index, as illustrated in Fig. 10.2.

Handling Missing Data

Managing missing data are a crucial step in data analysis. The research employs a systematic approach to address this issue. Initially, the Little's Missing Completely at Random (MCAR) test is used to assess the presence of missing data. If the data are deemed MCAR, the Likewise Deletion (LD) technique is employed. However, in cases where data are not MCAR (Missing at Random), the Multiple Imputation (MI) technique is chosen. This automated technique scans the data and employs the monotonous method, while a wholly conditional specification is utilized if the data exhibit a monotone pattern of missing values.

Principal Component Analysis (PCA)

PCA is a vital statistical technique employed to simplify complex data. It identifies components that account for the overall variability among the examined variables, creating linear combinations that explain standard and individual variability. The application of PCA, as outlined by DeCoster (1998) and Hair et al. (2019), is a critical step in reducing data complexity and revealing key insights. The steps involved in PCA are visually represented in Fig. 10.2.

Normalization Techniques

Given the diverse nature of data sources, normalization is imperative. This study utilizes two distinct normalization methods tailored to the data type and source. These techniques are illustrated in Fig. 10.2, providing clarity on their application.

Weighting Methods

Weighting variables is a pivotal step in constructing the CSI. In addition to the unweighting method, this study explores three primary weighting methods:

- *Equal Weighting*: Assigns equal weight to all variables.
- *Analytic Hierarchy Process (AHP) Weighting*: Utilizes a structured process to derive weights based on a hierarchical criterion.
- *PCA Weighting*: Employs PCA to derive weights by considering total variance and factors with low proportions of unique variance.

Table 10.9. Operationalization of Corporate Sustainability.

Variable	Operational Definition	Dimensions	Abbreviation	Number of Questions	Source
Environmental sustainability (ES)	Environmental sustainability means air, energy, biodiversity, marine protection, waste management, and environmental management	Air preservation	AP	7	Zhang et al. (2019); Gomes et al. (2014)
		Energy management	EM	9	Zhang et al. (2019); Gomes et al. (2014)
		Water reservation	WR	5	Zhang et al. (2019); Gomes et al. (2014)
		Waste management	WM	7	Zhang et al. (2019); Gomes et al. (2014)
		Biodiversity protection	BD	5	Gomes et al. (2014)
		Environmental management	EM	5	Zhang et al. (2019)
		Marine protection	MP	3	Gomes et al. (2014)
Social sustainability (SSI)	Social sustainability is a process for creating sustainable, successful places that promote well-being by understanding what people need from the places they live and work	Employees	EM	14	Turker (2009); Antolín-López et al. (2016)
		Customers	CU	7	Turker (2009); Antolín-López et al. (2016)
		Community	CO	13	Turker, (2009); Antolín-López et al. (2016)

		Government	GO	3	Turker (2009); Antolín-López et al. (2016)
		Shareholders	SU	3	Turker (2009); Antolín-López et al. (2016)
		NGOs	NG	3	Turker (2009); Antolín-López et al. (2016)
Economic sustainability	Economic sustainability is the achievement of long-term growth, cost efficiency, competitiveness, sustainable innovation, sustainable innovation, government relationship, and consideration of spin-offs and trade-offs	Long-term profits	LG	7	Svensson et al. (2018)
		Cost efficiency	CE	4	Svensson et al. (2018)
		Sustainable investment	SI	3	Svensson et al. (2018)
		Spin-off	SO	3	Svensson et al. (2018)
		Trade-off	TO	3	Svensson et al. (2018)

Source: *Constructed by the authors.*

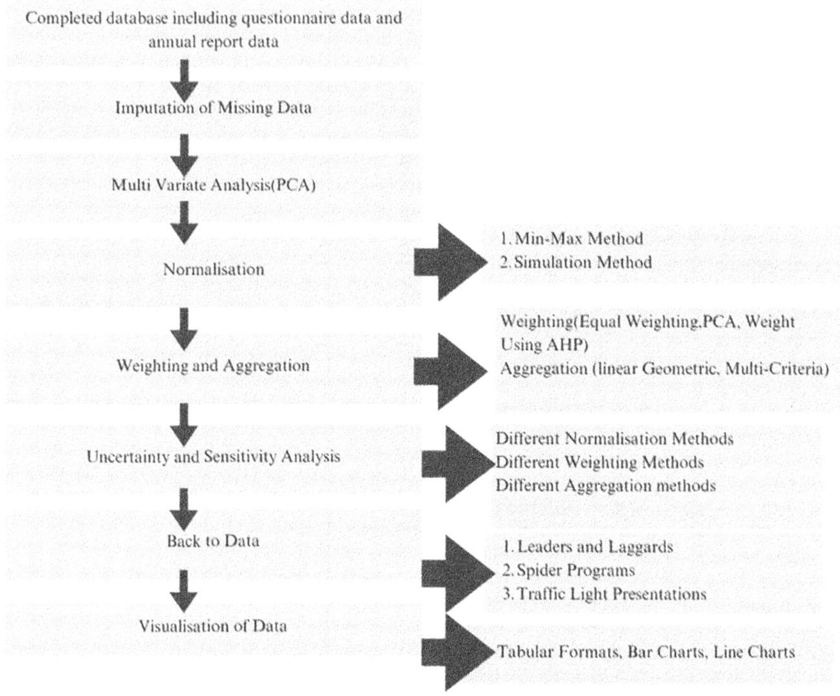

Fig. 10.2. OECD Methodology. *Source*: Authors' adaptation from OECD (2008).

In conclusion, the methodology employed to construct the CSI is characterized by meticulousness, adherence to data quality standards, and alignment with established frameworks. This comprehensive approach ensures that the CSI serves as a robust and reliable tool for assessing corporate sustainability, ultimately contributing to a more sustainable future for organizations and society as a whole.

Accordingly, 10 steps are to be followed to construct the index, as illustrated in Fig. 10.2.

In conclusion, the findings of this study provide a rigorous, structured, and well-grounded measurement framework for the holistic assessment of corporate sustainability. These dimensions, meticulously validated and enriched through expert opinions, literature mapping, and pilot surveys, serve as a valuable tool for researchers, policymakers, and practitioners alike. This framework not only fosters sustainable business practices but also contributes significantly to the broader objectives of sustainability on both corporate and societal levels.

Discussion

This section explains the sub-dimensions required to construct corporate sustainability.

Measurements of Environmental Sustainability

The measurement of environmental sustainability in this study encompasses several critical dimensions, each playing a vital role in assessing and improving corporate sustainability practices. These dimensions are supported by established literature and recognized best practices in environmental sustainability:

1. Air Protection: Air protection strategies involve measures to mitigate climate change and enhance indoor air quality. These strategies address the reduction of greenhouse gas emissions to combat global warming while also ensuring that indoor environments promote the health, comfort, and productivity of occupants (EPA, 2022).
2. Energy Preservation: Energy preservation includes both energy efficiency and the utilization of clean energy sources. Energy-efficient systems aim to reduce energy consumption, ultimately lowering greenhouse gas emissions. Clean energy, derived from renewable sources like solar and wind, contributes to a more sustainable energy portfolio (EPA, 2022).
3. Water Preservation: This dimension focuses on water efficiency and recycling. Water efficiency measures help in reducing wastage by optimizing water usage. Water recycling involves treating wastewater to make it reusable, reducing the strain on freshwater sources (UNEP, 2022).
4. Waste Management: Waste management strategies encompass waste reduction, reuse, recycling, and the proper management of toxic waste. These practices aim to minimize the environmental impact of waste generation and disposal (EPA, 2022).
5. Biodiversity Protection: Protecting biodiversity involves restoring natural habitats and safeguarding environmentally sensitive areas. These efforts contribute to the preservation of ecosystems and the species within them (CBD, 2022).
6. Environmental Management: This dimension involves enhancing environmental awareness, preventing pollution, investing in environmental management, and contributing to voluntary environmental schemes. It signifies a holistic approach to corporate sustainability (EPA, 2022).
7. Marine Conservation: To prevent the over-exploitation of marine resources, marine conservation practices aim to protect and sustainably manage ocean ecosystems and marine life (MarineBio, 2023).

These dimensions provide a comprehensive framework for evaluating and improving corporate sustainability efforts with respect to environmental factors. By addressing these aspects, organizations can contribute to a more sustainable future and reduce their environmental footprint.

Measurements of Social Sustainability

Social sustainability is a crucial dimension within the broader framework of corporate sustainability. It encompasses a range of factors that reflect a company's commitment to fostering positive social impact and relationships within society. Here, we elaborate on the components of social sustainability and provide insights from the literature:

1. Employee Sustainability: This aspect focuses on the welfare and well-being of employees. It includes fair compensation, ensuring employee health and safety, providing conducive working conditions, enhancing employee rights, supporting collective bargaining, promoting work dignity, protecting against discrimination, and facilitating employee organization. The literature emphasizes that a motivated and satisfied workforce contributes to increased productivity and long-term organizational success (Pfeffer, 2018; Welbeck et al., 2020).
2. Customer Sustainability: Customer sustainability revolves around delivering quality products and services, transparent customer information, ensuring high levels of customer satisfaction, and safeguarding customer rights. Research suggests that businesses that prioritize customer satisfaction tend to build stronger brand loyalty and trust, which can lead to sustained profitability (Reichheld, 2004; Welbeck et al., 2020).
3. Community Sustainability: This dimension underscores a company's role in the communities where it operates. It involves community engagement through donations, participation in local events, initiatives to enhance community health and safety, and efforts to preserve and improve community culture. Raising awareness about community issues and informing the public about the company's developments are also integral. Literature highlights the benefits of positive community relationships, including improved reputation and the potential for local support (Joung et al., 2013; Welbeck et al., 2020).
4. Government Sustainability: Adhering to ethical standards by avoiding bribery and corruption, fulfilling tax obligations, and complying with legal regulations are essential aspects of government sustainability. Companies that maintain strong ethical practices and legal compliance tend to face fewer regulatory risks and legal consequences, contributing to their long-term stability (Karlsson et al., 2018).
5. NGOs: Collaborative efforts with NGOs in addressing societal challenges and improving environmental performance are increasingly common. Early warning signs and proactive engagement with NGOs can help companies anticipate and address social and environmental issues more effectively (Matten & Moon, 2008).

In summary, social sustainability reflects a company's commitment to ethical and responsible practices that benefit employees, customers, communities, governments, suppliers, and NGOs. The literature underscores the importance of these dimensions in building strong stakeholder relationships, enhancing reputation, and ensuring long-term business success in an increasingly socially conscious world.

Measurements of Economic Sustainability

Economic sustainability is a fundamental component of corporate sustainability that focuses on the long-term growth and prosperity of an organization while considering the well-being of all stakeholders. This section elaborates on key aspects of economic sustainability and provides insights from the literature:

1. Long-Term Profits: Economic sustainability prioritizes long-term growth strategies that aim to improve shareholder wealth maximization rather than pursuing short-term profit maximization. This perspective aligns with principles found in Buddhist philosophy, emphasizing the importance of balance, ethical conduct, and long-term value creation (Svensson et al., 2018).
2. Cost Efficiency: Achieving cost efficiency is a crucial element of economic sustainability. It involves saving money by optimizing processes and enhancing the efficiency of product or service delivery. Cost efficiency not only reduces input costs but also helps companies avoid earning distortions from unethical practices such as bribery, child labor, and the sale of harmful products (Svensson et al., 2018).
3. Sustainable Investing: Economic sustainability aligns with sustainable investing, which seeks to address climate change, environmental degradation, and corporate social responsibility. Investors are increasingly considering environmental, social, and governance (ESG) factors when making investment decisions. This trend reflects a growing consensus that sustainable practices can enhance financial performance and reduce risks (Gibson et al., 2020).
4. Trade-offs: Economic sustainability necessitates a careful consideration of trade-offs in business decision-making. It involves evaluating both economic and non-economic impacts, as well as weighing the short-term and long-term consequences of decisions. Achieving economic sustainability often requires balancing profitability with social and environmental responsibility (Svensson et al., 2018).
5. Spin-offs: In the context of corporate sustainability, refer to strategic actions undertaken by a company that involve the creation of new entities or initiatives. These actions are driven by a desire to enhance long-term growth and sustainability. Spin-offs typically involve the establishment of separate entities or projects that were once part of the parent company but are now independently operated (Svensson et al., 2018).

In conclusion, economic sustainability is a multifaceted concept that encompasses long-term growth, cost efficiency, competitiveness, sustainable innovation, responsible investing, government relationships, and trade-offs. These elements collectively contribute to an organization's ability to thrive economically while fulfilling its social and environmental responsibilities.

Conclusion

The COVID-19 pandemic disrupted global economies and emphasized the need for businesses to navigate unprecedented challenges while remaining committed to sustainability. In this context, our study's comprehensive measurement framework for corporate sustainability is timely and vital. It not only addresses the urgent need for clarity in assessing sustainability but also provides a roadmap for organizations seeking to align their practices with the broader goals of society and the environment.

The three core dimensions of our framework – Environmental Sustainability, Social Sustainability, and Economic Sustainability – each play a pivotal role in shaping an organization's sustainable profile. Environmental Sustainability acknowledges the critical role of businesses in environmental conservation. It encompasses initiatives to reduce carbon emissions, protect natural habitats, conserve water resources, and minimize waste. Social Sustainability underscores the importance of stakeholders' well-being, including employees, communities, and customers. Ensuring fair labor practices, promoting diversity and inclusion, and engaging in philanthropic activities are all facets of this dimension. Economic Sustainability emphasizes the long-term financial viability of an organization while integrating sustainability principles. It involves responsible financial management, ethical investment strategies, and the pursuit of economic benefits in ways that do not compromise sustainability objectives.

For researchers, our framework provides a standardized and methodologically sound basis for conducting studies in the domain of corporate sustainability. It offers a systematic approach to evaluating corporate practices, enabling the development of more robust research methodologies and the generation of valuable insights. Researchers can use this framework to explore the relationships between sustainability practices and organizational performance, employee satisfaction, customer loyalty, and other key variables, contributing to the ever-growing body of knowledge in this field.

Policymakers will find our framework instrumental in assessing the impact of existing sustainability regulations and designing more effective policies.

In the context of the SDGs set for 2030, policymakers can use our framework as a tool to evaluate progress toward these global objectives. By aligning corporate practices with SDGs, governments can accelerate the achievement of critical targets related to climate action, poverty reduction, and social equity.

Businesses and practitioners will derive practical value from our framework. It serves as a diagnostic tool that allows organizations to identify areas where they excel in sustainability and areas that require improvement. By conducting assessments based on our framework, businesses can enhance their sustainability performance, reduce risks, and increase competitiveness. Furthermore, it supports responsible business practices by encouraging transparency, accountability, and responsible stakeholder engagement.

Nonetheless, it's essential to acknowledge that the landscape of corporate sustainability is dynamic and ever-evolving. As new challenges emerge, such as those related to climate resilience, supply chain sustainability, and ethical technology adoption, further research is necessary to adapt our framework to accommodate these evolving dimensions. Additionally, our framework can be customized to specific industries, as the priorities and challenges faced by, for example, the energy sector, differ significantly from those of the retail industry.

Limitations and Future Research

While this study contributes significantly to the field of corporate sustainability measurement, it is not without limitations. The research primarily draws on documents and expert opinions up to 2022, which may not encompass the most recent developments in the field. Additionally, the study relies on a bibliometric analysis of existing literature, which may not capture all emerging perspectives on the subject. Moreover, the expert opinions obtained may be subject to bias or may not represent the full diversity of viewpoints in the field.

Future research in the domain of corporate sustainability should consider the evolving landscape and incorporate emerging perspectives. Longitudinal studies tracking the evolution of corporate sustainability practices beyond 2022 would be valuable. Exploring the practical implementation of the proposed measurement framework in various industries and regions could provide insights into its adaptability and effectiveness. Moreover, research into the relationship between corporate sustainability practices and financial performance could shed light on potential trade-offs and synergies.

In conclusion, our study's contribution extends beyond the presentation of a measurement framework; it empowers researchers, policymakers, and businesses to engage more meaningfully with the complex and critical concept of corporate sustainability. As we continue to grapple with global challenges, such as climate change and social inequality, the need for effective and comprehensive measurement tools becomes increasingly urgent. Our framework provides a solid foundation for addressing these challenges and advancing the cause of sustainability in a post-COVID-19 world and beyond.

Constructing a robust CSI requires a meticulous approach that adheres to both established frameworks and data quality standards. This chapter outlines the methodology employed to create the CSI, with a focus on data selection, handling, and analysis.

References

Antolín-López, R., Delgado-Ceballos, J., & Montiel, I. (2016). Deconstructing corporate sustainability: a comparison of different stakeholder metrics. *Journal of Cleaner Production*, *136*, 5–17. https://doi.org/10.1016/J.JCLEPRO.2016.01.111

Aria, M., & Cuccurullo, C. (2017). Bibliometrix: An R-tool for comprehensive science mapping analysis. *Journal of Informetrics*, *11*(4), 959–975. https://doi.org/10.1016/J.JOI.2017.08.007

Berger, R. (2017). *Roland Berger Trend Compendium 2030*.

Carroll, A. B. (2015). Evolution of a definitional construct. *Business & Society*, *38*(3), 268–295.

CBD. (2022). *Home|convention on biological diversity*. https://www.cbd.int/

DeCoster, J. (1998). *Overview of factor analysis*. http://www.stat-help.com/factor.pdf

Elkington, J. (1997). The triple bottom line. In M. V. Russo (Ed.), *Environmental management: Readings and cases* (Vol. 2, pp. 49–66). https://books.google.com/books?hl=en&lr=&id=hRJGrsGnMXcC&oi=fnd&pg=PA49&dq=elkingston+1997&ots=0ftAFTMx9M&sig=qfQJ9DqDZZwBTCzt8L7qreFZVUY

EPA. (2022). *Air quality*. https://www.epa.gov/air-quality

Fields, R., O'Kelly III, R., Sanderson, L., & Russel Reynolds Associates. (2022). *2022 Global and Regional Trends in Corporate Governance*. https://Corpgov.Law.Harvard.Edu/. https://corpgov.law.harvard.edu/2022/02/21/2022-global-and-regional-trends-in-corporate-governance/

Freeman, R. E. (1999). Divergent stakeholder theory. *Academy of Management Review*, *24*(2), 233–236. https://doi.org/10.5465/AMR.1999.1893932

Gibson, R., Krueger, P., & Mitali, S. F. (2020). The sustainability footprint of institutional investors: ESG driven price pressure and performance. *SSRN Electronic Journal*. https://doi.org/10.2139/SSRN.2918926

Gomes, C. M., Kneipp, J. M., Kruglianskas, I., Da Rosa, L. A. B., & Bichueti, R. S. (2014). Management for sustainability in companies of the mining sector: An analysis of the main factors related with the business performance. *Journal of Cleaner Production*, *84*(1), 84–93. https://doi.org/10.1016/J.JCLEPRO.2013.08.030

Hair, J. F., Black, W. C., Babin, B. J., Anderson, R. E., Black, W. C., & Anderson, R. E. (2019). *Multivariate Data Analysis*.

Hesse, J., & Olsen, S. (2017). *What will work look like in 2030?* Strategy+business. https://www.strategy-business.com/article/What-Will-Work-Look-Like-in-2030

Joung, C. B., Carrell, J., Sarkar, P., & Feng, S. C. (2013). Categorization of indicators for sustainable manufacturing. *Ecological Indicators*, *24*, 148–157. https://doi.org/10.1016/j.ecolind.2012.05.030

Karlsson, N. P. E., Laurell, H., Lindgren, J., Pehrsson, T., Andersson, S., & Svensson, G. (2018). A cross-country comparison and validation of firms' stakeholder considerations in sustainable business practices. *Corporate Governance (Bingley)*, *18*(3), 408–424. https://doi.org/10.1108/CG-07-2017-0131

MarineBio. (2023). *Marine conservation*. MarineBio Conservation Society. https://www.marinebio.org/conservation/

Matten, D., & Moon, J. (2008). "Implicit" and "explicit" CSR: A conceptual framework for a comparative understanding of corporate social responsibility. *Academy of Management Review*, *33*(2), 404–424. https://doi.org/10.5465/AMR.2008.31193458

OECD. (2008). *Handbook on constructing composite indicators: Methodology and user guide*. OECD. https://doi.org/10.1787/9789264043466-EN

OECD. (2020, March 10). *Implementing the OECD guidelines on corporate governance of state-owned enterprises: Review of recent developments*. OECD. https://doi.org/10.1787/4CAA0C3B-EN

Pfeffer, J. (2018). *Dying for a paycheck: How modern management harms employee health and company performance – And what we can do about it*. https://philpapers.org/rec/PFEDFA

Reichheld, F. (2004). The one number you need to grow. *Harvard Business Review*, *82*(6), 133–133. https://www.nashc.net/wp-content/uploads/2014/10/the-one-number-you-need-to-know.pdf

Rosen, M. A. (2018). Issues, concepts and applications for sustainability. *Glocalism: Journal of Culture, Politics and Innovation*, *3*. https://doi.org/10.12893/GJCPI.2018.3.4

Statista. (2020). https://www.statista.com/

Svensson, G., Ferro, C., Høgevold, N., Padin, C., Carlos Sosa Varela, J., & Sarstedt, M. (2018). Framing the triple bottom line approach: Direct and mediation effects between economic, social and environmental elements. *Journal of Cleaner Production*, *197*, 972–991. https://doi.org/10.1016/j.jclepro.2018.06.226

Szmigiera, M. (2022, May 26). *Impact of the coronavirus pandemic on the global economy – Statistics & facts*. Statista. https://www.statista.com/topics/6139/covid-19-impact-on-the-global-economy/#dossierKeyfigures

Tseng, M. L., Chang, C. H., Lin, C. W. R., Wu, K. J., Chen, Q., Xia, L., & Xue, B. (2020). Future trends and guidance for the triple bottom line and sustainability: A data driven bibliometric analysis. *Environmental Science and Pollution Research*, *27*(27), 33543–33567. https://doi.org/10.1007/S11356-020-09284-0

Turker, D. (2009). Measuring corporate social responsibility: A scale development study. *Journal of Business Ethics*, *85*(4), 411–427. https://doi.org/10.1007/s10551-008-9780-6

UNEP. (2022). *About UN environment programme*. https://www.unep.org/about-un-environment

UNGC. (2015). *Guide for general counsel on corporate sustainability* (Version 2.0). Retrieved May 17, 2021, from https://www.unglobalcompact.org/library/5722

Waddock, S. (1997). The corporate social performance–financial performance link. *Strategic Management Journal*, *18*(4), 303–319. https://doi.org/10.1002/(SICI)1097-0266(199704)18:4<303::AID-SMJ869>3.0.CO;2-G

Welbeck, E. E. S., Owusu, G. M. Y., Simpson, S. N. Y., & Bekoe, R. A. (2020). CSR in the telecom industry of a developing country: Employees' perspective. *Journal of Accounting in Emerging Economies*, *10*(3), 447–464. https://doi.org/10.1108/JAEE-01-2019-0017

World Bank. (2020). The World Bank group's response to the COVID-19 pandemic. https://www.worldbank.org/en/who-we-are/news/coronavirus-covid19

World Economic Forum (WEF). (2020). *How COVID-19 could push 49 million into extreme poverty*. https://www.weforum.org/agenda/2020/05/impact-of-covid19-coronavirus-economic-global-poverty/

World Health Organisation (WHO). (2020). *Coronavirus disease (COVID-19)*. https://www.who.int/emergencies/diseases/novel-coronavirus-2019

Zhang, J., Djajadikerta, H. G., & Trireksani, T. (2019). Corporate sustainability disclosure's importance in China: financial analysts' perception. *Social Responsibility Journal*, *16*(8), 1169–1189.

Chapter 11

Leader Approach and Rural Entrepreneurship for Resilient Rural Areas: Perceptions by the Local Action Groups' Managers in Serbia

Vesna Paraušić and Nataša Kljajić

Institute of Agricultural Economics, Belgrade, Serbia

Abstract

This chapter in its first part analyzes the Leader approach in terms of concept, constituent elements, application, and its contribution to rural development and rural entrepreneurship. In the continuation of the text, authors analyze the application of this approach in Serbia, looking at the activities of the ministry in charge and the views of local action groups (LAGs)' managers on this matter. The aim of this chapter is to present the results and problems Serbia has seen so far in the implementation of the Leader approach for development of rural areas on a local level. The results indicate that the lack of systemic and continuous state support resulting, among other things, in the lack of a financial portfolio for the LAGs, is the main cause of low local entrepreneurial initiatives and projects implemented within the Leader approach. Future steps in the implementation of this approach in Serbia will depend on financial support for the LAGs from all levels of government, as well as from the possibility of using funds within the EU pre-accession assistance for rural development. Also, it will be necessary to launch larger innovative and entrepreneurial initiatives both by LAGs' managers and all stakeholders involved in local rural development.

Keywords: Rural development; local strategy; territorial partnerships; entrepreneurial initiatives; profile of the LAGs' managers in Serbia

Emerging Patterns and Behaviors in a Green Resilient Economy, 233–254

doi:10.1108/978-1-83549-780-720241012

Introduction

"Leader" is an acronym and means the networking of actors, actions and resources in the local development of rural communities (European Communities, 2006). This method of local development assumes that local communities in rural areas are extremely diverse in terms of their resources and priority needs and that local people are in the best position to correctly and realistically see the strengths, weaknesses and interests of their community (European Commission, 2021; European Communities, 2006; EU, 2021a). In fact, local rural development initiatives are most effective when they are managed by local stakeholders, and these areas will develop much more effectively if local stakeholders actively participate in formulation and realization of the local development strategies (LDSs), with transparent decision-making procedures and public administration support (European Commission, 2021; European Communities, 2006; EU, 2021a). This is a method of bottom-up guidance and sustainable local development of rural and other areas, through local stakeholders' mobilization and networking and realization of their initiatives and projects, primarily in terms of improving the quality and conditions of life and employment in local areas (European Commission, 2017, 2021; European Communities, 2006; EU, 2021a, 2021b).

Since the 1990s, the Leader approach has been an important measure in rural development policy in all EU countries financed through the EU's common agricultural policy (CAP) (EU, 2005). Under the cohesion policy, the Leader approach was further expanded in the 2014–2020 program period (N + 3), and named "Community-Led Local Development" (CLLD) today refers not only to the development of rural and fishing areas but other areas as well and their connection (EU, 2013a, 2013b, 2021a, 2021b; European Commission, 2021).

In Western Balkan countries to join the EU, including Serbia, the implementation of the Leader approach is almost in its infancy, and numerous prerequisites for its successful implementation have not yet been met. The bottom-up process of local rural development is fragmented, as a result of limited sources of funding and absence of continuous support (Bogdanov et al., 2018). This weakens young and fragile partnerships, at the same time deterring local stakeholders from further involvement in the local community (Bogdanov et al., 2018).

The issues of local entrepreneurial initiatives and CLLD are becoming increasingly important in Serbia. This is because both the public and civil sectors have realized that the survival of rural areas is increasingly threatened, that Leader provides great opportunities for their empowerment and resilience, especially with the support of the EU Instrument for Pre-Accession Assistance for Rural Development (IPARD), more precisely with support within the IPARD III Program for Serbia 2021–2027 (MAFWM, 2022). In general, the bottom-up approach offers a number of benefits and is very valuable for rural development in Serbia. Its affirmation can ensure local development only if based on the correct foundations of CLLD and rural entrepreneurship. Looking at the views of managers of LAGs in Serbia on this issue will certainly benefit public policymakers in drafting future policies aimed at greater application of the bottom-up approach to rural development.

This chapter is structured in several units. In addition to the introduction, overview of methodology, and conclusion, this chapter consists of the following units: (1) Leader approach – concept, constituent elements and application; and (2) Leader approach and rural entrepreneurship. What follows is an overview of the application of this approach in Serbia through the two following points: (1) Leader approach in Serbia: research background; and (2) Attitudes of interviewed LAGs' managers related to the Leader approach in Serbia.

Methodology

For the analysis of the selected thematic area in this chapter, the authors used desk research, as well as the interview technique, as the most common qualitative research technique in social research (DiCicco-Bloom & Crabtree, 2006).

As part of the desk research, the authors dealt with extensive scientific studies by national and foreign authors, covering the bottom-up approach to rural development and rural entrepreneurship. They also used official Serbian documents that directly or indirectly explain the research subject, as well as the corresponding EU documents and legislation.

A semi-structured interview technique was used in order to obtain the views of LAGs' managers in rural regions of Serbia on their previous experience with using Leader. For these needs, the authors designed the questionnaire consisting of 10 questions. The entire interviewing process included two segments.

The first segment included a semi-structured in-depth interview with the president and manager of the "Network of Local Action Groups of Serbia." This network is a national organization that gathers 12 LAGs recognized by the Ministry of Agriculture, Forestry and Water Management of the Republic of Serbia (MAFWM). The president of the network showed interest and was willing to contribute to the research and took part in two phone interviews in March 2023. Each interview lasted from 45 minutes to 1 hour. The author encouraged the interviewee to speak freely, broadly and in detail about preconceived topics of interest for the research, in order to better understand the implementation of the Leader approach in rural development in Serbia (Paraušić, 2023).

The second research segment included semi-structured interviews with the representatives, i.e., managers of 10 recognized LAGs in Serbia (Paraušić & Kljajić, 2023). As Serbia currently has 21 recognized LAGs, LAGs for the interview were randomly selected. An email interview was used, which gave LAGs' managers an opportunity to think about the questions and answer them when they had free time. This was very useful considering that interviewees were supposed to answer most questions by highlighting their opinions, attitudes or describing them. The entire process of email interviews lasted from March to April 2023.

For the purpose of analysis and to draw conclusions, the data were processed using descriptive statistics and inductive reasoning.

Leader Approach: Concept, Constituent Elements and Application

The development of the Leader approach as a measure of rural development in EU countries went through several stages of implementation and financing, together with the CAP development. Today, it is an integral part of a wider concept known as CLLD. CLLD focuses on (a) integrated territorial development of a specific sub-regional area, involving local stakeholders and local initiatives, (b) all areas (not only rural and fishing but also urban, peri-urban and coastal) and their connection and (c) all European structural and investment funds (EU, 2013a, 2021b; European Commission, 2017).

As part of the CAP and as a component of CLLD, Leader is based on the local initiatives and enables comprehensive, endogenous, bottom-up, and multi-sectoral development of the local rural communities (EU, 2013b, 2021a; European Commission, 2017; European Communities, 2006).

Leader is closely associated with the "Smart Village" concept, i.e., innovative development processes at the local level, which, based on local resources and needs, as well as the cooperation of all stakeholders, improves the sustainability and resilience of local rural communities (Adamowicz & Zwolińska-Ligaj, 2020; EU, 2021a). What is more, this concept is an integral part of the EU declaration "A Better Life in Rural Areas" (EU, 2016).

The European Commission sets precise conditions for a successful endogenous development process, emphasizing the need for proper and comprehensive application of all key principles of the Leader (Fig. 11.1).

LAGs design, prepare and implement LDSs, as planning and development documents of their territory, in accordance with the needs, interests and resources of local communities. Operative work of LAGs implies the cooperation of public, private and civil actors, where no single group has a dominant influence in decision-making (EU, 2021b, p. 202). This is important in order to ensure transparency and non-discrimination in the LDS realization, as well as to avoid conflicts

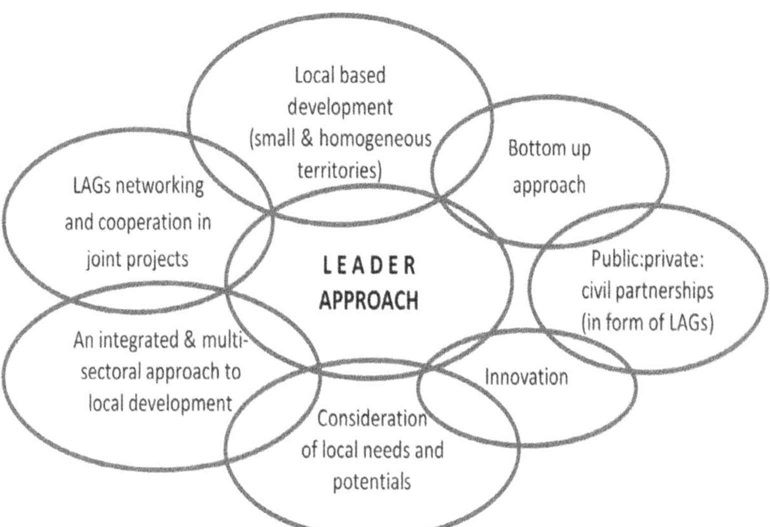

Fig. 11.1 Principles of the Leader. *Source*: Authors' presentation based on a literature review (European Communities, 2006; European Commission, 2017; EU, 2005).

of interest. In view of the confirmed positive contribution to local development, "Leader local development" is recognized as a measure of rural development in the new program period (CAP 2023–2027) as well, with mandatory application in the rural development programs (RDPs) in all EU countries (EU, 2021a).

EU countries actively foster revitalization of their rural areas and empower farmers through the CAP and Leader measure (Navarro et al., 2016; Nieto Masot et al., 2019; Ray, 2000; Vázquez-Barquero & Rodríguez-Cohard, 2016). Institutional, socio-economic, political, historical and cultural factors affect the scope and potential of Leader application and, above all, the way this instrument is managed in EU countries and/or regions (Konečný, 2019; Nieto Masot et al., 2019; Pollermann et al., 2020). Differences are most pronounced between the old and new member states (Konečný, 2019, p. 13). Despite these differences, there are similarities in Leader implementation results between countries and regions in the EU (Konečný, 2019; Nieto Masot et al., 2019). In general, the correct implementation of the Leader approach in EU rural areas has led to (a) improvements in the quality and living conditions of the rural population; (b) strengthening of the local capacities in the non-agricultural and entrepreneurial activities (in tourism or the processing of agricultural products), (c) creating new jobs and reducing poverty, (d) stopping the depopulation process and (e) improving social capital and social innovations (Adamowicz & Zwolińska-Ligaj, 2020; Dargan & Shucksmith, 2008; Esparcia Perez, 2000; European Commission, 2017; Konečný, 2019; Nieto Masot et al., 2019; Nordberg et al., 2020; Tirado Ballesteros & Hernández, 2019).

Leader Approach and Rural Entrepreneurship

The importance of entrepreneurship for stimulating balanced and sustainable regional development, as well as for the development of local communities in rural areas, is indisputable (Baumgartner et al., 2013; EU, 2016; European Commission, 2021).

In the field of agriculture and rural development, the so-called green entrepreneurship for green economy and effective social response to climate change are more and more taken into consideration (Gabriel Anton et al., 2022). At the farm level, entrepreneurial efforts are extremely important for good business performance and innovating agricultural processes (Grande et al., 2011). For strengthening sustainability and resilience of rural communities, numerous authors emphasize the importance of smart villages and endogenous rural development, as well as the importance of entrepreneurship and the diversification of rural population's activities (Adamowicz & Zwolińska-Ligaj, 2020; Vázquez-Barquero & Rodríguez-Cohard, 2016). For example, as Vázquez-Barquero and Rodríguez-Cohard (2016) point out, one of the important dimensions of endogenous development is the economic one, which is specifically aimed at local entrepreneurs, and which should enable them "to use the productive factors efficiently, introduce technological change and innovation, and reach productivity levels all of which make them competitive in the national and international markets" (Vázquez-Barquero & Rodríguez-Cohard, 2016, p. 3).

The connection between CLLD, more precisely Leader approach, and rural entrepreneurship is multiple and complex. First of all, the success of the Leader approach depends, among other things, on local entrepreneurship (the number and activities of local entrepreneurs) in rural areas, as well as on entrepreneurial orientation and entrepreneurial initiatives of networked local stakeholders (Coffey & Polese, 1985; Dargan & Shucksmith, 2008; Janković, 2020; Navarro et al., 2016; Paraušić et al., 2023). On the other hand, many activities of a social nature that are implemented in the community through LAGs' projects strengthen and foster the development of entrepreneurship in the local community, especially in the field of rural tourism (Nordberg et al., 2020).

Back in the second half of the last century, Coffey and Polese (1985, p. 86) pointed out that "areas with even severe physical disadvantages can prosper if their inhabitants have sufficient know-how and initiative-in short, entrepreneurial ability." In recent times, more and more studies point to the "rural or local entrepreneurial ecosystems development," as a type of community-led entrepreneurial local development management style, which successfully helps solve the systemic problems of communities, especially those in remote, devastated and sparsely populated rural areas (Miles & Morrison, 2020; Rego et al., 2018).

López et al. (2019) point to the importance of creating and implementing a rural entrepreneurship strategy in a sparsely populated rural area in Spain. In particular, these authors highlight the example of a non-profit organization, which cultivates an entrepreneurial style of local rural development management, in order to support ecological development, transfer of scientific results as well as provide support for youth training (López et al., 2019).

As Dargan and Shucksmith (2008, p. 284) point out, "the lack of a creative milieu and risk-friendly entrepreneurship, together with the concentration of power in the hands of government actors, remains a major constraint discouraging new bottom-up approaches." It should be noted in this regard that countries and regions differ significantly in terms of their entrepreneurial capacities (both individuals' and communities'), networking abilities (through LAGs, clusters, producers' organizations, etc.) and the potential of collective actions, and these differences depend on the level of economic development, as well as numerous other historical, inherited, social, institutional and other factors (Bogdanov et al., 2018; Dargan & Shucksmith, 2008; Konečný, 2019; López et al., 2019; Paraušić et al., 2017).

Some countries and regions simply do not have a history of collective action, individuals do not trust the community and work atomistically (Dargan & Shucksmith, 2008). Local development does not rely much on entrepreneurial initiatives and leadership capacities, especially in remote, peripheral, sparsely populated and underdeveloped rural areas (López et al., 2019). The effects of public policies to support entrepreneurship in these regions are quite weak (Neto et al., 2014), so the promotion of community-driven rural entrepreneurship often requires the combined efforts of the private sector, scientific community and government (Miles & Morrison, 2020).

Moreover, in the Western Balkans countries, the process of joining the CAP (under which the countries should develop the Leader approach) is still largely slow and difficult due to internal political pressures, the influence of various interest groups as well as the lack of a financial portfolio for the implementation of this approach (Bogdanov et al., 2018; Erjavec et al., 2021).

Public policies that support the local development of rural communities should encourage local initiatives, cooperation of local stakeholders from different sectors and territories as well as investments by private companies and entrepreneurs at the local level (Coffey & Polese, 1985; Neto et al., 2014; Santos et al., 2016). In addition, one of the basic tasks of local self-government units (LSGUs) is to create a stimulating business environment for stronger entrepreneurial activities, especially in rural areas (Janković Milić et al., 2014; Vujičić et al., 2013).

Leader Approach in Serbia: Research Background

Rural areas of Serbia are characterized by numerous systemic economic-social and institutional-infrastructural development limitations (Bogdanov et al., 2015; FAO, 2020; Government of Republic of Serbia, 2014; Joldžić et al., 2019; Paraušić & Domazet, 2018; Subić et al., 2017; Živojinović et al., 2019). Central/regional/local authorities cannot mitigate these developmental problems, which deepens the existing gap between rural and urban areas, and also gap between rural settlements in economically developed and underdeveloped regions.

Numerous of domestic authors agree that the key drivers of the development of rural areas are the following (Cizler, 2013; European Commission, 2019; Janković, 2020; Janković Milić et al., 2014; Vujičić et al., 2013):

- Analysis and appreciation of local heterogeneities;
- Respect of the needs and interests of the local population,
- Affirmation of strong local entrepreneurial initiatives, with effective local administration and respect for the principles of democratic decision-making, as well as
- Networking of all local stakeholders in the process of rural development.

Bearing in mind the European experiences, it is undeniable that the Leader approach is recognized as extremely useful for improving the quality of life and strengthening social capital, especially in remote, inaccessible and underdeveloped villages in Serbia (Government of Republic of Serbia, 2014; European Commission, 2019; MAFWM, 2022). Small priority projects that LAGs can implement within their LDSs can be different, and most often in practice these are projects of low value, such as support to rural events and exhibitions, support to farmers' and entrepreneurs' participation at fairs and events, support to branding and promotion of local identity and traditional local products, promotion of rural tourism and small investments in rural tourism, improvement of public spaces, organization of various cultural, sports and other collective events and the like (Nordberg et al., 2020; Paraušić & Kljajić, 2023). LAGs' projects could also help revitalize certain locations in rural areas through brownfield investments (Sredojević et al., 2019), which would be a double way to test new sustainable development practices in Serbia.

As a national measure of rural development, Leader is within the jurisdiction of MAFWM, Department for Rural Development, and it's recognized in the Agriculture and Rural Development Strategy of Serbia in the period 2014–2024 as a future direction of local rural development (Government of Republic of Serbia, 2014).

The lack of a complete and adequate planning and legal framework led to delays in the implementation of Leader, which further reflected in the creation of a disincentive framework for new initiatives by local actors (Bogdanov et al., 2018). Serbia officially started the implementation of the Leader in 2019, with the adoption of the appropriate rulebook in this area (MAFWM, 2019a). Based on the adopted rulebook, the Directorate for Agrarian Payments announced the First Public Call for subsidies for the establishment of Partnerships and the drafting of LDSs in rural areas (MAFWM, 2019b). The results of this public call were published in 2021, when, based on the criteria for evaluating the quality of LDSs (Fig. 11.2), a list of 21 Partnerships with positive scores of their LDSs was published by the MAFWM Evaluation Commission (Directorate for Agrarian Payments, 2021). With this, the Partnerships completed the establishment process and at the same time became the first Partnerships recognized by MAFWM.

After this, MAFWM slowed down the further process of the Leader development since the expected and planned call for subsidies for LDSs implementation programs (funding of priority mini-projects, more precisely projects of lesser value) did not follow, nor did another public call for the establishment of new Partnerships. Thus, despite the expectation that, through national support, the Partnerships would prepare to apply for funds under the IPARD Program for Serbia, this did not happen.

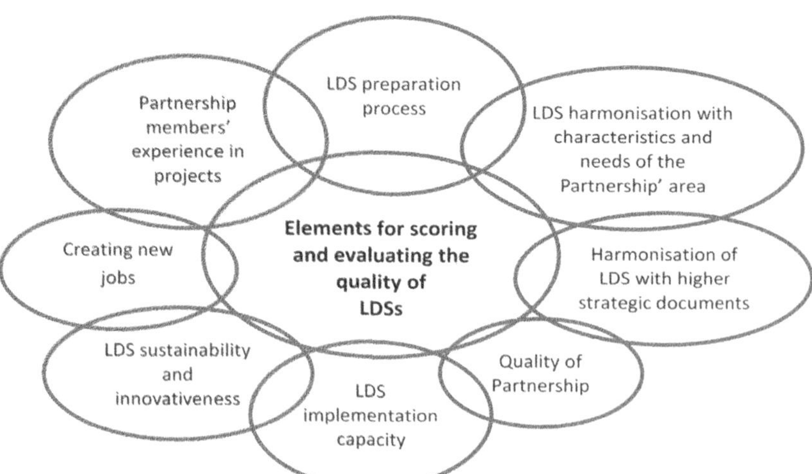

Fig. 11.2 Elements for Scoring and Evaluating the Quality of LDSs in Rural Areas in Serbia. *Source*: MAFWM (2019a, Annex 6).

Also, MAFWM is significantly late with the accreditation of Leader measure within the IPARD III Program (2021–2027) for Serbia (MAFWM, 2022). At the same time, it should be borne in mind that surveyed LAGs' managers have high expectations from these funds, considering that the amounts of support would be far higher than the national ones and could ensure the implementation of projects within the LDSs, as well as international recognition and cooperation for the Partnerships (MAFWM, 2022; Paraušić & Bekić Šarić, 2021; Paraušić & Kljajić, 2023).

All of the above indicates that Partnerships (LAGs) in Serbia face enormous limitations in terms of sources of funding, both for office work and LAGs staff, as well as for projects planned for implementation under LDSs. Not only do these restrictions slow down the implementation of the measure, but they also prevent further animation, stakeholder mobilization and the spread of activities at the local level. Also, there is a risk of loss of confidence and enthusiasm among the members of the already formed Partnerships, risk of human and material capacities weakening of the Partnerships, which all reduce national capacities for the Leader implementation through IPARD fund (Bogdanov et al., 2018; Paraušić, 2023; Paraušić & Kljajić, 2023). Based on an interview with the president of the "Network of Local Action Groups of Serbia," it is clear that one of the biggest challenges LAGs in Serbia face today is related to the absence of systemic and continuous financing of the Leader approach (Paraušić, 2023). Specifically, only a few LAGs are recognized as important and prioritized by LSGUs, for example, LAG "Srce Bačke" by LSGU Kula and "Panonski fijaker" by LSGU Sombor. Each year, these two LSGUs allocate funds for the office and managers from the local budget (Paraušić, 2023). However, the vast majority of LAGs do not receive funds from the local budget (they are not recognized by their LSGUs). They get a small share of funds for their work from donors (by responding to domestic and international calls) and practically rely on volunteer work (Paraušić, 2023).

In addition to financial obstacles, the correct implementation of this measure in practice is hampered by many inherited problems in most municipalities in rural areas of Serbia, such as (a) insufficiently strong capacity of local initiatives, which are mostly short-term and ad hoc in nature; (b) insufficient networking of local stakeholders with low level of trust between them; and (c) strong influence of politics and bureaucracy on the level of LSGUs, with the absence of a democratic decision-making culture at the local level (Bogdanov et al., 2018; Erjavec et al., 2021; Janković Milić et al., 2014; Paraušić et al., 2023; Vujičić et al., 2013).

The importance of proper understanding and support to the Leader approach by local (public) authorities is extremely important for its future application, bearing in mind, among other things, the fact that representatives of public authorities, at the decision-making level, should have at least 20% and at most 49% voting rights in the Partnership management board (Table 11.1). Although the recognized LAGs expect a lot from projects financed through the IPARD Program, they consider the participation of representatives of the public (governmental) sector in LAGs as a problem, primarily because the representatives of LSGUs are not sufficiently familiar with the bottom-up approach to rural development, they do not understand the concept, nor the essence of the Leader approach (Paraušić, 2023).

Table 11.1 LAG Composition According to MAFWM.

Sector	Sector Representatives	Composition of the Management Board of the Partnership
Public (governmental) partners	• LSGUs or municipalities: the most influential representatives; • Public institutions (like educational bodies, schools...), public service providers and similarly	Local public authorities should have minimum of 20% and maximum of 49% voting rights.
Private (economic/ business) partners	• Farmers; • Entrepreneurs; • Business companies; • Agricultural cooperatives; • Producer organizations	Civil society sector must make up minimum 51% of voting rights; Economic and social partners must include rural women's' representatives as well (minimum one voting right) and young people from the Partnership territory (minimum one voting right);
Social partners	• Individuals/citizens, including women and young people; • Civil society organization (in sport, culture, environment, tourism, ...)	
No single interest group should have more than 49% of the voting rights.		

Source: MAFWM (2019a, 2022).

MAFWM is aware of the existence of numerous problems in the implementation of the Leader approach, which are listed in the SWOT (Strengths, Weaknesses, Opportunities and Threats) matrix (MAFWM, 2022, pp. 99–100). Authors also found out many problems in the implementation of the Leader approach, like (Paraušić, 2023; Paraušić & Kljajić, 2023):

- Non-recognition of the importance of LAGs by local public authorities and lack of support (financial, logistical and any other) from LSGUs;
- Lack of funds in the national budget for rural development to finance the Leader approach and uncertain further MAFWM support for implementation of this measure from the national budget. LAGs have not yet been given the opportunity to use incentives for financing priority projects defined in LDSs, nor have there been any new MAFWM calls for the formation of new LAGs;
- MAFWM being late with the accreditation of Measure 5 within the IPARD III Program for Serbia 2021–2027 (absence of IPARD funding and uncertain time of accreditation of Measure 5);
- The result of all the above is the loss of enthusiasm of managers and members of LAGs, as well as the weakening of human and material resources of LAGs.

This further leads to low national capacities of LAGs for financing the Leader approach through the IPARD III Program.

Attitudes of Interviewed LAGs' Managers Related to the Leader Approach in Serbia

In this section, authors present the results of interviews with managers of 10 LAGs in Serbia, recognized by MAFWM during 2019. In order to examine their views on the functioning of the LAGs that they manage, as well as the general environment in which all LAGs function in Serbia today, the authors designed a questionnaire, which consisted of several sets of questions.

The first set of questions included examining the views of LAGs' managers on the following issues related to the LAGs they manage:

1. Description of LAGs (concise presentation of LAG purpose, goals, vision);
2. Dominant sphere of LAG involvement;
3. Availability of funds for the work of the LAG manager and office;
4. Sources of financing projects defined in LDS;
5. Assessment of the degree to which LAG succeeds in realizing projects planned under LDS;
6. Description of difficulties or challenges in LAG management.

The second segment of the questionnaire consisted of questions that were designed in order to see activities LAGs in Serbia are primarily involved in (area, directions of involvement), and so the respondents could give suggestions for improving the work of the LAGs they manage, as well as the business environment for the implementation of Leader approach in general. Finally, through an answer to one question, respondents described a typical LAG representative or manager in Serbia today.

Below is a summary of the interview results for the first segment of questions.

Question 1. Description of LAG (Brief Presentation of LAG Purpose, Goals and Vision).
• Strategic planning and comprehensive development of the rural area of the Partnership territory; • Improving the conditions and quality of life of the local population on the Partnership territory, through the development of human resources, small businesses and agriculture; • Connection of local actors from the Partnership territory and joint action of all local stakeholders in order to create effective local rural policies and sustainable rural development;

- Rural development based on a recognizable, innovative and creative community, which bases its development on local resources and values, development of human resources, small economy, agriculture, tourism, infrastructure, ...
- Active life in villages, connecting urban and rural areas and improving infrastructure;
- Allowing people in rural areas to take responsibility for improving their living conditions and get motivation for village development and entrepreneurship;
- Development and improvement of LAG area products based on domestic advantages, knowledge and entrepreneurship.

Source: Authors' presentation based on Paraušić and Kljajić (2023).

Question 2. Dominant Sphere of LAG Involvement.

- Promotion of entrepreneurship and support to small producers of food and other products, support to women and their associations on the Partnership territory;
- Promotion of local products, food, rural tourism, ...
- Visiting/organization of fairs/events;
- Education of local producers/associations on how to improve the quality of local products;
- Support for the diversification of the rural economy, through the promotion of agricultural product processing on the farm, the development of all forms of rural tourism and the like;
- Connecting urban and rural areas, cooperation of all local stakeholders, construction of infrastructure in villages;
- Focus on the processing activity, especially on the branding of local products, in order to increase the visibility of producers of agricultural food products on the market;
- Realization of activities in the field of culture, construction of infrastructure and education of stakeholders;
- Writing and implementation of LDS projects; technical assistance to members in the development of project proposals; advisory assistance to members for IPARD measures;
- The LAG is not involved because the LSGU, on whose territory the LAG is mostly located, has not supported the work of the LAG for years. We should be concerned with LDS realization.

Source: Authors' presentation based on Paraušić and Kljajić (2023).

Question 3. Availability of Funds for the Work of the LAG Manager and Office.
• Half (50%) of the surveyed representatives of LAGs pointed out the lack of funds for the LAG office and the work of managers; • There are several recognized LAGs, which are led by LSGU employees (at the Youth Office or at the Department of Economy and Agriculture; members of the Municipal Council or the like). Among other tasks in the Municipality, these persons are responsible for the LAG; • At the same time, there is a small number of LAGs in which managers are financed by the LSGU on whose territory the LAG is registered (through the project principle), and these are rare municipalities that have recognized the importance of bottom-up approach to rural development; • Most LAGs do not have permanent (continuous) and secure sources of funding for the work of the office and LAGs' managers.

Source: Authors' presentation based on Paraušić (2023) and Paraušić and Kljajić (2023).

Question 4. Sources of Financing Projects Defined in LDS.
• Responding to calls announced by higher government level; • Solely by responding to calls and invitations announced by the local, provincial and republican levels of government, as well as participation in international projects (project financing); • Responding to calls announced by the LSGU (for LAGs, nongovernmental organizations, associations and the like). • Modest funds from only one LSGU; • Donations, project applications at LSGUs Boljevac and Sokobanja and at relevant ministries; • MAFWM financed the establishment of the LAG and the process of creating and implementing LDSs, and funds are expected from MAFWM to finance projects planned in LDS.

Source: Authors' presentation on Paraušić and Kljajić (2023).

Question 5. Assessment of the Degree to Which LAG Succeeds in Realizing Projects Planned Under LDS.
• Out of 10 surveyed LAGs, even 6 of them pointed out that they realize a small number of projects due to the lack of financial resources.

Source: Authors' presentation on Paraušić and Kljajić (2023).

Question 6. Description of Difficulties or Challenges in LAG Management
• Absence of continuous financial support from the national and local levels for the work of the office and managers and uncertainty in solving funding issues; • The currently available funds (funds received from the LSGU) are not sufficient for the implementation of the planned projects; • Lack of financial resources, low human capacity, lack of recognition of the importance of the LAG by state authorities and local population; • Lack of calls related to LAGs by MAFWM and the impossibility of financing the work of managers; • Money and human resources, barriers between the two cities that make up the LAG; • A long period of waiting for the accreditation of Leader Measure 5 within the IPARD program, which leads to the lack of interest of LAG members in further work; • Distrust of the local population in the work of LAGs; • Misunderstanding of the Leader approach by certain local stakeholders, more precisely representatives of LSGUs and inertness of MAFWM.

Source: Authors' presentation on Paraušić and Kljajić (2023).

The views of LAGs' managers regarding the areas in which future LAGs should be involved were obtained based on the questions in the second segment of the questionnaire. These attitudes are generally uniform among the surveyed managers and are aimed at (Paraušić & Kljajić, 2023):

- Supporting small-scale farmers, young people and entrepreneurs in local rural areas covered by the LAG, in order to increase their income;
- Promotion of (a) local identity and collective events, (b) natural values of the LAG area, (c) local (traditional) food and (d) rural tourism;
- Promotion of the bottom-up approach, while encouraging the local population to take greater responsibility for the development of their community;
- Activating the resources and potential of local communities and local associations, connecting and strengthening ties between rural and urban areas, networking the public sector with civil society.

What follows are the suggestions of LAGs' managers regarding the more efficient work of the LAGs they manage, as well as regarding the improvement of the business environment for the implementation of the Leader approach in general in Serbia (Table 11.2).

Table 11.2 Proposals of LAGs' Managers for Improving the Work of LAGs in Serbia.

Suggestions for improving the work of the LAG led by the manager					
Recognition of the importance of LAGs by LSGUs	Permanent financing of LAGs (office, managers) from the budget of LSGUs	Support and participation of LSGUs in the realization of LAG's projects	Permanent financial allocations for Leader in national agrarian budget	Professional training and improvement of knowledge and skills of LAGs' managers	More calls at all levels of government so that the LAG could realize the planned projects
Suggestions for improving the environment for the implementation of the Leader approach					
The importance of LAG must be recognized and financially supported by authorities at all levels (state, province, municipality); Regular funding programs for LAG managers; Treat LAGs as mini-development agencies for the development of rural areas	Animating LSGUs to support LAGs in implementing projects from LDSs	Continuation of the started support of MAFWM implementation of the Leader approach	Urgent accreditation of Measure 5 within the IPARD III Program for Serbia 2021–2027	Urgent preparation of new LDSs for the next budget period from 2024 to 2027 (financing of the production of LDSs and animating the stakeholders)	Skills training, practical exercises, exchange of ideas and experiences to strengthen the resources of LAG managers

Source: Paraušić and Kljajić (2023).

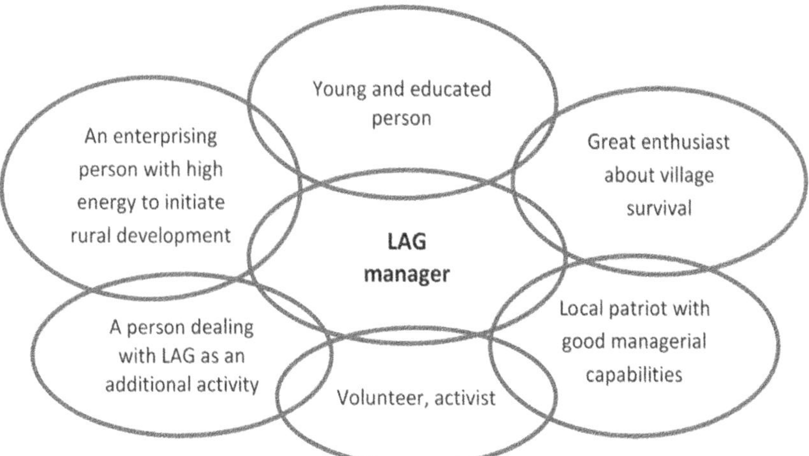

Fig. 11.3 Typical Profile of the LAG Manager in Serbia. *Source*: Authors' presentation based on Paraušić and Kljajić (2023).

Finally, when asked how they would describe a typical LAG manager in Serbia today, the respondents said:

- There are no rules; the situation is different from LAG to LAG. Most often, managers of LAGs are volunteers, enthusiasts. They mostly work in LSGUs, the private sector or civil society organizations. They have their regular job, and they deal with the LAG in addition to their regular job;
- Enterprising and young people, enthusiasts;
- Amateurs without previous experience and education in rural development.
- Young, educated and primarily enterprising people;
- Young, educated, enthusiastic, local patriots with good managerial skills;
- Managers are mostly young and ambitious people, with great energy to initiate the development of their rural areas, but they face the problem of insufficient sources of financing;
- Young, educated, enterprising, activists and great enthusiasts regarding village survival and rural development.

A typical profile of the LAG manager is given in Fig. 11.3.

Conclusion

Leader enables activation of local resources, as well as entrepreneurial ideas and initiatives of numerous local stakeholders, primarily in the segment of improving quality and living conditions and employment in rural areas. Considering the needs, problems and resources of the local community, the measure is implemented by LAGs, more precisely the local population (private and social partners), along with representatives of the local government, who implement smaller local projects of importance for the rural community.

The implementation of the Leader approach in Serbia is still in its infancy, and this is still a new and insufficiently understood concept of rural development. As a national rural development measure, Leader began in 2019, and at the beginning of 2023, only a list of recognized Partnerships is available, i.e., LAGs, whose LDSs have been positively evaluated by the MAFWM Evaluation Commission.

Entrepreneurial initiatives of the local population are of low capacity, due to the disinterest of stakeholders in projects of general interest and due to numerous institutional and inherited problems, which lead to the fact that local initiatives remain in the shadow of political interests and conflicts. The entrepreneurial abilities of LAGs' managers are largely limited and hindered by the absence of permanent sources of funding for the office work and the implementation of LAGs' projects. At the same time, MAFWM shows slowness, inconsistency and inefficiency in the implementation, i.e., financing of the Leader measure, which is why LAGs realize a small percentage of their LDSs.

All this leads to the fact that the capacities of existing LAGs are significantly low, as well as their ability to apply for project implementation through IPARD funds. In the same way, the possibilities of the existing LAGs to spread examples of good practice through the implementation of the project, and thus animate and interest the local population, socially responsible companies and various donors for wider involvement in community development, are limited.

In the coming period, effective Leader application in Serbia will depend on a number of factors, the key of which are (a) recognizing the importance of the bottom-up approach and strengthening the awareness of the local population that through joint and networked entrepreneurial initiatives, they can improve the environment for living and working in their communities (MAFWM and Agricultural Extension Service must play an important role here); and (b) the existence of a financial portfolio for the work of LAGs' managers and the implementation of LAGs' projects, more precisely, ensuring permanent sources of funding for LAGs' work (funds from the local budget, provincial/national budget, IPARD funding).

For now, the most important role of MAFWM is to continue the implementation of Leader as a national measure, and as soon as possible address Measure 5 under the IPARD III Program, which will provide recognized partnerships with significantly more financial resources for work than those available at the national/local level. In fact, only regular calls for co-financing of LAGs' activities by MAFWM, and in a later phase applying for IPARD funds, would lead to the implementation of LDSs, popularization of LAGs and strengthen their capacities.

If the former is absent, bearing in mind the processes of depopulation in Serbian villages, the much-needed revitalization of rural areas and improvement of conditions and quality of life in these areas cannot be expected.

The research results enrich the theoretical framework in the area of the Leader approach. The results of the realized empirical research contribute to a better understanding, clarification and demystification of this approach in Serbia and other countries that still do not apply Leader or are in its infancy. Research can benefit the scientific community, stakeholders and entrepreneurs in local rural communities, practitioners and nongovernmental organizations, as well as public policymakers (at all government levels) in drafting policies aimed at greater application of CLLD in rural areas. Also, the results can provide guidelines for organizing future more complex and complex research in the analyzed area.

Acknowledgment

This chapter was financially supported by the Ministry of Science, Technological Development and Innovation of the Republic of Serbia, Contract No. 451-03-47/ 2023-01//200009 dated February 3, 2023.

References

Adamowicz, M., & Zwolińska-Ligaj, M. (2020). The "Smart Village" as a way to achieve sustainable development in rural areas of Poland. *Sustainability*, *12*(16), 6503. htpps://doi.org/10.3390/su12166503

Baumgartner, D., Pütz, M., & Seidl, I. (2013). What kind of entrepreneurship drives regional development in European non-core regions? A literature review on empirical entrepreneurship research. *European Planning Studies*, *21*(8), 1095–1127. htpps://doi.org/10.1080/09654313.2012.722937

Bogdanov, N., Gjorgievski, P., & Lukeš, R. (2018). Regional aspects. In N. Bogdanov, B. Leveska Đoršoska, A. Palaco, P. Đorđijevski, & R. Lukeš (Eds.), *Application of the LEADER approach in the Western Balkan countries – From a local initiative to a mainstream concept in the rural areas* (pp. 9–27). Regional Rural Development Standing Working Group in SEE (SWG). https://seerural.org/wp-content/uploads/2018/06/LEADER-Report-WEB.pdf

Bogdanov, N., Nikolić, A., Dimitrievski, D., & Kotevska, A. (2015). Rural areas and rural development policy in Macedonia, Serbia, and Bosnia and Herzegovina. In A. Kotevska & A. Martinovska Stojcheska (Eds.), *The impact of socio-economic structure of rural population on success of rural development policy* (pp. 21–35). Association of Agricultural Economists of Republic of Macedonia. https://publicpolicy.rs/publikacije/d16435796b8009eb918aa100c03cfbba0d5423f3.pdf

Cizler, J. (2013). Opportunities for the sustainable development of rural areas in Serbia. *Problemy Ekorozwoju–Problems of Sustainable Development*, *8*(2), 85–91. https://ekorozwoj.pollub.pl/no16/k.pdf

Coffey, W. J., & Polese, M. (1985). Local development: Conceptual bases and policy implications. *Regional Studies*, *19*(2), 85–93. htpps://doi.org/10.1080/09595238500185101

Dargan, L., & Shucksmith, M. (2008). LEADER and innovation. *Sociologia Ruralis*, *48*(3), 274–291. htpps://doi.org/10.1111/j.1467-9523.2008.00463.x

DiCicco-Bloom, B., & Crabtree, B. F. (2006) The qualitative research interview. *Medical Education*, *40*(4), 314–321. htpps://doi.org/10.1111/j.1365-2929.2006.02418.x

Directorate for Agrarian Payments. (2021). *Ranking list of rated LSDs in rural areas*. Ministry of Agriculture, Forestry and Water Management of the Republic of Serbia. https://uap.gov.rs/wp-content/uploads/2019/02/rang-lista-partnerstava-za-teritorijalni-razvoj.pdf

Erjavec, E., Volk, T., Rednak, M., Ciaian, P., & Lazdinis, M. (2021). Agricultural policies and European Union accession processes in the Western Balkans: Aspirations versus reality. *Eurasian Geography and Economics*, *62*(1), 46–75. htpps://doi.org/10.1080/15387216.2020.1756886

Esparcia Perez, J. (2000). The LEADER programme and the rise of rural development in Spain. *Sociologia Ruralis*, *40*(2), 200–207. https://doi.org/10.1111/1467-9523.00142

European Communities. (2006). *The Leader approach*. A basic guide. Office for Official Publications of the European Communities. http://old.europe.bg/upload/docs/leader.pdf

European Commission. (2017). *Guidelines. Evaluation of LEADER/CLLD*. European Evaluation Helpdesk for Rural Development. https://ec.europa.eu/enrd/sites/default/files/evaluation_publications/twg-03-leader_clld-aug2017.pdf

European Commission. (2019). *Agricultural policy developments and EU approximation process in the Western Balkan countries*. Publications Office of the European Union. htpps://doi.org/10.2760/583399

European Commission. (2021, June 30). A long-term vision for the EU's rural areas – Towards stronger, connected, resilient and prosperous rural areas by 2040. https://eur-lex.europa.eu/legal-content/EN/TXT/DOC/?uri=CELEX:52021DC0345

European Union. (2005). Council Regulation (EC) No. 1698/2005 of 20 September 2005 on support for rural development by the European Agricultural Fund for Rural Development (EAFRD). *Official Journal of the European Union, L 277*. https://eur-lex.europa.eu/eli/reg/2005/1698/oj, pp. 25-27

European Union. (2013a). Regulation (EU) No. 1303/2013 of the European Parliament and of the Council of 17 December 2013 laying down common provisions on the European Regional Development Fund, the European Social Fund, the Cohesion Fund, the European Agricultural Fund for Rural Development and the European Maritime and Fisheries Fund and laying down general provisions on the European Regional Development Fund, the European Social Fund, the Cohesion Fund and the European Maritime and Fisheries Fund and repealing Council Regulation (EC) No. 1083/2006. http://data.europa.eu/eli/reg/2013/1303/oj

European Union. (2013b). Regulation (EU) No. 1305/2013 of the European Parliament and of the Council of 17 December 2013 on support for rural development by the European Agricultural Fund for Rural Development (EAFRD) and repealing Council Regulation (EC) No. 1698/2005. *Official Journal of the European Union, L 347*. http://data.europa.eu/eli/reg/2013/1305/oj, pp. 493-494, p. 520

European Union. (2016). *Cork 2.0 declaration "A Better Life in Rural Areas."* Publications Office of the European Union. https://ec.europa.eu/enrd/sites/default/files/cork-declaration_en.pdf

European Union. (2021a). Regulation (EU) 2021/2115 of the European Parliament and of the Council of 2 December 2021establishing rules on support for strategic plans to be drawn up by Member States under the common agricultural policy (CAP Strategic Plans) and financed by the European Agricultural Guarantee Fund (EAGF) and by the European Agricultural Fund for Rural Development (EAFRD) and repealing Regulations (EU) No. 1305/2013 and (EU) No. 1307/2013. *Official Journal of the European Union, L 435*. http://data.europa.eu/eli/reg/2021/2115/oj, p. 16, p. 25, pp.70-71, p. 80

European Union. (2021b). Regulation (EU) 2021/1060 of the European Parliament and of the Council of 24 June 2021 laying down common provisions on the European Regional Development Fund, the European Social Fund Plus, the Cohesion Fund, the Just Transition Fund and the European Maritime, Fisheries and Aquaculture Fund and financial rules for those and for the Asylum, Migration and Integration Fund, the Internal Security Fund and the Instrument for Financial Support for Border Management and Visa Policy. *Official Journal of the European Union, L 231/159*. http://data.europa.eu/eli/reg/2021/1060/oj, p. 164

FAO. (2020). *Empowering smallholders and family farms in Europe and Central Asia. Regional synthesis report 2019 based on country studies in eight countries in Europe and Central and Asia*. Food and Agriculture Organization of the United Nations. https://doi.org/10.4060/ca9586en

Gabriel Anton, S., Onofrei, M., Neta Gostin, I., & Oprică, L. (2022). Entrepreneurial opportunities in the green economy. In N. Marcu, G. R. Lădaru, & I. Neta Gostin (Eds.), *Entrepreneurial innovation in agri-food science* (pp. 70–85). "Alexandru Ioan Cuza" University Press & Institute of Agricultural Economics. https://www.iep.bg.ac.rs/images/stories/izdanja/Monografije/IO2%20-%20AGROECOINN.pdf

Government of Republic of Serbia. (2014). *The strategy of Agriculture and Rural Development of the Republic of Serbia 2014–2024*. Official Gazette of the RS No. 85. http://www.minpolj.gov.rs/download/strategija-poljoprivrede-i-ruralnog-razvoja-republike-srbije-za-period-2014-2024-godine/

Grande, J., Madsen, E. L., & Borch, O. J. (2011). The relationship between resources, entrepreneurial orientation and performance in farm-based ventures. *Entrepreneurship and Regional Development*, *23*(3–4), 89–111. htpps://doi.org/10.1080/08985620903183710

Janković, D. (2020). Društvene promene i ruralni razvoj: Značaj socijalnog kapitala, participacije i društvenih mreža/Social change and rural development: The importance of social capital, participation and social networks. Faculty of Agriculture, University of Novi Sad. http://ae.polj.uns.ac.rs/wp-content/uploads/2017/08/Dru%C5%A1tvene-promene-i-ruralni-razvoj-D_Jankovic.pdf

Janković Milić, V., Stanković, J., & Marinkovic, S. (2014). The capacity of local governments to improve business environment: Evidence from Serbia. *Zbornik radova Ekonomskog fakulteta u Rijeci, časopis za ekonomsku teoriju i praksu – Proceedings of Rijeka Faculty of Economics. Journal of Economics and Business*, *32*(2), 233–254. https://www.efri.uniri.hr/hr/volume_32_no_2_2014_volumen_32_svezak_2_2014/256/119

Joldžić, V., Batrićević, A., Stanković, V., & Paunović, N. (2019). Solving the problems of rural as environmentally desirable segment of sustainable development. *Economic Analysis*, *51*(1–2), 79–91. htpps://doi.org/10.28934/ea.18.51.12

Konečný, O. (2019). The leader approach across the European Union: One method of rural development, many forms of implementation. *European Countryside, 11*(1), 1–16. htpps://doi.org/10.2478/euco-2019-0001

López, M., Cazorla, A., & Panta, M. D. P. (2019). Rural entrepreneurship strategies: Empirical experience in the Northern Sub-Plateau of Spain. *Sustainability*, *11*(5), 1243. htpps://doi.org/10.3390/su11051243

MAFWM (Ministry of Agriculture, Forestry and Water Management of the Republic of Serbia). (2019a). Regulation on incentives for support of programmes related to the preparation and implementation of local rural development strategies. Official Gazette of the Republic of Serbia No. 3/2019 and 159/2020. https://www.pravno-informacioni-sistem.rs/SlGlasnikPortal/eli/rep/sgrs/ministarstva/pravilnik/2019/3/6/reg

MAFWM (Ministry of Agriculture, Forestry and Water Management of the Republic of Serbia). (2019b). Public call for the submission of requests for the approval of the right to an incentive for supporting programs related to the preparation of local rural development strategies in 2019. https://uap.gov.rs/wp-content/uploads/2019/02/Javni-poziv-Lider-2019.pdf

MAFWM (Ministry of Agriculture, Forestry and Water Management of the Republic of Serbia). (2022). IPARD III Programme for the Republic of Serbia for the period 2021-2027. http://www.minpolj.gov.rs/download/IPARD-III-Programme-for-the-Republic-of-Serbia-for-the-period-2021-2027-CLEAN-21-Jan-2022.pdf

Miles, M. P., & Morrison, M. (2020). An effectual leadership perspective for developing rural entrepreneurial ecosystems. *Small Business Economics*, *54*, 933–949. https://doi.org/10.1007/s11187-018-0128-z

Navarro, F. A., Woods, M., & Cejudo, E. (2016). The LEADER initiative has been a victim of its own success. The decline of the bottom-up approach in rural development programmes. The cases of Wales and Andalusia. *Sociologia Ruralis*, *56*(2), 270–288. htpps://doi.org/10.1111/soru.12079

Neto, P., Santos, A., & Serrano, M. M. (2014). Public policies supporting local networks for entrepreneurship and innovation: Effectiveness and added value analysis of LEADER program in the Alentejo region of Portugal. *International Journal of Entrepreneurship and Small Business, 21*(3), 406–435. https://doi.org/10.1504/IJESB.2014.060900

Nieto Masot, A., Cárdenas Alonso, G., & Costa Moreno, L. M. (2019). Principal component analysis of the Leader approach (2007–2013) in South Western Europe (Extremadura and Alentejo). *Sustainability, 11*(15), 4034. htpps://doi.org/10.3390/su11154034

Nordberg, K., Mariussen, Å., & Virkkala, S. (2020). Community-driven social innovation and quadruple helix coordination in rural development. Case study on LEADER group Aktion Österbotten. *Journal of Rural Studies, 79*, 157–168. https://doi.org/10.1016/j.jrurstud.2020.08.001

Paraušić, V. (2023). *Interview with the president of the Network of Local Action Groups of Serbia, Bojan Kovač*. [Unpublished material].

Paraušić, V., & Bekić Šarić, B. (2021). Implementation of the Leader approach in Serbia: Experiences and results. In J. Subić, P. Vuković, & J. V. Andrei (Eds.), *Sustainable agriculture and rural development* (pp. 345–352). Institute of Agricultural Economics. https://www.iep.bg.ac.rs/images/stories/izdanja/Tematski%20Zbornici/Tematski%20zbornik%202021.pdf

Paraušić, V., & Domazet, I. (2018). Cluster development and innovative potential in Serbian agriculture. *Economics of Agriculture, 65*(3), 1159–1170. htpps://doi.org/10.5937/ekoPolj1803159P

Paraušić, V., Domazet, I., & Simeunović, I. (2017). Analysis of the relationship between the stage of economic development and the state of cluster development. *Argumenta Oeconomica, 39*(2), 279–305. htpps://doi.org/10.15611/aoe.2017.2.12

Paraušić, V., & Kljajić, N. (2023). Email interview with managers of LAGs in Serbia. Unpublished material.

Paraušić, V., Kostić, Z., & Subić, J. (2023). Local development initiatives in Serbia's rural communities as prerequisite for the Leader implementation: Agricultural advisors' perceptions. *Economics of Agriculture, 70*(1), 117–130. htpps://doi.org/10.59267/ekoPolj2301117P

Pollermann, K., Aubert, F., Berriet-Solliec, M., Laidin, C., Pham, H. V., Raue, P., & Schnaut, G. (2020). LEADER as a European policy for rural development in a multilevel governance framework: A comparison of the implementation in France, Germany and Italy. *European Countryside, 12*(2), 156–178. htpps://doi.org/10.2478/euco-2020-0009

Ray, C. (2000). The EU LEADER programme: Rural development laboratory. *Sociologia Ruralis, 40*(2), 163–171. https://doi.org/10.1111/1467-9523.00138

Rego, C., Lucas, M. R., Vieira, C., & Vieira, I. (2018). Entrepreneurial ecosystems in low-density regions: Business incubation practices in Alentejo. In L. Cagica Carvalho (Ed.), *Handbook of research on entrepreneurial ecosystems and social dynamics in a globalized world* (pp. 45–74). IGI Global. htpps://doi.org/10.4018/978-1-5225-3525-6.ch003

Santos, A., Neto, P., & Serrano, M. M. (2016). A long-term mortality analysis of subsidized firms in rural areas: An empirical study in the Portuguese Alentejo region. *Eurasian Economic Review, 6*, 125–151. htpps://doi.org/10.1007/s40822-015-0035-4

Sredojević, Z., Kljajić, N., & Gajić, B. (2019). Brownfield investments as possibility of revitalization and sustainability of locations. *Economics of Agriculture, 66*(2), 589–599. htpps://doi.org/10.5937/ekoPolj1902589S

Subić, J., Kljajić, N., & Jeločnik, M. (2017). Obnovljivi izvori energije i navodnjavanje u funkciji održivog razvoja poljoprivrede – ekonomski aspekti (Renewable energy sources and irrigation in the function of sustainable agricultural development - economic aspects).Institute of Agricultural Economics. https://www.iep.bg.ac.rs/images/stories/dokumenti/Monografije/Mon%20Energija%20i%20navodnjavanje%20%20FINAL.pdf

Tirado Ballesteros, J. G., & Hernández, M. H. (2019). Promoting tourism through the EU LEADER programme: Understanding local action group governance. *European Planning Studies*, *27*(2), 396–414. htpps://doi.org/10.1080/09654313.2018.1547368

Vázquez-Barquero, A., & Rodríguez-Cohard, J. C. (2016). Endogenous development and institutions: Challenges for local development initiatives. *Environment and Planning C: Government and Policy*, *34*(6), 1135–1153. htpps://doi.org/10.1177/0263774X15624924

Vujičić, M., Ristić, L., & Ćirić, N. (2013). Local initiatives for rural vitality and social inclusion: Some experiences from Serbia. *Eastern European Countryside*, *19*, 105–126. htpps://doi.org/10.2478/eec-2013-0006

Živojinović, I., Ludvig, A., & Hogl, K. (2019). Social innovation to sustain rural communities: Overcoming institutional challenges in Serbia. *Sustainability*, *11*(24), 7248. htpps://doi.org/10.3390/su11247248

Chapter 12

Achieved Level of Development Within the Framework of the Smart Cities Concept in the Direction of Green Resilient*

Drago Cvijanović[a], Tibor Fazekaš[b], Otilija Sedlak[b] and Dragan Stojić[b]

[a]*University of Kragujevac, Serbia*
[b]*University of Novi Sad, Serbia*

Abstract

The aim of this chapter is to develop a conceptual model for the analysis of sustainable development and the ranking of cities based on selected standard criteria and metrics of smart cities. The conceptual framework contains standard and measurable indicators that influence the creation and survival of smart cities that could be self-sustaining, Green Resilient. We can measure the level of smartness of cities from two perspectives, first from the point of view of the degree of automation of services, infrastructure, buildings, transport, etc. and second from the point of view of planning the further development of the city in order to raise the quality of life of its citizens. Indicators should satisfy the principles of specificity, measurability, availability, relevance and timeliness (Schomaker, 1997). Researchers in the field of smart cities define different sets of characteristics, on which they construct a system of indicators that together describe the degree of development of a smart city. It must be taken into account the fact that there is no single set of indicators that would refer to the level of smartness of the city. It is a complex phenomenon, which occurs differently depending on the conceptual framework and the goal of classifying

*Extracts published in this chapter have been taken from: Sedlak, O., Fazekas, T., Horvat, A. M., Radovanov, B., Stojic, D., & Korhec, R. (2023). Measuring development level and defining criteria for ranking smart cities. *Civitas, 13*(1), 108–123.

Emerging Patterns and Behaviors in a Green Resilient Economy, 255–320

Published under exclusive licence by Emerald Publishing Limited
doi:10.1108/978-1-83549-780-720241013

cities according to the complex characteristics of smartness, especially if you take into account the fact that the general well-being and quality of life of citizens are more important than only indicators of the quality of city services.

Keywords: Smart city; general characteristics of the city; improvement of the environment in the city; green resilient city; environmental problems in cities; importance of city traffic

Introduction

The development of a conceptual model for the analysis of sustainable development and ranking of cities based on selected standard criteria and metrics of smart cities is considered. The aim of this research is to accentuate the differences in the corresponding characteristics and factors by measuring individual indicators, different factors for individual criteria of medium and small towns. Based on the determined situation in relation to various factors, guidelines and perspectives for further development will be determined through the built model. The measured values of individual factors will represent a database, on the basis of which cities can be ranked, i.e., identify advantages and disadvantages, determine their diversity, as well as comparative advantages in the region, in order to increase sustainability.

Given the multidisciplinarity of the research subject, it is necessary to analyze the various criteria and methods of measurement applied so far, in order to determine the conceptual framework of standard and measurable indicators that have an impact on the emergence and survival of smart cities. Monitoring and respecting the opinions of experts will enable the research to have a well-founded basis for sustainable development and the creation of a smart city. Each city has its own unique economic, social and administrative characteristics, as well as different priorities. The developed conceptual model will contain basic, standardized criteria (indicators) that will enable cities to compare themselves, as well as with the cities of Europe. In addition to technological changes, the process of European integration is the one that reduces economic differences, differences in social and environmental standards, and thus provides a common market. By determining the values of components, through the values of their factors or indicators, the basis for ranking cities in our environment will be made. This will create preconditions for combining competitiveness and sustainable development in the region. Technological factors and their development are of key importance for the growth of the city into a smart city. A necessary, but not a sufficient, condition for the development of smart cities is the correct functioning of infrastructure, mobile and virtual technologies, digital networks. In order for the city to become smart, it must also meet the condition that is related to both institutional and human factors. Institutional factors include adequate governance, policies and regulations, and the human factor encompasses different forms and levels of education.

Literature Review

Level of smartness of cities can be measured from two perspectives. First from the point of view of the degree of automation of services, infrastructure, buildings, transport, etc. and second from the point of view of planning the further development of the city in order to raise the level of quality of life of its citizens. Indicators should meet the principles of specificity, measurability, availability, relevance and timeliness (Schomaker, 1997). Researchers in the field of smart cities define different sets of characteristics, over which they construct a system of indicators that together describe the degree of development of a smart city (Leonova et al., 2018). It must be borne in mind that there is no single set of indicators that would relate to the level of smartness of the city. It is a complex phenomenon, which occurs differently depending on the conceptual framework and goal of classifying cities according to complex characteristics of smartness, especially if we take into account the fact that the general welfare and quality of life of citizens are more important than indicators of city services. Different authors understand the components that need to be taken into account when determining the degree of development of a smart city in different ways (Technopolis, 2013).

One of the significant research projects related to the categorization of smart cities in the EU was realized in the Center for Regional Sciences of the University of Technology in Vienna (Giffinger et al., 2007). The research adopted the concept according to which medium-sized cities are very similar to each other and, as such, represent a good research framework for finding common factors for defining a smart city. The working team selected the components of the economy, people, government, mobility, environment and quality of life of citizens. Six main functional segments that characterize the city were selected as a starting point: smart economy, smart mobility, smart environment, smart population, smart apartment and smart administration. Based on the set concept and identified six main characteristics important for the ranking of cities, the overall structure was adopted, which depicts each analyzed city individually. The result of this research is the formation of a ranking list of 70 European Union (EU) cities, by individual components and collectively.

Batagan (2011) builds a smart city indicator system for four groups of indicators: education, health, transportation, and public administration. Chourabi et al. (2012) state that the components are management and organization, technology, city authorities, city management policy, human community, infrastructure, environment. Carlia et al. (2013) set a framework for indicators that serve to classify performance within the measurement of the degree of development of smart cities and look at objective indicators (physical infrastructure, public areas and buildings and environmental indicators) and subjective indicators (satisfaction and well-being of citizens). Firnkorn (2015) observes cities from the point of view of the degree of development of intelligence in the short and long terms. For the formation of a smart city in the short term, within the next few years, one should start from a technical vision, which means collecting data and making these data available to experts who work on developing the elements of a smart city. The features of a smart city that should be considered in the long run, (according to this author, it is 30 years after the initiation of development in this direction) are a built strategy that combines all components, such as public services, public role, economic dynamism, transport and resources; special attention is paid to dynamism and flexibility, i.e., the power to adapt to change. Moreno (2015) believes that the degree of development of a smart city is determined by the availability of technology needed to meet the needs of citizens, focus on service design, constant use of information and communication technologies, openness, adaptability and the degree of horizontal and collaborative organization. Canteneur (2015a, 2015b) highlights the example of Vienna, whose management evaluates the degree of development of their city, as a smart city, from a social point of view, i.e., to what extent the quality of life of the inhabitants has been ensured and to what extent harmonization has been achieved between certain social strata, with special importance attached to the rational consumption of energy and the preservation of the environment.

Fields where generally high socio-economic benefits from smart city policy are to be expected were defined by authors Sassen and Kourtit (2021) are environmental and health transition, resource and energy transition, socio-demographic and spatial transition, cultural and community transition. Another group of researchers (Long, 2020; Monfaredzadeh & Krueger, 2015; Strüver et al., 2021) put actual smartness – in the sense of social justice and sustainability – at the center stage.

In 2016, the German Institute for Industrial Engineering in Stuttgart, Fraunhofer, launched the "Morgenstadt" (city of tomorrow) initiative to explore development potentials within urban systems, which support the transformation of sustainable smart cities (Frauenhofer Society, 2016). The institute also organizes research in cooperation with cities within the project "CityLabs" (city laboratories), the results of which are derived indicators of the level of development and proposals for corrective actions. Researchers at the institute list nine sectors that represent the most important determinants of sustainable urban development: mobility, buildings, water supply, city authorities, energy, finance, information and communication technologies, logistics and flexibility. In order to perform a single assessment, the institute evaluates 28 indicators grouped into four topics (quality of life, environmental protection, innovation and flexibility), which are measured for a large number of European and world cities. Based on the results of the research, in 2016, the online documentation "Morgenstadt City Index" was published with the values of indicators of the level of development of selected smart cities.

Under the coordination of the consulting company ABUD (Advanced Building and Urban Design) from Budapest, the European project SmartCEPS (Smart City Evaluation Platform and Service) was launched in 2017, funded through the Eurostars-2 program and the European Union Horizon 2020 research and innovation program. This project has two goals: to provide services to European cities for self-assessment of their performance on certain issues of a smart and sustainable city through an online platform and consulting. The issues considered in this project are the availability of common standards and experience, the approach to planning aimed at information and communication technologies and the disadvantage of small and medium enterprises in relation to large companies, which assess the benefits for entrepreneurship and attractiveness of the city for investors (ABUD, 2017).

In order to support the application of smart technologies in cities, the European Commission (EC) has launched two projects: "Lighthouse Project" and "Horizontal Activities." As part of the Horizontal Activities, the project "CITYkeys – Smart City performance measurement system" (Huovila et al., 2017) was launched in 2015, funded under the EU program "Horizon 2020." The aim was development of a framework for monitoring and comparing activities within European cities, in order to achieve their development into a smart city (EC, 2015a, 2015b, 2016, 2018, 2019; Majer et al., 2018). The project working group (Bosch et al., 2017) published a list of indicators of the development level of smart cities, divided into four areas: people, planet earth, prosperity and city leadership, with a total of 80 indicators.

Methodology

An Innovative Approach to the Creation of Criteria for Ranking Cities Within the Concept of Smart Cities

The most important measure of the reliability of the methods for the analysis of the competitiveness of cities is the way of selecting the cities to be compared, as well as the objectivity in the analysis, which is achieved by adequate selection of comparative indicators. In order to realize the most successful ranking of cities, it is necessary to identify three key aspects of the analysis:

- Ranking goal – is not defined only on the basis of the target group for which it is intended but also on the basis of the spatial coverage over which it is implemented, as well as on the basis of analyzed indicators.
- Ranking methodology – in addition to the choice of data collection and the methodology of their processing, it is necessary to consider all the limitation.
- Presentation of results – the way in which the results of the analysis are evaluated, interpreted and published has the greatest impact on decision-making.

The method of ranking cities is recommended as a very effective tool aimed at identifying and perceiving both good and bad characteristics of a city or as a way to direct local authorities in a relatively simple way to optimize key solutions important for its normal functioning.

Assessing or ranking cities based on their attributes has emerged as a highly effective approach. It benefits local governments by offering insights into areas requiring improvement, and it provides valuable guidance to potential investors seeking to implement business ideas in specific cities. This methodology is based exclusively on the objectivity of the surveyed citizens, which can also be the most sensitive point in terms of its reliability. By adequately choosing the content of the survey, as well as the methodology of selecting participants in the research, these negative impacts can be greatly reduced. In addition to this shortcoming, it should also be noted that it is questionable to comment on the results obtained based on the analysis of cities that differ greatly in size and status (capitals always have a specific status).

According to the conceptual variants of the smart city, the key conceptual components of the smart city can be identified and clarified. The three categories of key factors we have defined for our research are technology (hardware and software infrastructure), people (creativity, diversity and education) and institutions (governance and policy). Table 12.1 shows the basic components of a smart city that served as a starting point in our further analysis.

Research on the status and ranking of smart cities relies on defined criteria, on which measurements were made, statistical data were collected and surveys were conducted regarding the degree of satisfaction with these predefined items.

Our research represents a new approach and starting point: we assume that there are views on a number of generally accepted components of smart cities, but there are also new factors, such that they have not been taken into account so far. Furthermore, each factor has its own importance and weight and does not contribute equally to the level of smartness of the city or to the degree of satisfaction of citizens with the living conditions in the smart city.

In this sense, our research is focused on a set of given, defined indicators, which relate to certain characteristics of smart cities. Furthermore, the survey of experts is conducted on the degree of indicators' importance. Then, each expert can define several additional, new, hitherto unmentioned–unexplored characteristics, which may be important for the categorization of smart cities. Each descriptive characteristic is covered by one or more measured numerical indicators of smart cities, as well as one or more quantified values of opinions (citizens, service providers and members of city management) regarding the state or satisfaction with a feature of a smart city. Based on the results of the survey, the obtained average assessment of characteristics is formed by weights that are applied to the respective indicators.

The grades that experts can assign to individual characteristics in the survey range from 1 to 10.

By performing a concise assessment with a weighting procedure, it can be expected to obtain more reliable assessments of the rank of smart cities and especially the degree of satisfaction of its citizens. Indicators that belong to certain

Table 12.1. Basic Components of a Smart City.

Technological Factors	**Human Factors**	**Institutional Factors**
• Physical infrastructure • Smart technologies • Mobile technologies • Virtual technologies • Digital networks	• Human infrastructure • Social capital	• Management • Politics • Regulations/directives

Source: Authors' source.

characteristics are measurable values or opinions-assessments of citizens about the situation in the city and the degree of satisfaction.

Selection of Criteria and Survey Creation

Based on our research on the phenomenon of smart settlements, based on the studied scientific and professional literature and practical analyses listed in this chapter, we have formed a set of characteristics, which can largely cover most of the features, conditions and processes that potentially determine the achieved level of development within the concept of smart cities. The list of characteristics with the corresponding units of measurement, grouped by areas, is shown in Appendix 1.

The set of characteristics can be further expanded, based on other research, which may attach more importance to some other characteristics. There are a total of 116 features on our list. All these indicators are measurable quantities and can be accompanied by quantitative values. The relative importance of certain indicators is calculated on the basis of per capita values. All characteristics can be classified into the following six types:

- data in physical units of measure (number of pieces or quantities);
- data in monetary units (EUR);
- percentage amounts (participation of the city in the national economy);
- relations between two quantities;
- results of surveys of experts or citizens (values given according to the Likert scale (McLeod, 2014));
- binary variable (existence or not of certain characteristics: yes–no).

Expert opinions on the characteristics of cities are divided into six groups:

Group 1: The importance of general characteristics of the city, with 22 individual characteristics,

Group 2: The importance of strategic directions for the realization of the concept of smart cities, with 12 individual characteristics,

Group 3: The importance of the principle of forming a management strategy for improving the environment in the city, with 12 individual characteristics,

Group 4: The importance of solving environmental problems in cities, with 13 individual characteristics,

Group 5: The importance of city administration measures for improving living conditions, with 12 individual characteristics,

Group 6: The importance of elements of urban traffic, with 21 individual characteristics.

According to these groups, we have defined a total of 92 questions, which reflect the opinion of experts on the most important features of cities, from the point of view of reaching a certain degree of smartness (Appendix 2). Questions related to some characteristics can be found in several groups, in order to shed light on the problem from several different points of view, and at the same time, it allows to assess the reliability and validity of the survey, according to a certain quantitative procedure (correlation coefficient, regression coefficient and Cronbach's α-coefficient).

The possibilities of obtaining statistical data have determined a set of characteristics of cities for empirical research in this chapter, which aim to present the proposed innovative approach to the formation of a composite index that reflects the achieved level of development within the concept of smart cities.

Expert Survey Results

A total of 92 experts participated in the survey, and 84 correctly completed survey questionnaires were obtained. Of the 84 respondents, 41 were female and 43 male. The mean age of the subjects was 37.74 (±14.13) years. The length of work experience of the respondents averaged 15.89 (±13.89) years. Of all respondents, only two were unemployed, and the rest were part-time or full-time employees.

In the preliminary part of the survey, the experts stated about the attitude and interest of citizens and city authorities toward issues of quality of life in the city in general. The answers were given according to the Likert scale (European Statistical Office, 2021): 1 – slightly, 2 – weak, 3 – medium, 4 – sufficient and 5 – complete. Results show that there is a general disinterest in these questions: out of all given answers, as many as 41% have a grade of 2, and the average grades in all questions are between 2 (low interest) and 3 (medium interest). The results, sorted by average grade, are shown in Table 12.2.

For all six groups of problems related to the importance of certain characteristics of a smart city, the experts assigned ratings on the Likert scale from 1 (least important) to 10 (most important) for each item. The general average grade of all experts on all issues was 7.54. When the surveyed experts are observed individually, the lowest general grade was 3.41, and the highest was 9.80. The distribution of general average scores of 84 experts does not deviate significantly from normal flatness (measure of flatness $K = 3.11$) but is significantly negatively asymmetric (measure of asymmetry $S = -0.95$), so it does not follow the normal distribution (Jarque–Bera statistics is $JB = 12.66$, $p = 0.002$). Due to the deviation from the normal distribution, finding the extreme value in the general average grades of individual experts was performed by a non-parametric test, i.e., an extreme value is considered to be an average score less than $Q1 - 1.5 \cdot IQR$ or greater than $Q3 + 1.5 \cdot IQR$ (where Q1 is the first quartile of a series of general average expert scores, Q3 is the third quartile, and IQR is the interquartile range). The lower limit for the extreme value was 3.26 and the upper 12.01. Since the minimum and maximum values shown above belong to this interval, it follows that no extreme value was detected. The average score of any expert does not deviate significantly from the others, so it was not necessary to exclude the answers of some respondents from further data processing.

The internal consistency of the survey was checked using Cronbach's α-coefficient on three bases. First, individually by defined groups of questions and then by questions related to public services (education, health, electricity, gas

Table 12.2. Experts' Responses.

No.	Question	Average	Standard Deviation
1	How interested are the citizens in the quality of life as a part of the development of their city as a smart city?	2.85	1.05
2	How interested are the citizens in general issues concerning city development?	2.77	0.88
3	Are the citizens sufficiently engaged with general transport issues in their city?	2.55	0.86
4	Are the city authorities sufficiently engaged in improving public urban passenger transport?	2.30	0.90
5	In your opinion, are civic initiatives sufficiently present in order to improve public urban passenger transport as part of the smart city development?	2.20	0.85

Source: Authors' source.

and water supply, public security service, fire protection and cleanliness), which are in individual groups of questions. Third, the check was performed within individual groups of questions. Furthermore, clusters of questions that can be summarized in one factor have been identified using the principal components method. It was concluded that the grades assigned in the survey meet the condition of consistency and are a suitable basis for analysis and application in further research. A higher value of α indicates a higher level of internal consistency. An acceptable level of α is greater than or equal to 0.6, values greater than or equal to 0.8 are considered good, while values greater than or equal to 0.9 reflect the excellent internal consistency of the survey. The values of the α-coefficients by groups of questions are shown in Table 12.3.

Appendix 3 shows the results of a survey by groups of problems. For each question in each group, the medians, mean values and standard deviations of the scores assigned by the experts were calculated. All items by groups are ranked according to the average grade, from the most important question in the opinion of experts to the least important. The last columns of the tables show the normalized values of grades in the range of 0.5–1.0, which we will use as weights in the derivation of the modified index of competence of cities.

Comparative Analysis of Survey Results by Groups of Questions

When observing the answers of all surveyed experts to all questions, an average score of 7.54 was obtained, on a scale from 1 to 10. The medians, average scores and standard deviations of the answers of experts by groups of questions are shown in Table 12.4.

Table 12.3. Values of the Cronbach's α-Coefficients.

Group of Questions	α	Level of Internal Consistency
Group 1: The importance of general characteristics of the city	0.88	Good
Group 2: The importance of strategic directions for the realization of the smart cities concept	0.86	Good
Group 3: The importance of the principle of forming a management strategy for improving the environment in the city	0.94	Excellent
Group 4: The importance of environmental problems in cities	0.88	Good
Group 5: The importance of city administration measures for improving living conditions	0.82	Good
Group 6: The importance of urban transport	0.90	Excellent

Source: Authors' source.

A comparative analysis of the statistical significance of the differences between the arithmetic means of the scores assigned to individual groups, using the *t*-test, gave the results shown in Table 12.5.

In the above table, the values of $p < 0.05$ show the existence of a statistically significant difference between the mean values. The symbol * indicates fields that refer to a pair of groups of questions between whose mean values there is no statistically significant difference. According to these results, groups of questions can be classified into three clusters:

- **First cluster** with the highest average grades includes the following groups of questions:
  - The importance of city administration measures for improving living conditions (7.85)
  - The importance of environmental problems in cities (7.81)
  - The importance of urban transport (7.77)
- **Second cluster** with medium average grades includes the following groups of questions:
  - The importance of the principle of forming a management strategy for improving the environment in the city (7.59)

Table 12.4. Experts' Assessments on the Importance of Individual Groups of Indicators.

Rank	The Importance of Smart City Development Indicators	Median	Average	Standard Deviation
1	Group 5: The importance of city administration measures for improving living conditions	8.00	7.85	2.14
2	Group 4: The importance of environmental problems in cities	8.00	7.81	2.08
3	Group 6: The importance of urban transport	8.00	7.77	2.22
4	Group 3: The importance of the principle of forming a management strategy for improving the environment in the city	8.00	7.59	2.36
5	Group 2: The importance of strategic directions for the realization of the smart cities concept	8.00	7.25	2.38
6	Group 1: The importance of general characteristics of the city	8.00	7.14	2.27
	Average indicator value for all questions	8.00	7.54	2.26

Source: Authors' source.

- **Third cluster** with the lowest average grades includes the following groups of questions:
  - The importance of strategic directions for the realization of the smart cities concept (7.25)
  - The importance of general characteristics of the city (7.24).

Creation of the Database and Preliminary Data Processing

Systematization of Research Results and Creation of the Database

In order to conduct research related to the achieved level of development of selected European cities as smart cities, the basic characteristics were studied

Table 12.5. *t*-Test of the Significance of Differences Between Arithmetic Means.

Group	5	4	6	3	2	1
5		$t = 0.482$	$t = 0.942$	$t = 3.063$	$t = 6.789$	$t = 9.676$
		$p = 0.630$	$p = 0.346$	$p = 0.002$*	$p < 0.001$*	$p < 0.001$*
4			$t = 0.417$	$t = 2.259$	$t = 5.625$	$t = 7.703$
			$p = 0.676$	$p = 0.024$*	$p < 0.001$*	$p < 0.001$*
6				$t = 1.797$	$t = 5.073$	$t = 7.085$
				$p = 0.073$	$p < 0.001$*	$p < 0.001$*
3					$t = 3.285$	$t = 5.071$
					$p = 0.001$*	$p < 0.001$*
2						$t = 1.206$
						$p = 0.228$
1						

Source: Authors' source.

and statistical indicators and survey results were collected from the Eutrostat[1] (European Statistical Office, 2021) database and available documents (CEN-CENELEC, 2020; Mourshed et al., 2016; Paredes Muse et al., 2020). The data in these documents are published at the EU level, at the level of national economies and at the level of regional units according to the nomenclature of territorial units for statistics (NUTS) classification. In order to present the formulated methodology of creating a composite index and ranking of cities, 28 capitals of EU countries were selected together with data on the number of inhabitants on December 31, 2018. Data for the given cities, which are processed in this part of the research, refer to the size of cities, use of urban areas, population and demographic, living conditions, social exclusion and crime rate, economic activities and economic accounts of cities and households, structural business statistics, development digital economy and digital society, protection of intellectual property, labor market, education, scientific research and technological development, ecology, environmental protection and waste management, culture and tourism, urban transport, health care and the results of population satisfaction surveys. Names for groups of variables and Eurostat codes of tables in the database are presented in Appendix 4. The database contains a total of 26 data sets with 125 folders, containing a total of 342 variable lists. The data refer to the year of 2018. Most of the data were taken from the website of the European Statistical Service, while missing data were taken from some national and city statistical institutes or an assessment was made for 2018 for variables for which historical data are available, using a linear trend.

[1]https://ec.europa.eu/eurostat/data/database (European Statistical Office, 2021).

Display and Interpretation of Basic Statistical Structure Indicators and Mean Values

The variables included in the analysis can be divided into two basic groups: the first group contains basic, most important indicators related to the analyzed measured variables, while the second contains indicators derived from surveys of EU capitals' citizens regarding their attitudes on quality of life and characteristics of the city they live in. The results of the survey served us as control values, and the selected measured variables are included in the database for calculating the composite index, as a summary indicator for comparing and ranking EU capitals, in terms of competitiveness and "smartness" level of development.

Basic Indicators

The database includes a total of 48 variables, which reflect the characteristics of the examined cities. The variables are classified into the following subgroups (calculated values of the variables are presented in Appendix 5):

population,
living conditions,
employment,
economic development,
education,
health and social care,
culture,
tourism,
ecology,
information and communication technologies and
urban transport.

In order for characteristics to be comparable, the data were normalized within the range 0–100. Let K_{ij} be the *j*th characteristics for the city *i*. Then, the normalized values of the *j*th characteristics for the set of cities G_i are given:

$$N_{ij} = \frac{K_{ij} - \min_i\left(K_{ij}\right)}{\max_i\left(K_{ij}\right) - \min_i\left(K_{ij}\right)} \cdot 100, \forall i, j$$

The last column of the table in Appendix 5 shows the average normalized values of the measured characteristics of cities by groups of characteristics. Normalized values are equal to 0 if minimal and 100 if maximal. A comparative examination of normalized characteristics across cities reveals that among all the attributes studied, the group with the highest normalized values is Living Conditions. Specifically, the average share of the population with access to public city sewerage network and public drinking water supply network exceeds

85 out of 100 for all cities. At the second highest level are employment indicators (share of employed young people around 71/100, share of employed population around 61/100). The lowest normalized value is, surprisingly, research and development expenditures in educational institutions per capita in euros (around 23/100).

Results of Residents of EU Capitals' Survey

Appendix 6 contains items from survey questionnaires from which the data on the attitudes of residents of EU capitals regarding the quality of life in their cities were collected. The appendix also contains a *table of ranks awarded to individual items* from the survey of EU capitals. Data on the results of the survey are published on the EU website for years 2004, 2006, 2009, 2012 and 2015. Some survey questions are repeated from year to year, some are omitted, additional questions are formulated and some are given in a modified form. In processing the data, we took into account the results for the year 2015.

The answers to the questions asked can be grouped into five types:

- Type 1:
  - completely satisfied (a)
  - quite satisfied (b)
  - quite dissatisfied (c)
  - completely dissatisfied (d)
  - undecided (x)
- Type 2:
  - I totally agree
  - I partly agree
  - I partly disagree
  - I strongly disagree
  - indecisive
- Type 3:
  - always
  - sometimes
  - rarely
  - never
  - indecisive
- Type 4: Multiple options
- Type 5: Yes–no questions

For Types 1–3 in the statistical tables, the data for each city are presented in the form of a distribution of relative frequencies in percentages, within 100% range. We suggest the following rank calculation attributed to each city:

- let *a, b, c* and *d* be in the order of participation of individual answers in %.
- the rank for the *i*th city in relation to the *j*th item of the survey questionnaire (out of 100 points) is:

$$B_{ij} = \frac{100}{3} \cdot \frac{3 \cdot a + 2 \cdot b + 1 \cdot c + 0 \cdot d}{a + b + c + d}$$

Type 4 questions are used for analysis and are not included in the subsequent calculation. Type 5 questions are control questions; they repeat certain questions of Types 1–3, all with a positive connotation, so that the ratio of "YES" answers directly represents the number of points awarded to a given city. The obtained results are used for analysis only and do not enter the process of ranking the cities.

The following tables show the average amounts of points awarded to cities by individual groups of survey questions. The groups are formed according to the groups related to the basic measured indicators, with the proviso that the groups "Population" and "Information and communication technologies" were omitted (the latest data from the surveys are outdated, referring to 2006), while two new groups have been formed: "City Administration" and "Security." A higher number of points also means a higher level of quality of a given indicator. It is especially emphasized that the lowest average number of points (out of maximal 100) has been assigned to items "Possibility of finding a suitable apartment at an affordable price" (31.50) and "Possibility of finding a suitable job" (43.57), while the highest marks were given by the respondents to the items "High level of satisfaction with living conditions in this city" (80,79) and "The quality of life in this city" (77.45).

Creating a Composite Index and City Ranking According to Smart City Criteria

Methodology of Composite Index Formation

Let *n* cities G_i, $i = 1, 2, \ldots, n$ be investigated, for which composite indices should be calculated so that they reflect the degree of achieved development of the smart city property, and let data on m characteristics K_{ij}, $j = 1, 2, \ldots, m$, be available for each city. In order to create comparable results, the standardization of the indicator values was performed, according to the following procedure:

- Average value of the *j*th characteristics for the set of cities $i = 1, \ldots, n$:

$$\bar{K}_j = \frac{1}{n}\sum_i K_{ij}, \forall j$$

- Standard deviation of the *j*th characteristics:

$$\sigma_j = \sqrt{\frac{1}{n}\sum_i \left(K_{ij} - \bar{K}_j\right)^2}, \forall j$$

- Standardized value of the *j*th characteristics for the *i*th city:

$$S_{ij} = \frac{K_{ij} - \bar{K}_j}{\sigma_j}$$

Standardized values measure the difference in standard deviations between the given data and the average value. The higher the standardized value, the better the position of a given city in a city set.

In order to further clarify the cities' ranks according to individual measured indicators, the obtained standardized values are further normalized in the interval from 50 to 100. The normalization interval is set to 50–100 range so that possible weights also affect the characteristics with the lowest values. The city that has the weakest position for a given characteristic is awarded 50 points, and the city that is of the highest quality according to a given characteristic receives 100 points; the point numbers of other cities and for the given characteristic *j* are calculated according to:

$$Q_{ij} = 50 + \frac{S_{ij} - \min_i\left(S_{ij}\right)}{\max_i\left(S_{ij}\right) - \min_i\left(S_{ij}\right)} \cdot 50, \forall j$$

We calculate the competence index of cities in two ways:

a) in the traditional way,[2] as the sum of points obtained by individual characteristics:

$$I_i = \sum_j Q_{ij}, \forall i$$

b) in a modified way, as suggested in this chapter, by including the importance of certain characteristics in the form of weights, derived from the experts' opinions:

$$M_i = \sum_j A_j Q_{ij}, \forall i$$

where A_j denotes the weight value, i.e., average expert assessments of the importance of individual characteristics (as shown in section "An Innovative Approach

[2]See, e.g., Bosch et al. (2017), ABUD (2017), Carlia et al. (2013), Batagan (2011), and Giffinger et al. (2007).

to the Creation of Criteria for Ranking Cities Within the Concept of Smart Cities" of this chapter), which are then multiplied by the values of individual characteristics.

We hypothesize that by including the degree of importance of certain characteristics, more reliable and credible indices of competence of individual cities are obtained, in the way which better reflects the state and perspectives of cities in their efforts and aspirations on the way to an ideal position of "perfect smart city."

Appendix 7 shows the calculation of expert assessments from surveys with individual examined characteristics. The scores from the surveys are used as weights for the numerical values of the characteristics in the calculations of the competitiveness index of cities.

Ranking of EU Capitals

Table 12.6 shows the ranking of EU capitals formed according to the composite index calculation procedure, based on the values of the measured indicators. The order was set according to the two suggested methodologies for the measured indicators. According to the first methodology, the index is calculated as a

Table 12.6. Composite Indices and Ranking of EU Capitals Based on Basic Attributes, Based on Weighted Attributes, Based on the Degree of Citizens' Satisfaction and Based on Weighted Attitudes of the Surveyed Citizens.

No.	City	Number of Points (Rank)	Composite Index	City	Number of Points (Corrected Rank)	Composite Index (Corrected)
1	Stockholm, Sweden	3.795	100.0	Stockholm, Sweden	3.091	100.0
2	Copenhagen, Denmark	3.779	98.9	Copenhagen, Denmark	3.070	98.2
3	Prague, Czech Republic	3.740	96.1	Prague, Czech Republic	3.056	97.0
4	Helsinki, Finland	3.706	93.8	Helsinki, Finland	3.039	95.5
5	Amsterdam, Holland	3.577	84.7	Amsterdam, Holland	2.905	83.7
6	Paris, France	3.564	83.7	Paris, France	2.881	81.6
7	Vienna, Austria	3.555	83.1	Tallinn, Estonia	2.881	81.6
8	Tallinn, Estonia	3.532	81.5	Vienna, Austria	2.874	81.1
9	London, UK	3.504	79.5	Berlin, Germany	2.853	79.2

(*continued*)

Table 12.6. (*Continued*)

No.	City	Number of Points (Rank)	Composite Index	City	Number of Points (Corrected Rank)	Composite Index (Corrected)
10	Lisbon, Portugal	3.499	79.2	London, UK	2.850	78.9
11	Berlin, Germany	3.493	78.8	Ljubljana, Slovenia	2.832	77.4
12	Luxembourg	3.493	78.8	Luxembourg	2.832	77.4
13	Ljubljana, Slovenia	3.490	78.6	Lisbon, Portugal	2.819	76.2
14	Valletta, Malta	3.458	76.3	Bratislava, Slovakia	2.791	73.8
15	Bratislava, Slovakia	3.422	73.8	Valletta, Malta	2.779	72.8
16	Budapest, Hungary	3.417	73.4	Budapest, Hungary	2.764	71.4
17	Madrid, Hotel Spain	3.392	71.7	Madrid, Hotel Spain	2.752	70.4
18	Brussels, Belgium	3.391	71.6	Brussels, Belgium	2.748	70.0
19	Warsaw, Poland	3.380	70.8	Warsaw, Poland	2.736	68.9
20	Dublin, Ireland	3.315	66.3	Dublin, Ireland	2.721	67.6
21	Athens, Greece	3.291	64.5	Vilnius, Lithuania	2.669	63.1
22	Vilnius, Lithuania	3.276	63.5	Athens, Greece	2.668	63.0
23	Riga, Latvia	3.225	59.9	Riga, Latvia	2.625	59.3
24	Nicosia, Cyprus	3.201	58.2	Nicosia, Cyprus	2.615	58.3
25	Bucharest, Romania	3.184	57.0	Bucharest, Romania	2.613	58.2
26	Rome, Italy	3.183	56.9	Sofia, Bulgaria	2.568	54.3
27	Sofia, Bulgaria	3.164	55.6	Rome, Italy	2.567	54.2
28	Zagreb, Croatia	3.084	50.0	Zagreb, Croatia	2.519	50.0

Source: Authors' source.

simple sum of points obtained on the basis of the original values of the analyzed attributes of cities, while according to the second procedure, on the basis of values modified by weights obtained from surveys of experts on the importance of certain characteristics. According to both methodologies, the composite index of the highest value was assigned to Stockholm, and the lowest value to Zagreb. By introducing weights as an indicator of the importance of individual attributes, the order of the analyzed cities in certain positions is modified. The adjusted values show an improvement for Prague, Helsinki, Dublin, Nicosia and Bucharest, which means that in those cities, those indicators are relatively better, to which experts attach a greater degree of importance. In other cities, the adjusted values are unchanged or reduced. As a result of these changes, after the introduction of the weight of attribute importance, the relative position on the ranking list of cities has improved for Tallinn, Berlin, Ljubljana, Bratislava, Vilnius and Bucharest.

Conclusion

By observing the components of the smart city, which can be found in numerous literatures, and used by various institutions, the systematization of characteristics was performed, and the key components are presented in the overview in the first chapter.

Based on the presented research, previous literature and practical application, a set of characteristics was formed, which are considered comprehensive for the description and determination of the city rank according to the attributes and the definition of the composite index. Stemming from the list of characteristics, the set of characteristics is grouped into six areas.

Composite indices and ranking of EU capitals based on basic attributes, weighted attributes, the degree of citizens' satisfaction and weighted attitudes of the surveyed citizens were proposed. Formulated composite indices, derived from the attained quality levels of specific elements crucial to defining the "smartness" of cities, serve as concise summary indicators. These indices facilitate the efficient and effective ranking of cities within the smart city framework.

Continuing research in this area would mean further expanding the set of features or reducing them to a framework that may be of particular importance.

Based on the examined opinions of experts on the listed characteristics of cities, a total of 92 questions for evaluation of importance were also classified into six groups, as well as empirical research for the purpose of defining and formulating a composite index. The composite index can serve as an indicator of the level of development within the concept of smart cities.

The method of ranking cities offers a realistic view of their current state and is very effective in identifying and perceiving both good and bad characteristics of a city, i.e., as a means for local authorities to optimize key solutions important for cities' normal functioning.

Based on experts' survey, we determined the following:

- the importance of the general characteristics of the city;
- the importance of strategic directions for the realization of the concept of smart cities;

- the importance of the principle of forming a management strategy for improving the environment in the city;
- the importance of environmental problems in cities
- the importance of city administration measures to improve living conditions;
- the importance of urban transport;
- comparative analysis of survey results by groups of questions;
- systematization of research results and formation of a database;
- composite index formation methodology.

References

ABUD. (2017). *SmartCEPS – Smart city evaluation platform and service*. Retrieved June 23, 2021, from http://www.abud.hu

Batagan, L. (2011). Smart cities and sustainability models. *Informatica Economica*, *15*(3), 80–87.

Bosch, P., Jongeneel, S., Rovers, V., Neumann, H. M., Airaksinen, M., & Huovila, A. (2017). *CITYkeys list of city indicators, EC*. Retrieved March 23, 2023, from http://nws.eurocities.eu/MediaShell/media/CITYkeyslistofcityindicators.pdf

Canteneur, P. (2015a). Uber providing data to promote `smarter` urban transport solutions. *L`Atelier Weekly Newsletters*, January. Retrieved August 16, 2022, from https://atelier.bnpparibas

Canteneur, P. (2015b). Vienna nurtures a social vision of the smart city. *L`Atelier Weekly Newsletters*, July. Retrieved August 16, 2022, from https://atelier.bnpparibas

Carlia, R., Dotolia, M., Pellegrino, R., & Ranieri, L. (2013). *Measuring and managing the smartness of cities: A framework for classifying performance indicators, smart cities communities and social innovation research and competitiveness program*. Italian University and Research Ministry. Retrieved April 23, 2023, from www.researchgate.net/publication/262165246

CEN-CENELEC. (2020). *CEN-CENELEC guide 29. CEN/CENELEC workshop agreements: A rapid way to standardization*. Retrieved February 18, 2023, from https://ftp.cencenelec.eu/EN/EuropeanStandardization/Guides/29_CENCLCGuide29.pdf

Chourabi, H., Nam, T., Walker, S., Gil-Garcia, J. R., Mellouli, S., Nahon, K., Pardo, T. A., & Scholl, H. J. (2012). Understanding smart cities: An integrative framework. In *45th Hawaii international conference on system sciences*. Maui, HI, Jan. 4–7 (pp. 2289–2297). htpps://doi.org/10.1109/HICSS.2012.615

European Commission. (2015a). *CITY keys project*. Retrieved June 23, 2021, from www.citykeys-project.eu/citykeys/project

European Commission. (2015b). Quality of life in European cities 2015. *Flash Eurobarometer*, p. 419.

European Commission. (2016, July 25). *Horizon 2020, work programme 2016-2017. 17. Cross-cutting activities (focus areas)*. European Commission Decision C(2016)4614.

European Commission. (2018). *White paper on resilience management guidelines for critical infrastructures. From theory to practice by engaging end-users: Concepts, interventions, tools and methods*. Retrieved January 10, 2023, from https://smr-project.eu/fileadmin/user_upload/Documents/Resources/WP_7/DRS_7_WHITE_PAPER_final_April2018.pdf

European Commission. (2019). *European Commission website. Success stories. Cities work together towards a more resilient future*. Retrieved January 18, 2023, from https://ec.europa.eu/research-and-innovation/en/projects/success-stories/all/cities-work-together-towards-more-resilient-future

European Statistical Office. (2021). Retrieved June 30, 2021, from https://ec.europa.eu/eurostat/data/database

Firnkorn, J. (2015). A city becomes `smart` when it knows how to use its data. *L`Atelier*, Interview with Joerg Firnkorn, May. Retrieved August 16, 2022, from https://atelier.bnpparibas

Frauenhofer Society. (2016). *Morgenstadt – City of the future*. Retrieved December 23, 2022, from www.morgenstadt.de/en

Giffinger, R., Fertner, C., Kramar, H., Kalasek, R., Pichler-Milanović, N., & Meijers, E. (2007). *Smart cities: Ranking of European medium-sized cities*. Centre of Regional Science (SRF), Vienna University of Technology. Retrieved March 3, 2023, from http://www.smartcities.eu/download/smart_cities_final_report.pdf

Huovila, A., Airaksinen, M., Pinto-Seppä, I., Piira, K., Bosch, P., Penttinen, T., Neumann, H. M., & Kontinakis, N. (2017). CITYkeys smart city performance measurement system. Int. *Journal for Housing Science*, *41*(2), 113–125.

Leonova, T., Golovtcova, I., Mamedov, E., & Varfolomeeva, M. (2018). The integrated indicator of sustainable urban development based on standardization. *MATEC Web of Conferences*, *17*, 1039.

Long, J. (2020). *Constructing the narrative of the sustainability fix: Sustainability, social justice and representation in Austin, TX*. Retrieved August 23, 2022, from http://usj.sagepub.com/content/early/2014/12/05/0042098014560501.full.pdf+html

Majer, S., Wurster, S., Moosmann, D., Ladu, L., Sumfleth, B., & Thrän, D. (2018). Gaps and research demand for sustainability certification and standardisation in a sustainable bio-based economy in the EU. *Sustainability*, *10*, 2455.

McLeod, S. (2014). *Likert scale*. Retrieved April 23, 2023, from http://www.simplypsychology.org/Likert-scale.html/pdf

Monfaredzadeh, T., & Krueger, R. (2015). Investigating social factors of sustainability in a smart city. *International Conference on Sustainable Design, Engineering and Construction, Procedia Engineering*, *118*, 1112–1118. htpps://doi.org/10.1016/j.proeng.2015.08.452

Moreno, C. (2015). How smart is my city? Visions of the smart city in the 21st century. *L`Atelier Weekly Newsletters*, October. Retrieved August 16, 2022, from https://atelier.bnpparibas

Mourshed, M., Bucchiarone, A., & Khandokar, F. (2016, September 12–15). SMART: A process-oriented methodology for resilient smart cities. In *Proceedings of the 2016 IEEE international smart cities conference (ISC2)*, Trento, Italy (pp. 1–6).

Paredes Muse, L., Frazer, J., & Fidler, E. (2020, September 28–October 1). The IEEE P2784 standardization process workshop: The use of Delphi method and interactive evaluation tools to identify perceptions about smart cities. In *Proceedings of the 2020 IEEE international smart cities conference (ISC2)*, Piscataway, NJ, USA (pp. 1–6).

Sassen, S., & Kourtit, K. (2021). A post-corona perspective for smart cities: 'Should I stay or should I go?'. *Sustainability*, *13*(17), 9988. Retrieved April 16, 2023, from https://doi.org/10.3390/su13179988

Schomaker, M. (1997). *Development of environmental indicators in UNEP (United Nations Environment Programme)* (pp. 35–36). Land Quality Indicators and Use in Sustainable Agriculture and Rural Development.

Strüver, A., Saltiel, R., Schlitz, N., Hohmann, B., Höflehner, T., & Grabher, B. (2021). A Smart right to the city – Grounding corporate storytelling and questioning smart urbanism. *Sustainability*, *13*(17), 9590. Retrieved August 16, 2021, from https://doi.org/10.3390/su13179590

Technopolis. (2013). *Study on the contribution of standardization to innovation in European-funded research projects*. Retrieved March 18, 2023, from https://www.cencenelec.eu/research/news/publications/Publications/Study_Contribution_Standardization_Innovation_Final2013.pdf

Appendix 1 List of Characteristics and Factors for Ranking EU Medium-Sized Cities By Level of Smartness (Giffinger et al., 2007)

List of Smart City Features.

No.	Smart City Features	Measurement Unit
	Group 1: Smart Economy - level of economic development and economic relations in the city	
1	Formulated strategy of economic development of the city	Yes–no
2	Gross domestic product (GDP) per capita in the previous year	EUR per capita
3	GDP per employee in the previous year	EUR per capita
4	The share of the city GDP in the total GDP in the previous year	%
5	The share of the service sector in the GDP of the city in the previous year	%
6	Share of companies headquartered in the city out of the total number of registered companies in the country	%
7	The share of micro and small enterprises in the total number of registered enterprises in the city in relation to the national average	%/%
8	Number of registered new business ventures in the city in the previous year in relation to the number of active population	No. per capita
9	Total number of jobs in relation to the number of active population	%
10	Number of temporary jobs in relation to the total number of jobs in the city	%
11	Unemployment rate	%
12	Average value of household income in the city in relation to the average value of household income in the country	%
13	Number of inhabitants living below the poverty line in relation to the number of inhabitants	%
14	Number of employees in the information and communication technology (ICT) sector in relation to the total number of employees in the city	%
15	Number of knowledge-intensive jobs in relation to the total number of jobs	%
16	Number of registered patents in the city per employee in the previous year	No. per capita

Appendix 1 (*Continued*)

No.	Smart City Features	Measurement Unit
17	Investments in research and development in the city in the previous year in relation to GDP	%
18	Number of registered financial institutions (branches) in the city in relation to the number of inhabitants	No. per capita
19	Structure of city budget revenues in the previous year: own revenues in relation to total revenues	%
20	Total budget expenditures of the city in relation to the total revenues in the previous year	%
21	Number of high school students (four-year education) in relation to the number of inhabitants aged 15–19	%
22	Number of active students in relation to the population aged 19–30 years	%
	Group 2: Smart Environment – management of natural resources and preservation of the environment	
1	The city development strategy is formulated in accordance with the expected climate changes	Yes–no
2	Green areas in the city in relation to the total area	%
3	Share of the number of days in the year with higher values of the air quality index*	%
4	Number of patients with chronic diseases of the lower respiratory organs per capita	No. per capita
5	Individual activities of the population on environmental protection	Likert scale
6	Awareness of the need to protect the environment	Likert scale
7	Organized classes in environmental protection in schools	Yes–no
8	Degree of maintaining cleanliness in the city	Likert scale
9	Regularity of municipal waste collection	Yes–no
10	Frequency of harmful night noise in the central parts of the city	%
11	Water consumption in relation to GDP	000 lit./EUR
12	Electricity consumption in relation to GDP	000 kWh/EUR
13	Renewable energy consumption in relation to total energy consumption	%
14	The amount of waste collected in relation to GDP	%

(*Continued*)

Appendix 1 (*Continued*)

No.	Smart City Features	Measurement Unit
	Group 3: Smart Administration - transparency of the city administration and participation of residents in decision-making	
1	Formulated strategy for the development of the city as a smart city	Yes–no
2	Number of city deputies in relation to the number of inhabitants	%
3	Political engagement of the population	Likert scale
4	The importance of politics in everyday life	Likert scale
5	Participation of female deputies in the representative body	%
6	Prison maintenance costs relative to GDP	%
7	Satisfaction with the quality of work of preschool institutions	Likert scale
8	Satisfaction with the quality of schools	Likert scale
9	Satisfaction with the transparency of the administration	Likert scale
10	Satisfaction with the fight against corruption	Likert scale
	Group 4: Smart Housing - housing, living standard and quality of living	
1	Number of dwellings in relation to the number of households	%
2	Number of rented apartments in relation to the total number of apartments	%
3	Average size of living space per capita in relation to housing norms**	%
4	Satisfaction with housing conditions	Likert scale
5	Satisfaction with the location of the apartments	Likert scale
6	Percentage of households with water supply	%
7	Percentage of households with sewage	%
8	Percentage of households with electricity	%
9	Percentage of households with a gas pipeline	%
10	Number of general practitioners per 100,000 inhabitants in relation to the norms***	%
11	Number of specialist doctors per 100,000 inhabitants in relation to norms***	%

Appendix 1 (*Continued*)

No.	Smart City Features	Measurement Unit
12	Number of hospital beds per 1,000 inhabitants in relation to the EU13 average****	%
13	Satisfaction with the quality of health care	Likert scale
14	Organized programs to promote a healthy lifestyle	Yes–no
15	Number of visits to cultural events and performances per capita during the year in relation to the number of inhabitants	No. per capita
16	Number of visits to museums per capita during the year	No. per capita
17	Number of visits to public libraries during the year per capita	No. per capita
18	Satisfaction with the richness of the cultural life of the city	Likert scale
19	Level of protection of cultural monuments	Likert scale
20	Access to public service facilities	Yes–no
21	Public outdoor recreational areas per capita	m^2 per capita
22	Total areas intended for sports per capita	m^2 per capita
23	Number of visits to swimming pools per year per capita	No. per capita
24	Crime rate	%
25	Satisfaction with personal safety	Likert scale
26	Number of students per capita	No. per capita
27	Number of participants in additional education and retraining courses in relation to the number of unemployed	%
28	Number of accommodation capacities in preschool institutions in relation to the number of preschool children	%
29	Satisfaction with the quality of primary education	Likert scale
30	Satisfaction with the quality of secondary education	Likert scale
31	Satisfaction with the opportunity to participate in the education system	Likert scale
32	Number of hotel beds in relation to the number of inhabitants	%
33	Number of overnight stays of domestic tourists in relation to the number of inhabitants	%
34	Number of overnight stays of foreign tourists in relation to the number of inhabitants	%

(*Continued*)

Appendix 1 (*Continued*)

No.	Smart City Features	Measurement Unit
	Group 5: Smart Mobility - traffic and ICT	
1	Centralized electronic city traffic management system introduced	Yes–no
2	Percentage of urban area with restriction or ban of traffic for motor vehicles	%
3	Percentage of hard surface city roads for motor vehicles	%
4	Percentage of streets with a built pavement with a hard surface	%
5	Completeness of traffic signals	%
6	Percentage of city roads with bicycle paths	%
7	Frequency of traffic congestion	%
8	Possibility of quick exit from the city/entry into the city	Yes–no
9	Number of public transport lines per capita	%
10	Percentage of population using public transportation to get to work	%
11	Percentage of population using non-motorized private transportation to get to work	%
12	Number of trips by public transport per year in relation to the number of inhabitants	No. per capita
13	Satisfaction with access to public transport lines	Likert scale
14	Satisfaction with the quality of public transport	Likert scale
15	Satisfaction with safety in city traffic	Likert scale
16	Number of traffic accidents per capita	No. per capita
17	Number of ecological motor vehicles in relation to the total number of motor vehicles	%
18	Introduced benefits for users of ecological motor vehicles	Yes–no
19	Number of computers per household	No. per household
20	The existence of a high-speed internet network in the city	Yes–no
21	Number of internet connections per household	No. per household
22	Number of computers in schools in relation to the number of students	No. per capita
23	Access to free public wireless internet service	Yes–no

Appendix 1 (*Continued*)

No.	Smart City Features	Measurement Unit
	Group 6: Smart Population – human and social potentials	
1	A scientific center (research center, higher education institution) was established in the city.	Yes–no
2	Number of employees after graduating from high school in relation to the total number of employees	%
3	Number of employees with a university degree or scientific title in relation to the total number of employees	%
4	Percentage of employees who speak at least one foreign language	%
5	Share of population in the process of lifelong learning	%
6	Percentage of employees in creative jobs*****	%
7	Willingness to find a more suitable job	Likert scale
8	Knowledge of the facts about the European Union	Likert scale
9	Percentage of voters running in local elections	%
10	Organized public service to help the elderly	Yes–no
11	The issue of protection of the socially endangered population has been resolved.	Yes–no
12	Respect for the traditions and customs of ethnic communities	Likert scale
13	Readiness of the population for volunteer work	Likert scale

*Air Quality Index (AQI) is an indicator of the concentration of harmful substances in the air, with critical values of 7 and more

**Based on: 'Rulebook on conditions and norms for designing residential buildings and apartments', published in June 13, 2012, in "Sl. Glasnik RS" No. 58/2012.

***Normatives from Cooper, University of Pennsylvania (30.4 and 7.9 on 100,000 inhabitants)

****Based on www.gateway.euro.who.int (6.66 on 1,000 inhabitants)

*****Creative jobs: design, handicrafts, fine arts, multimedia, writing and communication, performing arts

Appendix 2 Questionnaire to Collect Expert Opinions on the Degree of Importance of Smart City Characteristics

Questionnaire

Research Topic: Characteristics and Factors of Smart Cities

This Likert scale is anonymous.

The results of the survey are used for internal research, in order to prepare a scientific paper (dissertation), and some questionnaires are a business secret.

Please, regardless of the current situation in a city, assess the degree of importance of individual items in general for medium-sized cities that are in the phase of intensive development. Please assign a score of 1–10 for a given item by placing a × in only one field in each row. Grade 1 indicates the least significant degree of a given item, which gradually increases to the maximum importance with Grade 10. Please assign your grades in terms of the relative importance of individual characteristics, i.e., a lower grade does not mean the absolute irrelevance of an item, but only that in your opinion, it is of a lower degree of importance compared to others, to whom you have assigned a higher grade. At the end of each table in the free rows, please enter the characteristics that you think are also more or less important and assign an appropriate grade.

Thank you for your cooperation.

1. Gender

M	F

2. Age group

Up to 20	21–30	31–40	41–50	Over 50

3. Education

Elementary school	High school	College	Undergraduate studies	Master studies	Doctoral studies

4. Years of working experience

Up to 1 year	1–3	3–5	5–7	7–10	Over 10

5. Current working status

Student	Part-time worker	Fully employed	Freelance	Unemployed

6. Your field of expertise

____

For the following questions, please tick one answer.

1. In your opinion, how interested are the citizens in the general issues concerning the development of the city?

Barely	Weakly	Moderately	Sufficiently	Absolutely

2. In your opinion, how interested are the citizens for the quality of life as part of the smart city development?

Barely	Weakly	Moderately	Sufficiently	Absolutely

3. In your opinion, how interested are the citizens in engaging with general transport issues in the city?

Barely	Weakly	Moderately	Sufficiently	Absolutely

4. In your opinion, how interested are the civic initiatives and activities aimed at improving public urban passenger transport as part of smart city development?

Barely	Weakly	Moderately	Sufficiently	Absolutely

5. In your opinion, how engaged are the city authorities in improving public urban passenger transport as part of the development of a smart city?

Barely	Weakly	Moderately	Sufficiently	Absolutely

Group 1. The Importance of General Characteristics of the City.

Characteristics	1	2	3	4	5	6	7	8	9	10
1. General life convenience										
2. Security										
3. Intelligent city (coverage of all areas by information and communication technologies)										
4. Health care										
5. Education										
6. Cultural institutions and events										
7. Tourism										
8. Employment										
9. Traffic										
10. Energy										
11. Water management										
12. Overpopulation and crowding										
13. Ecology										
14. Green city and public areas										
15. Waste management										
16. Quality of public services										
17. Citizen participation in governance										
18. University, research center										
19. Innovation centers										
20. Centers for additional education and retraining										
21. Career guidance advisory service										
22. Economic development										

Group 2. The Importance of Strategic Directions for Achieving the Concept of Smart Cities.

Characteristics	**1**	**2**	**3**	**4**	**5**	**6**	**7**	**8**	**9**	**10**
1. Digitalization										
2. Support of research and development activities										
3. Development of knowledge management										
4. Development of an innovative environment – development of business culture and incubation										
5. Support for cooperation between economic and other entities										
6. Development of a harmonized system of smart city services										
7. Modernization and sustainable functioning of public services										
8. Forming smart brands and encouraging their use										
9. Constant monitoring and development of the scope and quality of smart services										
10. Communication with the community, sharing/ disseminating information										
11. Education of user groups										
12. Support in finding jobs and employment										

Group 3. The Importance of the Principle of Forming a Management Strategy for Improving the Environment in the City.

Characteristic	**1**	**2**	**3**	**4**	**5**	**6**	**7**	**8**	**9**	**10**
1. Slowing down the expansion of the city										
2. More efficient traffic organization										
3. Development of public passenger transport										
4. Encouraging the population to increase energy efficiency										
5. Expanding the possibilities of renewable energy supply in the city										
6. Increasing green areas										
7. Restoration of vacant areas										
8. Development of selective waste collection										
9. Measures to reduce air, groundwater and surface water and soil pollution										
10. Generating energy from renewable sources										
11. Measurement of harmful gas emissions										
12. Existence of recycling centers										

Group 4. The Importance of Solving Environmental Problems in Cities.

Characteristic	1	2	3	4	5	6	7	8	9	10
1. Degree of air pollution										
2. State of groundwater and surface water and their impact on the environment										
3. Land degradation										
4. Noise and light pollution										
5. Image of the city, landscape problems										
6. Condition of green areas										
7. Cleanliness and tidiness in public areas and in public institutions										
8. Level of ecological awareness of the population										
9. Individual ecological activities of the population										
10. Developing awareness of the need to protect the environment										
11. Waste collection										
12. Illegal garbage disposal										
13. The impact of global climate change on weather conditions in the city										

Group 5. The Importance of City Administration Measures for Improving Living Conditions.

Characteristic	**1**	**2**	**3**	**4**	**5**	**6**	**7**	**8**	**9**	**10**
1. Making information and communication technology available to citizens										
2. Improving the complaints management system addressed to city authorities and public services										
3. Taking measures to raise the level of public and personal security of citizens										
4. Improving the structure of educational institutions and raising the level of quality of their services										
5. Improving the structure of health institutions and raising the level of quality of their services										
6. Improving the structure of social institutions and raising the level of quality of their services										
7. Organizational and financial support to cultural institutions and activities										
8. Undertaking activities in order to improve housing conditions										
9. Adaptation of traffic infrastructure in the city										
10. Introduction of an intelligent traffic management system in order to reduce congestion and increase the speed of travel in the city										
11. Development of a flexible public transport system										
12. Improving the environment, reducing pollution and forming new green areas										

Group 6. The Importance of Elements of Urban Traffic.

Characteristic	**1**	**2**	**3**	**4**	**5**	**6**	**7**	**8**	**9**	**10**
1. Construction, completeness and quality of city roads										
2. Existence of pedestrian zones and zones with traffic restrictions										
3. Construction of bicycle paths										
4. Parking										
5. Completeness of traffic signals and traffic signs										
6. Introduced intelligent traffic management system										
7. Roadside assistance service in the city										
8. Safety in city traffic										
9. Freight traffic in the city										
10. Reducing the use of private cars										
11. Coverage of the city territory by public transport (PT) lines and stops										
12. PT timetable										
13. Condition of means of transport in PT										
14. Use of PT by citizens										
15. Combined use of PT within a single service										
16. Price policy in PT										
17. Cooperation between PT service providers and cooperation with the city administration										
18. Financial support to PT										
19. Functioning of taxi service										
20. Reducing traffic jams										
21. Possibility of quick exit from the city and arrival to external roads, as well as fast entry into the city										

Appendix 3

Experts' Assessments of the Importance of the General Characteristics of the City.

Rank	Group 1. The Importance of General Characteristics of the City	Median	Average	Standard Deviation	Normalized
1	5. Education	8.00	8.00	2.07	1.00
2	2. Security	8.00	7.69	2.23	0.92
3	1. General life convenience	8.00	7.64	1.77	0.91
4	22. Economic development	8.00	7.62	1.62	0.90
5	8. Employment	8.00	7.57	2.52	0.89
6	4. Health care	8.50	7.46	2.59	0.86
7	9. Traffic	8.00	7.45	2.07	0.86
8	10. Energy	8.00	7.38	2.01	0.84
9	18. University, research center	8.00	7.30	2.22	0.82
10	14. Green city and public areas	8.00	7.24	2.15	0.80
11	6. Cultural institutions and events	8.00	7.21	2.04	0.80
12	11. Water management	7.00	7.18	2.13	0.79
13	16. Level and quality of public services	7.00	7.05	2.23	0.75
14	3. Intelligent city (coverage of all areas by information and communication technologies)	7.00	7.02	2.07	0.75
15	7. Tourism	7.00	7.01	1.91	0.75
16	20. Centers for additional education and retraining	7.00	6.86	2.35	0.71

Appendix 3 (*Continued*)

Rank	Group 1. The Importance of General Characteristics of the City	Median	Average	Standard Deviation	Normalized
17	19. Innovation centers	7.50	6.83	2.58	0.70
18	15. Waste management	8.00	6.74	2.60	0.67
19	12. Overpopulation and crowding	7.00	6.67	2.43	0.66
20	13. Ecology	6.50	6.65	2.40	0.65
21	21. Career guidance advisory service	6.50	6.40	2.25	0.59
22	17. Citizen participation in governance	6.00	6.06	2.52	0.50
	Average indicator value for all questions	8.00	7.14	2.27	0.78

In order to check the internal consistency within this group of questions, the questions were grouped into clusters each forming one factor. In order to check the justification of the application of factor analysis, two preliminary tests were performed. The first refers to the sample adequacy, the KMO test;[3] test values from 0.8 to 1.0 show complete suitability of the sample, values from 0.6 to 0.8 show moderate suitability and below 0.6 means that the data are not suitable for factor analysis. The second is the Bartlett test of sphericity,[4] which compares the correlation matrix of variables with the identity matrix. If there is a certain degree of agreement of the variables, then they are suitable for factor analysis; the test gives an approximate value of the Chi-square test and the risk of error for a given number of degrees of freedom; if the level of significance is $p < 0.05$, then the factor analysis can be considered valid. After preliminary tests, the main components method within the factor analysis was used to group the questions into subgroups and the internal consistency was checked using Cronbach's α. The following table shows the values of the KMO test, Bartlett's measure, the formed factors composed of variables and the corresponding values of the Cronbach's α.

General Characteristics of the City – Testing the Adequacy of Factor Analysis, Formed Factors and α-Coefficients.

---

[3]Kaiser–Meyer–Olkin measure of sampling adequacy.

[4]Bartlett's test for sphericity.

Description	Cluster Variables	Test Value	Inference
KMO		0.935	Adequate sample
Bartlett measure		$\chi^2 = 1{,}877.74$, $p = 0.000$	Adequate sample
Factor 1 – Cluster 1	2, 4, 9, 11, 10, 15, 8, 1, 3	$\alpha = 0.943$	Reliable test
Factor 2 – Cluster 2	17, 19, 14, 13, 20, 21, 16, 22	$\alpha = 0.948$	Reliable test
Factor 3 – Cluster 3	18, 6, 7, 5, 12	$\alpha = 0.867$	Reliable test

Experts' Assessments of the Importance of Strategic Directions for the Realization of the Concept of Smart Cities.

Rank	Group 2. The importance of strategic directions for achieving the concept of smart cities	Median	Average	Standard Deviation	Normalized
1	1. Digitalization	8.00	7.68	2.16	1.00
2	12. Support in finding jobs and employment	8.00	7.60	2.44	0.96
3	10. Communication with the community, sharing/disseminating information	8.00	7.58	2.36	0.95
4	7. Modernization and sustainable functioning of public services	8.00	7.44	2.38	0.88
5	2. Encouragement of research and development activities	8.00	7.33	2.45	0.83
6	3. Development of knowledge management	8.00	7.33	2.38	0.83
7	4. Development of an innovative environment – development of business culture and incubation	8.00	7.30	2.33	0.81
8	5. Support for cooperation between economic and other entities	8.00	7.12	2.34	0.72
9	11. Education of user groups	7.50	7.06	2.19	0.69

(*Continued*)

Rank	Group 2. The importance of strategic directions for achieving the concept of smart cities	Median	Average	Standard Deviation	Normalized
10	6. Development of a harmonized system of smart city services	8.00	6.98	2.52	0.65
11	9. Constant monitoring and development of the scope and quality of smart services	7.50	6.88	2.44	0.60
12	8. Forming smart brands and encouraging their use	7.00	6.68	2.50	0.50
	Average indicator value for all questions	8.00	7.25	2.38	0.78

Strategic Directions for Achieving the Concept of Smart Cities – Testing the Adequacy of Factor Analysis, Formed Factors and α-Coefficients.

Description	Cluster Variables	Test Value	Inference
KMO		0.946	Adequate sample
Bartlett measure		$\chi^2 = 1{,}416.94$, $p = 0.000$	Adequate sample
Factor 1 – Cluster 1	2, 1, 4, 6, 9, 3, 8, 5	$\alpha = 0.978$	Reliable test
Factor 2 – Cluster 2	10, 12, 11, 7	$\alpha = 0.942$	Reliable test

Experts' Assessments of the Importance of the Principle of Forming a Management Strategy for Improving the Environment in the City.

Rank	Group 3. The Importance of the Principle of Forming a Management Strategy for Improving the Environment in the City	Median	Average	Standard Deviation	Normalized
1	3. Development of public passenger transport	9.00	8.10	2.00	1.00
2	2. More efficient traffic organization	8.00	7.95	1.96	0.97

(*Continued*)

(*Continued*)

Rank	Group 3. The Importance of the Principle of Forming a Management Strategy for Improving the Environment in the City	Median	Average	Standard Deviation	Normalized
3	9. Measures to reduce air, groundwater and surface water and soil pollution	9.00	7.89	2.56	0.95
4	6. Increasing green areas	8.00	7.88	2.33	0.95
5	8. Development of selective waste collection	9.00	7.75	2.46	0.92
6	11. Measurement of harmful gas emissions	8.00	7.74	2.26	0.92
7	12. Existence of recycling centers	8.00	7.73	2.47	0.91
8	4. Encouraging the population to increase energy efficiency	8.00	7.64	2.15	0.89
9	5. Expanding the possibilities of renewable energy supply in the city	8.00	7.58	2.37	0.88
10	10. Generating energy from renewable sources	8.00	7.57	2.57	0.88
11	7. Restoration of vacant areas	8.00	7.35	2.26	0.83
12	1. Slowing down the expansion of the city	6.00	5.95	2.31	0.50
	Average indicator value for all questions	8.00	7.59	2.36	0.88

Principles of Forming a Management Strategy for Improving the Environment in the City – Testing the Adequacy of Factor Analysis, Factors Formed and α-Coefficients.

Description	Cluster Variables	Test Value	Inference
KMO		0.944	Adequate sample
Bartlett measure		$\chi^2 = 1{,}366.85$, $p = 0.000$	Adequate sample
Factor 1 – Cluster 1	8, 10, 9, 5, 12, 11, 6, 7, 3, 4, 2	$\alpha = 0.978$	Reliable test
Factor 2 – Cluster 2	35		Not tested

Experts' Assessments of Solving Environmental Problems in Cities.

Rank	Group 4. Solving Environmental Problems in Cities	Median	Average	Standard Deviation	Normalized
1	1. Degree of air pollution	9.00	8.56	1.82	1.00
2	2. State of groundwater and surface water and their impact on the environment	9.00	8.20	1.89	0.86
3	12. Illegal garbage disposal	8.00	8.17	1.85	0.85
4	7. Cleanliness and tidiness in public areas and in public institutions	9.00	8.14	2.04	0.84
5	11. Waste collection	9.00	8.06	2.26	0.81
6	10. Developing awareness of the need to protect the environment	8.50	8.00	2.15	0.79
7	6. Condition of green areas	8.00	7.87	1.96	0.74
8	8. Level of ecological awareness of the population	8.00	7.68	2.39	0.67
9	4. Noise and light pollution	8.00	7.55	1.86	0.62
10	9. Individual ecological activities of the population	8.00	7.44	2.31	0.58
11	3. Land degradation	8.00	7.43	1.93	0.57
12	5. Image of the city, landscape problems	7.50	7.25	1.81	0.50
13	13. The impact of global climate change on weather conditions in the city	8.00	7.24	2.24	0.50
	Average indicator value for all questions	8.00	7.81	2.08	0.72

Environmental Problems in Cities – Testing the Adequacy of Factor Analysis, Formed Factors and α-Coefficients.

Description	Cluster Variables	Test Value	Inference
KMO		0.866	Adequate sample
Bartlett measure		$\chi^2 = 1{,}030.38$, $p = 0.000$	Adequate sample
Factor 1 – Cluster 1	10, 9, 8, 11, 6, 7, 13, 5, 12	$\alpha = 0.943$	Reliable test
Factor 2 – Cluster 2	3, 1, 2, 4	$\alpha = 0.883$	Reliable test

Experts' Assessments of the Importance of City Administration Measures for Improving Living Conditions.

Rank	Group 5. The Importance of City Administration Measures for Improving Living Conditions	Median	Average	Standard Deviation	Normalized
1	5. Improving the structure of health institutions and raising the level of quality of their services	9.00	8.45	2.17	1.00
2	9. Adaptation of traffic infrastructure in the city	8.00	8.02	1.78	0.76
3	4. Improving the structure of educational institutions and raising the level of quality of their services	9.00	8.01	2.12	0.75
4	6. Improving the structure of social institutions and raising the level of quality of their services	8.50	8.00	2.11	0.74
5	12. Improving the environment, reducing pollution and forming new green areas	8.50	7.95	2.32	0.72
6	3. Taking measures to raise the level of public and personal security of citizens	8.00	7.87	2.20	0.67

(Continued)

Rank	Group 5. The Importance of City Administration Measures for Improving Living Conditions	Median	Average	Standard Deviation	Normalized
7	8. Undertaking activities in order to improve housing conditions	8.00	7.79	2.14	0.62
8	10. Introduction of an intelligent traffic management system in order to reduce congestion and increase the speed of travel in the city	8.00	7.68	2.22	0.56
9	1. Making information and communication technology available to citizens	8.00	7.64	1.93	0.54
10	11. Development of a flexible public transport system	8.00	7.61	2.39	0.52
11	2. Improving the complaints management system addressed to city authorities and public services	8.00	7.58	2.06	0.51
12	7. Organizational and financial support to cultural institutions and activities	8.00	7.57	2.10	0.50
	Average indicator value for all questions	8.00	7.85	2.14	0.66

City Administration Measures for Improving Living Conditions – Testing the Adequacy of Factor Analysis, Formed Factors and α-Coefficients.

Description	Cluster Variables	Test Value	Inference
KMO		0.961	Adequate sample
Bartlett measure		$\chi^2 = 1{,}291.06$, $p = 0.000$	Adequate sample
Factor 1 – Cluster 1	3, 2, 11, 1, 12, 4, 10, 7, 6	$\alpha = 0.972$	Reliable test
Factor 2 – Cluster 2	9,8,5	$\alpha = 0.926$	Reliable test

Experts' Assessments of the Importance of the Urban Traffic.

Rank	Group 6. The Importance of the Urban Traffic	Median	Average	Standard Deviation	Normalized
1	2. Existence of pedestrian zones and zones with traffic restrictions	9.00	8.45	1.58	1.00
2	8. Safety in city traffic	9.00	8.31	2.05	0.96
3	3. Construction of bicycle paths	9.00	8.24	1.68	0.94
4	4. Parking	9.00	8.21	2.24	0.93
5	5. Completeness of traffic signals and traffic signs	9.00	8.20	1.97	0.93
6	21. Possibility of quick exit from the city and arrival to external roads, as well as fast entry into the city	8.00	8.08	1.86	0.89
7	1. Construction, completeness and quality of city roads	9.00	8.07	2.08	0.89
8	12. PT Timetable	9.00	8.06	2.15	0.89
9	14. Use of PT by citizens	8.00	7.96	1.92	0.86
10	11. Coverage of the city territory by PT lines and stops	8.00	7.94	2.08	0.85
11	20. Reducing traffic jams	8.50	7.94	2.24	0.85
12	13. Condition of means of transport in PT	8.00	7.74	2.29	0.79
13	6. Introduced intelligent traffic management system	9.00	7.67	2.59	0.77
14	18. Financial support for PT	8.00	7.64	2.22	0.77
15	19. Functioning of taxi service	7.00	7.55	1.77	0.74
16	15. Combined use of PT within a single service	8.00	7.44	2.44	0.71
17	16. Price policy in PT	8.00	7.39	2.49	0.70
18	17. Cooperation between PT service providers and cooperation with the city administration	8.00	7.39	2.23	0.70
19	7. Roadside assistance service in the city	8.00	7.32	2.27	0.67
20	10. Reducing the use of private cars	7.00	6.83	2.73	0.53
21	9. Freight traffic in the city	7.00	6.71	2.59	0.50
	Average indicator value for all questions	8.00	7.77	2.22	0.80

Urban Traffic – Testing the Adequacy of Factor Analysis, Formed Factors and α-Coefficients.

Description	Cluster Variables	Test Value	Inference
KMO		0.931	Adequate sample
Bartlett measure		$\chi^2 = 1{,}842.68$, $p = 0.000$	Adequate sample
Factor 1 – Cluster 1	15, 17, 10, 16, 14, 13, 18, 6, 20, 21, 11, 12	$\alpha = 0.969$	Reliable test
Factor 2 – Cluster 2	4, 5, 8, 3, 1, 19, 7, 2, 9	$\alpha = 0.909$	Reliable test

Appendix 4

Codes in the EU Statistics Database for the Analysis of the Composite Index of Competitiveness of EU Capitals.

No.	Variable	Eurostat Code
1	Soil erosion	aei_pr_soiler
2	Agricultural production	agr_r_accts
3	Business demography	bd_enace2_r3
		bd_esize_r3
		bd_hgnace2_r3
		bd_size_r3
4	Crime	crim_gen_reg
5	Population and living conditions	demo_r_d2jan
		demo_r_d3area
		demo_r_d3dens
		demo_r_gind3
		demo_r_pjanaggr3
		demo_r_pjangroup
		demo_r_pjangrp3
		demo_r_pjanind2
		demo_r_pjanind3
		urb_cfermor
		urb_clivcon
		urb_cpop1
		urb_cpopcb
		urb_cpopstr
6	Population structure by level of education	edat_lfse_04
		edat_lfse_12
		edat_lfse_16
		edat_lfse_22
		edat_lfse_33

Appendix 4 (*Continued*)

No.	Variable	Eurostat Code
7	Education indicators	educ_regind
		educ_renrlrg1
		educ_renrlrg3
		educ_uoe_enra11
		educ_uoe_enra12
		educ_uoe_enra13
		educ_uoe_enra14
		educ_uoe_enra15
		educ_uoe_enrp03
		educ_uoe_enrp06
		educ_uoe_enrs03
		educ_uoe_enrs06
		educ_uoe_enrs09
		educ_uoe_enrt05
		educ_uoe_enrt06
		urb_ceduc
8	Production and collection of municipal waste	env_rwas_cov
		env_rwas_gen
9	Health care	hlth_co_disch2t
		hlth_rs_bdsrg
		hlth_rs_prsrg
10	Human resources in science and technology	hrst_st_rage
		hrst_st_rcat
		hrst_st_rsec
		hrst_st_rsec2
		hrst_st_rsex
11	Technology and knowledge-intensive sectors	htec_emp_reg
		htec_emp_reg2
		htec_emp_risced
		htec_emp_risced2
		htec_emp_risco
		htec_emp_risco2
12	Poverty and social exclusion	ilc_peps11

(*Continued*)

Appendix 4 (*Continued*)

No.	Variable	Eurostat Code
13	Copyright in industrial design in the EU	ipr_da_gdpr
		ipr_da_popr
		ipr_da_reg
		ipr_dfa_reg
		ipr_dr_reg
		ipr_ta_gdpr
		ipr_ta_popr
		ipr_ta_reg
14	Individual use of computers and the internet	isoc_r_blt12_i
		isoc_r_broad_h
		isoc_r_cux_i
		isoc_r_gov_i
		isoc_r_iacc_h
		isoc_r_iumd_i
		isoc_r_iuse_i
15	Employees and time spent at work	lc_rnum1_r2
16	Labor force and labor market statistics	lfst_r_lfe2ecomm
		lfst_r_lfe2eedu
		lfst_r_lfe2eftpt
		lfst_r_lfe2ehour
		lfst_r_lfe2emprc
		lfst_r_lfe2emprt
		lfst_r_lfe2emprtn
		lfst_r_lfe2en2
		lfst_r_lfe2estat
		lfst_r_lfp2acedu
		lfst_r_lfp2act
		lfst_r_lfp2actrt
		lfst_r_lfp2actrtn
		lfst_r_lfsd2pwn
		lfst_r_lfu2ltu
		lfst_r_lfu3pers
		lfst_r_lfu3rt
		urb_clma

Appendix 4 (*Continued*)

No.	Variable	Eurostat Code
17	Economic activities	nama_10r_2coe
		nama_10r_2emhrw
		nama_10r_2gdp
		nama_10r_2gfcf
		nama_10r_2gvagr
		nama_10r_2hhinc
		nama_10r_3empers
		nama_10r_3gdp
		nama_10r_3gva
		nama_10r_3popgdp
18		nrg_chddr2_a
		urb_cenv
19	Meteorological data and environment	pat_ep_ripc
		pat_ep_rtec
		pat_ep_rtot
20	Patent application	rd_e_gerdreg
		rd_p_persreg
21	Research and development	reg_area3
22	Area of regional units	sbs_cre_rreg
		sbs_r_3f_my
		sbs_r_3k_my_r2
		sbs_r_nuts03
		sbs_r_nuts06_r2
		urb_cecfi
23	Business unit statistics	tour_occ_nin2
		urb_ctour
24	Culture and tourism	tran_r_acci
		tran_r_mapa_nm
		tran_r_net
		tran_r_vehst
		urb_ctran
25	Transport	trng_lfse_04
26	Population participation in education and retraining	urb_percep

Source: Eurostat Database, https://ec.europa.eu/eurostat.

Note: The order of the variables is given in alphabetical order of the corresponding codes.

Appendix 5

Values of Measured Variables for the Capitals of the EU Member States.

	Groups of Questions	Average	Standard Deviation	Minimum	Maximum	Average Normalized
	Living conditions					
1	Share of population at risk of poverty or social exclusion (%)	22.30	5.61	12.20	32.80	47.73
2	Average area of dwellings in m^2 per inhabitant	32.88	8.21	16.74	47.79	42.75
3	Number of outdoor and indoor pools per 100,000 inhabitants	3.36	3.37	0.00	12.28	30.93
4	Share of population supplied with public city drinking water supply network (%)	45.60	4.49	86.20	100.00	83.51
5	Share of population supplied with public city sewerage network (%)	39.88	5.01	82.40	100.00	83.22
6	Part of the city territory intended for green urban areas and sports and recreational activities (%)	11.97	6.51	3.70	24.10	44.22
	Employment					
7	Share of active population 15–74 years (%)	68.20	4.49	58.50	77.10	45.43
8	Share of employed population 15–64 years (%)	70.86	6.13	54.70	80.40	61.23
9	Unemployment rate (%)	6.61	3.93	1.30	19.90	28.96

Appendix 5 (*Continued*)

	Groups of Questions	Average	Standard Deviation	Minimum	Maximum	Average Normalized
10	Share of young people aged 18–24 who are unemployed and do not participate in either formal or non-formal education (%)	9.73	3.18	3.50	17.90	36.90
11	Share of young people aged 15–34 who are employed and completed schooling no more than three years ago (%)	78.32	10.05	49.60	91.20	71.17
	Economic development					
12	Real growth rate of gross value added in basic prices in 2018 compared to the previous year, in %	3.16	1.73	0.90	8.20	32.88
13	GDP per capita in euros	43,150.57	21,068.51	7.938.30	92.628.78	35.45
14	Share of employees in sectors of high-tech manufacturing industry and knowledge of intensive service sectors in the total number of employees (%)	6.20	1.82	2.30	9.30	46.28
15	Expenditure on research and development in educational institutions per capita in euros	785.61	769.43	56.10	3.117.90	23.22

(*Continued*)

Appendix 5 (*Continued*)

	Groups of Questions	Average	Standard Deviation	Minimum	Maximum	Average Normalized
16	Number of employees in research and development per 1,000 inhabitants	8.85	4.80	1.47	20.49	39.43
17	The value of registered EU projects in euros per million euros of GDP	1,044.01	720.83	340.00	3.120.00	33.32
	Education					
18	Share of population aged 25–64 participating in education, further education or retraining (%)	12.95	7.68	1.40	32.20	37.62
19	Proportion of population aged 25–64 who have two years of college or higher education (%)	46.07	8.00	24.60	62.80	49.28
20	Share of population aged 25–64 who have completed four years of secondary school (%)	37.74	9.59	18.70	58.30	54.22
21	Proportion of young people aged 18–24 who dropped out of education (%)	8.42	3.68	2.70	17.50	35.67
22	Share of pupils and students at all levels of education in the total population (%)	23.20	3.91	18.20	35.40	29.96
23	Number of students in higher education institutions per 1,000 inhabitants	78.21	40.05	51.00	225.00	22.33

Appendix 5 (*Continued*)

	Groups of Questions	Average	Standard Deviation	Minimum	Maximum	Average Normalized
	Health and social protection					
24	Number of hospital beds per 1,000 inhabitants	4.77	1.96	2.31	10.23	37.16
25	Number of doctors per 100,000 inhabitants	418.75	154.06	230.67	920.18	31.71
26	Number of dentists per 100,000 inhabitants	82.34	30.27	26.48	163.52	44.85
27	Infant mortality per 1,000 newborn	3.15	0.81	1.22	4.52	51.78
28	Number of children 0–4 years covered by public or private day care institutions per 1,000 inhabitants	428.51	166.19	249.40	787.40	36.24
	Culture					
29	Number of seats in cinemas per 1,000 inhabitants	16.96	5.93	6.04	31.93	41.00
30	Average annual number of visits to cinemas per capita	3.36	1.36	1.43	6.27	41.89
31	Average annual number of museum visits per capita	3.47	2.62	0.61	10.95	33.13
32	Number of inhabitants per one theater	57,681.07	41,198.40	2.720.75	155.666.00	28.24
33	Number of public libraries per 100,000 inhabitants	4.25	4.71	0.06	19.48	27.75

(*Continued*)

Appendix 5 *(Continued)*

	Groups of Questions	Average	Standard Deviation	Minimum	Maximum	Average Normalized
	Tourism					
34	Number of beds in tourist accommodation facilities per 1,000 inhabitants	42.76	21.21	9.24	93.60	35.81
35	Number of tourist overnight stays in hotels and other accommodation facilities per 1,000 inhabitants	7,828.24	5,001.81	1.528.84	20.813.36	26.40
	Ecology					
36	Number of days in the year with ozone concentration over 120 μg/m³	10.46	10.06	0.00	33.40	32.12
37	Average annual concentration of nitrogen dioxide in the air in μg/m³	30.16	9.07	11.70	48.30	42.13
38	Average annual concentration of particles with a diameter over 10 μm in air	23.13	7.64	12.00	43.80	36.22
	Information and communication technologies					
39	Share of employees in information and communication technologies in total employment (%)	6.53	2.47	0.00	11.96	50.03
40	Share of households that bought goods or services online for personal use (%)	63.28	17.14	24.00	87.00	52.61

Appendix 5 (*Continued*)

	Groups of Questions	Average	Standard Deviation	Minimum	Maximum	Average Normalized
41	Share of households with broadband internet access (%)	90.21	5.74	75.00	97.00	59.58
42	Proportion of population who have never used a computer (%)	9.85	8.58	1.00	28.00	39.68
43	Share of population who used the internet to communicate with the authorities (%)	56.78	19.37	13.00	93.00	57.77
44	Share of households with internet access from home (%)	90.94	5.76	75.00	97.00	63.15
	Traffic					
45	Number of vehicles of all types per 1,000 inhabitants	513.70	147.13	352.56	832.80	47.64
46	Length of bicycle paths in km per 100,000 inhabitants	0.00	47.11	1.33	192.06	17.00
47	Number of registered cars per 1,000 inhabitants	351.68	136.12	229.09	677.20	36.86
48	The number of people killed in traffic accidents per 10,000 inhabitants	0.24	0.13	0.11	0.60	34.08

Appendix 6

Items from the Questionnaires Collected from Residents of the EU Capital Cities

The Questionnaire Items	Type
1. Quality of public transport, 2015.	1
2. School quality, 2015.	1
3. Quality of health services in hospitals, 2006.	1
4. Quality of health services of doctors, 2006.	1
5. Quality of green areas in the city, 2015.	1
6. Quality of sports fields and halls, 2015.	1
7. Cinema quality, 2006.	1
8. Quality of cultural institutions (concert halls, theaters, museums, libraries), 2015.	1
9. Quality of internet access from public places (internet cafes, libraries), 2006.	1
10. Quality of internet access at home, 2006.	1
11. Possibility of finding a suitable job, 2015.	1
12. Degree of integration of immigrants, 2015.	1
13. Possibility of finding a suitable apartment at an affordable price, 2015.	1
14. Efficiency of administrative services in the city, 2015.	1
15. Urban air pollution is a serious problem, 2009.	2
16. Noise pollution in the city is a serious problem, 2009.	2
17. The city is clean, 2009.	2
18. Resource spending is done responsibly, 2009.	2
19. There is a high level of life satisfaction in this city, 2015.	2
20. Living conditions in this city will be improved in five years, 2006.	2
21. Rarely or almost never have problems paying bills at the end of the month, 2006.	5
22. Rarely or almost never do I feel safe in the part of town where I live, 2006.	5
23. Quality of health services of hospitals and doctors, 2015.	1
24. Appearance of buildings and streets in the part of the city where I live, 2009.	1
25. Quality of public areas in the city: markets, squares, pedestrian zones, 2015.	1

Appendix 6 (*Continued*)

The Questionnaire Items	Type
26. Conditions for recreational activities near the city – walking, cycling, excursions, 2009.	1
27. The presence of foreigners does good to this city, 2015.	1
28. The largest number of inhabitants of this city can be trusted, 2015.	1
29. Poverty is a serious problem in this city, 2009.	1
30. This city is dedicated to the fight against climate change	1
31. This city is a healthy city, 2009.	
(According to WHO Healthy Cities – World Health Organization, https://www.who.int › healthy_settings › types › cities, A healthy city is one that continuously creates and improves the physical and social environment and expands common resources so that residents are able to provide mutual support in the realization of all functions of life and develop their maximal potential.)	1
32. You have difficulty in paying your bills at the end of the month, 2015.	3
33. Duration of commuting, 2009.	4
34. The main means of transport to the workplace, 2015.	4
35. The main means of transport to the workplace, 2009.	4
36. How often do you use public urban passenger transport? 2009.	4
37. Why don't you use public transport? 2009.	4
38. The most important quality of this city, 2015.	4
39. Condition of buildings and streets in my area, 2015.	1
40. Access to retail facilities, 2015.	1
41. Air quality in the city, 2015.	1
42. Noise level in the city, 2015.	1
43. Cleanliness in the city, 2015.	1
44. Security in the city, 2015.	1
45. Security of its immediate surroundings in the city, 2015.	1
46. Degree of trust in people who live in my immediate vicinity in the city, 2015.	1
47. Degree of trust in the city public administration, 2015.	1
48. Your current situation at work, 2015.	1
49. Financial situation of your household, 2015.	1
50. Quality and way of living, 2015.	1
51. The quality of my life in this city, 2012.	1

(*Continued*)

Appendix 6 (*Continued*)

The Questionnaire Items	Type
52. I am satisfied with public transport in my city, 2015.	5
53. This city is dedicated to the fight against climate change, 2015.	5
54. The noise level in the city is satisfactorily low, 2015.	5
55. The quality of cultural institutions in the city is satisfactory, 2015.	5
56. The financial situation of my household is satisfactory, 2015.	5
57. In this city, it is easy to find satisfactory housing at an affordable price, 2015.	5
58. Foreigners are satisfactorily integrated into life in this city, 2015.	5
59. The presence of foreigners is good for this city, 2015.	5
60. The quality of health services of doctors and hospitals is satisfactory, 2015.	5
61. The quality of schools in the city is satisfactory, 2015.	5
62. The largest number of people in this city can be trusted, 2015.	5
63. Administrative services of the city administration are efficient, 2015.	5
64. Satisfied with life in his city, 2015.	5
65. I am satisfied with my situation at work, 2015.	5

Notes: the order of the presented survey questions corresponds to the order as published on the official EU website; questions for 2004 are not listed, as they are repeated in later years.

Points Awarded to Individual Items from the Survey of Citizens of EU Capitals.

	Groups of Questions	Average	Standard Deviation	Minimum	Maximum
	Living conditions				
1	Quality of sports fields and halls	60.64	9.54	37.80	77.25
2	Degree of integration of immigrants	52.94	10.03	25.67	70.37
3	Possibility to find a suitable apartment at an affordable price	31.50	12.56	10.54	58.02
4	There is a high level of satisfaction with life in this city	80.79	7.76	56.96	93.66
5	Quality of public areas in the city: markets, squares, pedestrian zones	62.87	9.28	37.97	75.81
6	The presence of foreigners does good to this city	67.92	11.06	40.39	83.31
7	You have no difficulty paying your bills at the end of the month	76.01	11.24	45.14	93.88
8	The condition of buildings and streets in my area	55.74	13.23	25.31	77.97
9	Access to retail facilities	74.46	6.69	55.64	86.31
10	Quality and way of living	72.86	7.76	51.47	87.52
11	The quality of your own life in this city	77.45	7.02	59.29	88.32
	Employment				
12	Possibility of finding a suitable job	43.57	12.42	16.48	64.20
	Economic development				
13	Your current situation at work	68.23	8.09	46.87	80.88

(*Continued*)

(*Continued*)

	Groups of Questions	Average	Standard Deviation	Minimum	Maximum
14	The financial situation of your household	61.23	9.28	36.97	80.78
	Education				
15	School quality	65.02	8.61	50.92	76.86
	Health and social protection				
16	Quality of hospital and physician health services	58.55	12.86	35.01	79.56
	Culture				
17	Quality of cultural institutions (concert halls, theaters, museums, libraries	72.77	11.19	41.34	92.58
	Ecology				
18	The quality of green spaces in the city	67.49	12.70	32.31	82.31
19	The city is committed to combating climate change (e.g., reducing energy consumption in apartments, alternative transport instead of cars, etc.)	52.34	8.59	36.18	67.02
20	Air quality in the city	53.42	13.58	29.53	74.96
21	Noise level in the city	54.68	10.37	35.34	69.66
22	Cleanliness in the city	52.39	14.30	20.31	81.30
	City traffic				
23	Quality of public city transport	65.78	10.66	35.76	89.21
24	I am satisfied with the public transport in my city	70.14	15.43	30.00	95.00
	City administration				
25	Efficiency of administrative services in the city	49.11	8.19	32.96	66.96

(*Continued*)

	Groups of Questions	Average	Standard Deviation	Minimum	Maximum
26	Degree of trust in the city's public administration Security	52.22	10.26	31.91	73.77
27	Most of the inhabitants of this city can be trusted	54.38	10.58	35.34	73.64
28	Security in the city	65.21	12.33	36.64	82.98
29	Security of your immediate surroundings in the city	73.02	10.17	49.30	89.21
30	The degree of trust in the people who live in my immediate vicinity in the city	66.78	9.10	50.30	83.48

Points Awarded to Items Within Yes–No Questions.

	Yes–No Questions	Average Ratio of Yes Answers	Standard Deviation	Minimum	Maximum
31	This city is dedicated to fight against climate change	49.89	12.02	30.00	75.00
32	The noise level in the city is satisfactorily low	60.29	15.57	31.00	82.00
33	The quality of cultural institutions in the city is satisfactory	79.29	13.20	34.00	97.00
34	The financial situation of my household is satisfactory	70.75	12.41	33.00	90.00
35	In this city, it is easy to find satisfactory living space at an affordable price	23.96	14.90	4.00	62.00
36	Foreigners are satisfactorily integrated into life in this city	50.46	12.69	20.00	77.00

(*Continued*)

(*Continued*)

	Yes–No Questions	Average Ratio of Yes Answers	Standard Deviation	Minimum	Maximum
37	The presence of foreigners is good for this city	73.46	13.34	41.00	90.00
38	The quality of health services of doctors and hospitals is satisfactory	63.50	17.60	33.00	91.00
39	The quality of schools in the city is satisfactory	64.07	10.87	47.00	83.00
40	Most people in this city can be trusted	58.25	15.71	34.00	85.00
41	Administrative services of the city administration are efficient	48.79	12.40	27.00	80.00
42	I am satisfied with life in his city	89.93	6.05	67.00	98.00
43	I am satisfied with the situation at work	65.25	9.30	45.00	79.00

Appendix 7

Characteristics of Cities and the Associated Importance Assessments Obtained from Expert Surveys.

	Characteristics of the City	Experts' Assessments
	Living conditions	
1	Share of population at risk of poverty or social exclusion (%)	Economic development and economic development
2	Average area of dwellings in m^2 per inhabitant	Undertaking activities in order to improve housing conditions
3	Number of outdoor and indoor pools per 100,000 inhabitants	Convenience for life in general
4	Share of population supplied with public city drinking water supply network (%)	Water management
5	Share of population supplied with public city sewerage network (%)	Waste management
6	Part of the city territory intended for green urban areas and sports and recreational activities (%)	Green city and public areas
	Employment	
7	Share of active population 15–74 years (%)	Improving the structure of educational institutions and raising the level of quality of their services
8	Share of employed population 15–64 years (%)	Recruitment
9	Unemployment rate (%)	Support in finding jobs and employment
10	Share of young people aged 18–24 who are unemployed and do not participate in either formal or non-formal education (%)	Retirement and retraining centers
11	Share of young people aged 15–34 who are employed and completed schooling no more than three years ago (%)	Career guidance advisory service

(*Continued*)

Appendix 7 *(Continued)*

	Characteristics of the City	Experts' Assessments
	Economic development	
12	Real growth rate of gross value added in basic prices in 2018 compared to the previous year, in %	Economic development and economic development
13	GDP per capita in euros	Economic development and economic development
14	Share of employees in sectors of high-tech manufacturing industry and knowledge of intensive service sectors in the total number of employees (%)	Development of an innovative environment – development of business culture and incubation
15	Expenditure on research and development in educational institutions per capita in euros	Encouragement of research and development activities
16	Number of employees in research and development per 1,000 inhabitants	Encouragement of research and development activities
17	The value of registered EU projects in euros per million euros of GDP	Innovation centers
	Education	
18	Share of population aged 25–64 participating in education, further education or retraining (%)	User group education
19	Proportion of population aged 25–64 who have two years of college or higher education (%)	Education
20	Share of population aged 25–64 who have completed four years of secondary school (%)	Education
21	Proportion of young people aged 18–24 who dropped out of education (%)	Improving the structure of educational institutions and raising the level of quality of their services
22	Share of pupils and students at all levels of education in the total population (%)	Improving the structure of educational institutions and raising the level of quality of their services
23	Number of students in higher education institutions per 1,000 inhabitants	University, research center

Appendix 7 (*Continued*)

	Characteristics of the City	Experts' Assessments
	Health and social protection	
24	Number of hospital beds per 1,000 inhabitants	Improving the structure of health institutions and raising the level of quality of their services
25	Number of doctors per 100,000 inhabitants	Health care
26	Number of dentists per 100,000 inhabitants	Health care
27	Infant mortality in per mille	Improving the structure of health institutions and raising the level of quality of their services
28	Number of children 0–4 years covered by public or private day care institutions per 1,000 inhabitants	Improving the structure of social institutions and raising the level of quality of their services
	Culture	
29	Number of seats in cinemas per 1,000 inhabitants	Organizational and financial support to cultural institutions and activities
30	Average annual number of visits to bishops per capita	Organizational and financial support to cultural institutions and activities
31	Average annual number of museum visits per capita	Cultural institutions and events
32	Number of inhabitants per one theater	Cultural institutions and events
33	Number of public libraries per 100,000 inhabitants	Development of a harmonized system of smart city services
	Tourism	
34	Number of beds in tourist accommodation facilities per 1,000 inhabitants	Tourism
35	Number of tourist nights in hotels and other accommodation facilities per 1,000 inhabitants	Tourism
	Ecology	
36	Number of days in the year with ozone concentration over 120 $\mu g/m^3$	Degree of air pollution

(*Continued*)

Appendix 7 *(Continued)*

	Characteristics of the City	Experts' Assessments
37	Average annual concentration of nitrogen dioxide in the air in µg/m³	Degree of air pollution
38	Average annual concentration of particles with a diameter over 10 µm in air	Degree of air pollution
	Information and communication technologies	
39	Share of employees in information and communication technologies in total employment (%)	An intelligent city
40	Share of households that bought goods or services online for personal use (%)	Digitization
41	Share of households with broadband internet access (%)	Digitization
42	Proportion of population who have never used a computer (%)	Making information and communication technology available to citizens
43	Share of population who used the internet to communicate with the authorities (%)	Improving the grievance management system addressed to city authorities and public services
44	Share of households with internet access from home (%)	Digitization
	Urban transport	
45	Number of vehicles of all types per 1,000 inhabitants	Reducing traffic jams
46	Length of bicycle paths in km per 100,000 inhabitants	Construction of bicycle paths
47	Number of registered cars per 1,000 inhabitants	Reducing the use of private cars
48	The number of people killed in traffic accidents per 10,000 inhabitants	Safety in city traffic

Printed and bound by CPI Group (UK) Ltd, Croydon, CR0 4YY

19/08/2024

14542884-0002